CROWDS AND POWER

Other Continuum books by Elias Canetti

Audo-da-Fé
The Tongue Set Free
The Conscience of Words
Earwitness
The Human Province
The Voices of Marrakesh

CROWDS AND POWER

by

ELIAS CANETTI

Translated from the German by
Carol Stewart

CONTINUUM · NEW YORK

The Continuum Publishing Corporation
575 Lexington Avenue
New York, N.Y. 10022

Originally published as *Masse und Macht* by Claassen Verlag,
Hamburg, copyright © 1960 by Claassen Verlag Hamburg.

English translation copyright © 1962, 1973 by Victor Gollancz Ltd.

Printed in the United States of America

Library of Congress Cataloging in Publication Data

Canetti, Elias, 1905–
Crowds and power.

Translation of: Masse Und Macht.
Reprint. Originally published: New York: Seabury Press, 1978.
Bibliography: p. 485
1. Crowds. 2. Power (Social sciences) I. Title.
HM281.C3613   1981   303.3   81-70793
ISBN 0-8264-0211-9   AACR2
ISBN 0-8264-0089-2 (pbk.)

The author wishes to acknowledge with gratitude the
generous support given him in his research by the
Bollingen Foundation

The translator wishes to acknowledge very gratefully the
help and advice of the author in preparing this text

CONTENTS

THE CROWD

THE PACK

THE PACK AND RELIGION

THE CROWD IN HISTORY

THE CROWD

The Fear of being Touched

THERE IS NOTHING that man fears more than the touch of the unknown. He wants to *see* what is reaching towards him, and to be able to recognize or at least classify it. Man always tends to avoid physical contact with anything strange. In the dark, the fear of an unexpected touch can mount to panic. Even clothes give insufficient security: it is easy to tear them and pierce through to the naked, smooth, defenceless flesh of the victim.

All the distances which men create round themselves are dictated by this fear. They shut themselves in houses which no-one may enter, and only there feel some measure of security. The fear of burglars is not only the fear of being robbed, but also the fear of a sudden and unexpected clutch out of the darkness.

The repugnance to being touched remains with us when we go about among people; the way we move in a busy street, in restaurants, trains or buses, is governed by it. Even when we are standing next to them and are able to watch and examine them closely, we avoid actual contact if we can. If we do not avoid it, it is because we feel attracted to someone; and then it is we who make the approach.

The promptness with which apology is offered for an unintentional contact, the tension with which it is awaited, our violent and sometimes even physical reaction when it is not forthcoming, the antipathy and hatred we feel for the offender, even when we cannot be certain who it is—the whole knot of shifting and intensely sensitive reactions to an alien touch—proves that we are dealing here with a human propensity as deep-seated as it is alert and insidious; something which never leaves a man when he has once established the boundaries of his personality. Even in sleep, when he is far more unguarded, he can all too easily be disturbed by a touch.

It is only in a crowd that man can become free of this fear of being touched. That is the only situation in which the fear changes into its opposite. The crowd he needs is the dense crowd, in which body is pressed to body; a crowd, too, whose psychical constitution is also dense, or compact, so that he no longer notices who it is that presses against him. As soon as a man has surrendered himself to the crowd, he ceases to fear its touch. Ideally, all are equal there; no distinctions count, not even that of sex. The man pressed against him is the same as himself. He feels him as he feels himself. Suddenly it is as though every-thing were happening in one and the same body. This is perhaps one of the reasons why a crowd seeks to close in on itself: it wants to rid each individual as completely as possible of the fear of being touched. The more fiercely people press together, the more certain they feel that they do not fear each other. This reversal of the fear of being touched belongs to the nature of crowds. The feeling of relief is most striking where the density of the crowd is greatest.

The Open and the Closed Crowd

THE CROWD, suddenly there where there was nothing before, is a mysterious and universal phenomenon. A few people may have been standing together—five, ten or twelve, not more; nothing has been announced, nothing is expected. Suddenly everywhere is black with people and more come streaming from all sides as though streets had only one direction. Most of them do not know what has happened and, if questioned, have no answer; but they hurry to be there where most other people are. There is a determination in their movement which is quite different from the expression of ordinary curiosity. It seems as though the movement of some of them transmits itself to the others. But that is not all; they have a goal which is there before they can find words for it. This goal is the blackest spot where most people are gathered.

This is the extreme form of the spontaneous crowd and much more will have to be said about it later. In its innermost core it is not quite as spontaneous as it appears, but, except for these 5, 10 or 12 people with whom actually it originates, it is everywhere spontaneous. As soon as it exists at all, it wants to consist of *more* people: the urge to grow is the first and supreme attribute of the crowd. It wants to seize everyone within reach; anything shaped like a human being can join it. The natural crowd is the *open* crowd; there are no limits whatever to its growth; it does not recognize houses, doors or locks and those who shut themselves in are suspect. "Open" is to be understood here in the fullest sense of the word; it means open everywhere and in any direc-tion. The open crowd exists so long as it grows; it disintegrates as soon as it stops growing.

For just as suddenly as it originates, the crowd disintegrates. In its spontaneous form it is a sensitive thing. The openness which enables it to grow is, at the same time, its danger. A foreboding of threatening disintegration is always alive in the crowd. It seeks, through rapid increase, to avoid this for as long as it can; it absorbs everyone, and, because it does, must ultimately fall to pieces.

In contrast to the open crowd which can grow indefinitely and which is of universal interest because it may spring up anywhere, there is the *closed* crowd.

The closed crowd renounces growth and puts the stress on permanence. The first thing to be noticed about it is that it has a boundary. It establishes itself by accepting its limitation. It creates a space for itself which it will fill. This space can be compared to a vessel into which liquid is being poured and whose capacity is known. The entrances to this space are limited in number, and only these entrances can be used; the boundary is respected whether it consists of stone, of solid wall, or of some special act of acceptance, or entrance fee. Once the space is completely filled, no one else is allowed in. Even if there is an overflow, the important thing is always the dense crowd in the closed room; those standing outside do not really belong.

The boundary prevents disorderly increase, but it also makes it more difficult for the crowd to disperse and so postpones its dissolution. In this way the crowd sacrifices its chance of growth, but gains in staying power. It is protected from outside influences which could become hostile and dangerous and it sets its hope on *repetition*. It is the expectation of reassembly which enables its members to accept each dispersal. The building is waiting for them; it exists for their sake and, so long as it is there, they will be able to meet in the same manner. The space is theirs, even during the ebb, and in its emptiness it reminds them of the flood.

The Discharge

THE MOST IMPORTANT occurrence within the crowd is the *discharge*. Before this the crowd does not actually exist; it is the discharge which creates it. This is the moment when all who belong to the crowd get rid of their differences and feel equal.

These differences are mainly imposed from outside; they are distinctions of rank, status and property. Men as individuals are always conscious of these distinctions; they weigh heavily on them and keep them firmly apart from one another. A man stands by himself on a secure and well defined spot, his every gesture asserting his right to keep others at a distance. He stands there like a windmill on an enormous plain, moving expressively; and there is nothing between him and the next mill. All life, so far as he knows it, is laid out in distances— the house in which he shuts himself and his property, the positions he holds, the rank he desires—all these serve to create distances, to confirm and extend them. Any free or large gesture of approach towards another human being is inhibited. Impulse and counter impulse ooze away as in a desert. No man can get near another, nor reach his height. In every sphere of life, firmly established hierarchies prevent him touching anyone more exalted than himself, or descending, except in appearance, to anyone lower. In different societies the distances are differently balanced against each other, the stress in some lying on birth, in others on occupation or property.

I do not intend to characterize these hierarchies in detail here, but it is essential to know that they exist everywhere and everywhere gain a decisive hold on men's minds and determine their behaviour to each other. But the satisfaction of being higher in rank than others does not compensate for the loss of freedom of movement. Man petrifies and darkens in the distances he has created. He drags at the burden of them, but cannot move. He forgets that it is self-inflicted, and longs for liberation. But how, alone, can he free himself? Whatever he does, and however determined he is, he will always find himself among others who thwart his efforts. So long as they hold fast to *their* distances, he can never come any nearer to them.

Only together can men free themselves from their burdens of distance; and this, precisely, is what happens in a crowd. During the discharge distinctions are thrown off and all feel *equal*. In that density, where there is scarcely any space between, and body presses against body, each man is as near the other as he is to himself; and an immense feeling of relief ensues. It is for the sake of this blessed moment, when no-one is greater or better than another, that people become a crowd.

But the moment of discharge, so desired and so happy, contains its own danger. It is based on an illusion; the people who suddenly feel equal have not really become equal; nor will they *feel* equal for ever. They return to their separate houses, they lie down on their own beds, they keep their possessions and their names. They do not cast out their relations nor run away from their families. Only true conversion leads men to give up their old associations and form new ones. Such associations, which by their very nature are only able to accept a limited number of members, have to secure their continuance by rigid rules. Such groups I call crowd crystals. Their function will be described later.

But the crowd, as such, disintegrates. It has a presentiment of this and fears it. It can only go on existing if the process of discharge is continued with new people who join it. Only the growth of the crowd prevents those who belong to it creeping back under their private burdens.

Destructiveness

THE DESTRUCTIVENESS of the crowd is often mentioned as its most conspicuous quality, and there is no denying the fact that it can be observed everywhere, in the most diverse countries and civilizations. It is discussed and disapproved of, but never really explained.

The crowd particularly likes destroying houses and objects: breakable objects like window panes, mirrors, pictures and crockery; and people tend to think that it is the fragility of these objects which stimulates the destructiveness of the crowd. It is true that the noise of destruction adds to its satisfaction; the banging of windows and the crashing of glass are the robust sounds of fresh life, the cries of something new-born. It is easy to evoke them and that increases their popularity. Everything shouts together; the din is the applause of objects. There seems to be a special need for this kind of noise at the beginning of events, when the crowd is still small and little or nothing has happened. The noise is a promise of the reinforcements the crowd hopes for, and a happy omen for deeds to come. But it would be wrong to suppose that the ease with which things can be broken is the decisive factor in the situation. Sculptures of solid stone have been mutilated beyond recognition; Christians have destroyed the heads and arms of Greek Gods and reformers and revolutionaries have hauled down the statues of Saints, sometimes from dangerous heights, though often the stone they wanted to destroy has been so hard that they have achieved only half their purpose.

The destruction of representational images is the destruction of a hierarchy which is no longer recognized. It is the violation of generally established and universally visible and valid distances. The solidity of the images was the expression of their permanence. They seem to have existed for ever, upright and immovable; never before had it been possible to approach them with hostile intent. Now they are hauled down and broken to pieces. In this act the discharge accomplishes itself.

But it does not always go as far as this. The more usual kind of destruction mentioned above is simply an attack on all boundaries. Windows and doors belong to houses; they are the most vulnerable part of their exterior and, once they are smashed, the house has lost its individuality; anyone may enter it and nothing and no-one is protected any more. In these houses live the supposed enemies of the crowd, those people who try to keep away from it. What separated them has now been destroyed and nothing stands between them and the crowd. They can come out and join it; or they can be fetched.

But there is more to it than this. In the crowd the individual feels that he is transcending the limits of his own person. He has a sense of relief, for the distances are removed which used to throw him back on himself and shut him in. With the lifting of these burdens of distance he feels free; his freedom is the crossing of these boundaries. He wants what is happening to him to happen to others too; and he expects it to happen to them. An earthen pot irritates him, for it is all boundaries. The closed doors of a house irritate him. Rites and ceremonies, any- thing which preserves distances, threaten him and seem unbearable. He fears that, sooner or later, an attempt will be made to force the disintegrating crowd back into these pre-existing vessels. To the crowd in its nakedness everything seems a Bastille.

Of all means of destruction the most impressive is *fire*. It can be seen from far off and it attracts ever more people. It destroys irrevocably; nothing after a fire is as it was before. A crowd setting fire to something feels irresistible; so long as the fire spreads, everyone will join it and everything hostile will be destroyed. After the destruction, crowd and fire die away.

The Eruption

THE OPEN CROWD is the true crowd, the crowd abandoning itself freely to its natural urge for growth. An open crowd has no clear feel- ing or idea of the size it may attain; it does not depend on a known building which it has to fill; its size is not determined; it wants to grow indefinitely and what it needs for this is more and more people. In this naked state, the crowd is at its most conspicuous, but, because it always disintegrates, it seems something outside the ordinary course of life and so is never taken quite seriously. Men might have gone on disre- garding it if the enormous increase of population in modern times, and the rapid growth of cities, had not more and more often given rise to its formation.

The closed crowds of the past, of which more will be heard later, had turned into familiar institutions. The peculiar state of mind characteristic of their members seemed something natural. They always met for a special purpose of a religious, festal or martial kind; and this purpose seemed to sanctify their state. A man attending a sermon honestly believed that it was the sermon which mattered to him, and he would have felt astonished or even indignant had it been explained to him that the large number of listeners present gave him more satisfaction than the sermon itself. All ceremonies and rules pertaining to such institutions are basically intent on capturing the crowd; they prefer a church-full secure to the whole world insecure. The regularity of church-going and the precise and familiar repetition of certain rites safeguard for the crowd something like a domesticated experience of itself. These performances and their recurrence at fixed times supplant needs for something harsher and more violent.

Such institutions might have proved adequate if the number of human beings had remained the same, but more and more people filled the towns and the accelerating increase in the growth of populations during the last few centuries continually provided fresh incitements to the formation of new and larger crowds. And nothing, not even the most experienced and subtle leadership, could have prevented them forming in such conditions.

All the rebellions against traditional ceremonial recounted in the history of religions have been directed against the confinement of the crowd which wants to feel the sensation of its own growth again. The Sermon on the Mount in the New Testament comes to mind. It is enacted in the open, thousands are able to listen and there is no doubt that it is directed against the limiting ceremoniousness of the official temple. One remembers the tendency of Pauline Christianity to break out of the national and tribal boundaries of Judaism and to become a universal faith for all men. One remembers the contempt of Buddhism for the caste-system of contemporary India.

The *inner* history, too, of the several world religions is rich in occurrences of a similar kind. The Crusades developed into crowd formations of a magnitude no church building of the contemporary world could have held. Later, whole towns became spectators of the performances of the flagellants and these, in addition, wandered from town to town. Wesley, in the 18th Century, based his movement on sermons in the open air. He was perfectly aware of the importance of the enormous crowds which listened to him and sometimes in his Journals he worked out the numbers of those who were able to hear him. Each eruption from a closed locality means that the crowd desires to regain its old pleasure in sudden, rapid and unlimited growth.

I designate as *eruption* the sudden transition from a closed into an open crowd. This is a frequent occurrence, and one should not understand it as something referring only to space. A crowd quite often seems to overflow from some well-guarded space into the squares and streets of a town where it can move about freely, exposed to everything and attracting everyone. But more important than this external event is the corresponding inner movement: the dissatisfaction with the limitation of the number of participants, the sudden will to attract, the passionate determination to reach *all* men.

Since the French Revolution these eruptions have taken on a form which we feel to be modern. To an impressive degree the crowd has freed itself from the substance of traditional religion and this has perhaps made it easier for us to see it in its nakedness, in what one might call its biological state, without the transcendental theories and goals which used to be inculcated in it. The history of the last 150 years has culminated in a spate of such eruptions; they have engulfed even wars, for all wars are now mass wars. The crowd is no longer content with pious promises and conditionals. It wants to experience for itself the strongest possible feeling of its own animal force and passion and, as means to this end, it will use whatever social pretexts and demands offer themselves.

The first point to emphasise is that the crowd never feels saturated. It remains hungry as long as there is one human being it has not reached. One cannot be certain whether this hunger would persist once it had really absorbed all men, but it seems likely. Its efforts to endure, however, are somewhat impotent. Its only hope lies in the formation of double crowds, the one measuring itself against the other. The closer in power and intensity the rivals are, the longer both of them will stay alive.

Persecution

ONE OF THE most striking traits of the inner life of a crowd is the feeling of being persecuted, a peculiar angry sensitiveness and irritability directed against those it has once and forever nominated as enemies. These can behave in any manner, harsh or conciliatory, cold or sympathetic, severe or mild—whatever they do will be interpreted as springing from an unshakable malevolence, a premeditated intention to destroy the crowd, openly or by stealth.

In order to understand this feeling of hostility and persecution it is necessary to start from the basic fact that the crowd, once formed, wants to grow rapidly. It is difficult to exaggerate the power and determination with which it spreads. As long as it feels that it is growing —in revolutionary states, for example, which start with small but highly-charged crowds—it regards anything which opposes its growth as constricting. It can be dispersed and scattered by police, but this has only a temporary effect, like a hand moving through a swarm of mosquitoes. But it can also be attacked from within, namely by meeting the demands which led to its formation. Its weaker adherents then drop away and others on the point of joining turn back. An attack from outside can only strengthen the crowd; those who have been physically scattered are more strongly drawn together again. An attack from *within*, on the other hand, is really dangerous; a strike which has achieved any gains crumbles visibly. It is an appeal to individual appetites and the crowd, as such, regards it as bribery, as "immoral"; it runs counter to its clear-cut basic conviction. Everyone belonging to such a crowd carries within him a small traitor who wants to eat, drink, make love and be left alone. As long as he does all this on the quiet and does not make too much fuss about it, the crowd allows him to proceed. But, as soon as he makes a noise about it, it starts to hate and to fear him. It knows then that he has been listening to the enticements of the enemy.

The crowd here is like a besieged city and, as in many sieges, it has enemies before its walls and enemies within them. During the fighting it attracts more and more partisans from the country around. These slip through the enemy lines and collect in front of the gates, begging to be let in. In favourable moments their wish is granted; or they may climb over the walls. Thus the city daily gains new defenders, but each of these brings with him that small invisible traitor we spoke of before, who quickly disappears into a cellar to join the traitors already hidden there. Meanwhile the siege continues. The besiegers certainly watch for a chance to attack, but they also try to prevent new recruits reaching the city. To do this they keep on strengthening the walls from outside. (In this strange siege the walls are more important to the assailants than to the defenders.) Or they try to bribe newcomers to keep away. If they fail in both, they do what they can to strengthen and encourage that traitor to his own cause which each newcomer carries with him into the city.

The crowd's feeling of persecution is nothing but the intuition of this double threat; the walls outside become more and more constricting and the cellars within more and more undermined. The activities of the enemy outside on the walls are open and can be watched; in the cellars they are hidden and insidious.

But images of this kind never convey more than a part of the truth. Those streaming from outside, wanting to get into the city, are not only new partisans, a reinforcement and a support; they are also the *food* of the crowd. A crowd which is not increasing is in a state of fast—there are ways of holding out through such a fast and religions have developed a great mastery of these. I propose now to show how the world religions have succeeded in holding their crowds even when these are not in the stage of fierce and rapid growth.

Domestication of Crowds in the World Religions

RELIGIONS WHOSE claims to universality have been acknowledged very soon change the accent of their appeal. In the beginning their aim is to reach and to win all who can be reached and won. The crowd they envisage is universal; every single soul counts and every soul shall be theirs. But the fight they have to sustain leads gradually to a kind of hidden respect for adversaries whose institutions are already in existence. They see how difficult it is to hold one's ground; institutions which offer solidarity and permanence seem more and more important to them. Stimulated by those of their adversaries, they make great efforts to introduce institutions of their own, and these, if they succeed, grow in importance with time. The dead weight of institutions, which have a life of their own, then gradually tames the impetus of the original appeal. Churches are built to contain the existing faithful and are enlarged only with reluctance and circumspection when there is real need. There is, too, a strong tendency to collect the faithful in separate units. When they become many there is always a danger of disintegration, which must be continually countered.

A sense of the treacherousness of the crowd, is, so to speak, in the blood of all the historical world religions. Their own traditions, which are of a binding character, teach them how suddenly and unexpectedly they grew. Their stories of mass conversions appear miraculous to them, and they are so. In the heretical movements which the churches fear and persecute, the same kind of miracle turns against themselves and the injuries thus inflicted on their bodies are painful and unforgettable. Both the rapid growth of their early days and the no less rapid defections later keep their suspicion of the crowd always alive.

What they want in contrast to this is an obsequious flock. It is customary to regard the faithful as sheep and to praise them for their submissiveness. The churches entirely renounce the crowd's essential tendency to quick growth. They are satisfied with a temporary fiction of equality among the faithful—though this is never too strictly imposed—, with a defined density kept within moderate bounds, and with a strong direction. The goal they place in the far distance, in that other world which no man may enter so long as he is alive and which he has to earn by many efforts and submissions. Gradually the direction becomes the most important thing; the more distant the goal, the better the prospect of its permanence. The seemingly indispensable principle of growth has been replaced by something quite different: by repetition.

The faithful are gathered together at appointed places and times and, through performances which are always the same, they are transported into a mild state of crowd feeling sufficient to impress itself on them without becoming dangerous, and to which they grow accustomed. Their feeling of unity is dispensed to them in doses and the continuance of the church depends on the rightness of the dosage.

Wherever men have grown accustomed to this precisely repeated and limited experience in their churches or temples they can no longer do without it. They need it as they need food and anything else which is part of their existence. No sudden suppression of their cult, no prohibition by edict of the state, can remain without consequences. Any disturbance of their carefully balanced crowd-economy must ultimately lead to the eruption of an *open* crowd, and this will have all the elemental attributes which one knows. It will spread rapidly and bring about a real instead of a fictitious equality; it will find new and far more fervent densities; it will give up for the moment that far-off and scarcely attainable goal for which it has been educated, and set itself a goal here, in the immediate surroundings of this concrete life.

All suddenly prohibited religions revenge themselves by a kind of secularization. The character of their adherents' faith changes completely in an eruption of great and unexpected ferocity, but they do not understand this. They think they still hold their old faith and convictions and their only intention is to keep them. But, in reality, they have suddenly become quite different people. They are filled with the unique and violent feeling of the open crowd which they now compose, and at all costs they want to remain part of it.

Panic

Panic in a theatre, as has often been noted, is a *disintegration* of the crowd. The more people were bound together by the performance and the more closed the form of the theatre which contained them, the more violent the disintegration.

It is also possible that the performance alone was not enough to create a genuine crowd. The audience may have remained together, not because they felt gripped by it, but simply because they happened to be there. What the play could not achieve is immediately achieved by a *fire*. Fire is as dangerous to human beings as it is to animals; it is the strongest and oldest symbol of the crowd. However little crowd feeling there may have been in the audience, awareness of a fire brings it suddenly to a head. The common unmistakable danger creates a common fear. For a short time the audience becomes something like a real crowd. If they were not in a theatre, people could flee together like a herd of animals in danger, and increase the impetus of their flight by the simultaneity of identical movements. An active crowd-fear of this kind is the common collective experience of all animals who live together in herds and whose joint safety depends on their speed.

In a theatre, on the other hand, the crowd inevitably disintegrates in the most violent manner. Only one or two persons can get through each exit at a time and thus the energy of flight turns into an energy of struggle to push others back. Only one man at a time can pass between the rows of seats and each seat is neatly separated from the rest. Each man has his place and sits or stands by himself. A normal theatre is arranged with the intention of pinning people down and allowing them only the use of their hands and voices; their use of their legs is restricted as far as possible.

The sudden command to flee which the fire gives is immediately countered by the impossibility of any common movement. Each man sees the door through which he must pass; and he sees himself alone in it, sharply cut off from all the others. It is the frame of a picture which very soon dominates him. Thus the crowd, a moment ago at its apex, must disintegrate violently, and the transmutation shows itself in violent individual action: everyone shoves, hits and kicks in all directions.

The more fiercely each man "fights for his life", the clearer it becomes that he is fighting *against* all the others who hem him in. They stand there like chairs, balustrades, closed doors, but different from these in that they are alive and hostile. They push him in this or that direction, as it suits them or, rather, as they are pushed themselves. Neither women, children nor old people are spared: they are not distinguished from men. Whilst the individual no longer feels himself as "crowd", he is still completely surrounded by it. Panic is a disintegration of the crowd *within* the crowd. The individual breaks away and wants to escape from it because the crowd, as a whole, is endangered. But, because he is physically still stuck in it, he must attack it. To abandon himself to it now would be his ruin, because it itself is threatened by ruin. In such a moment a man cannot insist too strongly on his separateness. Hitting and pushing, he evokes hitting and pushing; and the more blows he inflicts and the more he receives, the more *himself* he feels. The boundaries of his own person become clear to him again.

It is strange to observe how strongly for the person struggling with it the crowd assumes the character of fire. It originated with the unexpected sight of flames or with a shout of "fire" and it plays like flames with the man who is trying to escape from it. The people he pushes away are like burning objects to him; their touch is hostile, and on every part of his body; and it terrifies him. Anyone who stands in his way is tainted with the general hostility of fire. The manner in which fire spreads and gradually works its way round a person until he is entirely surrounded by it is very similar to the crowd threatening him on all sides. The incalculable movements within it, the thrusting forth of an arm, a fist or a leg, are like the flames of a fire which may suddenly spring up on any side. Fire in the form of a conflagration of forest or steppe actually *is* a hostile crowd and fear of it can be awakened in any human being. Fire, as a symbol for the crowd, has entered the whole economy of man's feelings and become an immutable part of it. That emphatic trampling on people, so often observed in panics and apparently so senseless, is nothing but the stamping out of fire.

Disintegration through panic can only be averted by prolonging the original state of united crowd fear. In a threatened church there is a way of achieving this: people pray in common fear to a common God in whose hand it lies to extinguish the fire by a miracle.

The Crowd as a Ring

AN ARENA CONTAINS a crowd which is *doubly* closed. On account of this curious quality its examination may not be entirely without value.

The arena is well demarcated from the outside world. It is usually visible from far off and its situation in the city—the space which it occupies—is well known. People always feel where it is, even if they are not thinking of it. Shouts from the arena carry far and, when it is open at the top, something of the life which goes on inside communicates itself to the surrounding city.

But however exciting these communications may be, an uninhibited flow into the arena is not possible. The number of seats it contains is limited; its maximum density is fixed in advance. The seats are arranged so that people are not too closely crushed. The occupants are meant to be comfortable in them and to be able to watch, each from his own seat, without disturbing others.

Outside, facing the city, the arena displays a lifeless wall; inside is a wall of people. The spectators turn their backs to the city. They have been lifted out of its structure of walls and streets and, for the duration of their time in the arena, they do not care about anything which happens there; they have left behind all their associations, rules and habits. Their remaining together in large numbers for a stated period of time is secure and their excitement has been promised them. But only under one definite condition: the discharge must take place *inside the arena*.

The seats are arranged in tiers around the arena, so that everyone can see what is happening below. The consequence of this is that the crowd is seated opposite itself. Every spectator has a thousand in front of him, a thousand heads. As long as he is there, all the others are there too; whatever excites him, excites them; and he sees it. They are seated some distance away from him, so that the differing details which make individuals of them are blurred; they all look alike and they all behave in a similar manner and he notices in them only the things which he himself is full of. Their visible excitement increases his own.

There is no break in the crowd which sits like this, exhibiting itself to itself. It forms a closed ring from which nothing can escape. The tiered ring of fascinated faces has something strangely homogeneous about it. It embraces and contains everything which happens below; no-one relaxes his grip on this; no-one tries to get away. Any gap in the ring might remind him of disintegration and subsequent dispersal. But there is no gap; this crowd is doubly closed, to the world outside and in itself.

The Attributes of the Crowd

BEFORE I TRY to undertake a classification of crowds it may be useful to summarize briefly their main attributes. The following four traits are important.

1. *The crowd always wants to grow.* There are no natural boundaries to its growth. Where such boundaries have been artificially created—e.g. in all institutions which are used for the preservation of closed crowds—an eruption of the crowd is always possible and will, in fact, happen from time to time. There are no institutions which can be absolutely relied on to prevent the growth of the crowd once and for all.

2. *Within the crowd there is equality.* This is absolute and indisputable and never questioned by the crowd itself. It is of fundamental importance and one might even define a crowd as a state of absolute equality. A head is a head, an arm is an arm, and differences between individual heads and arms are irrelevant. It is for the sake of this equality that people become a crowd and they tend to overlook anything which might detract from it. All demands for justice and all theories of equality ultimately derive their energy from the actual experience of equality familiar to anyone who has been part of a crowd.

3. *The crowd loves density.* It can never feel too dense. Nothing must stand between its parts or divide them; everything must be the crowd itself. The feeling of density is strongest in the moment of discharge. One day it may be possible to determine this density more accurately and even to measure it.

4. *The crowd needs a direction.* It is in movement and it moves towards a goal. The direction, which is common to all its members, strengthens the feeling of equality. A goal outside the individual members and common to all of them drives underground all the private differing goals which are fatal to the crowd as such. Direction is essential for the continuing existence of the crowd. Its constant fear of disintegration means that it will accept *any* goal. A crowd exists so long as it has an unattained goal.

There is, however, another tendency hidden in the crowd, which appears to lead to new and superior kinds of formation. The nature of these is often not predictable.

Each of these four attributes will be found in any crowd to a greater or lesser degree. How a crowd is to be classified will depend on which of them predominates in it.

I have discussed open and closed crowds and explained that these terms refer to their growth. The crowd is open so long as its growth is not impeded; it is closed when its growth is limited.

Another distinction is that between *rhythmic* and *stagnating* crowds. This refers to the next two attributes, *equality* and *density*; and to both of them simultaneously.

The *stagnating* crowd lives for its discharge. But it feels certain of this and puts it off. It desires a relatively long period of density to prepare for the moment of discharge. It, so to speak, warms itself at its density and delays as long as possible with the discharge. The process here starts not with equality, but with density; and equality then becomes the main goal of the crowd, which in the end it reaches. Every shout, every utterance in common is a valid expression of this equality.

In the *rhythmic* crowd, on the other hand (for example the crowd of the dance), density and equality coincide from the beginning. Everything here depends on movement. All the physical stimuli involved function in a predetermined manner and are passed on from one dancer to another. Density is embodied in the formal recurrence of retreat and approach; equality is manifest in the movements themselves. And thus, by the skilful enactment of density and equality, a crowd feeling is engendered. These rhythmic formations spring up very quickly and it is only physical exhaustion which bring them to an end.

The next pair of concepts—the *slow* and the *quick* crowd—refer exclusively to the nature of the goal. The conspicuous crowds which are the ones usually mentioned and which form such an essential part of modern life—the political, sporting and war like crowds we see daily—are all *quick* crowds. Very different from these are the religious crowds whose goal is a heaven, or crowds formed of pilgrims. Their goal is distant, the way to it long, and the true formation of the crowd is relegated to a far off country or to another world. Of these slow crowds we actually see only the tributaries, for the end they strive after is invisible and not to be attained by the unbelieving. The slow crowd gathers slowly and only sees itself as permanent in a far distance.

This is a mere indication of the nature of these forms. We shall have to consider them more closely.

Rhythm

RHYTHM IS ORIGINALLY the rhythm of the feet. Every human being walks, and, since he walks on two legs with which he strikes the ground in turn and since he only moves if he continues to do this, whether intentionally or not, a rhythmic sound ensues. The two feet never strike the ground with exactly the same force. The difference between them can be larger or smaller according to individual constitution or mood. It is also possible to walk faster or slower, to run, to stand still suddenly, or to jump.

Man has always listened to the footsteps of other men; he has certainly paid more attention to them than to his own. Animals too have their familiar gait; their rhythms are often richer and more audible than those of men; hoofed animals flee in herds, like regiments of drummers. The knowledge of the animals by which he was surrounded, which threatened him and which he hunted, was man's oldest knowledge. He learnt to know animals by the rhythm of their movement. The earliest writing he learnt to read was that of their tracks; it was a kind of rhythmic notation imprinted on the soft ground and, as he read it, he connected it with the sound of its formation.

Many of these footprints were in large numbers close together and, just by looking quietly at them, men, who themselves originally lived in small hordes, were made aware of the contrast between their own numbers and the enormous numbers of some animal herds. They were always hungry and on the watch for game; and the more there was of it, the better for them. But they also wanted to be more themselves. Man's feeling for his own increase was always strong and is certainly not to be understood only as his urge for self-propagation. Men wanted to be more, *then* and *there*; the large numbers of the herd which they hunted blended in their feelings with their own numbers which they *wished* to be large, and they expressed this in a specific state of communal excitement which I shall call the *rhythmic* or *throbbing* crowd.

The means of achieving this state was first of all the rhythm of their feet, repeating and multiplied. Steps added to steps in quick succession conjure up a larger number of men than there are. The men do not move away but, dancing, remain on the same spot. The sound of their steps does not die away, for these are continually repeated; there is a long stretch of time during which they continue to sound loud and alive. What they lack in numbers the dancers make up in intensity; if they stamp harder, it sounds as if there were more of them. As long as they go on dancing, they exert an attraction on all in their neighbour-hood. Everyone within hearing joins them and remains with them. The natural thing would be for new people to go on joining them for ever, but soon there are none left and the dancers have to conjure up increase out of their own limited numbers. They move as though there were more and more of them. Their excitement grows and reaches frenzy.

How do they compensate for the increase in numbers which they cannot have? First, it is important that they should all do the same thing. They all stamp the ground and they all do it in the same way; they all swing their arms to and fro and shake their heads. The equival-ence of the dancers becomes, and ramifies as, the equivalence of their limbs. Every part of a man which can move gains a life of its own and acts as if independent, but the movements are all parallel, the limbs appearing superimposed on each other. They are close together, one often resting on another, and thus _ensity is added to their state of equivalence. Density and equality become one and the same. In the end, there appears to be a single creature dancing, a creature with fifty heads and a hundred legs and arms, all performing in exactly the same way and with the same purpose. When their excitement is at its height, these people really feel as one, and nothing but physical exhaustion can stop them.

Thanks to the dominance of rhythm, all throbbing crowds have something similar in their appearance. The following account of one such dance was written in the first third of the last century. It describes the haka of the New Zealand Maoris, which was originally a war dance.

"The Maoris placed themselves in an extended line, in ranks four deep. This dance, called Haka, to a stranger witnessing it for the first time, is calculated to excite the most alarming fears; the entire body of performers, male and female, bond and free, were mixed together, without reference to the rank they held in the community. All the male performers were quite naked, except for the cartouche-box around the body, filled with ball cartridges. All were armed with muskets or bayonets put on the ends of spears or sticks; the young women, including the wives of the chief who joined in the dance, were exposed to the waist.

"In the chant that accompanied the dance, proper time was kept; as was equally well displayed in the various performances of agility exhibited in these hakas, especially in the perpendicular jump from the ground which was often repeated in a simultaneous manner, as if the whole body of performers were actuated by *one* impulse. The implements with which they armed themselves were brandished at the same moment, and the distortions of countenance, with the long tresses of hair that often adorn either sex, gave them the appearance of an army of Gorgons.

"The countenances of all were distorted into every possible shape permitted by the muscles of the human face; every new grimace was instantly adopted by all the performers in exact unison. Thus, if one commenced screwing up his face with a rigidity as if the appliance of a vice had been made use of, he was instantly followed by the whole body with a similar gesticulation, so that at times the whites of the eyes were only visible, the eyeballs rolling to and fro. They almost rolled their eyes out of their sockets, and distended their mouths, like hammer-headed sharks, from ear to ear. Their tongues were thrust out of the mouth with an extension impossible for an European to copy; early and long practice only could accomplish it. Altogether their countenances presented so horrible a spectacle that I was glad to relieve myself by withdrawing my gaze. . . .

"Every part of their body was in separate activity, fingers, toes, eyes, tongues as well as arms and legs. With the flattened hand they struck themselves on the left breast, or on the thigh. The noise of their chant was deafening. At least 350 performers took part in the haka. It is easy to imagine the effect of these dances in times of war, in raising the bravery, and heightening the antipathy that is felt by the contending parties against each other."

The rolling of the eyes and the thrusting out of the tongue are signs of defiance and challenge. But though war is usually a matter for men, that is, for *free* men, *everyone* abandons himself to the excitement of the haka. The crowd here knows neither age, sex nor rank; all act as equals. But what distinguishes this dance from others of a similar purpose is the exceptionally extreme *ramification* of equality. It is as though each body was taken to pieces, not only the arms and legs, but also the fingers, toes, tongues and eyes; and then all the tongues got together and did exactly the same thing at the same moment; all the toes and all the eyes became equal in one and the same enterprise. Each part of each dancer is seized by this feeling of equality; and it is always represented in action of increasing violence. The sight of 350 human beings, who together leap from the ground, together thrust out their tongues and together roll their eyes, must make an impression of invincible unity. Density here is not only a density of people, but also, and equally, one of their several limbs. One could imagine fingers and tongues coming together on their own to fight. The rhythm of the haka gives substance to each one of these equalities; mounting together to their common climax they are irresistible. For everything happens under the supposition that it is *seen*. The enemy is watching and the essence of the haka is the intensity of the common threat. But, once in existence, the dance becomes something more as well. It is practised from an early age, assumes many shapes and is performed on all kinds of occasion. Many travellers have been welcomed with a haka; the report quoted above derives from one such occasion. When one friendly group meets another, they salute each other with a haka, which looks so much in earnest that the innocent spectator fears the immediate outbreak of a battle. At the funeral ceremonies of a great chief, after all the phases of violent lament and self-mutilation customary with the Maoris, or after a festive and abundant meal, everyone suddenly jumps up, reaches for his musket and forms into a haka.

In this dance, in which all may participate, the tribe feel themselves a crowd. They make use of it whenever they feel a need to be a crowd, or to appear as one in front of others. In the rhythmic perfection it has attained the haka serves this purpose reliably. Thanks to it their unity is never seriously threatened from within.

Stagnation

THE *stagnating* crowd is closely compressed; it is impossible for it to move really freely. Its state has something passive in it; it waits. It waits for a head to be shown it, or for words, or it watches a fight. What really matters to it is *density*. The pressure which each member feels around him will also be felt as the measure of the strength of the formation of which he is now part. The more people who flow into that formation, the stronger the pressure becomes; feet have nowhere to move, arms are pinned down and only heads remain free, to see and to hear; every impulse is passed directly from body to body. Each individual knows that there must be a number of people there, but, because they are so closely jammed together, they are felt to be one. This kind of density allows itself time; its effects are constant over a certain period; it is amorphous and not subject to a practised and familiar rhythm. For a long time nothing happens, but the desire for action accumulates and increases until it bursts forth with enhanced violence.

The *patience* of a stagnating crowd becomes less astonishing if one realizes fully the importance this feeling of density has for it. The denser it is, the more people it attracts. Its density is the measure of its size, but is also the stimulus to further growth; the densest crowd grows fastest. Stagnation before the discharge is an exhibition of this density; the longer a crowd remains stagnant, the longer it feels and manifests its density.

For the individuals who compose such a crowd the period of stagnation is a period of marvels; laid down are all the stings and weapons with which at other times they arm themselves against each other; they touch one another, but do not feel confined; a clutch is a clutch no longer; they do not fear each other. Before they set forth, in whatever direction this will be, they want to make sure that they will remain together when they do. They want to grow closer together beforehand and, to do this, they need to be undisturbed. The stagnating crowd is not quite sure of its unity and therefore keeps still for as long as possible.

But this patience has its limits. The discharge must come sometime. Without it, it would be impossible to say that there really was a crowd. The outcry which used to be heard at public executions when the head of the malefactor was held up by the executioner, and the outcry heard today at sporting occasions, are the *voice* of the crowd. But the outcry must be spontaneous. Rehearsed and regularly repeated shouts are no proof that the crowd has achieved a life of its own. They may lead to it, but they may also be only external, like the drill of a military unit. Contrasted with them, the spontaneous and never quite predictable outcry of a crowd is unmistakable, and its effect enormous. It can express emotions of any kind; *which* emotions often matters less than their strength and variety and the freedom of their sequence. It is they which give the crowd its "feeling" space.

They can also, however, be so violent and concentrated that they immediately tear the crowd apart. This is what happens at public executions; one and the same victim can be killed only once. If he happens to be someone thought inviolable, there will, up to the very last moment, be some doubt as to whether he can in fact be killed; and this doubt will accentuate the inherent stagnation of the crowd. All the sharper and more effective, then, will be the sight of the severed head. The succeeding outcry will be terrible, but it will be the last outcry of this particular crowd. We may say that, in this case, the crowd pays for the lengthened period of stagnant expectation, which it will have enjoyed intensely, with its own immediate death.

Our modern arrangements for sport are more practical. The spectators can *sit*: universal patience is made visible to itself. They are free to stamp their feet, but they stay in the same place; they are free to clap their hands. A definite time is allowed for the occasion, and in general, they can count on its not being shortened. For this time, at least, they will remain together. Within it, however, anything may happen. No-one can know whether, or when, or on which side, goals will be shot; and, apart from these longed-for occurrences, there are many other lesser events which can lead to vociferous eruptions, many occasions on which the crowd will hear its own voice.

The final disintegration and scattering of this crowd is made somewhat less painful by being determined in advance. It is known, too, that the beaten side will have an opportunity of taking its revenge; everything is not over for good. The crowd can really feel comfortable at a match; first it can jam the entrances and then it can settle down in the seats. It can shout as opportunity arises and, even when everything is over, it can hope for similar occasions in the future.

Stagnant crowds of a much more passive kind form in *theatres*. Ideally, actors play to full houses; the desired number of spectators is fixed from the start. People arrive on their own. There may be small aggregations in front of the box-office, but people find their way separately into the auditorium. They are taken to their seats. Everything is fixed: the play they are going to see, the actors who will perform, the time the curtain will rise, and the spectators themselves in their seats. Late-comers are received with slight hostility. There they all sit, like a well-drilled herd, still and infinitely patient. But everyone is very well aware of his own separate existence. He has paid for his seat and he notices who sits next to him. Till the play starts, he leisurely contemplates the rows of assembled heads. They awaken in him an agreeable but not too pressing feeling of density. The equality of the spectators really consists only in the fact that they are all exposed to the same performance. But their spontaneous reactions to it are limited. Even their applause has its prescribed times; in general people clap only when they are supposed to. The strength of the applause is the only clue to the extent to which they have become a crowd; it is the only measure of this, and is valued accordingly by the actors.

Stagnation in the theatre has become so much a rite that individuals feel only gentle external pressure, which does not stir them too deeply and scarcely ever gives them a feeling of inner unity and togetherness. But one should not underestimate the extent of their real and shared

expectation, nor forget that it persists during the whole of the performance. People rarely leave a theatre before the end of the play;
even when disappointed they sit it through, which means that, for that
period anyway, they stay together.

The contrast between the stillness of the listeners and the din of the
apparatus inflicting itself on them is even more striking in *concerts*.
Here everything depends on the audience being completely undisturbed; any movement is frowned on, any sound taboo. Though the
music performed draws a good part of its life from its rhythm, no
rhythmical effect of any sort on the listeners must be perceptible. The
continually fluctuating emotions set free by the music are of the most
varied and intense kind. Most of those present must feel them and, in
addition, must feel them together, at the same time. But all outward
reactions are prohibited. People sit there motionless, as though they
managed to hear *nothing*. It is obvious that a long and artificial training
in stagnation has been necessary here. We have grown accustomed to
its results, but, to an unprejudiced mind, there are few phenomena of
our cultural life as astonishing as a concert audience. People who allow
music to affect them in a natural way behave quite differently; and
those who hear it for the first time, never having heard any before,
show unbridled excitement. When French sailors played the Marseillaise to the aborigines of Tasmania these expressed their satisfaction by
such strange contortions of their body and such astounding gestures
that the sailors shook with laughter. One young man was so enchanted
by it that he tore out his hair, scratched his head with both hands and
repeatedly uttered loud, piercing cries.

A meagre remnant of physical discharge is preserved even in our
concerts. Clapping is offered as thanks to the performers: a brief,
chaotic noise in exchange for a long, well-organized one. If applause
is suppressed and people disperse as quietly as they have sat, it is because
they feel that they are within the sphere of religious devotion.

It is from this sphere that the stillness of the concert originally derives.
The *standing together* before God is a practice common to many religions. It is characterized by the same features with which we have become familiar in secular crowds, and it can lead to just as sudden and
violent discharges.

Perhaps the most impressive case is the famous "Standing on
Arafat", the climax of the pilgrimage to Mecca. On a ritually appointed
day, 600-700,000 pilgrims gather on the plain of Arafat, some hours
distance from Mecca. They group themselves in a large circle round
"The Mount of Mercy", a bare hill which rises in the middle of the

plain. They take up their positions towards two o'clock, when the sun is hottest, and remain standing there until it sets. They are all bareheaded and dressed in the white robes of pilgrims. In passionate tension they listen to the words of the preacher who speaks to them from the summit of the hill. His sermon is an uninterrupted glorification of God and the pilgrims respond with one formula, repeated a thousand times: "We wait for your commands, O Lord. We wait for your commands." Some sob with excitement, some beat their chest. Many faint in the terrible heat. But it is essential that they should endure through the long burning hours on the sacred plain. Only at sunset is the signal for departure given.

Subsequent events, which are amongst the most enigmatic of all known religious observances, will be described and interpreted later, in another context. All we are interested in here is this hour-long moment of stagnation. Hundreds of thousands of human beings in a state of mounting excitement are kept there on that plain. They stand before God, and, whatever happens to them, may not abandon their station. Together they take their places and together they receive the signal for departure. They are set on fire by the sermon and they set themselves on fire with their own voices. Their "waiting" is contained in the formula they use, which recurs again and again. The sun, moving with imperceptible slowness, immerses everything in the same blazing light, the same burning glow. It is the embodiment of stagnation.

Every gradation of stiffening and of stillness can be found among religious crowds, but the highest degree of passivity ever attained by a crowd is that imposed on it from outside, by force. In a battle two crowds meet, each of which wants to be stronger than the other. With the help of battle-cries each tries to prove, to the enemy as to itself, that it is the stronger. The aim of the battle is to silence the other side. Their loud and united voice is a threat rightly feared; when they have all been cut down, it is silenced for ever. The stillest crowd is the crowd of enemy dead. The more dangerous they were, the stronger the desire to see them in a motionless heap. The experience of seeing them thus, as a defenceless heap of dead, evokes an intense and peculiar emotion, for it was only a short time before that they were experienced as a living host, which fought and shouted for blood. In former times, this *stilled crowd* of the dead was by no means felt to be lifeless. It was assumed that, in a way of their own, they would go on living somewhere else, all of them together still; and basically their life would be as one had known it. The enemy who lay on the battlefield as corpses represented for the beholder an extreme case of a stagnating crowd.

But this conception can be carried still one degree further. Instead of the slaughtered enemy, it can be *all* the dead *everywhere* who lie in the common earth and await resurrection. Everyone who dies and is buried adds to their number. All who have ever lived belong there, and there are so many of them that they cannot be counted. The earth between them is their density and, though they lie there separately, they are felt to be close to each other. They will lie there for an eternity, until the Day of the Last Judgment. Their life stagnates until the moment of resurrection, and this moment coincides with that of their assembly together before God, who will judge them. Nothing happens in between. As a crowd they lie there; as a crowd, they rise again. There is no more sublime proof of the reality and significance of the stagnating crowd than the development of this conception of Resurrection and Last Judgment.

Slowness, or the Remoteness of the Goal

THE SLOW CROWD is characterized by the remoteness of its goal. It is composed of people who move with great persistence towards an immovable goal, and who keep together in all circumstances. The road is long, the obstacles unknown and dangers threaten them from all sides. No discharge is permitted before the goal has been reached.

The slow crowd has the form of a train. Sometimes it includes from the beginning everyone who is going to belong to it, as with the Exodus of the Children of Israel from Egypt. Their goal is the Promised Land and they are a crowd so long as they believe in this goal. The story of their wandering is the story of their belief. Often the difficulties are so great that they begin to doubt. They hunger and thirst and, as soon as they grumble, they are threatened with disintegration. Again and again must the man who leads them strive to re-establish their faith. Again and again he succeeds, or, if *he* does not, the threat of enemies does. Their wandering stretches over forty years and contains many examples of the formation of quick, transitory crowds. Much could be said about these, but the point now is that here they are all subordinated to the more comprehensive conception of a single slow crowd moving onwards to its goal, the country that was promised it. The adults in it grow old and die; children are born and grow up. But even if all the individuals are different, the Exodus as a whole remains the same. No new groups join it; from the start it had been decided who belonged to it and had a claim on the Promised Land. It is a crowd which cannot grow by leaps and bounds and thus one question remained paramount during the whole migration: how was such a crowd to avoid disintegration.

There is a second type of slow crowd which can better be compared to a network of streams. It starts with small rivulets gradually running together. Into the stream thus formed other streams flow and these, if enough land lies ahead, will in time become a river whose goal is the sea. The annual pilgrimage to Mecca is perhaps the most impressive example of this type of slow crowd. From the remotest parts of the Islamic world caravans of pilgrims set out, all in the direction of Mecca. Some of these begin small; others are equipped with great splendour by princes and, from the start, are the pride of the countries where they originate. But all of them in the course of their wanderings encounter other caravans with the same goal; and so they grow and grow until, near their goal, they become enormous rivers. Mecca is the sea into which they flow.

Such caravans are so constituted that the pilgrims have ample scope for ordinary experiences, quite unconnected with the purpose of their journey as a whole. They live the recurring day, contend with many dangers and, as they are mostly poor, have difficulty in providing themselves with food and drink. They live in alien and continually changing surroundings and are far more exposed to dangers than they are at home; and these dangers are not always related to their enterprise. Thus they remain to a large extent individuals, living their separate lives as people do anywhere. But as long as they stick to their goal—and most pilgrims do—they are also always part of a slow crowd which exists however they behave in relation to it, and which will continue to exist until the goal is reached.

A third variant of the slow crowd is to be found in formations which have reference to an invisible goal, not attainable in this life. The world where the blessed await all those who have merited their place in it is a well-defined goal and belongs to the faithful alone. They see it clearly and distinctly in front of them; they do not have to be satisfied with a vague symbol. Life is a pilgrimage towards it, but between them and their goal stands death. The way ahead is difficult to know, for it is nowhere marked; many go astray and get lost. But the hope of the world beyond still colours the life of the believer to such a degree that we are entitled to speak of a slow crowd to which all the followers of a faith belong in common. The anonymity of this crowd is particularly impressive. Its members do not know each other, for they live dispersed in many cities and countries.

But what does it look like from *inside* and what chiefly distinguishes it from a *quick* crowd?

The *discharge* is denied to the slow crowd. We could say that this was its most important distinguishing mark and, instead of slow crowds, we could speak of crowds which have no discharge. But the first term is preferable, for the discharge cannot be entirely renounced. It will always be contained in the conception of the final state. It is only postponed to a far distance; where the goal is, there too is the discharge. A vision of it is always strongly present, though its actuality lies at the end of the way.

The slow crowd tends to lengthen and protract the process which leads to the discharge. The great religions have developed a particular mastery of this business of delay. Their concern is to keep the followers they have won and, in order to do this and also to win new ones, they have to assemble them from time to time. Such assemblies will result in violent discharges and, once these have happened, they have to be repeated and, if possible, surpassed in violence. Their regular recurrence, at least, is essential if the unity of the faithful is not to be lost. But the events likely to happen in the course of services enacted, as these are, by rhythmic crowds, cannot be controlled over large distances. The central problem of the universal religions is how to dominate believers spread over wide stretches of the earth. The only way to do it is by a conscious slowing down of crowd events. Distant goals must gain in importance, near ones losing more and more of their weight until, in the end, they appear valueless. An earthly discharge is too brief; only one which is removed into the world beyond has permanence.

In this way goal and discharge coincide; and the goal is inviolate. A promised land here on earth can be occupied and laid waste by enemies; the people to whom it was sworn can be expelled from it. Mecca was conquered and plundered by the Carmathians and the holy stone Kaaba carried off; for many years no pilgrimage could be undertaken. But the heaven of the blessed is secure from all such devastations. It subsists on faith alone and is only vulnerable there. The disintegration of the slow crowd of Christianity set in as soon as faith in this other world began to decay.

Invisible Crowds

OVER THE WHOLE earth, wherever there are men, is found the conception of the *invisible dead*. It is tempting to call it humanity's oldest conception. There is certainly no horde, no tribe, no people which does not have abundant ideas about its dead. Man has been obsessed by them; they have been of enormous importance for him; the action of the dead upon the living has been an essential part of life itself.

They were thought of as being together, just as men are together, and generally it was assumed that there were a great many of them. "The old Bechuana, in common with all other South African natives, believed all space to be full of the spirits of their ancestors. Earth, air and sky were crowded with ghosts who could exercise a baleful influence on the living if they chose." "The Boloki folk in the Congo believe that they are surrounded by spirits who try to thwart them at every twist and turn and to harm them every hour of the day and night. The rivers and creeks are crowded with the spirits of their ancestors, and the forests and bush are full also of spirits, ever seeking to injure the living who are overtaken by night when travelling by road or canoe. I never met among them a man daring enough to go at night through the forest that divided our village from the next, even though a large reward was offered. Their invariable reply was: 'There are too many spirits in bush and forest.' "

Men usually believe that the dead live together in a distant country, under the earth, on an island, or in a heavenly house. The following is part of a song from the Pygmies in Gaboon.

> "The gates of the cave
> Are shut.
> The gates of the cave
> Are shut.
> The souls of the dead are crowding there in droves,
> Like a swarm of flies,
> Like a swarm of flies, dancing at evening time.
> A swarm of flies dancing at evening time
> When the night has grown dark,
> When the sun has vanished,
> When the night has grown dark,
> A swarm of flies.
> The whirling of dead leaves
> In a howling tempest."

But it is not only that the numbers of the dead increase and a feeling of their density prevails. They also move about and undertake expeditions together. To ordinary people they remain invisible, but there are people with special gifts, called Shamans, who have power to conjure up and subdue the spirits and turn them into their servants. Among the Chukchee in Siberia "a good Shaman has whole legions of auxiliary spirits and, when he calls them all, they come in such numbers that they surround the small sleeping tent where the exorcism takes place, like a wall on all sides."

The Shamans *tell* what they see. "In a voice trembling with emotion, the Shaman calls out through the snow hut:

'The space of heaven is filled with naked beings rushing through the air; men, naked men, naked women who rush through the air and rouse gale and snowstorm.

'Do you hear it roaring? Roaring like the wing-beat of great birds high in the air. That is the fear of naked men. That is the flight of naked men. The spirits of the air breathe out storm. The spirits of the air drive the whirling snow over the earth.' "

This mighty vision of naked spirits in their flight comes from the Eskimos.

Some peoples imagine their dead, or certain of them, as fighting hosts. The Celts of the Scottish Highlands have a special word for the host of the dead: *sluagh*, meaning "spirit-multitude". "The spirits fly about in great clouds like starlings, up and down the face of the world, and come back to the scenes of their earthly transgressions. With their venomous unerring darts they kill cats and dogs, sheep and cattle. They fight battles in the air as men do on the earth. They may be heard and seen on clear, frosty nights, advancing and retreating, retreating and advancing against one another. After a battle their crimson blood may be seen staining rocks and stones." The word *gairm* means shout or cry, and *sluagh-ghairm* was the battle-cry of the dead. This word later became "slogan". The expression we use for the battle-cries of our modern crowds derives from the Highland hosts of the dead.

Two widely separated northern peoples, the Lapps in Europe and the Tlinkit Indians in Alaska, share the same conception of the Aurora Borealis as a battle. "The Kolta Lapps imagine that they see in the Northern Lights those who have fallen in war and who, as spirits, continue their fight in the air. The Russian Lapps see in the Lights the spirits of the slain. They live together in a house where they assemble from time to time and there stab each other to death; the floor is covered with blood. The Northern Lights announce the start of these battles between the souls of the slain. Among the Tlinkit of Alaska all those who do not fall in battle, but die of disease, pass into the under-world. In heaven are only the brave warriors who have died in wars. From time to time heaven opens to receive new spirits; these show themselves to the Shaman as fully armed warriors and their souls appear as the Aurora Borealis and especially as those flames which resemble arrows and sheaves of light and pass and overtake each other and change places, very much as the Tlinkits themselves fight. A strong Aurora Borealis announces, so they believe, great slaughter. It is the dead seeking for new comrades."

The Germanic peoples believe that enormous numbers of warriors are gathered together in Valhalla. All those who have fallen in battle since the beginning of the world go to Valhalla. Their numbers grow continually, for there is no end to wars. In Valhalla they revel and gorge themselves; food and drink is renewed eternally. Each morning they seize their weapons and go out to fight. They kill each other in sport, but they stand up again; it is not real death. Through 640 gates they re-enter Valhalla, 800 men in a row.

But it is not only the spirits of the dead which are imagined in such numbers, invisible to ordinary living men. In an old Jewish text we read: "Man ought to know and should remember that the space be-tween heaven and earth is not empty, but is all filled with troops and multitudes. Some of these are pure, full of grace and goodness; but others are unclean creatures, tormentors and doers of harm. They all fly to and fro in the air. Some of them want peace, others seek war; some do good, some evil; some bring life, but others bring death."

In the religion of the old Persians, the demons—*Daevas*—form a specific host under a high command of their own. In their holy book, the *Zend-Avesta*, there is a formula for their innumerability: "Thous-ands of thousands of those *Daevas*, their ten thousands of ten thousands, their numberless myriads."

The Christian Middle Ages gave serious thought to the number of *devils*. In Caesarius von Heisterbach's *Dialogue of Miracles* is a report of how they once thronged the choir of a church in such numbers that they disturbed the chant of the monks. These were beginning the third psalm, "Lord, how are they increased that trouble me." The demons flew from one side of the choir to the other and mingled with the monks, so that the latter no longer knew what they were singing until, in their confusion, each side was trying to shout down the other. If so many demons can gather together in one single place to interrupt one

single service, how many of them must there be in the whole world!
"But we know already from the Gospel", adds Caesarius, "that a
legion entered into one man."

Later he tells how a wanton priest on his deathbed said to a kins-
woman who sat near him, "Do you see that great barn opposite us?
Under its roof are as many separate straws as there are demons now
gathered round me." They lay in ambush for his soul, waiting to carry
it to punishment. But they also tried their luck at the deathbeds of the
pious. At the funeral of a good abbess there were more devils gathered
together than there are leaves on the trees of a great forest; round a
dying abbot more than the grains of sand on the sea shore. These
particulars came from a devil who had been there in person and gave
an account of it all to a knight with whom he fell into conversation.
He did not disguise his disappointment over these fruitless endeavours
and admitted that he had been present, sitting on an arm of the Cross,
when Jesus expired.

It is clear that the importunity of these devils was as monstrous as
their numbers. Whenever Richalm, a Cistercian abbot, closed his eyes
he saw them around him as thick as dust. There were more precise
estimates of their numbers, two of which are known to me, but they
differ widely: one is 44,635,569; the other is 11 billion.

There is a natural and wide contrast between men's conception of
devils and their conception of angels and saints. With the latter everything is calm. There is no more striving, for the goal has been reached.
But they, too, are gathered together, a heavenly host, "a multitude of
angels, patriarchs, prophets, apostles, martyrs, confessors, virgins and
other righteous ones." Ranged in great circles, they stand round the
throne of their Lord, like courtiers turned towards their king. Head
pressed close to head, their bliss is grounded in their nearness to him.
He has accepted them forever and, in as much as they will never leave
him, they will never separate from each other. They remain in contemplation of him, and they sing his praises. It is the only thing they
still do, and they do it together.

The minds of the faithful are full of such images of invisible crowds.
Whether these are the dead, or devils, or saints, they are imagined as
large, concentrated hosts. It could be argued that religions *begin* with
these invisible crowds. They may be differently grouped, and in each
faith a different balance between them has developed. It would be
both possible and fruitful to classify religions according to the way in
which they manipulate their invisible crowds. Here the higher religions
—by which I mean all those which have attained universal validity—

exhibit a superior degree of certainty and clarity. These invisible hosts are kept alive by religious teaching. They are the life-blood of faith. The hopes and desires of men cling to them. When they fade, faith weakens and, whilst it dies slowly away, fresh hosts come to take the place of the faded.

One of these crowds, and perhaps the most important of all, has not been mentioned yet. It is the only one which, in spite of its invisibility, seems natural to us today: I mean *posterity*. For two, or perhaps three, generations a man can count his posterity; from then on it lies entirely in the future. It is precisely when it has become numberless that posterity is visible to no-one. It is known that it must increase, first gradually and then with growing acceleration. Tribes and whole peoples trace their origin back to a common ancestor and the promises claimed to have been given to him show how glorious, and especially how numerous, a progeny he desired; innumerable as the stars in heaven and the sand on the shores of the sea. In the *Shi-King*, the classical Book of Songs of the Chinese, there is a poem in which progeny is compared to a swarm of locusts:

"The locusts' wings say 'throng, throng';
Well may your sons and grandsons
Be a host innumerable.
The locusts' wings say 'bind, bind';
Well may your sons and grandsons,
Continue in an endless line.
The locusts' wings say 'join, join';
Well may your sons and grandsons
Be forever at one."

Large numbers, unbroken succession—a kind of density throughout time—and unity: these are the three wishes for progeny pronounced here. The use of the swarm of locusts as a symbol for the crowd of progeny is particularly striking in that it exhibits them not as harmful vermin, but as praiseworthy in their exemplary power of increase.

The feeling for posterity is as alive today as it ever was, but the image of abundance has detached itself from our own progeny and transferred itself to future humanity as a whole. For most of us, the hosts of the dead are an empty superstition, but we regard it as a noble and by no means fruitless endeavour to care for the future crowd of the unborn; to want their good and to prepare for them a better and a juster life. In the universal anxiety about the future of the earth, this feeling for the unborn is of the greatest importance. Disgust at the thought of their malformation, the thought of what they may look like if we continue to conduct our grotesque wars, may well do more than all our private fears for ourselves to lead to the abolition of these wars, and of war altogether.

If we now consider the *fate* of the invisible crowds we have spoken of, we shall conclude that some of them have disappeared completely, and others in large part. Among the latter are the devils. In spite of their former numbers, they are no longer to be found anywhere in their familiar shape. But they have left their traces. The fact that they were small is proved by the striking instances adduced by Caesarius von Heisterbach, who was contemporary with the time of their flowering. Since then they have given up all the traits which might remind us of a human figure and become much smaller still. It is greatly changed, and in even larger numbers, that they turn up again in the 19th century as *bacilli*. Instead of the souls, they now attack the bodies of men; and to these they can be very dangerous. Only a tiny minority of people have looked into a microscope and really seen them there. But everyone has heard of them and is continually aware of their presence and makes every effort not to come into contact with them—though this, considering their invisibility, is a somewhat vague endeavour. Their power to harm and their concentration in enormous numbers in very small spaces is undoubtedly taken over from devils.

An invisible crowd which has always existed, but which has only been recognized as such since the invention of the microscope, is the crowd of *spermatozoa*. 200 million of these animalcules set out together on their way. They are equal among themselves and in a state of very great density. They all have the same goal and, except for one, they all perish on the way. It may be objected that they are not human beings and that it is therefore not correct to speak of them as a crowd in the sense the word has been used. But this objection does not really touch the essentials of the matter. Each of these animalcules carries with it everything of our ancestors which will be preserved. It contains our ancestors; it *is* them, and it is overwhelmingly strange to find them here again, between one human existence and another, in a radically changed form, all of them within *one* tiny invisible creature, and this creature present in such uncountable numbers.

Classification of Crowds according to Their Prevailing Emotion

THE CROWDS WE have become acquainted with are filled with all kinds of emotions, and scarcely anything has been said about these. The first aim of our enquiry was a classification according to formal principles, but the statement that a crowd is open or closed, slow or quick, visible or invisible, tells us very little about what it feels, what its content is.

Now this content is by no means always to be found in a pure state. There are occasions when the crowd runs through a whole series of emotions in quick succession. People can spend hours in a theatre and the experiences they share there are of the most varied kind. In a concert their feelings are even more detached from the occasion and may be said, in fact, to attain the maximum of variety. But these occasions are artificial; their richness is an end-product of high and complex cultures. Their effect is moderated because in them, extremes cancel each other out. They serve, on the whole, to soften and diminish the passions at whose mercy people feel when alone.

The main emotional types of crowd can be traced much further back than this. They make a very early appearance; their history is as old as that of humanity itself, and in two cases even older. Each of these types is distinguished by a homogeneous colour; a single passion dominates them. Once they have been properly understood, it is impossible ever to confound them again.

I propose to distinguish five types of crowd in accordance with their emotional content. The oldest of these are the baiting crowd and the flight crowd. These are to be found among animals as well as amongst men and it is probable that their formation among men has time and again been influenced by the example of animals. The prohibition, the reversal and the feast crowd, on the other hand, are specifically human. A description of these five main types is indispensable, and its interpretation can afford insights of considerable importance.

Baiting Crowds

THE BAITING CROWD forms with reference to a quickly attainable goal. The goal is known and clearly marked, and is also near. This crowd is out for killing and it knows whom it wants to kill. It heads for this goal with unique determination and cannot be cheated of it. The proclaiming of the goal, the spreading about of who it is that is to perish, is enough to make the crowd form. This concentration on killing is of a special kind and of an unsurpassed intensity. Everyone wants to participate; everyone strikes a blow and, in order to do this, pushes as near as he can to the victim. If he cannot hit him himself, he wants to see others hit him. Every arm is thrust out as if they all belonged to one and the same creature. But the arms which actually do the hitting count for most. The goal is also the point of greatest density. It is where the actions of all the participants unite. Goal and density coincide.

One important reason for the rapid growth of the baiting crowd is that there is no risk involved. There is no risk because the crowd have immense superiority on their side. The victim can do nothing to them. He is either bound or in flight, and cannot hit back; in his defencelessness he is victim only. Also he has been made over to them for destruction; he is destined for it and thus no-one need fear the sanction attached to killing. His permitted murder stands for all the murders people have to deny themselves for fear of the penalties for their perpetration. A murder shared with many others, which is not only safe and permitted, but indeed recommended, is irresistible to the great majority of men. There is, too, another factor which must be remembered. The threat of death hangs over all men and, however disguised it may be, and even if it is sometimes forgotten, it affects them all the time and creates in them a need to deflect death on to others. The formation of baiting crowds answers this need.

It is so easy and everything happens so quickly that people have to hurry to get there in time. The speed, elation and conviction of a baiting crowd is something uncanny. It is the excitement of blind men who are blindest when they suddenly think they can see. The crowd advances towards victim and execution in order to rid itself once and for all of its own deaths. But what actually happens to it is the opposite of this. Through the execution, though only after it, it feels more menaced than ever by death; it disintegrates and disperses in a kind of flight. The greater the victim, the greater the fear. It can only hold together if a series of similar events follow each other in quick succession.

The baiting crowd is very old. It goes back to the most primitive dynamic unit known among men: the hunting pack. I shall say more later about packs, which are smaller than crowds, and differ from them in many other respects also. Here I only want to treat of a few general occasions which give rise to the formation of baiting crowds.

Among the death penalties which a horde or a people can inflict on an individual, two main forms can be distinguished. The first is *expulsion*. The individual is marooned where he is at the mercy of wild animals without any kind of defence, or where he will starve. The people to whom he formerly belonged will have nothing to do with him any more; they are not allowed to shelter him or give him food; any intercourse with him defiles them and makes them guilty. Solitude in its most rigorous form is the ultimate penalty here; separation from one's group is a torture which very few can survive, especially under primitive conditions. A variant of this isolation is handing over to the enemy. This is particularly cruel and humiliating for men who suffer it otherwise than after fighting. For them it is a double death.

The other way of punishing is collective killing. The condemned man is taken out to a field and stoned. Everyone has a share in his death; everyone throws a stone and it is under their joint impact that the transgressor collapses. No-one has been appointed executioner; the community as a whole does the killing. The stones stand for the community; they are the monument both to its decision and to its deed. Even where stoning is no longer customary, the inclination for collective killing persists. Death by *fire* can be compared to it; fire represents the multitude which desires the condemned person's death. The victim is assailed from all sides by the flames, which set on him simultaneously and kill him. The religions of hell go further. Collective killing by fire —fire stands as a symbol for the crowd—is associated with the idea of expulsion, namely, expulsion to hell, and surrender to diabolic enemies. The flames of hell reach up to the earth and fetch down the heretic who is forfeit to them. The studding of a victim with arrows and the shooting of a condemned man by a detachment of soldiers both present the executing group as the delegates of the whole community. With the burying of men in ant-heaps, as practised in Africa and elsewhere, the ants stand for the multitude and do its painful business.

All forms of public execution are connected with the old practice of collective killing. The real executioner is the crowd gathered round the scaffold. It approves the spectacle and, with passionate excitement, gathers from far and near to watch it from beginning to end. It wants it to happen and hates being cheated of its victim. The account of Christ's condemnation contains the root of the matter. The cry of "Crucify Him!" comes from the crowd; it is the crowd which is truly active here. On another occasion it might have done everything itself and stoned Jesus. The tribunal pronouncing judgement—normally in front of a limited number of people only—stands for the multitude which later attends the execution. The sentence of death, which sounds abstract and unreal when pronounced in the name of justice, becomes real when it is carried out in the presence of the crowd. It is actually for the sake of the crowd that justice is done and it is the crowd we have in mind when we speak of the importance of justice being public.

In the Middle Ages executions were carried out with pomp and solemnity, and as slowly as possible. Sometimes the victim exhorted the spectators with pious speeches. He declared his concern for them and expatiated on the manner of life which had led him to where he stood, so that they might avoid his fate. The crowd felt flattered by his concern and to him it may have been a last satisfaction to stand there once more as an *equal* amongst them, a good man like themselves, with them renouncing his former life and condemning it. This repentance in the face of death, which priests do their utmost to bring about in malefactors and infidels, has another significance besides the professed purpose of soul-saving. It transfuses the emotional state of the baiting crowd with premonitions of a future festal crowd. All who are present feel confirmed in their righteous convictions and in their belief in a heavenly reward.

In revolutionary periods executions are accelerated. Samson, the Paris executioner, boasted that his assistants only needed "a minute per person". Much of the feverish excitement of such times is due to the rapid succession of innumerable executions. It is important for the crowd that the executioner should show it the severed head. This, and this alone, is the moment of discharge. Whoever the head has belonged to, it is degraded now; during the short moment it stares at the crowd it becomes a head like all other heads. Though it may have started on the shoulders of a king, it is made level with them by this lightning process of public degradation. The crowd here consists of staring heads and it attains its feeling of equality during the moment that the head stares back at it. The greater the former power of the executed man, the greater the distance which used to separate him from the crowd and the stronger, therefore, the excitement of the discharge. In the case of a king, or person with similar power, there is, in addition, the satisfaction of *reversal*. The right of capital punishment which had been his so long, has been turned against him. Those he used to kill have now killed him. It is impossible to over-rate the importance of this reversal. There is a type of crowd which is created by reversal alone.

The effect of displaying the victim's head to the crowd is by no means confined to the discharge. The impact of his downfall is tremendous. By it he becomes no more than they are. They recognize him as one of themselves and thus he makes them all equal to one another, for they all see themselves in him. But the severed head of the victim is also a threat. They have looked into those dead eyes with such passion that now they cannot free themselves from him. His head has become part of the crowd and so the crowd itself is struck at in his death. Terrified and stricken by a mysterious disease, it begins to disintegrate, and finally disperses in a kind of flight from him.

Once a baiting crowd has attained its victim it disintegrates rapidly. Rulers in danger are well aware of this fact and throw a victim to the crowd in order to impede its growth. Many political executions are arranged solely for this purpose. The spokesman of radical parties, on the other hand, often fail to understand that the public execution of a dangerous enemy may cut deeper into their own flesh than into that of the enemy party. It may well be that the crowd of their partisans will scatter after such an execution, and that they will not regain their strength for a long time, and perhaps never.

Disgust at collective killing is of very recent date and should not be over-estimated. Today everyone takes part in public executions through the newspapers. Like everything else, however, it is more comfortable than it was. We sit peacefully at home and, out of a hundred details, can choose those to linger over which offer a special thrill. We only applaud when everything is over and there is no feeling of guilty connivance to spoil our pleasure. We are not responsible for the sentence, nor for the journalists who report its execution, nor for the papers which print them. None the less, we know more about the business than our predecessors, who may have walked miles to see it, hung around for hours and, in the end, seen very little. The baiting crowd is preserved in the newspaper reading public, in a milder form it is true, but, because of its distance from events, a more irresponsible one. One is tempted to say that it is the most despicable and, at the same time, most stable form of such a crowd. Since it does not even have to assemble, it escapes disintegration; variety is catered for by the daily re-appearance of the papers.

Flight Crowds

THE *flight crowd* is created by a threat. Everyone flees; everyone is drawn along. The danger which threatens is the same for all. It is concentrated at a definite point and makes no distinctions there. It can threaten the inhabitants of a city, or all those who belong to a particular faith, or speak a particular language.

People flee together because it is best to flee that way. They feel the same excitement and the energy of some increases the energy of others; people push each other along in the same direction. So long as they keep together they feel that the danger is distributed, for the ancient belief persists that danger springs at one point only. They argue that, whilst the enemy is seizing one of them, all the others can escape. The flanks of the flight are uncovered but, since they are extended, they think it impossible for danger to attack all of them at the same time. No-one is going to assume that he, out of so many, will be the victim and, since the sole movement of the whole flight is towards salvation, each is convinced that he personally will attain it.

For the most striking thing about a mass flight is the force of its direction. The crowd has, as it were, become all direction, away from danger. Since the goal of safety and the distance from it are the only things which matter, all the previously existing distances between men become unimportant. Strange and widely dissimilar creatures who have never come near each other before suddenly find themselves together. In their flight all the distances between them disappear, though the differences of course do not. The flight crowd is the most comprehensive of all crowds. It contains absolutely everybody and the picture of diversity which it thus presents is further complicated by the differing speeds of the fugitives: there are young and old among them, strong and weak, those less and those more burdened. But the picture is misleading. Its motley colours are only incidental and, measured against the overpowering force of direction, utterly insignificant.

The impetus of the flight continues to multiply so long as everyone recognizes that there are others fleeing with him. He may press them forwards, but he must not push them aside. The moment he starts to think only of himself and to regard those around him purely as obstacles, the character of the mass flight changes completely and it turns into its exact opposite; it becomes a panic, a struggle of each against all who stand in his way. This reversal generally occurs when the direction of the flight has been repeatedly impeded. To block the crowd's way is enough to make it break out in another direction. If its way is repeatedly blocked, it soon no longer knows where to turn. It grows confused about its direction and thus loses its coherence. The danger which, till then, had united its members and given them wings, now sets each man up as an enemy of the next. Everyone is intent only on saving himself.

The mass flight, on the other hand, contrary to the panic, derives its energy from its coherence. As long as it remains one powerful and undivided river and does not allow itself to be dispersed and split, so long does the fear by which it is driven remain bearable. Once a mass flight is under way it is characterized by a kind of exaltation—the exaltation of common movement. No one person is in any less danger than any other and, though he continues to run or ride with all his might to save his own life, he still occupies a recognized place amongst all the others and sticks to it throughout the turmoil.

The flight can last for days or weeks and, during it, some remain behind, either stricken by the enemy, or because their strength is gone. Everyone who falls by the way acts as a spur to the others. Fate has overtaken him and exempted them. He is a sacrifice offered to danger. However important he may have been to some of them as a companion in flight, by falling he becomes important to all of them. The sight of him gives new strength to the weary; he has proved weaker than they are; the danger was aimed at him and not at them. The isolation in which he remains behind, and in which they still see him for a short time, heightens for them the value of their being together. Anyone who falls has thus an incalculable importance for the cohesion of the flight.

The natural end of the flight is the attainment of the goal; once this crowd is in safety it dissolves. But the danger can also be arrested at its source. An armistice may be declared and the city from which people were fleeing be no longer in danger. They fled together, but they return singly, and soon everything is again as separate as it used to be. But there is also a third possibility, which may be called the oozing away of the flight in sand. The goal is too far off, the surroundings are hostile and the people starve and grow exhausted. It is no longer only a few, but hundreds and thousands who collapse and remain behind. This physical disintegration sets in only gradually, for the original impetus lasts for a long time; people crawl on even when every chance of salvation has vanished. Of all types of crowd, the flight crowd is the one which exhibits the greatest tenacity; its remnants keep together until the very last moment.

There is no dearth of examples of mass flights. Our own time alone is rich in them. Until the last war one would have thought first of the fate of Napoleon's *Grande Armée* in its retreat from Moscow, for this is the most striking example we know of, and we know it in all its details: an army composed of men of so many different countries and languages, the terrible winter, the immense stretch of country they had to traverse, most of them on foot—this was a retreat which was bound to degenerate into a mass flight. The first civilian flight from a metropolis of comparable size was probably that which took place when the Germans approached Paris in 1940. This famous exodus did not last long, for an armistice was soon concluded, but such was the extent and intensity of the movement that for the French it has become the central mass memory of the last war.

I do not intend to accumulate examples from recent times, for they are still fresh in everyone's memory. But it is worth pointing out that mass flight has always been known to men, even in the times when they still lived together in quite small groups. It played a part in their imagination long before they could have experienced it in actual numbers. One remembers the vision of the Eskimo Shaman: "The space of heaven is filled with naked beings rushing through the air. Men, naked men, naked women who rush through the air and rouse gale and snowstorm. Do you hear it roaring? Roaring like the wing-beat of great birds high in the air. That is the fear of naked men. That is the flight of naked men."

Prohibition Crowds

A SPECIAL TYPE of crowd is created by a *refusal*: a large number of people together refuse to continue to do what, till then, they had done singly. They obey a prohibition, and this prohibition is sudden and self-imposed. It can be an old prohibition which has been forgotten, or one which is resuscitated from time to time. But, in any case, it strikes with enormous power. It is as absolute as a command, but what is decisive about it is its negative character. Contrary to appearances, it never really comes from outside, but always originates in some need in those it affects. As soon as the prohibition has been enunciated the crowd begins to form. Its members all refuse to do what the outside world expects them to do. What, till then, they had done without any fuss, as if it was natural to them and not at all difficult, they now suddenly refuse to do in any circumstances; and the firmness of their refusal is the measure of their togetherness. From the moment of its birth this crowd is transfused with the negativeness of prohibition, and this remains its essential characteristic as long as it exists. Thus one could also speak of a negative crowd. It is formed by resistance; the prohibition is a frontier nothing can cross, a dam nothing can pierce. Each person watches the other to see whether he remains part of the dam. Anyone who gives way and transgresses the prohibition is outlawed by all the others.

In our own time the best example of a negative, or prohibition, crowd is the *strike*. The majority of workers are accustomed to do their work regularly at certain hours. The actual tasks vary from man to man, one doing one thing and another something quite different. But large groups start work at the same time and leave it at the same time. They are equals in relation to this common moment of starting and stopping work. In addition, most of them do their work with their hands and all of them alike get paid for working. Their wages, however, differ according to the work they do, and it is clear in general that their equality does not go very far and is not pronounced enough to lead by itself to the formation of a crowd. But when a strike breaks out the workers' equality becomes far more stringent. It consists then in their common refusal to continue work; and this refusal is something which permeates the whole man. The conviction created by a prohibition on work is both keen and strongly resistant.

The moment of standstill is a great moment, and has been celebrated in workers' songs. There are many things which contribute to the workers' feeling of relief at the start of a strike. The fictitious equality, which they had heard made so much of, had never really meant more than that they all used their hands. Now it has suddenly become a real equality. As long as they were working they had very varied things to do, and everything they did was prescribed. But, when they stop work, they all do the same thing. It is as though their hands had all dropped at exactly the same moment and now they had to exert all their strength *not* to lift them up again, however hungry their families. Stopping work makes the workers equals. Their concrete demands are actually of less importance than the effect of this moment. The aim of the strike may be a wage increase, and they certainly feel at one in this aim. But by itself it is not sufficient to make a crowd out of them.

The hands that drop infect other hands. Their inaction spreads to the whole of society. Sympathetic strikes prevent others, who had not been thinking of a stoppage, from following their normal occupations.

The essence of a strike is to prevent others working while the strikers are idle. The more nearly they achieve this, the greater their chance of victory.

Within the actual strike it is essential that everyone should abide by the undertaking not to work. Spontaneously from within the crowd itself there springs up an organization with the functions of a state. It is fully conscious of the shortness of its life and has only a very small number of laws; but these are strictly kept. Pickets guard the entrances to the place where the strike started, and the workplace itself is forbidden ground. The interdict on it lifts it out of its everyday triviality and endows it with a special dignity. In its emptiness and stillness it has something sacred. The fact that the strikers have taken over responsibility for it turns it into a common possession and, as such, it is protected and invested with a higher significance. Anyone who comes near it is examined about his convictions. Anyone who approaches it with profane intentions, wanting to work there, is treated as an enemy or traitor.

The organization sees to it that food and money are fairly distributed. What they have must last for as long as possible, so it is important that everyone should receive equally *little*. It does not occur to the strong to think that they should have more, and even the greedy are satisfied with their portion. As there is usually only a very little for everyone, and as distribution is settled in good faith and publicly, it adds to the pride which the crowd feels in its equality. There is something deeply serious and worthy of respect about such an organization and, when the ferocity and destructiveness of crowds are mentioned, one cannot help remembering the responsibility and dignity of these structures sprung spontaneously from crowds. An examination of the prohibition crowd is essential if only for the reason that it exhibits such entirely different, and indeed, contrary, qualities. As long as it remains true to its nature, it is averse to destruction.

But it is true that it is not easy to keep it in this state. When things go badly and want reaches proportions difficult to bear, and especially if it is assailed or besieged, the negative crowd tends to revert to a positive and active one. The strikers are men who have suddenly denied themselves the normal activity of their hands and, after a time, it can cost them no small effort to go on not using them. As soon as they feel the unity of their stand threatened, they incline towards destruction, and particularly towards destruction in the sphere of their own familiar activity. It is here that the most important task of the organization begins. It must keep the character of the prohibition crowd intact and prevent any positive or separate action. It must also recognize when the moment has come to lift the prohibition to which the crowd owes its existence. If its insight corresponds to the feeling of the crowd it will, by withdrawing the prohibition, decree its own dissolution.

Reversal Crowds

"DEAR FRIEND, the wolves have always eaten the sheep; are the sheep going to eat the wolves this time?" This sentence, which comes from a letter which Madame Jullien wrote to her son during the French Revolution, contains the essence of reversal. So far a few wolves have held down many sheep. Now the time has come for the many sheep to turn against the few wolves. It is true that sheep are not carnivorous, but, in its very absurdity, the sentence is full of meaning. Revolutions are times of reversal; those who have been defenceless for so long suddenly find teeth. Their numbers have to make up for the experience in viciousness which they lack.

Reversal presupposes a stratified society. A clear separation of classes, one enjoying more rights than the other, must have lasted for some time, and made itself felt in men's daily life before the need for reversal arises. The stratification may have occurred as the result of internal events, or the higher group may have acquired the right to give orders to the lower one by conquering the country and thus setting itself above the natives.

Every command leaves behind a painful *sting* in the person who is forced to carry it out. The nature of these stings will be examined in more detail later. All I want to say here is that they are indestructible. People who are habitually ordered about are full of them, and feel a strong urge to get rid of them. They can free themselves in two different ways. They can pass on to others the orders which they have received from above; but, for them to be able to do this, there must be others below them who are ready to accept their orders. Or they can try to pay back to their superiors themselves what they have suffered and stored up from them. One man alone, weak and helpless as he is, will only rarely be fortunate enough to find an opportunity for this, but, if many men find themselves together in a crowd, they may jointly succeed in what was denied them singly: together they can turn on those who, till now, have given them orders. A revolutionary situation can be defined as this state of reversal, and a crowd whose

discharge consists mainly in its collective deliverance from the stings
of command should be called a *reversal crowd*.

The French Revolution is usually considered to have begun with the
storming of the Bastille. It actually began earlier with a massacre of
hares. In May 1789 the States General were assembled at Versailles.
They were deliberating the abolition of feudal rights, among them the
hunting rights of the nobility. On June 10th, a month *before* the storming of the Bastille, Camille Desmoulins, who was present as a deputy,
wrote to his father: "The Bretons are provisionally carrying out some
of the articles of their *cahiers de doléance*. They are killing pigeons and
game. And here in this part some 50 young people are creating havoc
among hares and rabbits. They are said to have killed between four
and five thousand head of game under the eyes of the wardens in the
plain of St. Germain." Before they dare attack the wolves, the sheep
turn against hares. Before the reversal directed against superiors, they
turn on the lowliest available quarry.

But the real event is the Day of the Bastille. The whole city provided itself with arms. The rising was directed against the king's
justice, embodied in the stormed and conquered building. Prisoners
were set free, who were then able to join the crowd. The Governor
responsible for the defence of the Bastille, and his assistants, were
executed. But thieves, too, were strung from the lamp posts. The Bastille was razed to the ground and carried away stone by stone. Justice
in its two main aspects—the right of inflicting capital punishment and
the right of mercy—was taken over by the people. The reversal had,
for the moment, accomplished itself.

Crowds of this type form in the most diverse circumstances; they
may be revolts of slaves against their masters, of soldiers against their
officers, of coloured people against the whites who have settled in their
midst. But, in all cases, the one group will have been subject for a long
time to the commands of the other group; the rebels are always driven
to act by the stings they carry within them; and it always takes a long
time before they can do so.

Much of the surface activity of revolutions, on the other hand, is
due to baiting crowds. Single people are hunted and, when caught, are
killed by the crowd, with or without the formality of a trial. But the
revolution by no means consists solely of this. The baiting crowds
which quickly attain their natural goal are not the whole of it. Once
started, the reversal goes on spreading. Everyone tries to get into a
position where he can free himself of his stings of command; and everyone has a large number of these. The reversal is a process which takes

hold of the whole of a society and, even if attended with success from the start, it comes to an end only slowly and with difficulty. The successive baiting crowds run their brief course on the surface while the waves of reversal rise slowly from the depths.

But the process may be much slower even than this; the reversal may be promised for heaven: "The last shall be first." Between the present state and that other stands death. In the other world men will live again. The poorest here, if he has done no evil, will stand highest there. He will live on as a new man and one, moreover, who has a better position. The believer is promised deliverance from his stings. But nothing is said about the precise circumstances of this deliverance. Though physical proximity is part of the concept of heaven, there is no actual indication that the crowd is the substratum of this reversal.

At the centre of this kind of promise stands the idea of revival. Cases of people brought back to life by Christ are reported in the Gospels. The preachers of the famous "revivals" in Anglo-Saxon countries made every possible use of death and resurrection, threatening the assembled sinners with the most fearful pains of hell until they were reduced to an indescribable state of terror, imagining a lake of fire and brimstone yawning to swallow them and the hand of the Almighty thrusting them down in the horrible abyss. It was said of one of the preachers that the terror inspired by the fierceness of his invective was heightened still further by the hideousness of his visage and the thunder of his tones. People came from 40, 50 or 100 miles away to hear such preachers. Men brought their families with them in covered wagons and came provided with bedding and food for several days. Round about 1800, one part of Kentucky was roused to a state of feverish excitement by meetings of this kind. The meetings were held in the open because no building then existing in the State could have held the enormous crowds. In August 1801 20,000 people gathered at Cane Ridge and the memory of this meeting still lingered in Kentucky after the lapse of a century.

The preachers went on terrifying their listeners until the latter fell down to the ground and remained lying there as though dead. It was God's commands that threatened them and from which they fled, seeking refuge in a semblance of death. And it was the conscious and declared intention of the preachers thus to strike them down. The place looked like a battlefield; right and left whole rows of people fell to the ground. The comparison with a battlefield was made by the preachers themselves. To achieve the moral reversal they wanted this utmost and ultimate terror seemed essential. The success of the preaching was measured by the number of the "fallen". An eyewitness who kept a precise journal reports that, in the course of this meeting, which lasted for several days, 3,000 people fell helpless to the ground—nearly one sixth of those present. Those who fell were carried to the meeting house nearby. At no time was the floor less than half covered with people lying there. Some lay quiet, unable to speak, or move. At times they would come to themselves for a few moments, then a deep groan, a piercing shout or a fervent prayer for mercy would show that they were alive. "Some talked but could not move. Some beat the floor with their heels. Some, shrieking in agony, bounded about like a fish out of water. Many lay down and rolled over and over for hours at a time. Others rushed wildly over stumps and benches and plunged shouting 'Lost! Lost!' into the forest."

When the fallen came to themselves they were changed people. They rose and shouted 'Salvation!' They were "new-born" and ready to begin a good and pure life; their old sinful existence was left behind them. But the conversion could only be believed in if a kind of death had preceded it.

There were also phenomena of a less extreme nature which tended to the same end. A whole meeting would suddenly break out weeping: many people were seized with irresistible jerks. Others, usually in groups of four or five, started barking like dogs. After a few years, when the excitement had begun to take milder forms, people would burst out, first singly and then in chorus together, into a "holy laugh".

But everything that happened, happened within a crowd, crowds more highly-charged and excited than almost any others we know of.

The reversal aimed at in these revivals differs from that in revolutions. What is involved here is men's relation to the divine commands. Men have been acting contrary to them and now the fear of God's punishment has come over them. This fear, increased in every possible way by the preacher, has driven them into a state of unconsciousness. They feign death like hunted animals, but their fear is so great that they really lose consciousness. When they come to themselves they declare their readiness to submit to God's commands and prohibitions, and thus their acutest fear of his immediate punishment subsides. It is, as it were, a process of domestication: a man allows himself to be tamed by the preacher to become God's obedient servant.

The process is exactly the opposite of what happens in a revolution. As we saw earlier, the essential there is liberation from the burden of all the stings resulting from long submission to some kind of domination. Here the essential is a new submission, submission to the commands of God, and a willingness, therefore, to accept all the stings they may implant. The only factor common to both processes is the reversal itself, and the psychic scene where it takes place—in both cases the crowd.

Feast Crowds

THE FIFTH TYPE of crowd is the *feast crowd*. There is abundance in a limited space, and everyone near can partake of it. The produce of all kinds of cultivation is exhibited in great heaps: a hundred pigs lie bound in a row; mountains of fruit are piled up; huge vessels of a favourite drink are prepared and stand waiting to be drunk. There is more of everything than everyone together can consume and, in order to consume it, more and more people come streaming in. As long as there is anything there they partake of it, and it looks as though there would be no end to it. There is an abundance of women for the men, and an abundance of men for the women. Nothing and no-one threatens and there is nothing to flee from; for the time being, life and pleasure are secure. Many prohibitions and distinctions are waived, and unaccustomed advances are not only permitted but smiled on. For the individual the atmosphere is one of loosening, not discharge. There is no common identical goal which people have to try and attain together. The feast *is* the goal and they are there. The density is very great, but the equality is in large part an equality simply of indulgence and pleasure. People move to and fro, not in one direction only. The things which are piled up, and of which everyone partakes, are a very important part of the density; they are its core. They were gathered together first, and only when they were all there did people gather round them. It may take years before everything is ready and people may have to endure a long period of want for this brief abundance. But they live for this moment and work steadily towards it. Men who can otherwise rarely see each other are ceremoniously invited with their own groups. The arrival of the various contingents is vigorously acclaimed and each fresh arrival raises the level of universal joy.

But another feeling also plays its part. By common enjoyment at this one feast people prepare the way for many future feasts. Earlier occasions of the same kind are recalled in ritual dances and dramatic performances; the tradition of them is contained in the actuality of the present feast. Those feasting remember the first founders of their celebrations, whether these are their ancestors, the mythical creators of the delights they are enjoying, or, as in later and colder societies, simply the rich donors. In any case they feel assured of the future repetition of similar occasions. The feasts call to one another; the density of things and of people promises increase of life itself.

The Double Crowd: Men and Women.
The Living and the Dead

THE SUREST, and often the only, way by which a crowd can preserve itself lies in the existence of a second crowd to which it is related. Whether the two crowds confront each other as rivals in a game, or as a serious threat to each other, the sight, or simply the powerful image of the second crowd, prevents the disintegration of the first. As long as all eyes are turned in the direction of the eyes opposite, knee will stand locked by knee; as long as all ears are listening for the expected shout from the other side, arms will move to a common rhythm.

People are in physical proximity to their own kind and acting within a familiar and natural unit. All their curiosity and expectation, meanwhile, is directed towards a second body of men divided from them by a clearly defined distance. The sight of it fascinates them and, if they cannot see it, they can still hear it, and all their own actions turn on its actions and intentions. The confrontation calls for a special kind of watchfulness, raising the specific density within each group. Neither can disband until the other does. The tension between the two groups exerts its pressure on everyone belonging to either. If the tension happens to be that arising out of a ritual game, then the pressure manifests itself in a kind of shame; people make every effort to avoid the humiliation of their own side in front of the enemy. But if the enemy threatens them, if it is really a matter of life and death, then the pressure transforms itself into the armour of united and resolute defence.

But in any case, given that they are about equal in size and intensity, the two crowds keep each other alive. The superiority on the side of the enemy must not be too great, or, at least, must not be thought to be so. Once the feeling spreads that there is no chance of standing firm, people will try to save themselves in mass flight and, if this proves hopeless, the crowd will disintegrate in a panic, everyone fleeing for himself. But this is not what interests us here. For the formation of a *two-crowd structure* it is important that both sides should feel roughly equal in strength.

In order to understand the origin of this structure we have to start from three basic antitheses. The first and most striking is that between men and women; the second that between the living and the dead; and the third that between friend and foe. This last is the one people almost invariably have in mind today when they speak of two opposing crowds.

The connection between the first antithesis—that of men and women—and the formation of specific crowds is not immediately apparent. Men and women live together in families. They may tend to have different activities, but one scarcely thinks of them as confronting each other in separate, excited groups. One has to go to reports of more primitive conditions of life to acquire a real conception of the form this antithesis may take.

Jean de Léry, a young French Huguenot, was, in 1557, a witness of a big feast among the Tupinambu in Brazil.

"We were ordered to stay in the house where the women were. We did not yet know what they would do, but suddenly we heard a deep voice from the house where the men were, less than thirty paces from us and the women. It sounded like the murmur of prayers.

"As soon as the women, about 200 in number, heard this, they all jumped up, pricked their ears and pressed closely together in a heap. Soon afterwards the men raised their voices. We distinctly heard them all singing together and encouraging themselves by repeating over and over again the exclamation: 'He, he, he, he!' We were amazed when the women answered them with the same cry: 'He, he, he, he!' For more than a quarter of an hour they howled and screamed so loud that we did not know how to keep our countenances. In the midst of their howling they sprang in the air with great violence, their breasts shaking and their mouths foaming. Some fell unconscious to the ground, like people who have the falling sickness. It seemed to me that the devil had got into them and had made them mad.

"Quite near us we heard the uproar of the children, who were in a separate room by themselves. Though I had now lived among the natives for over half a year, and had got on quite well with them, I cannot deny that I was terrified. I asked myself how the thing would end and wished myself back in our fort."

The witches' sabbath calmed down in the end, the women and children fell silent and Jean de Léry heard the men sing in chorus so marvellously that he longed to see them and could not bear not to be with them. The women tried to hold him back, for they knew that they themselves were prohibited from joining the men. But he managed to sneak in among the men, nothing untoward happened to him and, with two other Frenchmen, he attended the feast.

Here the men and women are strictly separated from each other in different but adjacent houses. They cannot see each other, but this causes the one group to listen all the more intently for the noise of the other. They utter the same cries and work themselves into a state of crowd excitement which is common to both of them. The real events are enacted among the men, but the women take part in kindling the crowd. It is remarkable how, as soon as they distinguish the first sounds from the men's house, they press together into a dense mass and respond more and more wildly to the wild shouts which they soon hear from thence. They are full of fear because they are shut in—in no circumstances are they allowed out—and, as they thus cannot know what is happening among the men, their excitement takes on a particular tinge. They jump high in the air as though to jump out. The hysterical symptoms that de Léry notes in them are characteristic of a prevented mass flight. Their natural tendency would be to flee to the men but, since a heavy prohibition lies on this, they flee, as it were, on the same spot.

The sensations of de Léry himself are worth noticing. He feels the excitement of the women, but cannot really belong to their crowd, for he is both a stranger and a man. In the midst of it and yet separated from it, he inevitably fears that he may become its victim.

It is apparent from another part of the report (not quoted here) that the particular contribution of the women is not unimportant. The sorcerers of the tribe, or *Caraibs* as de Léry calls them, strictly forbid the women to leave their house, but they command them to listen attentively to the men's singing.

The assemblage of women can have a significant effect on the crowd of their men even when they are much further apart. There are times when the women are called on to make a contribution to the success of warlike expeditions. Three instances of this follow, drawn respectively from Asia, America and Africa, that is, from peoples between whom there was never any contact and who certainly could not influence each other.

Among the Kafirs of the Hindu-kush the women perform the war dance whilst the men are absent on a raid. In this way they give the warriors strength and courage and keep them wakeful lest they should be surprised by a wily enemy.

"Among the Jivaros in South America it is customary for the women during the whole time that the men are absent on the warpath to assemble every night in one house and perform a special dance with rattles of snail shells around the waist and chanting conjurations. This war dance of the women is supposed to have a special power: it protects their fathers, husbands and sons against the lances and bullets of the enemy; it lulls the enemy into security so that he will not apprehend the danger before it is too late; and lastly it prevents him taking revenge for the defeat inflicted upon him."

Mirary is the name given in Madagascar to an old dance of the women which might be performed only in the actual moment of fighting. When a battle was imminent the women were informed by messengers. They then let down their hair and started the dance. In this way they were in communion with the fighters. When the Germans were marching on Paris in 1914 the women in Tananarive danced the *Mirary* for the protection of the French soldiers. It seems to have worked in spite of the intervening distance.

Throughout the world there are feasts where men and women dance in separate groups. But they are visible to, and usually dance towards, each other. It is unnecessary to describe them, for they are widely known, and I have intentionally limited myself to a few extreme cases where the degree of separation, of distance and of excitement is particularly striking. It is certainly possible to speak of the double crowd as something deeply rooted in the lives of these people. The two crowds in these cases are favourably disposed towards each other. The excitement of the one side is supposed to further the well-being and success of the other. Men and women belong to the same people and are dependent on each other.

In the legends of Amazons, which are by no means confined to Greek antiquity, examples being found even among the natives of South America, the women have separated from the men for good and make war on them as a hostile people would.

But before we examine war, the most violent expression of what seems the inescapably dangerous essence of double crowds, it is desirable to consider briefly the age-old antagonism between the living and the dead.

Everything which happens in connection with the dying and the dead is coloured by the image of the much larger number of beings on the other side whom the dead man will eventually join. The loss weakens the living and, if it is a man in his prime, is particularly painful for his people. They resist it as well as they can, but they know that their resistance is not much use. The crowd on the other side is larger and stronger than theirs and the dying man is dragged over to it. All their attempts to prevent it are made in full awareness of this superiority. Everything that might irritate the spirits must be avoided, for they have power to harm the living. Some peoples believe that the crowd of the dead is the reservoir from which the souls of the new-born are taken. Thus it depends on them whether the woman have children or not. Sometimes the spirits come as clouds and bring rain; they can also withhold the plants and animals which serve as food; and they can fetch new victims for themselves from among the living. The dead man, who was surrendered only after strong resistance, must be appeased, for he is now a member of that powerful host.

Dying is thus a fight, a fight between two enemies of unequal strength. The piercing cries, and the wounds self-inflicted in sorrow and despair, are perhaps also intended to express this fight. The dead man must not believe that he was given up easily; he was fought for.

It is a unique kind of fight, a fight which is always lost however bravely it is fought. From the very beginning the living are in flight; they make a pretence of accepting battle only in the hope of detaching themselves from the enemy in a rear-guard action. The fight is also intended as flattery of the dying man who will soon increase the enemy's force. They want him to be well-disposed towards them when he arrives there, or, at least, not hostile. If he is angry when he arrives among the dead, he may incite them to fresh assaults.

The essence of this fight between the living and the dead is that it is intermittent. One can never know when something is going to happen. Nothing may happen for a long time, but one cannot count on this; each new blow comes suddenly out of the dark. There is no declaration of war; after a single death everything may be over, or it may go on for a long time as in plagues and epidemics. The living are always on the retreat. Nothing is ever really over.

I shall say more later about the relation of the living to the dead. All I wanted to do here was to show them as a double crowd, whose component parts continually interact.

The third type of double crowd is that which forms in war, and this is the one which concerns us most today. After the experiences of the last fifty years one would give much to understand and to be able to dissolve it.

The Double Crowd: War

WAR HAS TO DO with killing. The enemy ranks are "thinned". It is killing wholesale; as many of the enemy as possible are cut down. The aim is to transform a dangerous crowd of live adversaries into a heap of dead. The victor is the one who kills the largest number. The adversary in war is the growing crowd of one's neighbours. Their increase is frightening in itself, and the threat it contains is enough to release the aggressive drive of one's own corresponding crowd. During the war each side seeks to obtain superiority of numbers at the crucial spot, and to exploit the enemy's weakness in every possible way before he can increase his own numbers. The detailed conduct of war exactly mirrors the nature of war as a whole. Each side wants to constitute the larger crowd of living fighters and it wants the opposing side to constitute the larger heap of dead. In this rivalry between growing crowds lies an essential, and it may even be the prime, cause of wars. As well as killing enemies, one can also make slaves of them, especially of the women and children; and these slaves will serve to increase one's own crowd. But the war is not a true war unless its first aim is a heap of enemy dead.

All the only too familiar phrases in both modern and ancient languages describing the events of war point to precisely this fact. People speak of massacre, butchery and carnage; rivers run red with blood; the enemy is cut down to the last man; quarter is neither given nor taken.

It is, however, important to realize that the heap of the dead is also felt to be a unit; some languages have a special word for it. The German word *Walstatt* for battlefield contains the old root *Wal*, which means "those who are left dead on the field." *Valr* in old Norse means "the corpses on the battlefield". *Valhalla* is nothing but "the dwelling of the fallen warriors". The word *wuol*, meaning "defeat" is derived by ablaut from the old High German *wal*. The corresponding word *wol* in Anglo-Saxon means "plague, pestilence". All these words, whether they refer to those who are left on the field of battle, to defeat, or to plague and pestilence, have one thing in common: they contain the idea of a *heap of dead*.

This conception is found everywhere and is by no means purely Germanic. The prophet Jeremiah saw in a vision the whole earth as one field of rotting corpses: "And the slain of the Lord shall be at that day from one end of the earth even unto the other end of the earth; they shall not be lamented, neither gathered nor buried; they shall be dung upon the ground."

The prophet Mohammed had such a strong sense of the heap of his dead enemies that he addressed them in a kind of triumphal sermon. After the battle of Bedr, his first great victory over his enemies from Mecca, he gave orders that the enemy slain should be thrown into a pit. Only one of them was buried beneath earth and stones and this was because his body had swelled so much that it was impossible to remove his armour, and thus he was left to lie where he had fallen. "As the others were thrown in the pit, the apostle stood and said 'O people of the pit! Have you found that what God threatened is true? For I have found that what my Lord promised me is true.' His companions said: 'Are you speaking to dead people?' He replied 'They *hear* what I say to them.'"

Crowded together in the pit, and in safe keeping there, he had assembled those who had formerly refused to listen to his words. I know no more striking instance of the attribution of a residue of life and crowd-like character to the heap of enemy dead. They could no longer threaten, but they could be threatened. Anything could be perpetrated on them with impunity. Whether they felt it or not, the victor assumed that they did, in order to heighten his own triumph. They lay so close in the pit that none of them could move. If one of them awoke he would find nothing but dead men round him; his own people would stifle him; the world to which he returned would be a world of the dead, and the dead would be those who had been closest to him living.

Among the peoples of antiquity the Egyptians were not reckoned truly warlike, the energy of their Old Kingdom being directed more to the building of Pyramids than to conquest. But some campaigns were undertaken even at this early period. One of them was described by Une, a high judge who had been appointed by his king Pepy as commander-in-chief against the Bedouin. His report, as inscribed in his tomb, runs as follows:

"This host went happy and hacked to pieces the land of the Bedouin.
This host went happy and destroyed the land of the Bedouin.
This host went happy and overthrew its towers.
This host went happy and cut down its figs and vines.
This host went happy and threw fire into its villages.
This host went happy and slaughtered its armies, many ten thousands.
This host went happy and brought home prisoners, a large multitude."

This powerful image of destruction culminates in the line announcing the slaughter of tens of thousands of enemies. In the New Kingdom the Egyptians began, though they did not long continue, a planned policy of aggression. Rameses II undertook prolonged wars against the Hittites. A hymn in his praise runs as follows: "He treadeth down the land of the Khatti and maketh it a heap of corpses like Sekhmet when she rageth after the pestilence." Already in myth the lion-headed goddess Sekhmet has wrought terrible carnage amonst rebellious humans. She remains the goddess of war and slaughter, and the poet of this song of praise associates the image of the Hittite heap of dead with that of the victims of a plague—a conjunction already familiar to us.

In his famous report on the battle of Kadesh, which he fought against the Hittites, Rameses II tells how he was cut off from his own men and how, through superhuman strength and courage, he won the battle alone. His men "found that all peoples amongst whom I had forced my way were lying slaughtered in heaps in their blood, even all the best warriors of Khatti, and the children and brethren of their prince. I had caused the field of Kadesh to become white, and one knew not where to tread because of their multitude." The corpses were clothed in white, and it was their numbers which changed the colour of the field. It is a most terrifying and graphic description of the result of a battle.

But it is a result which only soldiers see. The battle may be fought abroad and people at home want a share in the heap of the dead. Merenptah, the son and successor of Rameses II, won a great battle against the Libyans. We hear how their whole camp, with all its treasures and all the relations of their prince, fell into the hands of the Egyptians and was first plundered and then burnt. The booty included 9,376 prisoners, but this was not enough; in order to prove the number of the dead to the people at home the private parts of the fallen were cut off; or, if they were circumcised, the hands were taken instead. All this booty was loaded on to donkeys. Rameses III also fought against the Libyans; on this occasion the trophies numbered 12,535. It is clear that these ghastly loads are simply epitomes of the mound of enemy dead which, in them, is made transportable and capable of demonstration to the whole people. Each of the fallen contributes part of his body to the heap and—and this is important—all these parts are identical.

Other peoples preferred heads. Among the Assyrians a reward was offered for every head of an enemy; a soldier sought to procure as many as possible for himself. A relief from the time of King Assurbanipal shows the scribes in their large tents noting down the number of severed heads. Each soldier brings his heads, throws them on a common heap, gives his name and that of his detachment and then goes away. The Assyrian kings had a passion for these mounds of heads. When with the army they presided at the bringing in of the trophies and themselves distributed the rewards to the soldiers. When absent they had the whole heap of heads brought to them; if that was impossible they made do with those of the enemy leaders.

Thus the immediate and quite concrete goal of war is clear, and we need search for no further illustrations of it. Written history abounds in them; indeed one forms the impression that they are its favourite subject matter and that only by great and repeated efforts has it been made to turn its attention to humanity's other memories.

If we consider both warring parties simultaneously war presents a picture of two doubly interlocked crowds. An army, itself as large as possible, is bent on creating the largest possible heap of enemy dead. And exactly the same is true of the other side. Thus every participant in the war belongs simultaneously to two crowds. From the point of view of his own people he belongs to the crowd of living fighters; from that of the enemy to the potential and desired crowd of dead.

In order to maintain a bellicose spirit each side has to assert, over and over again, first how strong it is itself—that is, how many fighters it disposes of; and second, how weak the enemy is—that is, how many of them are already dead. From the earliest times war reports have been characterized by these twofold statistics: on the one side, so many men on the move; on the other, so many dead. There is a strong tendency to exaggerate, particularly the number of enemy dead.

None of those involved in a war like admitting that the number of living enemies is too great for them. Even if aware of it, they keep silent about it and try to redress the balance by skilful distribution of the fighting troops. The self-sufficiency and mobility of army units is increased and, as has been said before, everything possible is done to ensure superiority on the spot. Only *after* the war do people speak openly of the losses on their own side.

The fact that wars can last so long, and may be carried on well after they have been lost, arises from the deep urge of the crowd to maintain itself in the acute stage; not to disintegrate; to remain a crowd. This feeling is sometimes so strong that people prefer to perish together with open eyes, rather than acknowledge defeat and thus experience the disintegration of their own crowd.

But how does a belligerent crowd *form*? What, from one moment to another creates that uncanny coherence? What is it that suddenly moves men to risk their all? The phenomenon is so mysterious that it must be approached with a measure of caution.

War is an astonishing business. People decide that they are threatened with physical destruction and proclaim the fact publicly to the whole world. They say "I can be killed", and secretly add "because I myself want to kill this or that man." The stress properly belongs on the second half of this sentence. It should run: "I want to kill this or that man, therefore I can be killed myself." But when it is a question of a war starting, of its eruption and the awakening of a bellicose spirit within the nation, the first version will be the only one openly admitted. Even if in fact the aggressor, each side will always attempt to prove that it is threatened.

The threat consists in someone arrogating to himself the right to kill one. Every single person on one's own side stands under the same threat and is made equal by it, for it is directed against everybody. From a given moment, which is the same for everyone—the moment of the declaration of war—the same thing can and may happen to everyone. Life within a community is normally a protection against physical destruction, but now this has come very close, just *because* one belongs to a community. One and the same terrible threat has been pronounced against all counting themselves members of one nation. Singly, but simultaneously, a thousand people have been told "You shall die", and they unite in order to ward off this danger of death. Quickly they seek to attract all those who might be similarly threatened and, for the sake of their common defence, submit to a common direction of action.

On both sides those involved usually come together very quickly, whether in physical actuality or in imagination and feeling. The outbreak of a war is primarily an *eruption of two crowds*. As soon as these crowds have formed, the supreme purpose of each is to preserve its existence through both belief and action. To abandon the crowd would be to abandon life itself. A belligerent crowd always acts as though everything outside it were death. The individual may have survived many wars but, with each new war, he surrenders himself afresh to the same illusion.

Death, which in truth threatens every man all the time, must have been proclaimed as a collective sentence before people will oppose it actively. There are, as it were, *declared times of death*, times when it turns on a definite, arbitrarily selected group as a whole. It is "Death to the French" or "Death to the English". The enthusiasm with which men accept such declarations has its root in the individual's cowardice before death; no one likes facing it alone. It is easier in a duel, when two enemies, as it were, execute sentence on each other; and the death that thousands approach together is entirely different. The worst that can happen to men in war is to perish together; and this spares them death as individuals, which is what they most fear.

But they do not even believe that this worst will happen, for they see that there is a possibility of deflecting the common sentence passed on them and of turning it against others. The *death-conductor* here is the enemy, and all they must do is to forestall his doing the same thing. But they have to be quick; this business of killing does not admit of even a moment's hesitation. And the enemy is there, ready to their hand. It was he who first pronounced sentence, who first said "You shall die". What he intended for others recoils on him. It is always the enemy who started it. Even if he was not the first to speak out, he was certainly planning it; and if he was not actually planning it, he was thinking of it; and, if he was not thinking of it, he would have thought of it. The wish to see death is everywhere and one does not have to go deep into men to bring it to light.

The curious and unmistakable high-tension which characterizes all the processes of war has two causes: people want to forestall death, and they are acting as a crowd. Without the latter element there is no chance whatsoever of success in the first. As long as the war lasts they must remain a crowd, and the war really ends as soon as they cease to be one. War offers the crowd the hope of a definite duration of life, and this is a considerable factor in its popularity. It can be shown that the coherence and duration of wars in modern times is associated with the greatly increased size and density of the double crowds involved in them.

Crowd Crystals

CROWD CRYSTALS are the small, rigid groups of men, strictly delimited and of great constancy, which serve to precipitate crowds. Their structure is such that they can be comprehended and taken in at a glance. Their unity is more important than their size. Their rôle must be familiar; people must know what they are there for. Doubt about their function would render them meaningless. They should preferably always appear the same and it should be impossible to confound one with another; a uniform or a definite sphere of operation serves to promote this.

The crowd crystal is *constant*; it never changes its size. Its members are trained in both action and faith. They may be allotted different parts, as in an orchestra, but they must appear as a unit, and the first feeling of anyone seeing or experiencing them should be that this is a unit which will never fall apart. Their life outside the crystal does not count. Even where the unit is a merely professional one, as with orchestral players, no one thinks of their private existence; they are the orchestra. In other cases they wear uniform, and it is only in uniform that one sees them together; out of it they are entirely different people. Soldiers and monks are the most important examples of this type. With them the uniform expresses the fact that members of a crystal *live* together. Even when they appear separately, people always think of the rigid unit to which they belong, the monastery or the regiment.

The clarity, isolation and constancy of the crystal form an uncanny contrast with the excited flux of the surrounding crowd. The process of rapid, uncontrollable growth, and the threat of disintegration, which together give the crowd its peculiar restlessness, do not operate within the crystal. Even in the midst of the greatest excitement the crystal stands out against it. Whatever the nature of the crowd it gives birth to, and however much it may appear to merge with it, it never completely loses the sense of its own identity and always recombines again after the disintegration of the crowd.

The *closed* crowd differs from the crystal not only by being larger, but because its sense of itself is more spontaneous and does not permit of any real allocation of functions. All it has in common with the crystal is defined limits and regular repetition. But the crystal is *all* limits; everyone belonging to it constitutes part of its boundary, whereas the closed crowd has its boundary imposed on it from outside, if only by the shape and size of the building where it meets. Within this boundary where its members touch each other, it remains fluid, and sudden surprises and unexpected changes of behaviour are therefore always possible. Enclosed though it is, it can always attain that degree of density and fervour which leads to an eruption. The crowd crystal, on the other hand, is solid throughout; the nature of its activity is prescribed and it remains precisely conscious of all its utterances and movements.

Another astonishing thing about these crowd crystals is their historical permanence. It is true that new ones continually arise, but the old obstinately persist side by side with them. They may, for a time, withdraw into the background, lose something of their edge and cease to be indispensable; the crowds belonging to them may have died away or been completely suppressed. But, as harmless groups, without effect on the outside world, the crystals go on living on their own. Small groups of religious communities continue to exist in countries which, as a whole, have changed their faith. The return of the moment when they are needed is as certain as the appearance of new crowds, ripe for the stimulation and release which they may be precisely qualified to give. All such torpid, semi-retired groups may be brought out again and re-activated. They can be revitalized and, with minor changes of constitution, reinstated as crowd crystals. There is scarcely any major political revolution which has not on occasion remembered such old, demoted groups, seized and galvanized them, and used them so intensively that they have appeared as something completely new and dangerously active.

I shall show later how individual crowd crystals function. Only by giving concrete examples is it possible to show how they actually precipitate crowds. The crystals themselves are variously constituted and give rise, therefore, to quite different crowds. The reader will, almost imperceptibly, make the acquaintance of a number of them in the course of this enquiry.

Crowd Symbols

CROWD SYMBOLS is the name I give to collective units which do not consist of men, but which are still felt to be crowds. Corn and forest, rain, wind, sand, fire and the sea are such units. Every one of these phenomena comprehends some of the essential attributes of the crowd. Although they do not consist of men, each of them recalls the crowd and stands as symbol for it in myth, dream, speech and song.

It is desirable to distinguish sharply and clearly between these symbols and crowd crystals. A crowd crystal is a group of men which is striking because of its coherence and unity. It is imagined and experienced as a unit, but it invariably consists of real men in action: soldiers, monks, an orchestra. Crowd symbols, on the other hand, are never made up of men, and they are only *felt* to be a crowd.

It may seem, at first sight, that they are not important enough to warrant detailed examination. But it will be seen that, through them, the crowd itself can be approached in a new and profitable way. They shed a natural light on it, which it would be foolish to exclude.

Fire
The first thing to be said about fire is that it is always the same. Whether it is large or small, wherever it starts, and however long or short the time it lasts, there is in our imagination always a sameness

about it, which is independent of the particular occasion. The image of fire is like a scar, strongly marked, irremovable and precise.

Fire spreads; it is contagious and insatiable. The violence with which it seizes whole forests and steppes and cities is one of the most impressive things about it. Until its onset tree stood by tree, and house by house, each distinct and separate from the next. But fire joins what was separate, and in the shortest possible time. Isolated and diverse objects all go up in the same flames. They become so much the same that they disappear completely. Houses, trees, creatures—the fire seizes them all. It is in the highest degree contagious; over and over again one is surprised by the feebleness of the resistance it encounters. The more life a thing has, the less it can defend itself against fire; only minerals, the most lifeless of all substances, are a match for it. Its headlong ruthlessness knows no bounds; it wants to swallow up everything, and is never sated.

Fire is sudden; it can originate anywhere. No one is ever surprised when fire breaks out; here, there, or somewhere, it is always expected. Its very suddenness is impressive and people invariably search for a cause. The fact that often none can be found adds to the awe inherent in the idea of fire. It has a mysterious ubiquity; it can appear anywhere and at any time.

Fire is multiple. Not only does one know that there must be fires in many, indeed in innumerable places, but the individual fire itself is multiple: we speak of flames and of tongues of flame. In the *Vedas* fire is called "The one Agni, manifoldly ablaze".

Fire is destructive; it can be fought and tamed; it goes out. It has an elemental enemy to contend with, namely water in the form of rivers and cloudbursts. Their enmity is proverbial; the expression "fire and water" denotes animosity of the most extreme and irreconcilable kind. In ancient prefigurations of the end of the world either one or the other is victorious. The deluge ends all life by water; the universal conflagration destroys the world by fire. Sometimes they appear together in one and the same mythology, both therefore diminished. But, in this temporal existence, man has learnt to dominate fire. Not only can he always ally himself with water in the fight against it, but he has also succeeded in dividing it and in storing it thus. He keeps it captive in hearths and ovens, and feeds it as he feeds an animal; he can starve it, or he can choke it. This brings us to the last important characteristic of fire: it is treated as though it were alive. It lives restlessly, and it dies. It may be completely smothered in one place, but it will go on living in another.

If we consider the several attributes of fire together we get a surprising picture. Fire is the same wherever it breaks out: it spreads rapidly; it is contagious and insatiable; it can break out anywhere, and with great suddenness; it is multiple; it is destructive; it has an enemy; it dies; it acts as though it were alive, and is so treated. All this is true of the crowd. Indeed it would be difficult to list its attributes more accurately. Let us go through them in turn. The crowd is the same everywhere, in all periods and cultures; it remains essentially the same among men of the most diverse origin, education and language. Once in being, it spreads with the utmost violence. Few can resist its contagion; it always wants to go on growing and there are no inherent limits to its growth. It can arise wherever people are together, and its spontaneity and suddenness are uncanny. It is multiple, but cohesive. It is composed of large numbers of people, but one never knows exactly how many. It can be destructive; and it can be damped and tamed. It seeks an enemy. It dies away as quickly as it has arisen, and often as inexplicably; and it has, as goes without saying, its own restless and violent life. These likenesses between fire and the crowd have led to the close assimilation of their images; they enter into each other and can stand for each other. Fire is one of the most important and malleable of the crowd symbols which have always played a part in the history of mankind. We must now consider some of these affinities between fire and the crowd more closely.

The dangerous traits of the crowd are often pointed out and, among these, the most striking is the propensity to incendiarism. This propensity has its roots in the burning of forests. The forest, itself an age-old crowd symbol, is set on fire by men in order to create space for settlements, and there is good reason to believe that it was through the experience of such conflagrations that men learnt how to deal with fire. There is a clear prehistoric connection between forest and fire. Fields were situated in burnt-out clearings in forests and, whenever they needed to be renewed or enlarged, more forest had to be burnt.

Animals flee from the burning forest; mass fear is the natural and perpetual reaction of animals to large fires; and it was once man's reaction too. But man has taken possession of fire. He holds the firebrand in his hand and need not fear it. His new power has overlaid his old fear, and the two of them have entered into a strange alliance.

The crowd which used to run from fire now feels strongly attracted by it. As is well known, conflagrations of all kinds have a magical effect on men. Men are not satisfied with the hearths and ovens which each domiciliary group maintains privately for itself; they want a fire which is visible from afar, which they can all surround and where they can all be together. If the conflagration is large enough, a curious reversal of their old mass fear commands them to hurry to its site, and they feel there something of the glowing warmth which formerly united them. In periods of peace they have to go without this experience for a long time, but one of the strongest instincts of the crowd, as soon as it has formed at all, is to create such a fire for itself and to use its attraction to further its own growth.

The matchbox that modern man carries in his pocket is a small remnant of these ancient and deeply significant associations. It represents the serried tree trunks of a wood, all reduced to an agreeable uniformity, and each provided with a combustible head. It is possible to light several, or indeed all, of them together and thus create an artificial conflagration. One may feel tempted to do this, but it is not usually done, because the tiny size of the ensuing conflagration would deprive fire of all its ancient splendour.

But the attraction of fire may go even further than this. Not only do men rush to it and surround it, but there are old ceremonies by which they actually identify themselves with it. One of the finest examples of these is the famous fire-dance of the Navajo Indians.

"The Navajos of North Mexico prepare a huge fire around which they dance all night in presenting eleven distinct acts between sunset and sunrise. As soon as the disc of the sun has disappeared the performers dance wildly into the clearing almost naked, bedaubed with paint, and allowing their long hair to flow freely as they whirl about. They carry dancing staffs with tufts of feathers at the ends, and with wild bounds approach the high flames. Those Indians dance with a clumsy constraint half crouching, and creeping, in fact the fire is so hot that the performers have to wriggle on the ground in order to get near enough to set alight the feathers at the ends of their dancing sticks. A disc representing the sun is held aloft and around this the wild dancing continues; each time the symbol is lowered and raised a new dance begins. Towards sunrise the sacred ceremonies draw to a close. Men daubed with white come forward and light pieces of bark at the dying embers, then they spring again into a wild chase round the fire, throwing sparks, smoke, and flames all over their bodies. They actually leap among the embers, trusting to the white clay to prevent serious burns."

They dance fire itself; they become fire; their movements are those of flames. What they hold in their hands and set alight appears as though it was they themselves who were burning. Finally they throw the sparks from the smouldering ashes up into the air, continuing until the rising sun takes over the fire from them, as they had taken it over from the sun at its setting.

The fire here, then, is still a live crowd. Just as other Indians, dancing, become buffaloes, so these act fire. For later peoples this living fire, into which the Najavos transform themselves, becomes a mere crowd symbol.

Behind every recognized crowd symbol one can find the concrete crowd which nourishes it; nor need one depend here on guesswork alone. The human urge to *become* fire, to re-activate this ancient symbol, is still alive in later and more complex cultures. Besieged cities which have abandoned all hope of relief often set fire to themselves. Kings in the last straits of despair burn themselves with their whole court. (Examples of this can be found among the old Mediterranean cultures as well as among the Indians and Chinese.) The Middle Ages, which believed in hell-fire, were satisfied with the burning of a single heretic instead of a whole audience. They, as it were, despatched representatives to hell, and saw to it that they really burnt.

An analysis of the significance which fire has acquired in different religions is of the greatest interest, but it would have little value unless treated at length and must therefore be reserved for another occasion. It seems appropriate, however, to speak here of the significance of impulsive incendiarism in relation to the individual who commits it, an individual who is really isolated and outside the sphere of any religious or political faith.

Kräpelin describes the case of a lonely old woman who, starting as a small child, committed arson about 20 times in her life. Six times she was accused of it, and 24 years of her life were spent in penitentiaries. "If only it would burn" she thinks to herself; arson is a fixed idea, she feels driven to it as though by an invisible power, and particularly when she has matches in her pocket. She certainly likes watching fire, but she also likes confessing, and confessing very circumstantially. She must, early in her life, have experienced fire as a means of attracting people; the commotion around a fire was probably her first experience of a crowd, and it was easy later for fire to take the place of the crowd. Her self-accusation results from her feeling that everyone is watching her. She likes this feeling and, through it, transforms herself into the fire that people are watching. Thus she has a double relationship with arson. Isolated at an early age by her lamentable history, she has had, particularly during her endless prison terms, no opportunity of mingling with crowds and now she wants, first of all, to be part of the crowd staring at the fire—a fire which is reflected in all eyes and under whose powerful compulsion all eyes turn in the same direction. When the initial blaze is over and the crowd threatens to disperse and escape her, she keeps it alive by suddenly transforming *herself* into the fire. This she achieves very simply: she confesses that she caused it. The fuller and more detailed her story, the longer she will be stared at; the longer she herself will remain the fire.

Cases of this kind are not as rare as one might think. Though not always so extreme, they provide irrefutable proof of the connection between fire and the crowd, even in isolated individuals.

The Sea

The sea is multiple, it moves, and it is dense and cohesive. Its multiplicity lies in its waves; they constitute it. They are innumerable; the sea-farer is completely surrounded by them. The sameness of their movement does not preclude difference of size. They are never entirely still. The wind coming from outside them determines their motion; they beat in this or that direction in accordance with its command. The dense coherence of the waves is something which men in a crowd know well. It entails a yielding to others as though they were oneself, as though there were no strict division between oneself and them. There is no escape from this compliance and thus the consequent impetus and feeling of strength is something engendered by all the units together. The specific nature of this coherence among men is unknown. The sea, while not explaining, expresses it.

Waves are not the only multiple element in the sea. There are also the individual drops of water. It is true that they only become drops in isolation, when they are separated from each other. Their smallness and singleness then makes them seem powerless; they are almost nothing and arouse a feeling of pity in the spectator. Put your hand into water, lift it out and watch the drops slipping singly and impotently down it. The pity you feel for them is as though they were human beings, hopelessly separated. They only begin to count again when they can no longer be counted, when they have again become part of a whole.

The sea has a *voice*, which is very changeable and almost always audible. It is a voice which sounds like a thousand voices, and much has been attributed to it: patience, pain, and anger. But what is most impressive about it is its persistence. The sea never sleeps; by day and by night it makes itself heard, throughout years and decades and centuries. In its impetus and its rage it brings to mind the one entity which shares these attributes in the same degree; that is, the crowd. But the sea has, in addition, the constancy which the crowd lacks. It is always there; it does not ooze away from time to time and disappear. To remain in existence is the greatest, though as yet fruitless, desire of the crowd; and this desire is seen fulfilled in the sea.

The sea is all-embracing; nor can it ever be filled. If all the streams and rivers and clouds, all the waters of the earth, flowed into it, they would not really increase it; it would remain unchanged; we should still feel that it was the same sea. Thus in its size, too, it serves as a model for the crowd, which always wants to grow and would like to become as large as the sea and, in order to do so, draws in more and more people. The word "ocean" is the final expression of the solemn dignity of the sea. The ocean is universal, it reaches everywhere, it touches all lands; the ancients believed that the earth itself swam on it. If it were possible, once and for always, to fill the ocean, the crowd would have no image of its own insatiability, of its deepest and darkest urge, which is to absorb more and more people. The ocean lies before its eyes as the mythical justification for its own unconquerable urge towards universality.

Thus the sea is changeable in its emotions: it can soothe or threaten or break out in storms. But it is always there. One knows where it is; it lies open and manifest, not appearing suddenly where there was nothing before. It lacks the mystery and suddenness of fire which, like a ravening animal, springs out at man from nowhere and thus may be expected anywhere; the sea is to be expected only where it is known to be.

But there is, nevertheless, mystery in it, a mystery lying not in suddenness, but in what it contains and covers. The life with which it teems is as much part of it as its enduring openness. Its sublimity is enhanced by the thought of what it contains, the multitudes of plants and animals hidden within it.

The sea has no interior frontiers and is not divided into peoples and territories. It has one language, which is the same everywhere. There is thus no single human being who can be, as it were, excluded from it. It is too comprehensive to correspond exactly to any of the crowds we know, but it is an image of stilled humanity; all life flows into it and it contains all life.

Rain

All over the world, and particularly where it is rare, rain, before it falls, is felt to be a unit. As a cloud it approaches and covers the sky;

the air grows dark before it rains and everything is shrouded in grey-ness. During this moment when it is imminent, rain is more strongly felt as a unit than while it is actually falling, for it is often ardently longed for, and may indeed be literally vital. Even when prayed for, however, it does not always appear; magic is called in aid and there are numerous and varied methods of luring it.

Rain falls in drops. There are many of them, they can be seen, and the direction of their movement is particularly noticeable. All languages speak of rain *falling*. It is seen as parallel streaks, and the number of the falling drops emphasises the uniformity of their direction. There is no movement which makes more impression on man than that of falling; compared with it all others seem secondary and derived. From a very early age falling is what one fears most; it is the first thing in life which one is armed against. Children learn to beware of it and, after a certain age, it becomes ridiculous or dangerous. In contrast to man, rain is what *should* fall, and there is nothing which falls so often or in such multiplicity.

It is possible that the heaviness and hardness of the fall is somewhat diminished by the great number of the falling drops. These can be heard hitting the ground, and it is a pleasant sound; they can be felt on the skin, and it is a pleasant sensation. Three senses at least—sight, hearing and touch—participate in the experience of rain, and to all these senses it is something multiple. It is easy to protect oneself against rain. Only rarely is it a serious menace; usually it is something beneficent and dense which wraps men round.

There is a sameness in the impact of rain-drops, and the parallel lines of their fall and the uniformity, both of their sound and of their wetness on the skin, all serve to accentuate this sameness.

The density of rain is variable. Rain can be heavy or light and the number of the drops is subject to large fluctuations. One can by no means count on its continuous increase; on the contrary, one knows that it will end and its drops ooze away in the earth without trace.

In so far as rain has become a crowd symbol, it does not stand, as fire does, for the phase of raging and irresistible increase. Nor is it ever as constant as the sea, and only rarely as inexhaustible. Rain is the crowd in the moment of discharge, and stands also for its disintegration. The clouds whence it comes dissolve into rain; the drops fall because they can keep together no longer, and it is not clear whether, or when, they can coalesce again.

Rivers

The most striking thing about a river is its direction. It moves between unmoving banks, and these render its flux continuously apparent. The unresting and uninterrupted flow of its waters, the definiteness of its main direction—even if this changes in detail—the determination with which it makes towards the sea, its absorption of other, smaller streams—all this has an undeniably crowd-like character. And thus the river has become a symbol for the crowd, though not so much for the crowd in general as for some of its specific forms. The width of a river is limited; it cannot grow indefinitely or unexpectedly, and hence its use as a crowd symbol is always in some degree provisional only. It stands for processions; the people watching from the pavements are like trees on river-banks, the solid bordering the flowing. Demonstrations in large cities have a similar river-like character: tributaries come from various districts to feed the main stream. Rivers are especially a symbol for the time when the crowd is forming, the time before it has attained what it will attain. Rivers lack the contagiousness of fire and the universality of the sea. But, in place of these, they have an impetus which seems inexhaustible and which, because there is never a time when it is not being fed, is present from the beginning. Hence the fact that their origins are sometimes taken more seriously than their goal.

A river is the crowd in its vanity, the crowd exhibiting itself. This being seen is as important as the element of direction. There is no river without banks; its bordering verdure is like a lane of people. All river-like formations, such as processions and demonstrations, want to be *seen*. They show as much as possible of their surface, extending as far as they can and offering themselves to the largest possible number of spectators. They want to be admired or feared. They have a provisional goal, but it is not really important. The important thing is the stretch which separates them from it, the length of street they have to traverse. The density among their participants need not be very high. It is higher among the spectators, and between spectators and participants a special kind of relationship develops, resembling the love-play of two snake-like creatures, the one slowly and tenderly drawing its length through the embrace of the other.

Growth, of course, is determined at source and takes place only through precisely defined tributaries. In addition to water, a river also carries along with it many other different things and its appearance is much more effectively changed by these than the appearance of the sea is changed by marine freights, which disappear on the enormous expanse of water.

Summing up, we may conclude that the river is only a limited crowd symbol and differs in this respect from fire, sea, forest or corn. It is the symbol of a movement which is still under control, before the eruption and the discharge; it contains the threat of these rather than their actuality. It is the symbol of the *slow* crowd.

Forest

The forest is *higher* than man. It may be enclosed and overgrown with all kinds of scrub; it may be hard to penetrate, and still harder to traverse, but its real density, that which makes it a forest, is its foliage; and this is overhead. It is the foliage of single trees linked together which forms a continuous roof; it is the foliage which shuts out the light and throws a universal shadow.

Man stands upright like a tree and he inserts himself amongst the other trees. But they are taller than he is and he has to look up at them. No other natural phenomenon of his surroundings is invariably above him and, at the same time, so near and so multiple in its formation as the concourse of trees. For clouds pass, rain dries up, and the stars are distant. Of all the multiple phenomena affecting him from above, none is as perpetually near him as the forest. Tree-tops are attainable; trees can be climbed and their fruit picked and brought down; people have lived in them.

The direction in which a forest draws men's eyes is that of its own growth. A forest grows steadily upwards; the equality of its trees is approximate, consisting, in fact, only in uniformity of direction. Once in the forest, man feels sheltered. He is not at its point of greatest density, the top, where it goes on growing. On the contrary, the density is overhead and protects him. Thus the forest is the first image of awe. It compels men to look upwards, grateful for the protection above. Looking up at trees becomes looking up in general. The forest is a preparation for the feeling of being in church, the standing before God among pillars and columns. Its most harmonious and therefore most perfect expression is the vault of a dome, the trunks of many trees intertwined in a supreme and indivisible unity.

Another, and no less important, aspect of the forest is its multiple immovability. Every single trunk is rooted in the ground and no menace from outside can move it. Its resistance is absolute; it does not give an inch. It can be felled, but not shifted. And thus the forest has become the symbol of the *army*, an army which has taken up a position, which does not flee in any circumstances, and which allows itself to be cut down to the last man before it gives a foot of ground.

Corn

Corn, in more than one way, is a diminished and subjugated forest. It grows where forest stood before, and it never grows as high. It is man's work and entirely in his power. He sows it and reaps it and, by ancient rites, contributes to its growth. It is as pliant as grass and subject to the influence of every wind. The blades move together in accordance with the wind; the whole field bows down simultaneously. In storms it is struck down completely and remains lying thus for long periods. But it has a mysterious ability to straighten itself and, so long as it has not been too badly maltreated, will suddenly stand there again, the whole field of it. The full ears are like heavy heads; they nod to one or turn away as the wind blows.

Corn is usually shorter than man, but, even when it has grown above his head, he remains its master. It is cut all together, as it grew and was sown together. Even the grasses which man does not use remain together throughout their existence. But how much more striking is the sameness of the fate of blades of corn, sown, harvested, threshed and stored together! As long as corn is growing, it remains rooted on the same spot; no one blade can get away from the other blades, and anything which happens to one happens to all. The blades vary in size, but no more than men; a cornfield as a whole generally appears uniform in height. Its rhythm when excited by the wind is that of a simple dance.

Men readily see their own equality before death in the image of corn. But blades of corn are cut simultaneously and this brings a quite specific death to mind: a common death in battle, whole rows of men mown down together. The cornfield is a battlefield.

The pliancy of corn becomes submissiveness. It is like an assemblage of loyal subjects, incapable of conceiving the idea of resistance. Tremulously obedient they stand there, responsive to every command. When the enemy comes they are mercilessly trampled down.

The heaps of seed from which corn originates are as significant as the heaps of grain it finally becomes. Whether it bears seven or one hundredfold, the latter are many times larger than the former. By growing and standing together it increases; and this increase is its blessing.

Wind

The strength of wind varies, and, with it, its voice. It can whine or howl, and, loud or soft, there are few sounds of which it is not capable. Thus it affects men as something living, long after other natural phenomena have become inanimate. Apart from its voice, the most striking thing about wind is its direction; in order to name it, it is essential to know which quarter it comes from. Since man is entirely surrounded by air, the buffettings he receives from wind are felt as something peculiarly physical. One feels entirely contained in wind, it gathers everything to itself and, in a storm, everything that it seizes is driven along together.

Wind is invisible, but the movement it imparts to clouds and waves, leaves and grasses, makes its multiplicity apparent. In the hymns of the *Vedas* the storm gods or *Maruts*, always appear in the plural. "Their numbers are stated as thrice seven or thrice sixty. . . . They are brothers of equal age, having the same birthplace and the same abode. . . . The noise made by the Maruts is thunder and the roaring of winds. They cause the mountains to quake, they shatter trees and, like wild elephants, devour the forests. They are often called singers: the singing of the wind. They are mighty, fierce, terrible like lions, but also playful like children or calves."

The age-old identification of wind and breath is proof of how concentrated wind is felt to be; it has the density of breath. Its invisibility, on the other hand, enables it to stand for invisible crowds, and thus for spirits. They come roaring like a storm, a wild host; or they are spirits in flight, as in the vision of the Eskimo Shaman.

Flags are wind made visible. They are like bits cut from clouds, nearer and more varied in colour, tethered and given permanent shape. In their movement they are truly arresting. Nations use them to mark the air above them as their own, as though the wind could be partitioned.

Sand

Sand has various qualities relevant to this discussion, but two of these are especially important. The first is the smallness and sameness of its parts. This is one quality, not two, for grains of sand are felt to be the same only because they are so small. The second is the endlessness of sand. It is boundless; there is always more of it than the eye can take in. Where it appears in small heaps it is disregarded. It is only really striking when the number of grains is infinite, as on the sea-shore or in the desert.

Sand is continually shifting, and it is because of this that, as a crowd symbol, it stands midway between the fluid and the solid symbols. It forms waves like the sea and rises in clouds; dust is refined sand. Also important is the fact that sand is a threat, confronting man as something hostile and aggressive. The monotony, vastness and lifelessness of the desert, consisting as it does of innumerable, homogeneous particles, opposes to man a power which is almost invincible. Sand suffocates man as the sea does, but more maliciously because more slowly.

Man's relationship to the sand of the desert anticipates the struggle he wages with growing power against huge swarms of tiny enemies. Locusts, like sand, wither vegetation, and man, as cultivator, fears them as he fears sand, for they leave desert behind them.

It is puzzling that sand should ever have become a symbol of progeny. The fact that it has—and the Bible provides many instances of it—proves the intensity of man's desire for immense numbers of descendants. The stress here is not primarily on quality. It is true that people wish for a troop of strong and upright sons, but, for the remoter future, the sum of the life of generations, they want more than this. They want their posterity to be a crowd, and the largest, most boundless and least countable crowd they know is that of sand. How little the individual quality of descendants matters can be seen from the similar symbol of the Chinese, who equate progeny with a swarm of locusts, extolling their numbers and cohesion as a model for man's posterity.

Another symbol which the Bible uses for posterity is the stars. Here, too, the essential is their innumerability. There is no mention of the brightness of single, special stars. What is important is the fact that they remain; that they never pass away, but are always there.

The Heap

Every heap which has human significance has been collected. The unity of a heap of fruit or grain is the result of activity. Many hands were occupied with the picking or harvesting. These are tied to a definite season and are of such decisive importance that the oldest division of the year is derived from them. Men celebrate in feasts their joy over the various heaps they have managed to collect. They exhibit them with pride and often their feasts are arranged round them.

The things which have been collected are all of the same kind, one species of fruit or grain. They are piled as closely as possible and the more there is of them and the denser the pile, the better. It is close at hand and does not have to be fetched from far off. The heap must be large and people boast of it. Only if it is large enough will it last all of them for any length of time. As soon as they have got used to the gathering of things for these heaps, people go on and on making them larger and larger. They love to remember the years which brought the richest harvest and, as soon as annals are kept, these are recorded in them as the years of greatest happiness. From year to year and place to place harvests vie with each other. Whether they belong to the community or to individuals the heaps of produce stand as exemplars to be guarded and cherished.

It is true that they are then used up, sometimes quickly on special occasions, at other times slowly according to need. The time of their existence is limited. The idea of decrease is contained in them from the beginning and their re-assembly is subject to the rhythm of the seasons. All harvesting is a rhythmic heaping, and feasts are celebrated in accordance with this rhythm.

Stone Heaps

But there are also heaps of an entirely different kind, which are not edible. Such heaps are of stone and are erected precisely because it is difficult to take them to pieces. They are meant to endure for a long time, for a kind of eternity, and should never decrease but remain always as they are. They do not make their way into people's bellies, nor are they always lived in. In their oldest form each separate stone stands for the man who has contributed it to the heap. Later the size and weight of the individual stone increases and each can only be mastered by a number of men working together. Such monuments may represent different things, but each contains the concentrated effort of innumerable difficult journeys. Sometimes it is a mystery how they were erected at all, and the less they can be explained, and the more distant the origin of the stone, the greater the imagined number of their builders and the stronger the impression they make on later generations. They represent the rhythmic exertion of many men, of which nothing remains but these indestructible monuments.

Treasure

Treasure, like all other heaps, is something which has been collected. But, in contrast to fruit and grain, it consists of units which are inedible and imperishable. What is essential is that each of these units should have a special value; it is only confidence in their retaining it which tempts men to amass treasure. A hoard of treasure is a heap which should be left to grow undisturbed. The man it belongs to may be powerful, but there are always others equally powerful to rob him. The prestige treasure gives its owner carries danger with it; fights and wars have arisen over treasure and many a man would have lived longer if his treasure had been smaller. Thus it is often of necessity kept secret. The peculiarity of treasure lies in the tension between the splendour it should radiate and the secrecy which is its protection. The lust of counting, of seeing numbers mount up, derives largely from treasure and is most comprehensible there. None of the other enumerations whose desired result is the highest possible figure—those of cattle, or of men, for example—share the same concentration of countable units. The image of the owner secretly counting his treasure is deeply engraved in the minds of men; and no less imperishable is their hope of discovering treasure for themselves, treasure which has been so well hidden that it lies forgotten in its hiding-place and no longer belongs to anyone. Disciplined armies have been corroded and overcome by their greed for treasure, and many victories turned to defeat. The transformation, even before battle, of an army into a band of treasure-seekers is described by Plutarch in his life of Pompey.

"As soon as Pompey landed his fleet near Carthage, 7,000 of the enemy deserted and came over to him. His own army consisted of six legions at full strength. Here, they say, a rather absurd thing happened to him. It seems that some of his soldiers came across some hidden treasure and got a considerable amount of money. The story of this got abroad and all the rest of the army fancied that the place must be full of money which had been buried by the Carthaginians at some time of calamity. And so, for many days, Pompey could do nothing at all with his soldiers who were all busy looking for treasure. He merely went about laughing at the sight of so many thousands of men together digging up the ground and turning it over, until in the end they got tired of it and asked him to lead them wherever he liked; they had already, they said, suffered enough for their foolishness."

But apart from the heaps or hoards which are irresistible because they are hidden, there are others which are collected quite openly, as a kind of voluntary tax, and in the understanding that they will fall into the hands of one person, or of a few. To this group belong all kinds of lottery; they are quick accumulations of treasure. It is known that, immediately after the announcement of the result, they will be handed over to the fortunate winners. The smaller the number of these, the larger the treasure and the greater, therefore, its attraction.

The greed which unites people on such occasions presupposes an absolute confidence in the units composing the treasure. It is difficult to

exaggerate the strength of this confidence. A man identifies himself
with the unit of his money; doubt cast on it offends him and, if it is
shattered, his self-confidence is shaken. He feels slighted and humiliated by the lowering of the value of his monetary unit and, if this
process is accelerated and inflation occurs, it is *men* who are depreciated
until they find themselves in formations which can only be equated
with flight-crowds. The more people lose, the more united are they
in their fate. What appears as panic in the few who are fortunate
enough to be able to save something for themselves, turns into mass-
flight for all those others who have become equals by being deprived
of their money. I shall describe in a later chapter the consequences of
this phenomenon which, particularly in our own time, have been of
incalculable general importance.

THE PACK

The Pack: Kinds of Pack

CROWD CRYSTALS and crowds, in the modern sense of the word, both derive from an older unit in which they are still one. This unit is the *pack*. Among the small hordes which roam about as bands of ten or twenty men it is the universal expression of communal excitement.

Characteristic of the pack is the fact that it cannot grow. It is surrounded by emptiness and there are literally no additional people who could join it. It consists of a group of men in a state of excitement whose fiercest wish is *to be more*. In whatever they undertake together, whether hunting or fighting, they would fare better if there were more of them. For a group consisting of so few, every single man who joined it would be a distinct, substantial and indispensable addition. The strength he brought with him might be a tenth or twentieth part of their total strength. The position he occupied would be clear to all; he would really count in the economy of the group, in a way that scarcely any of us count today.

In the pack which, from time to time, forms out of the group, and which most strongly expresses its feeling of unity, the individual can never lose himself as completely as modern man can in any crowd today. In the changing constellation of the pack, in its dances and' expeditions, he will again and again find himself at its edge. He may be in the centre, and then, immediately afterwards, at the edge again; at the edge and then back in the centre. When the pack forms a ring round the fire, each man will have neighbours to right and left, but no-one behind him; his back is naked and exposed to the wilderness. Density within the pack is always something of an illusion. Men may press closely together and enact a multitude in traditional rhythmic movements, but they are not a multitude; they are a few, and have to make up in intensity what they lack in actual numbers.

Of the four essential attributes of the crowd which we have come to know, two are only fictitious as far as the pack is concerned, though these are the two which are most strenuously desired and enacted. Hence the other two must be all the more strongly present in actuality. *Growth* and *density* are only acted; *equality* and *direction* really exist. The first thing which strikes one about the pack is its unswerving direction; equality is expressed in the fact that all are obsessed by the same goal, the sight of an animal perhaps, which they want to kill.

The pack is limited in more ways than one. Not only do relatively few people belong to it, but these few know one another well. They have always lived together, they meet daily and, in many joint enterprises, have learnt to value each other accurately. The pack can expect no addition; people who live in such conditions are too few, and too widely scattered. But in one respect it is superior to the crowd with its capacity for indefinite growth. Since it consists entirely of people who know each other well, it can always form again, even if scattered by adverse circumstances. It can count on continuing; its existence is guaranteed as long as its members are alive. It will develop rites and ceremonies and those participating in them can be counted on to appear. They know where they belong and are not tempted to stray. Temptations to do so are indeed so few that the habit of giving way to them has no chance of developing.

But, in so far as packs do grow, growth takes place in discrete quanta, and by mutual agreement of the participants. A pack formed from a second group may come across the first pack and, unless they fight, they may join forces for temporary purposes. But the separate consciousness of the two quanta will always be preserved. It may disappear temporarily in the heat of joint action, but not for long. It will in any case come to the fore again during the distribution of honours or other ceremonies. The feel of the pack is always stronger than the individual's sense of what he himself is apart from it. At a certain level of communal life the quantum-feeling of the pack is decisive, and unshakeable.

I am here deliberately opposing all the usual concepts of tribe, sib, clan, with a different kind of unit, the unit of the pack. Those well-known sociological concepts, important as they are, all stand for something static. The pack, in contrast, is a unit of *action*, and its manifestations are concrete. To explore the origins of the behaviour of crowds we have to start from the pack. It is their oldest and most limited form, and it existed long before crowds in the modern sense were known. It appears in various shapes, all of them easy to grasp, and, over tens of thousands of years, its active force has been such that there are traces of it everywhere and, even in our entirely different world, formations still exist which derive directly from it.

From earliest times the pack has had *four* different forms, or functions. They all have something fleeting about them, and each changes easily into another, but it is important to determine first of all the respects in which they differ. The truest and most natural pack is that from which our word derives, the hunting pack; and this forms wherever the object of the pack is an animal too strong and too dangerous to be captured by one man alone. It also forms whenever there is a prospect of a mass of game, so that as little as possible of it shall be lost. If the slaughtered animal is very large, a whale or an elephant for example, its size means that it can only be brought in and divided up by numbers of men working together, even if it was originally struck down by one or two individuals. Thus the hunting pack enters the stage of *distribution*. Distribution need not always be preceded by hunting, but the two stages, or states, are closely connected and should be examined together. The object of both is the *prey*; and the prey alone, its behaviour and nature, whether alive or dead, determines the behaviour of the pack which forms with it as object.

The second type of pack is the war pack, and this has much in common with the hunting pack and is, indeed, connected with it by many transitional states. It postulates a second pack of men, and is always directed against what it feels to be one, even where this has not yet had time to form. In earlier times its object was often a single life, one man on whom it had to take revenge. In the certainty with which it knows its victim it comes particularly close to the hunting pack.

The third type is the *lamenting pack*. This forms when a member of a group is torn from it by death. The group is small and feels every loss as irreplaceable, and unites for the occasion into a pack. It may be primarily concerned with keeping back the dying man, or with snatching from him, before he disappears completely, as much of his life as it can incorporate into itself; or it may want to propitiate his soul so that it does not become an enemy to the living. In any case, action of some kind is felt to be necessary, and there are no human beings anywhere who forgo it entirely.

Fourthly, I shall summarise a variety of phenomena which, in spite of all their diversity, have one thing in common: the intent to increase. *Increase packs* are formed so that the group itself, or the living beings, whether plants or animals, with which it is associated, should become *more*. They manifest themselves in dances to which a definite mythical significance is attributed. Like the other packs they are found everywhere where there are men living together; and what they express is always the group's dissatisfaction with its numbers. One of the essential attributes of the modern crowd, namely its urge to grow, thus appears very early, in packs which are not themselves capable of growth. There are rites and ceremonies which are intended to compel growth and, whatever one may think of their effectiveness, the fact remains that, in the course of time, they have resulted in the formation of large crowds.

A detailed examination of the four different types of pack leads to surprising conclusions. All four share a tendency to change into one another, and there is nothing which has greater consequences than this transmutation of packs. The instability of the far larger crowd is already to be found in these small and seemingly more solid formations. Their mutations often give rise to peculiar religious phenomena. I shall show how hunting packs change into lamenting packs, and how special myths and cults have formed around this process. In such cases the mourners want it forgotten that they were the hunters. The victim they bewail serves to purge them from the blood-guilt of the hunt.

The choice of the term "pack" for this older and more limited kind of crowd is intended to remind us that it owes its origin among men to the example of animals, the pack of animals hunting together. Wolves, which man knew well and from whom many of the dogs he uses derive, had impressed him very early. Their occurrence as mythical animals among so many peoples, the conception of a were-wolf, the stories of men who, disguised as wolves, assailed and dismembered other men, the legends of children brought up as wolves—all these things and many others prove how close the wolf was to man.

A pack of hounds, trained to hunt together, is a living remnant of this old association. Men have learnt from wolves. There are dances in which they, as it were, practise being wolves. Other animals, of course, have also contributed to the development of similar abilities among hunting peoples. I use the word "pack" for men as well as for animals, because it best expresses the joint and swift movement involved, and the concreteness of the goal in view. The pack wants its prey; it wants its blood and its death. In order to attain what it is after, it must have speed, cunning and endurance, and must not allow itself to be deflected. It urges itself on with its joint clamour, and the importance of this noise, in which the voices of all the individual creatures unite, should not be under-rated. It can swell and diminish, but it is persistent; it contains the attack. The prey, when it is finally captured and killed, is eaten by the whole pack together. Every member is customarily allowed a share; even among animals the rudiments of a distribution pack can be found. I use the same word "pack" for the three other basic formations I have mentioned. It is true that it would be difficult to find animal models for these, but I do not know of any better word to express the concreteness, directness and intensity of the processes involved.*

The Hunting Pack

THE HUNTING PACK moves with all its force towards a living object which it wants to kill in order subsequently to incorporate it. Its end is always a kill; overtaking and surrounding are the means to this end. It pursues a single, large animal, or many smaller animals fleeing together.

The prey is always in movement and has to be chased. What matters is the speed of the pack; it should be able to run faster than the quarry in order to tire it out. If it is a number of animals who are being chased, and if the pack succeeds in surrounding them, then their mass flight turns into a panic; each of the hunted animals will try to escape on its own from the circle of its enemies.

The hunt extends over a large and changing area. If the quarry is a single animal, the pack will continue to exist as long as this fights for its life. The excitement mounts during the hunt; the shouts the hunters exchange increase their thirst for blood.

The concentration on one continually moving object which disappears from sight and suddenly reappears, which is often lost and must be sought for again, which is never released from the hunters' deadly intent or from its own state of mortal fear—this concentration is shared by all the hunters *together*. Each of them has the same object in view and is closing in on it. The gradually diminishing distance between the pack and its quarry diminishes for *each* of them. The hunt has a joint and deadly pulse, which goes on beating for a long time and over changing ground, becoming more and more violent as it nears the animal. Once this is within reach and can be hit, each of the hunters has a chance of killing it, and each tries to do so. The spears and arrows of all the pursuers are concentrated on *one* creature; they are prolongations of the rapacious looks directed towards it during the hunt.

For every process of this kind has its natural end. Once its goal has

* The German word for pack is *Meute*, which derives from the mediaeval Latin *Movita*, meaning movement. The Old French *Meute* has two meanings, "rebellion or insurrection" and also "the hunt". The human element is still well to the fore, and the word comprises exactly what is meant here. The ambiguity it contains is precisely what I am concerned with.

been reached, the pack undergoes a sudden change, as sharp and clear-cut as its goal had been. Its fury abates the moment the kill has taken place. Everyone suddenly stands still around the outstretched victim. From among those present a ring forms, consisting of all to whom a share of the game is due. They could fall on it with their teeth, like wolves who devour their prey alive, but men postpone this act of incorporation to a later moment. The *distribution* is carried out peaceably and according to definite rules.

Whether the kill consists of a single large animal or of several smaller ones, it must, if it was a pack which hunted it down, be distributed among all the members of that pack. And this process of distribution is exactly the opposite of the process by which the pack was formed. Each man now wants something for himself, and wants as much as possible. If distribution were not precisely regulated and governed by something resembling law, with experienced men to watch over its execution, it would inevitably end in bloodshed. The law of distribution is the oldest law.

There are two basically different versions of this law. According to one, distribution is limited to the actual hunters; according to the other, women and men who had nothing to do with the hunt can also participate. The person in charge of the distribution, who sees that it is carried out in an orderly manner, originally derived no profit from the office. He may even, as is the case among some Eskimo whale-hunters, renounce his share for the sake of honour. The feeling of the common ownership of prey can be carried to great lengths. Among the Korjaks in Siberia the ideal hunter invites everyone to partake of his kill and is himself satisfied with what is left over.

The law of distribution is complex and variable. The portion of honour is not always allotted to the man who dealt the fatal blow. Sometimes the right to it belongs to the man who was the first to sight the game. But even those who were only distant witnesses of the kill may have a claim to part of the prey. When this is the case, spectators are counted as accomplices of the deed; they share the responsibility for it and partake of its fruits. I mention this extreme and not very common instance in order to demonstrate the strength of the feeling of unity which radiates from the hunting pack. Whatever the way in which distribution is regulated, the two decisive factors are the *sighting* and the *killing* of the prey.

The War Pack

THE ESSENTIAL difference between the hunting pack and the war pack lies in the fact that the latter is only one half of a formation. As long as it is simply a question of an excited group in pursuit of a single man whom it wants to punish, we are dealing with a formation resembling a hunting pack. But if the hunted man belongs to a second group which does not want to abandon him, it rapidly becomes a case of pack against pack. The enemies do not differ very much from each other. They are all human beings, males, and warriors. In the original form of warfare they are so much alike that it is difficult to distinguish one from the other. Their method of attack and their weapons are more or less similar. They both utter wild and threatening shouts, and their reciprocal intentions are the same. The hunting pack, in contrast, is *one-sided*. The animals which are being pursued do not try to surround or to hunt men; they are in flight and, if they fight back, this only happens during the moment of killing. For the most part they are no longer in a state to defend themselves against man.

The factor determining the shape of the war pack is that there are *two* packs, both of them out to do exactly the same thing to each other. The duplication of the pack is unquestioned, and the cleavage between the two remains absolute so long as a state of war exists. To find out what it is they really intend to do to each other it is sufficient to read the following report. It is the story of the expedition of a South American tribe, the Taulipang, against their enemies, the Pishauko. The account was taken down word for word from a Taulipang man, and it contains all that one need know about the war pack. The narrator is full of enthusiasm for the enterprise; he describes it from within, from his own side, in a kind of nakedness which is as truthful as it is terrible, and is virtually unparalleled among such records.

"In the beginning there was friendship between the Taulipang and the Pishauko. Then they started to quarrel over women. First the Pishauko mudered single Taulipang whom they assailed in the forest. Then they killed a young Taulipang and his wife, then three Taulipang in the forest. Thus the Pishauko gradually wanted to do away with the whole tribe of the Taulipang.

"Then Manikuza, the war-chief of the Taulipang, called all his men together. The Taulipang had three leaders: Manikuza the head-chief, and two sub-chiefs, one of whom was a small, stout, but very brave

man; the other was his brother. Then there was the old chief, Manikuza's father. Among his people there was also a small, very brave man
from the neighbouring tribe of the Arekuna. Manikuza had a fermented
mass of Kashiri prepared, five big gourds full. Then he had six canoes
fitted up. The Pishauko lived in the mountains. The Taulipang took
two women along; they were to set fire to the houses. They travelled
there, I don't know on which river. They ate nothing, no pepper, no
bigger fish, no game, only small fish, until the war should be over.
They also took paint and white clay with them, for painting their bodies.

"They came near to the settlement of the Pishauko. Manikuza sent
five men to the house of the Pishauko to find out whether they were
all there. They were all there. It was a big house with very many
people, surrounded by a stockade. The spies came back and reported
this to the chief. Then the old man and the three chiefs blew on the
fermented mass of Kashiri. They also blew on the paint and the white
clay and the war-clubs. The old men had only bows and arrows with
iron heads, no fire-arms. The others had guns and shot. Each had a
sack of shot and six boxes of powder with him. All these things too
were blown on (blowing on of magic power). Then they painted themselves with red and white stripes, beginning from the forehead, a red
stripe above and a white one below, across the whole face. On their
chest they painted three stripes each, a red stripe above and a white
one below, and the same on both upper arms, so that the warriors
would be able to recognize each other. The women also painted
themselves in the same way. Then Manikuza ordered water to be
poured into the mass of kashiri.

"The spies said there were a great many people in the houses. There
was a very big house, and three smaller ones stood further apart. The
Pishauko were many more than the Taulipang, who were only fifteen
men apart from the one Arekuna. Then they drank kashiri, a gourdful
each, a lot of kashiri to make themselves brave. Manikuza said: 'This
one here shoots first! Whilst he is loading his gun, the other shoots.
One after the other!' He disposed his people in three groups of five
men each, in a wide circle around the house. He said: 'Don't fire a
useless shot! When a man falls, let him lie and shoot at the man still
standing!'

"Then they advanced, divided into three groups, the women behind
them with the gourds full of drink. They arrived at the edge of the
savanna. Manikuza said: 'What shall we do now? They are very many.
Perhaps it is best we turn back and fetch more people.' But the
Arekuna said: 'No! Forward! When I burst into many people I find

nobody to kill!' (meaning: All these many people are too few for my club since I kill very fast.) Manikuza replied: 'Forward! Forward Forward!' He urged them all on. They came near the house. It was night. A sorcerer was in the house who was just blowing on a sick man. He said: 'There are people coming!' and thus warned the inhabitants of the house. The master of the house, the chief of the Pishauko said: 'Let them come! I know who it is! It is Manikuza! But he won't get back from here!' The sorcerer went on warning them and said: 'The people have arrived!' The chief said: 'It is Manikuza! He won't get back! He will end his life here!'

"Then Manikuza cut through the liana which bound the palisade together. The two women broke in and set fire to the house, one at the entrance, the other at the exit. There were a great many people in the house. Then both retired outside the stockade. The fire seized the house. An old man climbed up to extinguish the fire. Many people came out of the house, they shot a lot with their guns, but without aiming, for they saw nobody; only to frighten the enemies. The old chief of the Taulipang wanted to shoot a Pishauko with an arrow, but he missed him. The Pishauko was in his earth-hole. As the old man was fitting his second arrow the Pishauko shot him down with his gun. Manikuza saw that his father was dead. Then the warriors did much shooting. They had surrounded the whole house and the Pishauko had no way out by which to flee.

"Then a Taulipang warrior named Ewama forced his way in. Behind him came one of the sub-chiefs; behind him his brother; behind him Manikuza, the war-chief; behind him the Arekuna. The others remained outside to kill any Pishauko who wanted to escape. The other five burst in among their enemies and struck them down with their clubs. The Pishauko shot at them, but they hit no one. Manikuza killed the chief of the Pishauko. The sub-chief killed the sub-chief of the Pishauko. His brother and the Arekuna killed very fast, and many. Only two maidens fled, they still live on the upper reaches of the river, married to Taulipang. All the others were killed. Then they fired the house. The children wept. All the children were thrown into the fire. Among the dead there was a Pishauko who was still alive. He had smeared himself all over with blood and lay down among the dead, to make the enemies believe that he was dead. The Taulipang seized the fallen Pishauko one after the other and cut them right in two with a forest-knife. They found the man who was still alive, and seized and killed him. Then they took the fallen chief of the Pishauko, bound him with outstretched arms to a tree and shot at

him with the rest of their ammunition until he fell to pieces. Then they
seized a dead woman. Manikuza pulled her genitals apart with his
fingers and said to Ewama: 'Look, here, here is something good for
you to enter!'

"The remaining Pishauko who were still in the three other smaller
houses fled and scattered in the mountains of the region. There they
still live today, deadly enemies of the other tribes and secret murderers,
pursuing especially the Taulipang.

"The Taulipang buried their old chief on the spot. Apart from him,
they had only two men slightly wounded with shot in the belly. Then
they returned home shouting 'Hei-hei-hei-hei-hei!' "

The quarrel starts over women, and a few single men are killed:
only the deaths caused by the *other* side are really noticed. From this
moment on, an unshakeable conviction reigns that the enemy want to
exterminate the whole tribe of the Taulipang. The chief, who knows
his people well, now calls them together. There are not many of
them, only sixteen counting the man from the neighbouring tribe,
and they all know what they can expect of one another in a fight.
They keep a strict fast, being allowed to feed only on miserable small
fish. A strong fermented drink has been prepared and they drink it
before the battle in order to "make themselves brave". They make a
kind of uniform with paint "so that the warriors should be able to
recognise each other". Everything regarded as connected with war,
and particularly the weapons, are "blown on", and so endowed with
magic power, and blessed.

As soon as they arrive in the vicinity of the hostile settlement, spies
are sent out to discover whether all of the enemy are there. They are,
and it is essential that they should be, for they are all to be killed at the
same time. It is a large house with a great many people in it, a superior
and dangerous power. The sixteen men have every reason to drink for
courage. The chief gives his instructions exactly as an officer would.
Once arrived near the enemy's house he begins to feel his responsibility.
"They are very many" he says, and hesitates. Should they return and
fetch reinforcements? But there happens to be in his troop a man who
can never have enough enemies to kill. His resolution imparts itself
to the chief, who then gives the order to advance.

It is night, but the people in the house are awake. A sorcerer is
holding a session; he is treating a sick man and everyone is gathered
round. The sorcerer, more suspicious than the rest, is alert and senses
the danger. "There are people coming", he says, and, soon after,
"The people have arrived". But the chief knows exactly who it is.

He has one enemy, and of that man's enmity he is certain. But he is also certain that, if he comes, his enemy will lose his life. "He won't get back. He will end his life here." The blindness of the man who is to perish is as remarkable as the hesitation of the attacker. The man who is threatened does nothing, though disaster is already on him.

The house is soon in flames, set on fire by the women, and the inmates try to force their way out. They cannot see those who are shooting at them out of the darkness, but they themselves are well illuminated targets. Their enemies press in and club them, and the story of their destruction is completed in a few sentences. It is not a question of fighting, but of sheer annihilation. The weeping children are thrown into the fire. One after another, the dead are cut into pieces. A survivor who had smeared himself with blood and lain down amongst them in the hope of escape, shares their fate. The dead chief is tied to a tree and shot at until he falls to pieces. The rape of a dead woman is the ghastly climax. Everything perishes completely in the fire.

The few who escape from the smaller neighbouring houses flee to the mountains and live there as "secret murderers".

There is nothing to be added to this description of a war pack. Of all the innumerable similar reports this one is the most truthful, because most naked. It contains nothing extraneous; nothing has been improved or glossed over by the narrator.

The sixteen men who set out brought no booty home; their victory in no way enriched them. They did not leave a single woman or child alive. Their goal was the annihilation of the hostile pack so that nothing, literally nothing, of it should remain. They describe their own actions with relish; it was others who were, and remained, murderers.

The Lamenting Pack

THE MOST IMPRESSIVE description of a lamenting pack known to me comes from the *Warramunga* in Central Australia.

"Even before the sufferer had breathed his last the lamentations and self-inflicted wounds began. When it was known that the end was near, all the native men ran at full speed to the spot. Some of the women, who had gathered from all directions, were lying prostrate on the body of the dying man, while others were standing or kneeling around, digging the sharp ends of yam-sticks into the crown of their heads, from which the blood streamed down over their faces, while all the time they kept up a loud continuous wail. Many of the men, rushing up to the scene of action, flung themselves also higgedly-piggledy on the sufferer, the women rising and making way for them, till nothing was to be seen but a struggling mass of bodies all mixed up together. Presently up came a man yelling and brandishing a stone knife. On reaching the spot he suddenly gashed both his thighs with the knife, cutting right across the muscles, so that, unable to stand, he dropped down on the top of the struggling bodies, till his mother, wife, and sisters dragged him out of the scrimmage, and immediately applied their mouths to his gaping wounds, while he lay exhausted and helpless on the ground. Gradually the struggling mass of dusky bodies untwined itself, disclosing the unfortunate sick man, who was the object or rather victim, of this well-meant demonstration of affection and sorrow. If he had been ill before, he was much worse when his friends left him; indeed it was plain that he had not long to live. Still the weeping and wailing went on; the sun set, darkness fell on the camp, and later in the evening the man died. Then the wailing rose louder than before, and men and women, apparently frantic with grief, rushed about cutting themselves with knives and sharp-pointed sticks, while the women battered each other's heads with clubs, no one attempting to ward off either cuts or blows.

"An hour later a funeral procession set out by torch light through the darkness, carrying the body to a wood about a mile off, where it was laid on a platform of boughs in a low gum-tree. When day broke next morning, not a sign of human habitation was to be seen in the camp where the man had died. All the people had removed their rude huts to some distance, leaving the place of death solitary; for nobody wished to meet the ghost of the deceased, who would certainly be hovering about, along with the spirit of the living man who had caused his death by evil magic, and who might be expected to come to the spot in the outward form of an animal to gloat over the scene of his crime.

"But in the new camp the ground was strewed with men lying prostrate, their thighs gashed with the wounds which they inflicted on themselves with their own hands. They had done their duty by the dead and would bear to the end of their life the deep scars on their thighs as badges of honour. On one man the dints of no less than twenty-three wounds were counted which he had inflicted on himself at various times. Meantime the women had resumed the duty of lamentation. Forty or fifty of them sat down in groups of five or six, weeping and wailing frantically with their arms round each other, while the actual and tribal wives, mothers, wives' mothers, daughters,

sisters, mothers' mothers, sisters' husbands' mothers, and grand-
daughters, according to custom, once more cut their scalps open with
yam-sticks, and the widows afterwards in addition seared the scalp-
wounds with red-hot fire sticks."

One fact immediately stands out from this description (to which
many similar ones might be added): What matters is the *excitement*
itself. Many intentions play their part in the event, and it will be
necessary to discuss them, but the essential thing is the excitement as
such, the state of having something to lament in common. The ferocity
of the lament, its duration, its resumption the next day in the new
camp, the amazing rhythm in which it increases and, even after complete exhaustion, starts afresh—all this is proof of the fact that what
matters here is the reciprocal stimulation to lament. Even from this
single case, typical of the Australian aborigine, it will be readily
understood why this excitement is described as that of a pack, and why
it seems necessary to introduce the term lamenting pack.

The whole thing begins with the news that death is near. The men
run to the spot at full speed and find the women already there. Those
most closely related to the dying man lie in a heap on top of him.
An important fact is that lament is not deferred until after death, but
begins as soon as hope for the sick person has been given up. Directly
they believe that he will die, those around him become unable to withhold their lament. The pack breaks out; it has been waiting for its
opportunity and will not allow its victim to escape. The tremendous
violence with which it falls on its object seals its fate. It is scarcely
conceivable that a dangerously sick man should ever recover from such
treatment. In the rabid howling of his people he is almost smothered;
it is probable that he is sometimes actually stifled. In any event, his
death is accelerated. The feeling, so natural to us, that a man should
be allowed to die in peace, would be utterly incomprehensible to these
people, intent as they are on their own excitement.

What does it mean, this heap which forms on top of a dying man,
this mass of bodies obviously struggling to be as close to him as
possible? We are told that the women, who are lying there at first,
get up in order to make room for the men, as though these too, or at
least some of them, had a right to be closest to him. Whatever explanation the natives may give of the formation of this tangle, what actually
happens is that a heap of bodies completely absorbs the dying man into
itself.

The physical closeness of the members of the pack, their *density*,
could be carried no further. Together with the sufferer, they form one

heap; he still belongs to them; they hold him back amongst themselves. Since he is unable to rise and stand with them, they lie down with him. Everyone with a right to him fights to become part of the heap of which he is the centre. It is as though they wanted to die with him. Their self-inflicted wounds, the way they throw themselves down on the heap or elsewhere, the collapse of the wounded—all this is meant to show the seriousness of their intention. It may also be correct to say that they want to be *equal* with him. But they do not really intend to do away with themselves. What they do want, and try by their behaviour to ensure, is the continuance of the heap to which he belongs. The essence of the lamenting-pack consists in its assimilation to the dying man, so long as death has not actually occurred.

Equally essential, however, is the way it rejects him as soon as he is really dead. It is the sudden change from furious attachment to, and retention of, the *dying* to frightened rejection and isolation of the *dead* which creates the specific tension of the lamenting pack. During the same night his body is hastily carried away. Every trace of his existence is destroyed, his tools, his hut and everything belonging to him; even the camp where he lived with the rest is destroyed and burnt. Suddenly and decisively they have turned against him. He has become dangerous because he has left them. Because he is dead, he may become jealous of the living and take his revenge on them. All the signs of their affection, and even their physical proximity, could not hold him back. His rancour makes an enemy of him; with a hundred tricks and ruses he may sneak back amongst them, and they must be equally cunning to protect themselves against him.

They continue the lament in the new camp. The excitement which gave them their powerful feeling of unity is not relinquished immediately. They need it more than ever now, for the group is in danger. They make an exhibition of pain by continuing to wound themselves. It is like a war, but it is they who inflict on themselves what an enemy might. A man who carried on his body the scars of twenty-three such wounds regarded them as badges of honour, as though he had received them in war.

We must consider whether this is the only significance of the dangerous wounds which men inflict on themselves on such occasions; and the women apparently go even further than the men in this; they certainly persevere longer in lament. There is much anger in this self-mutilation, anger at impotence in the face of death. It is as though they were punishing themselves for death, as though the individual wanted to exhibit the mutilation through loss of the whole group by the mutilation of his own body. But the destruction is also directed against their poor dwellings and, in this respect, reminds us of that destructiveness of the crowd which we know already, and have explained in a previous chapter. By destroying all isolated objects the pack fulfills itself and thus also prolongs its existence. It also emphasises the breach with the time in which it first recognised and then suffered impending disaster. Everything begins anew, and begins in a potent state of common excitement.

To recapitulate the factors essential to the development of a lamenting pack: The first is a violent movement towards the dying man and the formation of an equivocal throng around him, which stands midway between life and death; the second is a terrified flight away from the dead man, and from everything which might have been touched by him.

The Increase Pack

IF WE OBSERVE the life of any primitive people we immediately come on the hunting, the war, or the lamenting packs which are central to its existence. The course which these three types of pack take is clear; there is something elemental about all of them. Even where one or other has receded into the background, there are usually remnants of it to be found, which prove its past existence and significance.

In the *increase pack*, however, we have a formation of greater complexity. It is of immense importance, being the specific propelling force behind the spread of men. It has conquered the earth for him and has led to ever richer civilisations. The full range of its effectiveness has never been properly understood because the concept of propagation has distorted and obscured the actual processes of increase. These can, from their very beginning, only be understood in conjunction with the processes of *transformation*.

Early man, roaming about in small bands through large and often empty spaces, was confronted by a preponderance of animals. Not all of these were necessarily hostile; most, in fact, were not dangerous to man. But many of them existed in enormous numbers. Whether it was herds of buffaloes or springboks, shoals of fish, or swarms of locusts, bees or ants, their numbers rendered those of man insignificant.

For the progeny of man is sparse, coming singly and taking a long time to arrive. The desire to be *more*, for the number of the people to whom one belongs to be larger, must always have been profound and urgent, and must, moreover, have been growing stronger all the time. Every occasion on which a pack formed must have strengthened the desire for a larger number of people. A larger hunting pack could round up more game. The quantity of game was never something that could be relied on; it might suddenly be abundant and then, the more hunters there were, the larger the kill would be. In war men wanted to be stronger than a hostile horde and were always conscious of the danger of small numbers. Every death they had to lament, especially that of an experienced and active man, was an incisive loss. Man's weakness lay in the smallness of his numbers.

It is true that the animals dangerous to man often lived singly or in small groups as he did. Like them he was a beast of prey, though one which never wanted to be solitary. He may have lived in bands about the size of wolf-packs, but wolves were content with this and he was not. In the enormously long period of time during which he lived in small groups, he, as it were, incorporated into himself, *by transformations*, all the animals he knew. It was through the development of transformation that he really became man; it was his specific gift and pleasure. In his early transformations into other animals he acted and danced many of the species which appear in large numbers. The more perfect his representation of such creatures was, the intenser his awareness of their numbers. He felt what it was to be many and, each time, was made conscious of his own isolation in small groups.

It is certain that man, as soon as he was man, wanted *to be more*. All his beliefs, myths, rites and ceremonies are full of this desire. There are many instances of this and we shall encounter a number of them in the course of our enquiry. Since everything in man directed towards increase is endowed with such elemental force, it may seem strange that, at the beginning of this chapter, stress should have been laid on the complexity of the increase-pack. But a little reflection will show why it appears in so many different forms. One must be on the watch for it everywhere, and it does indeed appear where one expects to find it. But it also has its secret hiding-places and will suddenly appear where least expected.

For, originally, man does not think of his own increase detached from that of other creatures. He transfers his desire for increase to everything around him. Just as he wants the enlargement of his own horde through a plentiful supply of children, so he also wants more game and more fruit, more cattle and more grain, more of whatever he feeds on. For him to prosper and increase there must be plenty of everything he needs to live.

When rain is rare he sets himself to bring about rainfall. Creatures like him need water most of all. Thus, in many parts of the world, rain and increase rites are identical. Whether the people dance rain themselves, as among the Pueblo Indians, or thirstily surround their magician as he conjures the rain for them, in all cases their state is that of an increase pack.

To understand the close connection between increase and transformation we must touch on the rites of the Australian aborigines. These were thoroughly investigated by several explorers over half a century ago.

The *ancestors* of which the legends of the aborigines treat are remarkable beings; their nature is dual, part human and part animal, or, more precisely, both at once. It was they who introduced ceremonies and these are performed because commanded by them. Each of them associates man with a specific animal or plant. Thus the kangaroo-ancestor is simultaneously man and kangaroo, and the emu-ancestor man and emu, but two animals are never represented in one ancestor. Man is always, as it were, half of them, the other half being a specific animal; and it cannot be sufficiently emphasised that both man and animal are simultaneously present in the one figure, their properties being mingled in what appears to us a most naïve and startling manner.

It is clear that these ancestors are nothing but the products of transformation. The men who repeatedly succeeded in looking and feeling like a kangaroo became the kangaroo totem. Such a transformation, frequently practised and made use of, assumed the character of an acquisition and was handed on from one generation to another by the dramatic representation of myths.

The ancestor of the actual kangaroos surrounding man became at the same time the ancestor of the group of men calling themselves kangaroo. The transformation which stands at the origin of this two-fold progeny was publicly represented on communal occasions. One or two men represented a kangaroo, the others taking part in the traditional transformation as spectators. Another time they might be the ones to dance the kangaroo, their ancestor. The delight in the transformation, the particular weight which it acquired in the course of time, and its preciousness for new generations of men, were expressed in the sanctity of the rites during which it was practised. The successful and established transformation became a kind of endowment; it was cherished like the treasure of words which constitutes a language, or that other treasure of objects, by us felt to be purely material: weapons, ornaments and certain sacred utensils.

The transformation, which was a cherished tradition, and, as totem, the sign of the relationship existing between certain men and the kangaroos, signified also a connection with their *number*. The numbers of the kangaroos were always larger than those of men, and since they were connected with man, he desired their increase. When they increased, he also increased; the increase of the totem animal was identical with his own.

Thus the strength of the link between increase and transformation cannot be overrated; the two go hand in hand. Once a transformation has become fixed and, in its precise shape, can be cultivated as a tradition, it ensures the increase of *both* the creatures which, in it, have become one and indivisible. One of these creatures is always man. With each totem he ensures the increase of yet another animal. A tribe which consists of many totems has appropriated to itself the increase of all of them.

The great majority of Australian totems are animals, but there are also plants among them. Since these are usually plants on which man feeds, it is not particularly surprising that there should be rites for their increase. It seems natural that man should like plums and nuts and want plenty of them. Some of the insects which we regard as vermin, such as certain grubs, termites and grasshoppers, are delicacies to the aborigines, and so they, too, occur as totems. But what are we to say when we encounter people who designate scorpions, lice, flies or mosquitoes as their totem? In these cases it is impossible to speak of usefulness in the vulgar sense of the word, for such creatures are as much plagues for the aborigine as they are for us. It can only be their immense number which attracts him; in establishing a relationship with them he means to ensure their numbers for himself. The man who is descended from a mosquito-totem wants his people to become as numerous as mosquitoes.

I cannot conclude this very provisional and summary reference to the double figures of the Australian aborigines without mentioning another kind of totem which is also found among them. The following list will surprise the reader, for it is already well-known to him in another connection. Among their totems are to be found clouds, rain, wind, grass, burning grass, fire, sand, the sea and the stars. This is the list of the natural crowd symbols which I have already interpreted at length. No better proof could be found of the antiquity and importance of these symbols than their existence in Australia as totems.

It would, however, be wrong to assume that all increase packs are connected with totems, and that they always allow themselves as much

time to fructify as among the Australian aborigines. There are operations of a simpler and more compact kind whose aim is the direct and
immediate attraction of the desired animals. The following description
of the famous buffalo dance of the Mandan, a tribe of North American
Indians, was written in the first half of the last century.

"Buffaloes, it is known, are a sort of roaming creatures, congregat-
ing occasionally in huge masses, and strolling away about the country
from east to west, or from north to south, or just where their whims or
strange fancies may lead them; and the Mandans are sometimes, by
this means, most unceremoniously left without anything to eat; and
being a small tribe, and unwilling to risk their lives by going far from
home in the face of their more powerful enemies, are often times left
almost in a state of starvation. In any emergency of this kind, every
man musters and brings out of his lodge his mask (the skin of a buffalo's
head with the horns on), which he is obliged to keep in readiness for
this occasion; and then commences the buffalo dance which is held
for the purpose of making "buffalo come" (as they term it), of inducing the buffalo herds to change the direction of their wanderings, and
bend their course towards the Mandan village.

"The dance takes place in the public arena in the centre of the village.
About ten or fifteen Mandans at a time join in the dance, each one with
the skin of the buffalo's head, or mask, with the horns on, placed over
his head, and in his hand his favourite bow or lance, with which he is
used to slay the buffalo.

"The dance always has the desired effect; it never fails, nor can it,
for it cannot be stopped but is going incessantly day and night, until
"buffalo come". Drums are beating and rattles are shaken, and songs
and yells incessantly are shouted, and lookers-on stand ready with
masks on their heads, and weapons in hand, to take the place of each
one as he becomes fatigued, and jumps out of the ring.

"During this time of general excitement, spies or 'lookers' are kept
on the hills in the neighbourhood of the village, who, when they
discover buffaloes in sight, give the appropriate signal, 'by throwing
their robes', which is instantly seen in the village, and understood by the
whole tribe. These dances have sometimes been continued in this village
two or three weeks without stopping an instant, until the joyful
moment when buffaloes made their appearance. So they *never* fail;
and they think they have been the means of bringing them in.

"The mask is put over the head, and generally has a strip of the
skin hanging to it of the whole length of the animal, with the tail
attached to it, which, passing down over the back of the dancer, is

dragging on the ground. When one becomes fatigued of the exercise he signifies it by bending quite forward, and sinking his body towards the ground; when another draws a bow upon him and hits him with a blunt arrow, and he falls like a buffalo and is seized by the bystanders, who drag him out of the ring by the heels, brandishing their knives about him; and having gone through the motions of skinning and cutting him up, they let him off, and his place is at once supplied by another, who dances into the ring with his mask on; and by this taking of places, the scene is easily kept up night and day, until the desired effect has been produced, that of 'making buffalo come'."

The dancers represent buffaloes and hunters simultaneously. They are disguised as buffaloes, but bows, arrows and spears characterize them as hunters. As long as a man goes on dancing he is regarded as a buffalo, and acts as one. When he tires, he is a tired buffalo, and he is not allowed to leave the herd without being killed. It is because he has been hit by an arrow, and not from weariness, that he sinks down. Throughout his death-struggle he remains a buffalo; he is carried off by the hunters and cut up. He was first "herd" and then prey.

The idea that, by a violent and long-continuing dance, a pack can attract a herd of real buffaloes presupposes two things. The Mandan know from experience that a crowd grows and attracts into its orbit everything of the same kind which is near; wherever there are a large number of buffaloes together, more buffaloes approach. But they also know that the excitement of dancing increases the intensity of the pack. Its strength depends on the violence of its rhythmic movement; what the pack lacks in numbers it makes up in violence.

The buffaloes, whose aspect and motion are so well known, resemble men in that they like dancing and allow themselves to be lured to a festivity by their disguised enemies. The dance lasts for a long time, for it has to take effect over large distances. From far off, the buffaloes sense a pack and succumb to its attraction so long as the dance continues. If the dancing stopped, there would no longer be a proper pack any more and the buffaloes, which might still be a long way off, would be free to turn elsewhere. There are always other scattered herds, and any of these might deflect them. The dancers must become and remain the strongest attraction. As an increase pack in a state of continuing excitement they are stronger than a loosely-grouped herd and draw the buffaloes irresistibly into their orbit.

The Communion

IN THE *common meal* we find an increase ceremony of a special kind. In accordance with a particular rite each of the participants is handed a piece of the slain animal. They eat together what they captured together. Parts of the same animal are incorporated into the whole pack. Some part of *one* body enters into all of them. They seize, bite, chew and swallow the same thing. All those who have eaten of it are now joined together through this one animal; it is present in all of them.

This rite of common incorporation is a *communion*. A special significance is attributed to it; it should take place in such a way that the animal which is eaten feels honoured, and will return, bringing with it many of its kind. Its bones are not broken, but are carefully kept. If everything is done as it should be, they will reclothe themselves with flesh and the animal will rise up and allow itself to be hunted again. But, if things are done in the wrong way, the animal will feel insulted and withhold itself. It will flee away with all its brethren; none of them will ever be seen again, and men will starve.

There are feasts at which people imagine that the animal of which they partake is present in person. Thus, among certain Siberian peoples, the bear is treated as a guest at his own meal. He is honoured by being offered the best parts of his own body. He is addressed in solemn and persuasive words and begged to intercede with his brethren. If one knows how to win his friendship he will even willingly allow himself to be hunted. Such communions may lead to an enlargement of the hunting pack; women and those men who were not present at the hunt participate in them. But they may, on the other hand, be confined to the small group of the actual hunters. The inner process, in as far as it relates to the character of the pack, is always the same: the *hunting pack* changes into a *pack of increase*. One particular hunt has been successful and its members partake of their prey, but, in the solemn moment of the communion, their mind is filled with the idea of all future hunts. The image of the invisible crowd of the animals they desire is clearly present to all who partake of the meal and they are meticulously intent on making it real.

The original communion of hunters is preserved even in cultures where the desires are for increase of an entirely different nature. Agricultural peoples are intent on the increase of the corn which is their daily bread, but they will still solemnly partake in common of the body of an animal, as in the days when they were exclusively hunters.

In the higher religions a new factor enters into the communion: the idea of the increase of the faithful. If the ceremony of the communion remains intact and is properly performed, the faith will go on spreading and will attract more and more believers. But even more important, of course, is the promise of revival and resurrection. The animal of which the hunters ceremoniously partook was to live again; it was to rise up and again allow itself to be hunted. This resurrection becomes the essential aim of higher communions but, instead of an animal, it is the body of a god which is eaten, and the faithful relate his resurrection to their own.

More will be said of this aspect of communion when we come to deal with the religions of lament. My present point is the transition of a hunting pack into a pack of increase; the increase of food is ensured by a certain ritual of eating, food being originally thought of as something living. Also apparent here is the urge to preserve the precious psychical substance of the pack by transmuting it into something new. Whatever this substance may be—and perhaps substance is not the right word for it—everything possible is done to prevent its dissolution or dispersal.

The connection between the common meal and the increase of food may also be a direct and immediate one, with no element of revival or resurrection in it, as in the New Testament miracles of the feeding of thousands of hungry people with a few small loaves and fishes.

Inward and Tranquil Packs

T HE FOUR MAIN types of pack can be grouped in several ways. We can distinguish first between inward and outward packs.

The *outward* pack, which is the more striking and therefore easier to characterise, moves in the direction of a goal lying outside it. It covers large distances and its movement has an intensity greater than that of normal life. Both hunting and war packs are outward packs. The game to be hunted has to be found and captured; the enemy to be fought has to be looked for. However intense the excitement which a war-dance or hunting dance achieves within a limited space, the true activity of the outward pack is directed outside itself, into a distance.

The *inward* pack is concentric. It forms around a man who has died and must be buried. Its urge is to retain something, not to reach it.

The lament for the dead man stresses in every possible way the fact that he belongs to those gathered together round his corpse. When he sets out, it is alone; it is a dangerous and terrible journey until he arrives where the other dead expect and receive him. Since it is impossible to hold him back, he is, as it were, *ex*corporated. The pack which laments him represents a kind of body, a whole from which, though not lightly, he is released and sundered.

The increase pack, too, is an inward pack. A band of dancers forms a nucleus which, it is intended, shall be joined from outside by something as yet invisible. More people are meant to join those who are already there, more animals those which are hunted or bred, more fruit that which is gathered. The dominant feeling is faith in the existence of all the things which are to join the actual visible units which are so dearly prized. These are all there, somewhere, and only need to be attracted. Ceremonies tend to be performed in places where a large, though invisible, number of these beings is suspected.

The *communion* is a significant transition from an outward to an inward pack. Through the incorporation of a particular animal captured in hunting, and through the solemn consciousness of the fact that some of this animal is contained in all those who have eaten of it, the pack turns in on itself. In this state it awaits the revival of the eaten animal and, above all, its increase.

Another distinction is that between *tranquil* and *noisy* packs. It is sufficient to recall how vociferous the lament is; it would have no meaning at all unless it made itself heard as stridently as possible. As soon as all the noise is over, the lamenting pack disperses and everyone is simply himself again. Hunting and war are, by their very nature, noisy. Silence may often be necessary to outwit the enemy, but then the climax of the assault is all the noisier. The barking of dogs and the shouts by which the hunters stimulate their excitement and thirst for blood are decisive elements in every hunt. And vehemence of challenge and the strident threatening of the enemy have always been indispensable in war; battle-cries and the din of battle echo throughout history, and, even today, war cannot dispense with the roar of explosions.

The *tranquil* pack is one of expectation. It is full of patience, a patience which is particularly striking when people are gathered together in this way. It appears wherever the goal of the pack is one which is not attainable by rapid and intense activity. "Tranquil" is possibly a somewhat misleading word here; the term "expectation pack" might be clearer, for this type of pack can be characterised by all kinds of activity, such as chants, exorcisms or sacrifices. What these have in common is the fact that they aim at something remote, which *cannot* be present for some time.

It is this kind of expectation and stillness that has entered into those religions which profess belief in another world. Thus there are people who pass this life in the hope of a better one after it. But the most illuminating example of the tranquil pack is the communion. The process of incorporation necessitates, if it is to be perfect, a concentrated stillness and patience. The awe in face of something held to be sacred and full of profound meaning, which is yet contained in oneself, imposes for a time a quiet and dignified demeanour.

The Pack's Determination.
The Historical Permanence of Packs

PEOPLE *know* the man whose death they lament. Only those who were close to him, or who know precisely who he was, have a right to join the lamenting pack. Their pain increases with the degree of their familiarity with him; those who knew him best lament most, and the crown of the lament is the mother from whose womb he came. Strangers are not mourned and, originally, it was not everyone who could become the centre of a lamenting pack.

This determination in relation to an object is characteristic of all packs. Not only do those who belong to a pack know each other well, but they also know their goal. When out hunting, they know what their quarry is and, when they go to war, they know who their enemy is; when they lament, their grief is for someone they knew and, in their rites of increase, they know precisely what it is that should increase.

The determination of the pack is terrible and unchanging, but it also contains an element of intimacy. A sort of tenderness for their prey can be discerned in primitive hunters. In lament and in rites of increase this familiar tenderness seems natural, but it sometimes lights even on an enemy, once he ceases to be excessively feared.

The pack makes for the same goals over and over again. It is as endlessly repetitive as all other life-processes of man. This determination and repetition have given rise to formations which have proved uncannily constant. They are always there and ready for use, and it is this fact which explains how they can still be made to play a part in more complex civilizations. In an earlier chapter I spoke of *crowd crystals*, giving as examples units of monks or of soldiers. It is as such crowd crystals that packs are used, over and over again, whenever, in fact, the quick formation of crowds is desired.

But many of the genuinely archaic elements still persisting in modern cultures find their expression in a pack. The nostalgia for a simple and natural existence, released from the growing constraints and fetters of our time, signifies exactly this; it is a desire for life in *isolated packs*. Fox-hunting in England, ocean voyages in small boats with a minimum crew, expeditions to little known countries, even the dream of living with a few others in a natural paradise where everything grows of itself without human effort—all these are archaic situations and have one thing in common: the vision of a small number of people who know each other well and who participate in a clear and uncomplicated enterprise of a definite or limited nature.

In addition there remains to this day one unashamedly primitive pack—the pack which operates under the name of *lynch law*. The word is as shameless as the thing, for what actually happens is a negation of law. The victim is not thought worthy of it; he perishes like an animal, with none of the forms usual amongst men. He differs in looks and behaviour from his murderers, and the cleavage these feel or imagine between themselves and him makes it easier for them to treat him like an animal. The longer he manages to evade them in his flight, the greedier the pack which they become. A man in his prime, who is a good runner, offers them an opportunity for a hunt which they seize eagerly. The very nature of the chase prevents it being frequent, and its rarity heightens its attraction. The brutalities they permit themselves may be explained by the fact that they cannot *eat* the man. They probably think themselves human because they do not actually sink their teeth in him.

The sexual accusation in which this sort of pack often originates transforms the victim into a dangerous being. His actual or supposed misdeeds are imagined, and the association of a black man with a white woman, the vision of their physical proximity, emphasises the difference between them in the eyes of the avengers, the woman becoming whiter and whiter and the man blacker and blacker. She is innocent, for he, being a man, is the stronger. If she consented it was because she was deluded by his supposed prowess. It is the thought of his superiority in this which they find intolerable and which forces them to unite against him. Like a wild animal—for has he not mauled a woman?—he is chased and killed by all of them together. His murder appears to them both permissible and mandatory, and it fills them with undisguised satisfaction.

Packs in the Ancestor Legends of the Aranda

WHAT DOES A PACK look like in the minds of the Australian aborigines? Two of the ancestor legends of the Aranda give a clear picture of this. The first is the story of Ungutnika, a famous kangaroo of mythical times. The following are his adventures with the wild dogs.

"He was not as yet fully grown, a little kangaroo, and after a short time he set out to go to a place After he had travelled about three miles, he came to an open plain, upon which he saw a mob of wild dogs, lying down close to their mother who was very large. He hopped about looking at the wild dogs, and presently they saw and chased him and, though he hopped away as fast as he could, they caught him on another plain, and, tearing him open, ate first his liver, and then, removing the skin, they threw it on one side and stripped all the meat off the bones. When they had done this they again lay down.

"Ungutnika was not, however, completely destroyed, for the skin and bones remained, and, in front of the dogs, the skin came and covered the bones, and he stood up again and ran away, followed by the dogs, who caught him this time at Ulima, a hill. Ulima means the liver, and is so called because on this occasion the dogs did not eat the liver, but threw it on one side, and the hill, which is a dark looking one, arose to mark the spot. The same performance was once more gone through, and again Ungutnika ran away, this time as far as Pulpunja, which is the name given to a peculiar sound made in imitation of little bats, and at this spot Ungutnika turned round and, jeering derisively at the dogs, made the noise. He was at once caught, cut open, and again reconstructed himself, much to the wonder of his pursuers. After this he ran straight towards Undiara, followed by the dogs, and when he reached a spot close to the water-hole they caught and ate him, and, cutting off his tail, buried it at the place where it still remains in the form of a stone, which is called the Kangaroo Tail Churinga." At the increase ceremonies it is always dug out, shown around and carefully rubbed.

Four times the kangaroo is chased by the pack of wild dogs. It is killed, torn to pieces and eaten. The first three times the skin and bones are left untouched. As long as these are intact he can stand up again; his flesh grows and covers his bones and the dogs chase him again. Thus the same animal is eaten *four times*. The flesh which has been eaten is suddenly there again. One kangaroo has become four, and yet is always the same animal.

The chase, too, is the same, only its location changing. The places where the miraculous events occur are forever marked in the landscape. The thing which has been killed does not give up; it comes to life again and jeers at the pack, which is surprised afresh each time. But the pack does not give up either; it must kill its prey, even if it has already swallowed it. The determination of the pack and the repetitiveness of its action could be represented in no clearer or simpler manner.

Here increase is achieved through a kind of resurrection. The animal is not full-grown and has not yet produced young. But, instead of this, it has quadrupled itself. One sees that increase and propagation are by no means identical. From bones and skin the animal stands up again under the eyes of its pursuers, and incites them to further chase.

The tail, which was buried, remains there as a stone, to commemorate and attest the miracle. The power of the fourfold resurrection is now contained in it and, if properly treated, as it is in the relevant ceremonies, time and again it will procure fresh increase.

The second legend begins with a single man in pursuit of a large and very strong kangaroo. He has seen it and he wants to kill and eat it. He follows it over great stretches of country; it is a wearisome chase and they both have to camp at various places, but always a certain distance apart from each other. Wherever the animal stays it leaves traces in the landscape. At one place, hearing a noise, it reared up on its hind legs and there is now a stone, twenty-five feet high, which represents it standing thus. Later on it scratched a hole in the ground to get water, and this hole remains to the present day.

But at last the animal feels utterly worn out and lies down. A number of men come up and meet the hunter. They ask him "Have you got big spears?" and he replies "No, only little ones. Have you got big spears?" They reply "No, only little ones." Then the hunter says "Put down your spears on the ground", and they reply "Very well. Put yours down too." Then the spears are thrown down and all the men advance on the kangaroo together, the original hunter keeping in his hand his shield and his Churinga, or sacred stone.

"The kangaroo was very strong and tossed them all about; then they all jumped upon him, and the *hunter*, getting underneath, *was trampled to death*. The kangaroo also appeared to be dead. They buried the hunter with his shield and Churinga, and then took the body of the kangaroo into Undiara. The animal was not then really dead, but soon died, and was placed in the cave, but not eaten. The rock ledge in the cave arose where the body was put, and when the animal was dead its spirit part went into this. Shortly afterwards the men died, and their spirit parts went into the water-pool close by. Tradition says that great numbers of kangaroo animals came at a later time to the cave, and there went down into the ground, their spirits also going into the stone."

In this story the one-man hunt changes into the hunt of a whole pack. The animal is attacked without weapons. It is to be buried under a heap of men; the united weight of all the hunters together is to stifle it. But it is very strong and kicks, and the men have a difficult task. In the confusion of the fight the original hunter finds himself beneath the heap and it is he, and not the kangaroo, who is trampled to death. He is buried with his shield and sacred Churinga.

The story of a pack which is hunting a special animal and which, by mistake, kills the foremost hunter instead is found throughout the world. It ends with the lament for the dead. The hunting pack changes into the lamenting pack and this transmutation forms the nucleus of many important and widely spread religions. Here too, in this legend of the Aranda, the burial of the victim is referred to. Shield and Churinga are buried with him, and the mention of the latter, which is regarded as sacred, imparts a tone of solemnity to the whole event.

The animal itself, which only died later, is buried at another place. Its cave becomes a centre for the kangaroos. In later periods great numbers of them come to the same rock and enter into it. Undiara, as it is called, becomes a sacred place where members of the kangaroo totem enact their ceremonies. They serve the increase of this animal and, so long as they are properly performed, there will always be sufficient numbers of kangaroos in the neighbourhood.

This legend is remarkable in that it unites together two quite distinct, but equally essential, religious processes. The first, as we have already seen, is the transmutation of the hunting into the lamenting pack. The second, which occurs in the cave, is the change of a hunting into an increase pack. To the Australian aborigine the second process is by far the more important; it stands at the very centre of his cult.

The fact that the two processes occur next to each other supports one of the main theses of this enquiry. All the four main types of pack exist everywhere where there are human beings. Thus transmutations of one kind of pack into another are also always possible. Depending on which transmutation is stressed, different basic forms of religion develop. As the two most important forms I distinguish the religions of lament from those of increase. But there are also, as I shall show, religions of hunting and of war.

There are intimations of war even in the legend I have quoted. The interchange about spears between the first hunter and the band of men he meets contains the possibility of a fight. By throwing all their spears on the ground, they renounce this and only when they have done so do they unite to attack the kangaroo.

Here we come on the second point which seems to me remarkable in this legend: the heap of men who throw themselves on top of the kangaroo; the solid mass of human bodies which is to stifle it. These heaps of human bodies occur frequently among the Australian aborigines. They are found over and over again in their ceremonies. At one point during the ceremonies accompanying the circumcision of the young men the candidate lies on the ground and a number of men lie down on top of him, so that he carries their full weight. In some tribes a heap of men throw themselves on to a dying person and press themselves closely to him from all sides. This occurrence, which I have already described, is of particular interest. It represents the transition to that heap of the dying and the dead which has often been spoken of in this book. A few instances of compact heaps among the aborigines are discussed in the next chapter. Here it is sufficient to say that the dense heap of *living* bodies, intentionally and violently brought into being, is no less important than the heap of the dead. If the latter seems more familiar to us, it is because it has assumed such monstrous proportions in the course of history. It must often seem that only when dead are human beings really close to each other in large numbers. But the heap of the living is, in fact, equally familiar to us. A crowd, in its core, is nothing else.

Temporary Formations among the Aranda

THE TWO LEGENDS cited in the last chapter are taken from the book by Spencer and Gillen about the Aranda tribe, whom they call the Arunta. The greater part of this famous work is devoted to a description of the tribe's feasts and ceremonies. It is impossible to conceive an exaggerated idea of their multiformity. The wealth of the physical groupings of men which form in the course of the ceremonies is particularly striking. Some of them are formations which are very familiar to us because they have kept their importance to this day, but there are others which astonish us by their extreme strangeness. The more important of them are briefly enumerated below.

Frequent in the course of those secret ceremonies which are carried out in silence, is the Indian or single file. In single file the men turn out to fetch their sacred Churingas from the caves and other hiding places where they are kept. They travel for an hour perhaps before they reach their goal. The young men who are taken on these expeditions are not allowed to ask questions. When the old man who is their leader wants to explain to them certain features in the landscape, connected with the legends of their ancestors, he uses sign language.

During the actual ceremonies there is usually only a very small number of performers, who are made up as the ancestors of a totem and act them. Generally there are two or three performers, but sometimes only one. The young men form a circle, running round and round them, and uttering shouts. This running round and round in a circle is very frequent and is mentioned over and over again.

On another occasion, during the Engwura ceremonies which represent the most important and solemn event in the life of the tribe, the young men lie down flat on the ground in a row with their heads on a long low mound, and remain mute in this position for many hours. This lying down in a row is often repeated and may last for eight hours at a time, from 9 o'clock at night until 5 in the morning.

There is another, much denser formation, which is very impressive. The men move together into a close group, the older men in the middle, the younger ones on the outside. This cylindrical formation, in which all the participants are packed together as closely as possible, sways backwards and forwards for two full hours without stopping, everyone singing throughout. Then they all sit down, and in this position, still closely packed together, they continue singing for perhaps another two hours.

Sometimes the men stand in two rows opposite each other and sing. For the crucial ceremony which ends the ritual part of the Engwura the young men form into a dense square and, accompanied by the old men, cross to the other side of the river-bed where the women and children await them.

This ceremony is very rich in details, but, as we are here only concerned with groupings, I shall single out the *heap on the ground*, formed by all the men together. The three old men who between them carry their most sacred object, which represents the pouch in which the babies of primeval times were contained, are the first to throw themselves headlong on the ground, hiding with their bodies this object which the women and children are not allowed to see. Then all the other men, and principally the young ones for whose initiation these ceremonies are performed, throw themselves on top of the three old men and all remain lying together in a chaotic heap on the ground.

Nothing can be identified any longer; only the heads of the three old men can be seen projecting from the pile of bodies. Everyone remains lying there for a few minutes, then they all try to get up and disentangle themselves. Similar heaps on the ground are also formed at other times, but this is the biggest and most important occasion mentioned by the observers I am quoting.

During the ordeals by fire the young men lie down full length on smoking boughs, but not, of course, on top of one another. Fire ordeals occur in many different forms, one of the most frequent being the following: The young men move to the ground beyond the river bed, where the women await them in two groups. The women come forward to attack the men, throwing a hail of burning boughs over them. On another occasion the long row of young men stands opposite a row of women and children. The women dance and the men, with all their strength, throw fire-sticks over their heads.

During one ceremony of circumcision six men lie on the ground together and form a table. The novice lies on top of them and is operated on in this position. The lying down on top of a novice, which belongs to the same ceremony, was noted in the preceding chapter.

If we try to find the meaning behind these formations we may say as follows:

The *single file* expresses migration. Its importance in the traditions of the tribe is very great. It is often supposed that the ancestors wandered even beneath the earth. It is as though the young men, one after the other, had to tread in the footprints of their ancestors. Their silence and the way they move contain the respect owed to sacred journeyings and destinations.

The *running round and round* and the dancing in a circle appear to give stability to the performances enacted in the centre. These are protected from everything alien outside the circle. They are applauded, reverenced, and taken possession of.

The *lying down in a row* could be an enactment of death. The novices remain in this position entirely mute and, for long hours, nothing stirs. Then they suddenly jump up and are alive again.

The *two rows* set up against each other, and interacting thus, represent cleavage into two hostile packs, the other sex sometimes standing for the enemy. The *dense square* already appears to be a formation for protection from all sides. It presupposes movement in hostile surroundings and is well-known in later history.

There still remain the densest formations of all: the *swaying cylinder*, entirely compact of men, and the chaotic *heap on the ground*. The cylinder, in its very movement, is an extreme example of a ryhthmic crowd, a crowd as dense and closed as possible, with room in it for nothing but the men who compose it.

The heap on the ground protects a precious secret. It indicates the existence of something which must be covered and held on to with all one's strength. It is in such a heap that a dying man is comprehended and thus, immediately before death, accorded a last honour. The heap is the measure of his preciousness to his people; with him in its midst it resembles and recalls the heap of the dead.

THE PACK AND RELIGION

The Transmutation of Packs

ALL FORMS OF pack, as I have described them, have a tendency to change into one another. Though, in general, the pack is repetitive, each reappearance closely resembling earlier appearances, there is always something fluid about it during the course of any individual manifestation.

The very attainment of the goal it was pursuing is inevitably followed by a change in its structure. The communal *hunt*, if successful, leads to distribution. Apart from "pure" cases, where the aim is butchery of the enemy, *victories* degenerate into looting. *Lament* ends with the removal of the dead man. As soon as he is where people want him to be, and they can feel partially safe from him, the excitement of the pack abates and its members scatter. But their relationship to the dead man does not really finish here. They assume that he goes on living somewhere else and may be summoned back to help and advise the living. In the conjuration of the dead the lamenting pack re-forms, as it were. But its aim now is the opposite of its original one. In some form or other the dead man, previously banished, will be recalled to his people. The successful *increase pack* becomes a feast of distribution. The buffalo dance of the Mandan ends with the arrival of the buffaloes.

It is thus clear that each type of pack is linked with an opposite into which it changes. But, in addition to this change into its opposite, which seems natural, there is also an entirely different kind of movement: the transmutation into one another of quite distinct types of pack.

This is exemplified in the Aranda legend quoted above. A strong kangaroo is trampled to death by a number of men together. During the struggle the foremost hunter falls victim to his comrades and is solemnly buried by them. The hunting pack is transmuted into a lamenting pack. The meaning of communion has already been discussed at length; there the hunting pack changes into an increase pack. At the beginning of wars stands yet another transmutation. A man is killed and the members of his tribe lament him. Then they form into a troop and set out to avenge his death on the enemy; the lamenting pack changes into a war pack.

The transmutation of packs is an extraordinary process. It occurs everywhere and can be investigated in the most diverse spheres of human activity. Without precise knowledge of it, no social event whatever, of any kind, can be understood at all.

Some of these transmutations have been taken out of their wider context and *fixed*. They have acquired a special significance and have become rituals. They are reproduced over and over again in exactly the same way. They have become the very substance, the core, of every important faith. The dynamics of packs, and the particular kind of interplay between them, explain the rise of the world religions.

It is not possible to give an exhaustive interpretation of religions here; that will be the subject of a separate work. But, in the following pages, I propose to examine a few social and religious structures with reference to the nature of the packs prevailing in them. It will be shown that there are religions of hunting and of war, of increase and of lament. Among the Lele in the former Belgian Congo the hunt, in spite of its meagre productivity, stands at the centre of social life. The Jivaros in Ecuador live exclusively for war. The Pueblo tribes in the South of the United States are distinguished by the atrophy of war and hunting, and by an amazing suppression of lament; they live entirely for peaceful *increase*.

For an understanding of the *religions of lament* which, in historical times, have spread over the whole earth and have unified it, we shall turn to Christianity and to one of the derivatives of Islam. Description of the Muhurram festival of the Shiites will confirm the centrality of lament in this type of religion. A final chapter is devoted to the descent at Easter of the Holy Fire in the Church of the Sepulchre in Jerusalem. It is the Feast of the Resurrection, into which the Christian lament is taken up; its meaning and its justification.

Hunting and the Forest among the Lele of Kasai

IN A SEARCHING recent study the English anthropologist, Mary Douglas, has succeeded in establishing the unity of life and religion in an African people. This work is characterized by a remarkable clarity of observation and openmindedness and absence of prejudice. The best tribute, however, is to summarize and quote from it.

The Lele, a tribe of about 20,000 people, live in the Belgian Congo, in a region near the Kasai river. Their villages, compact squares containing from 20 to 100 huts, are always set in the grassland, but never far from the forest. Their staple food is maize, which they cultivate in the forest. Fresh clearings are made each year and only one crop of maize is expected from each. In these clearings raffia palms also grow, all of whose products are used. The young leaves provide the material from which the Lele weave their raffia cloth. Unlike their neighbours all the Lele men can weave; woven squares of this material are used as a kind of currency. The palm also provides an unfermented wine which is highly prized. Though palms and bananas grow best in the forest, they are also planted round the village; groundnuts are planted only there. All other good things come out of the forest: water, firewood, salt, maize, manioc, oil, fish and animal flesh. Both sexes, the women equally with the men, spend the greater part of their time working in the forest, yet the Lele regard the forest as almost exclusively a male sphere. On every third day the women are excluded from it and must lay in their supplies of food, firewood and water the day before. "The prestige of the forest is immense. The Lele speak of it with almost poetic enthusiasm. . . . They often contrast the forest with the village. In the heat of the day, when the dusty village is unpleasantly hot, they like to escape to the cool and the dark of the forest. Work there is full of interest and pleasure, work elsewhere is drudgery. They say, 'Time goes slowly in the village, quickly in the forest'. Men boast that in the forest they can work all day without feeling hunger, but in the village they are always thinking about food."

But the forest is also a place of danger. No mourner may enter it, nor any one who has had a nightmare. A bad dream is interpreted as a warning not to enter the forest on the next day. All kinds of natural dangers may hurt the man who disregards it. A tree may fall on his head, he may cut himself with a knife or fall from a palm tree. The danger for a man is one of personal mishap, but a woman who breaks the injunction against entering the forest may endanger the whole village.

"There seem to be three distinct reasons for the great prestige of the forest: it is the source of all good and necessary things, food, drink, huts, clothes; it is the source of the sacred medicines; and, thirdly, it is the scene of the hunt, which in Lele eyes is the supremely important activity."

The Lele have a craving for meat. To offer a vegetable meal to a guest is regarded as a grave insult. Much of their conversation about social events dwells on the amount and kind of the meat provided. Nevertheless, unlike their southern neighbours, they breed neither goats nor pigs. The notion of eating animals reared in the village revolts them. Good food, they say, should come out of the forest, clean and wholesome like antelope and wild pig. Rats and dogs are unclean and designated by the same word, *hama*, which they use for pus and excreta. Goats and pigs are also unclean, just because they are reared in the village. The Lele's craving for meat has never led them to eat anything which is not the product of the forest or of hunting, though they keep dogs and poultry successfully and, if they wished, could make a success of goat herding too.

"The separation of women from men, of forest from village, the dependence of village on forest, and the exclusion of women from the forest are the principal recurring themes of their ritual."

The grassland has no prestige. It is dry and barren, a neutral sphere between forest and village, and it is left exclusively to the women.

The Lele believe in a God who created men and animals, rivers, and all things. They believe also in *spirits* whom they fear and speak of cautiously and reluctantly. The spirits have never been men, and have never been seen by men. If a man were to set eyes on a spirit, he would be struck blind and die of sores. The spirits inhabit the deep forest, especially the sources of streams. They sleep in the day, but roam about at night. They suffer no death or illness. They control the fertility of women and prosper men's hunting. They can strike a village with sickness. Water pigs are regarded as the animals most highly charged with spiritual power, because they spend their days wallowing in the sources of the streams, which are the favourite haunt of the spirits. The pig is a sort of dog, owned by a spirit; he lives with him and obeys him like a hunter's dog. If an animal is disobedient the spirit punishes him by allowing him to be killed by a hunter; by the same act the hunter is rewarded.

The spirits exact all kinds of requirements from men; in particular, however, "they require all persons living in a village to be at peace with each other. . . . Good hunting is the clearest sign that all is well with the village. The small amount of meat which each man, woman and child may receive when a wild pig is killed cannot explain the joy which is shown in talking about it for weeks afterwards. The hunt is a kind of spiritual barometer whose rise and fall is eagerly watched by the entire village."

It is a striking fact that child-bearing and hunting are coupled together, as if they were equivalent male and female functions. 'The village is spoilt' say the Lele, 'hunting has failed, women are barren, everyone is dying'. If, on the other hand, things are going well, they say, 'Our village is soft and good now. We have killed three wild pigs and many antelopes, four women have conceived, we are all healthy and strong!'

The activity which has the highest prestige is the *communal* hunt, not the private hunter's or trapper's success. "The method is to get a cordon of men armed with bows and arrows around a section of the forest, which is then combed by beaters and their dogs. Young boys and old men who can hardly walk try to join the hunt, but the most valued members are the dog owners, who have the heavy work of scrambling through the undergrowth, shouting to control and encourage their dogs. The game startled by them rushes out on to the arrows of the waiting hunters. This is probably the most effective method of hunting in dense forest. It depends on surprising the game and on quick shooting at very short range.

"What is strange in a people proud of their hunting is the general lack of individual skills. A man going into the forest for any purpose carries his bow and a few arrows, but these are intended for birds or squirrels. He does not expect to take large game by himself. They know none of the specialised techniques of the single hunter. They do not stalk, do not know how to imitate the calls of animals, do not camouflage or use decoys, seldom penetrate into deep forest alone. All their interest is centred on the communal hunt. A man walking in the forest might come on a herd of pig wallowing in a marsh, creep up to them so close as to hear their breathing, then, rather than risk a long shot, he will tiptoe away agog to call out the village.

"The Lele hunt the grassland only in the dry season when they fire the grass. On this annual occasion several villages combine to ring around the burning countryside. This is the time when young boys expect to make their first kill, for the slaughter, I am told, is terrific. This is the only occasion when the hunting unit is more than the male population of one village, as it is in all forest hunting. Ultimately the village is a political and a ritual unit because it is a single hunting unit. It is not surprising that the Lele think of theirs as a hunting culture first and foremost."

Of particular significance is the *distribution* of the game. It is shared out according to strict rules which emphasise the religious meaning of the hunt. There are three cult groups among the Lele, each of which enjoys a food privilege forbidden to outsiders. The first group, the Begetters, consists of men who have begotten a child. They are entitled to the "chest" of game and also to the flesh of all young animals. Within this group there is a sub-division of men who have begotten a male and a female child; from them is selected the second and more exclusive group, that of the Pangolin men, who are so called because only they are allowed to eat the flesh of the pangolin. The third group is that of the Diviners; they receive the head and the intestines of the wild pig.

No large animal can be killed without itself and its distribution becoming the object of a religious act. "Of all animals the wild pig has most significance; it is shared in the following manner: the head and entrails are reserved to the Diviners, the chest to the Begetters, the shoulders go to the men who carried it home, the throat to the dog-owners, the back, one haunch and one foreleg belong to the man who shot it, the stomach goes to the group of village-smiths who forge the arrows."

The structure of Lele society is, as it were, re-affirmed by each hunt. The excitement of the hunting pack has widened and become the driving emotion of the whole community. Without distorting the author's findings, we can speak here of a *hunting religion*, in the most literal sense of the words. Such a religion has never before been described in so completely convincing and indubitable a manner. We are also given a precious insight into the development of the forest as a crowd symbol. The forest contains everything which is valuable, and the things which are most valuable are fetched from it by the whole pack together. The animals which are the object of the hunting pack live in the forest; and also the dreaded spirits by whose sufferance men hunt.

The War Booty of the Jivaros

THE JIVAROS ARE the most warlike people in the whole of South America today. A great deal can be learnt from an examination of the part which war and booty play in their customs and ceremonies.

There is no question of over-population among them; they do not go to war to conquer new territory. On the contrary, their living-space is too large rather than too small; there are about 20,000 people in an area of over 25,000 square miles. They have no large settlements and dislike even living in villages. Each family, in the widest sense of the word, lives in a house by itself, with the oldest man as its head, and may be separated from the next family by several miles. They have no political organization; in times of peace the father is the highest authority in each family, answerable to no-one. If their hostile intentions did not lead them to seek each other out, one group of Jivaros would scarcely ever encounter another in the vast spaces of their virgin forests.

Blood revenge, or rather death, is what cements them. In their eyes there is no such thing as natural death; if a man dies it is because an enemy has bewitched him from a distance. It is the duty of the relatives to find out what sorcerer was responsible for his death, and to revenge it on him. Every death is thus a murder, and every murder can only be avenged by a counter-murder. But, whilst the fatal witchcraft of the enemy is effective at a distance, the physical, or blood revenge, which is a duty, only becomes possible by actually getting hold of the enemy.

The Jivaros seek one another out in order to take vengeance and thus blood revenge can be called the cement of their society.

The family which lives together in one house forms a very compact unit. Everything a man undertakes he undertakes in common with the other men of his household. For larger and more dangerous expeditions the men of several relatively near houses combine, and it is only then, when purposing a serious punitive campaign, that they elect a chief, an experienced and usually elderly man to whom they voluntarily submit themselves for the period of the war.

The war pack is thus the true dynamic unit of the Jivaros; apart from the static unit of the family, it is the only important one, and all their feasts are arranged round it. They assemble for a week before going to war, and assemble again after it, when they have returned victorious, for a whole series of big celebrations.

The war expeditions are pure *destruction*. All enemies are killed, apart from a few young women and perhaps some children, who are received into families. The enemy's possessions, which are extremely scanty, his domestic animals, his patches of cultivation and his house, are destroyed. The only object the Jivaros really want is the enemy's severed head. But for this they have a true passion, and the highest aim of every warrior is to return home with at least one such head.

The head is treated in a particular way and shrinks to the size of about an orange. From then on it is called a *Tsantsa*. The owner of a *tsantsa* gains a special prestige from it. After some time has passed, a year or two perhaps, a great feast is celebrated, the centre of which is the properly prepared head. Everyone is invited to this feast; they eat, drink and dance a great deal, all according to strict ceremonial. The feast is wholly religious in character and close examination reveals that the desire for increase, and the means of achieving it, constitute its very essence. It is not possible to enter into all the details here; they have been described at length by Karsten in his paper, "Blood Revenge, War and Victory Feasts among the Jivaro Indians." It is sufficient to mention one of the most important dances, during which all the animals they hunt are addressed in a series of impassioned conjurations, and, after them, the sexual act of man himself, which serves his own increase.

This dance is the actual introduction to the great feast. All the men and all the women arrange themselves in a circle round the central pillar of the house and, holding hands, move round in slow time, first whistling shrilly and then enunciating the names of all the animals whose flesh they like eating. After each name they utter a resounding cry, 'Hej'.

> "Hej! Hej! Hej!
> The howling monkey, hej!
> The red one, hej!
> The brown monkey, hej!
> The black monkey, hej!
> The capuchin monkey, hej!
> The grey monkey, hej!
> The wild hog, hej!
> The green parrot, hej!
> The long-tailed one, hej!
> The house-pig, hej!
> The fat one, hej!
> Women's clothing, hej!
> Girdle, hej!
> Basket, hej!"

This conjuration lasts for about an hour, the dancers moving alternately to right and to left. Every time they stop in order to move in the opposite direction, they whistle loudly and utter shouts of "Tshi, tshi, tshi, tshi" as if thereby to preserve the continuity of the conjuration.

Another conjuration is concerned with women and their fecundity.

> "Hej, hej, hej!
> Woman, hej!
> Woman, hej!
> Copulation, hej!
> Copulation, hej!
> May the *tsantsa* grant copulation!
> Mating, hej!
> Coupling, hej!
> Woman, hej!
> Woman, hej!
> May it be true, hej!

We will do it, hej!
May it be good, hej!
Enough, hej!"

In the centre of these conjurations and all the other acts of the feast stands the *tsantsa*, the captured and shrunken head of the enemy. The spirit is always close to the head and is extremely dangerous. Everything possible is done to subdue it; once mastered, it becomes very useful. It takes care of the increase of pigs, poultry, and manioc, and ensures every kind of prosperity. But it is not easy to subdue it completely. At first it is full of vindictiveness; the things it could do to one are inconceivable. But there is an amazing number of rites and observances for subjugating it, and, by the end of the feast, which lasts for several days, full power will have been acquired over the head and over the spirit which belongs to it.

Set beside our own more familiar habits of war, we have to say that the *tsantsa* takes the place of what we call booty. It is in order to win the heads that the Jivaros go to war; it is their *only* booty but, small as this booty finally appears, especially when shrunk to the size of an orange, it comprises all that matters to them. The head procures for them all the increase they desire, that of the animals or plants on which they feed, of the objects they make and, finally, of their own people. It is booty of a gruesome concentration, and its capture alone is not sufficient; lengthy operations have to be undertaken to make it what it should be. These operations culminate in the communal excitement of the feast, and especially in its wealth of conjurations and dances. The *tsantsa* feast as a whole is sustained by an increase pack. The war pack, when it has been lucky, becomes the increase pack of the feast; the transmutation from one into the other is the true dynamic of Jivaro religion.

The Rain Dances of the Pueblo Indians

THE RAIN DANCES are increase dances intended to procure rainfall. They, as it were, stamp the rain up out of the ground. The pounding of the dancers' feet is like the fall of rain. They go on dancing through the rain if it begins during the performance. The dance which represents rain finally becomes it. Through rhythmic movement a group of about 40 people transforms itself into rain.

Rain is the most important crowd symbol of the Pueblo peoples. It was always important, even for their forebears who may have lived

elsewhere, but, since they settled on their arid plateaux, its importance
has increased and has fundamentally determined the character of their
religion. The maize they live on, and the rain without which this
maize would not grow, stand at the centre of all their ceremonies. All
the magical methods used to attract rain are brought together and
heightened in their rain dances.

Observers have stressed the fact that there is nothing wild about
these dances. This is due to the nature of rain itself. Approaching as a
cloud, it forms a unit which is high overhead, distant, soft and white;
when it is near, it arouses feelings of tenderness in men. When it discharges itself, it must disintegrate; it is as isolated drops that rain
reaches men and the soil into which it sinks. The dance which, through
transformation into rain, is to allure it thus represents the flight and
disintegration of a crowd even more than its formation. The dancers
desire the presence of clouds, but these are not intended to remain
gathered in the sky, but to pour down as rain. The clouds are friendly
crowds, how much so can be seen from the fact that they are equated
with the *ancestors*. "The dead come back in the rain clouds, bringing
the universal blessing. People say to their children when the summer
afternoon clouds come up the sky 'Your grandfathers are coming', and
the reference is not to individual dead relatives, but applies imperson-
ally to all forbears. . . .

"The priests in their retreat before their altars sit motionless and
withdrawn for eight days, summoning the rain.

> "From wherever you abide permanently
> You will make your roads come forth,
> Your little wind-blown clouds,
> Your thin wisps of clouds
> Replete with living waters,
> You will send forth to stay with us.
> Your fine rain caressing the earth,
> Here at Itiwana,
> The abiding place of our fathers,
> Our mothers,
> The ones who first had being,
> With your great pile of waters
> You will come together."

What one desires is "a great pile of waters", but this great pile,
gathered in clouds, disintegrates into drops. The stress of the rain-
dances is on disintegration. It is a *gentle* crowd that one desires, not a

dangerous animal which has to be captured, or an obnoxious enemy who has to be fought. It is equated with the crowd of the ancestors who, to these people, are peaceful and benevolent.

The blessing which the raindrops bring to the soil results in that other crowd on which they live: their maize. Every harvest betokens a bringing together in heaps; rain is the reverse process. The clouds are dispersed as drops, whereas every single corn cob harvested is already a stable collection of grains.

Men grow strong and women fertile on this food. The word "children" occurs often in their prayers. The priest speaks of the living members of the tribe as children, but he also speaks of "all the little boys, all the little girls, all those whose roads are ahead". These are what we would call the future of the tribe. The priest, whose image is more precise, sees them as all those whose roads lie ahead.

Thus the essential crowds in the life of the Pueblos are those of ancestors and children, rain and maize; or, if we want to range them in a causal sequence: ancestors, rain, maize and children.

Of the four types of pack, two—the hunting and the war pack—are almost atrophied among them. There is still some communal rabbit hunting, and there is a society of warriors, but the function of these is only that of police, and there is little occasion for policing in our sense of the word. The lamenting pack has been suppressed to an astonishing degree. They make very little fuss about death and try to forget the dead as individuals as quickly as possible. Four *days* after the occurrence of death, the "chief speaks to the people telling them that they shall not remember any more. 'It is now four *years* he is dead.'" Death is removed into the past, and grief thus stilled. The Pueblos do not hold with lamenting packs; they *isolate* grief.

There remains the increase pack, which is highly developed and active amongst them. They put the whole stress of their communal life on it; it could be said that they live for increase alone, and in a purely positive sense. That Janus head, common to so many peoples—one's own increase on the one hand and the decrease of the enemy on the other—is unknown amongst them; they are not interested in wars. Rain and maize have made them gentle; their life depends entirely on their own ancestors and their own children.

On the Dynamics of War. The First Death. The Triumph

THE INNER, or pack, dynamics of war are basically as follows. From the lamenting pack around a dead man there forms a war pack bent on avenging him; and from the war pack, if it is victorious, a triumphant pack of increase.

It is the *first* death which infects everyone with the feeling of being threatened. It is impossible to overrate the part played by the first dead man in the kindling of wars. Rulers who want to unleash war know very well that they must procure or invent a first victim. It need not be anyone of particular importance, and can even be someone quite unknown. Nothing matters except his death; and it must be believed that the enemy is responsible for this. Every possible cause of his death is suppressed except one: his membership of the group to which one belongs oneself.

The quick-forming lamenting pack operates as a crowd crystal; it, as it were, opens out, everyone who feels the same threat attaching himself to it. Its spirit changes into that of a war pack.

War is kindled by the death of one man, or, at most, a few; but it leads to the death of tremendous numbers. The lament for these, when victory has been won, is very subdued in comparison with the original lament. Victory is felt to be a decisive decrease of the enemy, if not his annihilation, and it reduces the impetus of the lament for one's own dead. They have been sent as a vanguard into the land of the dead and have drawn many more of the enemy after them. Thus they have disburdened their people of that fear without which they would not have gone to war.

When the enemy has been beaten the threat which united people vanishes and it is each for himself again; the war pack is on the point of scattering for the sake of pillage, in the same way that the hunting pack merges into the stage of distribution of the prey. Where the sense of being threatened has not been universal, it will have been the promise of loot which effectively drove people to war, and, in such a case, they must be allowed their loot. A war-lord of the old kind would scarcely have dared refuse it to them, but the danger of an army disintegrating completely through pillage is so great that leaders have always been concerned with finding some means of re-establishing a fighting spirit. The most effective means to this end are *victory feasts*.

The true significance of victory feasts is the confrontation of the decrease of the enemy with one's own increase. The whole people is assembled, men, women and children. The victors march in the same formations in which they set out to fight. By showing themselves to the people they infect them with the spirit of victory. More and more people come until finally everyone is present who is capable of leaving his dwelling.

But the victors do not only show themselves; they also bring things with them. They come as agents of increase, and their booty is exhibited to the people. There is an abundance of everything which men want or value, and everyone will receive some of it. The victorious commander or king may decree large distributions to the people, or he may promise tax reliefs or other benefits. The booty consists not only of gold and goods; prisoners are led out too, their numbers a visible manifestation of the decrease of the enemy.

In societies which pride themselves on being civilized the exhibition of captured enemies suffices. Others, which to us appear barbarous, want more. They want to *experience* an actual decrease of the enemy, and to experience it *together*, relieved from the pressure of an immediate threat. This leads to the public executions of prisoners familiar in the victory feasts of many war-like peoples.

Such executions reached fantastic proportions in the capital of the kingdom of Dahomey. In the so-called 'Annual Custom', which lasted for several days, the king presented his people with a bloody spectacle, hundreds of prisoners being beheaded in the sight of everyone.

The king sat on a platform among his dignitaries while the people stood below in a dense throng. At a sign from the king the executioners set to work. The heads of the murdered prisoners were thrown onto a heap; several such heaps were to be seen. There were processions through streets lined with the naked corpses of executed enemies hanging from gallows; to spare the modesty of the king's innumerable wives these had been mutilated. On the last day of the feast the court was reassembled on a platform and a large presentation of gifts to the people took place. Strings of shell-money were thrown down among them to be scrambled for. Their manacled enemies were hurled down to them; these too were beheaded. People fought for the corpses; it was said that in their frenzy they ate them. Everyone wanted to get a piece of the enemy dead; it might be called a communion of triumph. Human beings were followed by animals, but the chief thing was the enemy.

There are eighteenth century reports by European eye-witnesses of these feasts. At this period the white nations had representatives in trading-stations on the coast. The material of their trade was slaves and they came to Abomey, the capital, in order to buy slaves from the king. He was accustomed to sell a proportion of his prisoners to the Europeans and his war expeditions were undertaken for this purpose. At that time the Europeans did not mind this at all, though they did not like having to witness the terrible mass-executions; their presence, however, was required by court etiquette. They tried to persuade the king to sell them for slaves the victims destined for execution. This made them feel humane and was also good for business. But, to their amazement, the king, in spite of his avarice, refused to renounce his victims. When there was a dearth of slaves and business was bad, this obstinacy annoyed them. They did not understand that power was more important to the king than possessions. His people were used to the spectacle of victims. From the crude and public exhibition of the mass decrease of their enemies they gained the assurance of their own increase; and this was the direct fount of the king's power. The spectacle had a twofold effect. It was an infallible way of convincing the people of their increase under the king's rule, and thus of maintaining them in the state of a religiously devoted crowd. It also, however, kept alive the terror of the king's command, for he personally decreed the executions.

Among the Romans the greatest public occasion was the *Triumph*. The whole city came together for it. But, when the empire reached the height of its power and the need for continuous conquest had lost its urgency, the feeling of being victorious became an institution in its own right, recurring periodically with the dates of the calendar. Fighting now took place before the assembled people in the *arena*. It had no political consequences, but remained significant as a means of re-awakening and keeping alive the feeling of victory. As spectators the Romans did not fight themselves, but, as a crowd, they decided who was the victor and acclaimed him as in former times. The feeling of victory was all that mattered; war itself, no longer seeming so necessary, declined in importance.

Among historical peoples of this kind war becomes the actual means of increase. Whether it procures them booty to live on or slaves to work for them, they reject other, more patient means of increase, and think them contemptible. A kind of state religion of war develops, with the speediest possible increase as its aim.

Islam as a Religion of War

DEVOUT MOHAMMEDANS assemble in four different ways.

1) They assemble several times daily for prayer, summoned by a voice from on high. The small rhythmic groups formed on these occasions may be called *prayer packs*. Each movement is exactly prescribed and orientated in one direction—towards Mecca. Once a week, at the Friday prayer, these packs grow to crowds.
2) They assemble for the Holy War against unbelievers.
3) They assemble in Mecca, during the great Pilgrimage.
4) They assemble at the Last Judgement.

As in all religions, invisible crowds are of the greatest importance, but in Islam, more strongly than in any of the other world religions, these are invisible *double* crowds, standing in opposition to each other.

When the trumpet of the Last Judgement sounds the dead all rise from their graves and rush to the Field of Judgement "like men rallying to a Standard". There they take up their station before God, in two mighty crowds separated from each other, the faithful on one side and the unbelieving on the other; and each individual is judged by God.

All the generations of men are thus assembled and to each man it seems as though he had only been buried the day before. None has any notion of the immeasurable spaces of time he may have lain in his grave; his death has been without dream or remembrance. But the sound of the Trumpet is heard by all. "On that day men will come in scattered bands." "On that day We will let them come in tumultuous throngs." The "bands" and "throngs" of this great moment recur repeatedly in the Koran; it is the most comprehensive idea of a crowd the Mohammedan can imagine. No one can conceive of a larger number of human beings than that of all those who have ever lived; and here they are pressed closely together on one spot. This is the only crowd which cannot grow, and it is also the densest, for each single man stands face to face with his Judge.

But, notwithstanding its size and density, it remains, from beginning to end, divided into two. Each man knows what he may expect; there is hope for some and terror for the others. "On that day there shall be beaming faces, smiling and joyful. On that day there shall be faces veiled with darkness, covered with dust. These shall be the faces of the wicked and the unbelieving." Since the justice of the sentence is absolute—for each deed has been recorded and can be proved in writing—no one can escape from that half of the crowd to which he rightfully belongs.

The bi-partition of the crowd in Islam is unconditional. The faithful and the unbelieving are fated to be separate for ever and to fight each other. The War of Religion is a sacred duty and thus, though in a less comprehensive form, the double crowd of the Last Judgement is prefigured in every earthly battle.

The Mohammedan has a very different image in mind when he thinks of another no less sacred duty: the pilgrimage to Mecca. This is a slow crowd, formed gradually by tributaries from many different countries. Depending on the distance of the faithful from Mecca, it can stretch over weeks, months and even years. The obligation to perform this journey at least once in a lifetime colours a man's whole earthly existence. Anyone who has not been on this pilgrimage has not really lived. The experience of it draws together, so to speak, the whole territory over which the Faith has spread, and assembles it in the place where it originated. The crowd of pilgrims is peaceful and wholly devoted to the attainment of its goal. Its task is not to subjugate infidels, but simply to reach the appointed place: to have been there.

It is regarded as a quite especial miracle that a city the size of Mecca should be able to contain the multitudes of the pilgrims. Ibn Jubayr, the Spanish Moor who was in Mecca as a pilgrim at the end of the 12th century, and who left a detailed description of it, was of the opinion that not even the largest city in the world could hold so many people; but Mecca, he thought, was endowed with a special faculty of expansion and should be compared to the womb which grows smaller or larger according to the size of the foetus it contains.

The greatest moment of the pilgrimage is the day on the Plain of Arafat. 700,000 people are supposed to assemble there. If the number falls short of this, it is made up by angels, who stand invisible among the people.

But when the days of peace are over, the Holy War comes into its own again. "Mohammed" says one of the greatest experts on Islam "is the prophet of *fighting* and of war. . . . What he first achieved in his Arabian sphere he leaves as a testament for the future of his community: the fight against the infidels, the expansion, not so much of the faith as of its sphere of power, which is the sphere of power of Allah. What matters to the fighters for Islam is not so much the conversion as the subjection of infidels." The Koran, the book of the prophet inspired by God, leaves no doubt of this.

"When the sacred months are over, slay the idolaters
wherever you find them.
Arrest them, besiege them and lie in ambush for them."

The Religions of Lament

THE FACE OF the earth has been changed by the religions of lament and, in Christianity, they have attained a kind of universal validity. The pack which sustains them is only of short duration. What is it then which has endowed them with their power of resistance? What is it that has procured for these religions originating in lament their peculiar persistence during millennia?

The legend around which they form is that of a man or a god who perishes unjustly. It is always the story of a pursuit, a hunt, or a baiting, and there may also be an unjust trial. In the case of a hunt, the wrong creature will have been struck down, the foremost hunter instead of the animal which was being pursued. This animal, in a kind of reversal, may have attacked the hunter and wounded him fatally, as in the story of Adonis and the boar. This is the one death which should not have taken place, and the grief it arouses is beyond all measure.

It may be that a goddess loves and laments the victim, as Aphrodite Adonis. In her Babylonian shape the goddess's name is Ishtar, and Tammuz is the beautiful dead youth. Among the Phrygians it is the mother goddess Cybele who grieves for Attis, her young lover. "Raving, she harnesses her lions, and, taking with her her Corybantes who are as mad as herself, she drives about all over Ida, howling for Attis. One of the Corybantes slashes his forearms with a sword, another lets down his hair and rushes to and fro over the mountains; one blows a horn, another bangs on a drum and yet another clashes cymbals together. All Ida is noise and madness."

In Egypt it is Isis who has lost her husband Osiris. She searches for him without wearying. Full of sorrow she wanders through the land and cannot rest until she finds him. "Come to your house" she wails. "Come to your house. . . . I do not see you, yet my heart yearns for you and my eyes desire you. Come to her who loves you, who loves you, blessed one. Come to your sister, come to your spouse, to your spouse, you whose heart stands still. Come to your wife. I am your sister, born of the same mother. Do not stay far from me. Gods and men have turned their face towards you, and weep for you together. I call after you and weep till my cries can be heard in heaven, but you do not hear me. Yet I am your sister, whom you loved on earth; you loved none but me, my brother."

But it can also happen—and this is the later and no longer mythical case—that a group of relatives and disciples lament the dead, as they do Jesus, or Husain, the Grandson of the Prophet and the true martyr of the Shiites.

The hunt, or pursuit, is pictured in all its details; it is a *precise* story, very concrete and personal. Blood always flows; even in the most humane of all Passions, that of Christ himself, we find wounds and blood. Each of the things which compose the Passion is felt to be unjust; the further removed from mythical times, the stronger becomes the tendency to prolong the passion and to fill it out with human details. The hunt, or baiting, is always experienced from the point of view of the victim.

Around his end a lamenting pack forms, but the lament has a particular tone; the dead man has died for the sake of the people who mourn him. Whether he was their great hunter, or had another and higher value for them, he was their saviour. His preciousness is stressed in every possible way; it is he, above all, who should not have died. His death is not recognised by the mourners. They want him alive again.

In the description of the archaic lamenting pack, as found among the Australian aborigines, I pointed out that the lament already begins around the *dying* man. The living try to hold him back and they cover him with their bodies. They take him into the heap they form; they press themselves closely to him on all sides and strive to keep him. Often they call him to come back even after death has occurred, and it is only when they are quite certain that he will not come that the second phase begins, that of pushing him away to the world of the dead.

This is the time when people hurry to be together and all who want to lament are welcome. In such religious cults the lamenting pack opens out into a continually growing crowd. This happens first at the dead man's own feast, when his passion is represented. Whole towns join in such feasts and sometimes great bands of pilgrims who have come from far away. But the opening out of the lamenting pack also happens over long periods of time with the gradual increase in the numbers of believers. It begins with the few faithful who stand beneath the cross; they are the kernel of the lament. At the first Whitsuntide there were possibly 600 Christians; at the time of the Emperor Constantine about 10 million. But the core of the religion remains the same; it is the lament.

Why is it that so many join the lament? What is its attraction? What does it give people? To all those who join it the same thing happens: the hunting or baiting pack expiates its guilt by becoming a lamenting pack. Men lived as ·pursuers and as such, in their own fashion, they continue to live. They seek alien flesh, and cut into it, feeding on the torment of weaker creatures; the glazing eye of the victim is mirrored in their eyes, and that last cry they delight in is indelibly recorded in their soul. Most of them perhaps do not divine that, while they feed their bodies, they also feed the darkness within themselves. But their guilt and fear grow ceaselessly, and, without knowing it, they long for deliverance. Thus they attach themselves to one who will die for them and, in lamenting him, they feel *themselves* as persecuted. Whatever they have done, however they have raged, for this moment they are aligned with suffering. It is a sudden change of side with far-reaching consequences. It frees them from the accumulated guilt of killing and from the fear that death will strike at them too. All that they have done to others, another now takes on himself; by attaching themselves to him, faithfully and without reserve, they hope to escape vengeance.

Thus it appears that religions of lament will continue to be indispensable to the psychic economy of men for as long as they remain unable to renounce pack killing.

Of all the traditional religions of lament which could be adduced for closer consideration that of the Islamic Shiites is the most illuminating. The cults of Tammuz and Adonis, of Osiris and Attis are also relevant. But they all belong to the past and are known only from cuneiform or hieroglyphic texts, or from the writings of the classical authors of antiquity, and, though these reports are invaluable, it will be more convincing if we concern ourselves with a faith which still exists today in a living and unweakened form.

The most important of all the religions of lament is Christianity, and something will have to be said about it in its Catholic form. But from among the crucial moments of Christianity, the moments of true mass excitement, I propose to choose for description, not a moment of genuine lament, which has become rare, but another: the Feast of the Resurrection in the Church of the Sepulchre in Jerusalem.

The lament itself, as an impassioned pack opening out to become a true crowd, manifests itself with unforgettable power at the Muharram Festival of the Shiites.

The Muharram Festival of the Shiites

ISLAM EXHIBITS all the unmistakable traits of a religion of war, but it has, nevertheless, branched out into a religion of lament more concentrated and more extreme than any to be found elsewhere: the faith of the Shiites. This is the official religion of Iran and the Yemen, and is strongly represented in India and Iraq.

The Shiites believe in a spiritual and temporal leader whom they call the Imam. His position is more important than the Pope's. He is the bearer of the divine light, and is infallible. Only the believer who adheres to the Imam can be saved. "Whosoever dies without knowing the true Imam of his time dies the death of an unbeliever."

The Imam descends in the direct line from the Prophet. Ali, Mohammed's son-in-law, the husband of his daughter Fatima, is held to have been the first Imam. The Prophet entrusted Ali with special knowledge which he kept from his other adherents, and which is passed on in his family. He explicitly nominated Ali his successor as teacher of his doctrine, and as ruler. By command of the Prophet he is the Chosen One; he alone has the right to the title "Ruler of the Faithful". Ali's sons, Hasan and Husain, as grandsons of the Prophet, inherited the office from him; Hasan was the second Imam, and Husain the third. Anyone else claiming dominion over the faithful was a usurper.

The political history of Islam after the death of Mohammed fostered the formation of a legend around Ali and his sons. Ali was not immediately elected a Khalif. During the twenty-four years following the death of Mohammed three others of the "Companions" held this highest position in succession. It was only after the death of the third that Ali came to power; and his rule was brief. During a Friday Service in the big mosque of Kufa in Iraq he was murdered by a fanatical enemy with a poisoned sword. His eldest son, Hasan, sold his rights for the sum of several million dirhem and retired to Medina, where he died a few years later from the effects of a dissipated life.

The sufferings of his younger brother, Husain, became the very core of the Shiite faith. He was the opposite of Hasan, reserved and serious, and he lived quietly in Medina. Though he had become the head of the Shia on his brother's death, he refrained from all political activity for a long time. But when the ruling Khalif in Damascus died, and his son wanted to assume the succession, Husain refused to do homage to him. The inhabitants of the turbulent city of Kufa wrote to him and asked him to come to them. They wanted him as Khalif and said that, once he was there, everyone would join his banner. Husain set out with his family, his wives and children and a small number of adherents, on the long journey through the desert. By the time he arrived in the neighbourhood of the town, its inhabitants had already forsaken his cause again. The governor sent a strong troop of horsemen against him, who demanded his surrender. When he refused they cut off his access to water. He and his small band were surrounded and, on the plain of Kerbela on the tenth day of the month of Muharram, in the year 680 of our era, Husain and his men, defending themselves bravely, were attacked and cut down. Eighty-seven of his people died with him, including several of his own and his brother's family. Thirty-three lance thrusts were counted on his body, and thirty-four gashes from swords. The commander of the hostile troop ordered his men to trample the body of Husain beneath the feet of their horses. The head of the prophet's grandson was cut off and sent to the Khalif in Damascus. The Khalif struck it on the mouth, but an old "companion" of the Prophet, who was present, protested, saying "withdraw your staff, for have I not seen the mouth of the Prophet kiss this mouth?"

The "afflictions of the family of the Prophet" are the real theme of Shiite devotional literature. "True members of this group should be recognizable by the emaciation of their bodies through want, their lips being parched with thirst and their eyes running from incessant weeping. The true Shiite is as persecuted and as wretched as the family whose rights he maintains and suffers for. Soon it becomes regarded as the vocation of the Prophet's family to suffer tribulation and persecution."

From the day of mourning at Kerbela onwards, the history of this family is one of continuous suffering and affliction. Stories about them in prose and verse are handed down in a rich literature of martyrology. They are the subject of the assemblies of the Shiites in the first third of the month of Muharram, the tenth day of which—Ashura—is kept as the anniversary of the tragedy of Kerbela. "Our days of remembrance are our mourning assemblies." Thus a Shiite prince ends a poem in which he remembers the many afflictions of the Prophet's family. Weeping, lamenting and mourning for the misfortunes of the Alids, for their persecution and martyrdom, is the essential concern of the true faithful. There is an Arab saying, "More moving than the Shiite tear" and, according to a modern Indian belonging to this faith, "To weep for Husain is the prize of our life and our soul; otherwise we would be the most ungrateful of creatures. Even in Paradise we shall mourn for Husain . . . grief for Husain is the sign of Islam. For a Shiite it is impossible not to weep. His head is a living grave, the true grave of the head of the decapitated martyr."

Emotionally the contemplation of the personality and fate of Husain stands in the centre of the faith; they are the mainspring of the believer's religious experience. His death is interpreted as voluntary self-immolation, and it is through his sufferings that the saints gain paradise. The conception of a mediator was originally alien to Islam, but among the Shia since Husain's death it has become preponderant.

Husain's grave on the plain of Kerbela very early became the most important place of pilgrimage for the Shiites. "4,000 angels surround Husain's grave, angels that are weeping day and night, and whatever pilgrim comes, even from the frontiers, these angels go to meet him." Whoever visits this shrine gains the following advantage: the roof of his house will never fall in on him; he will never be drowned, or burnt to death, or attacked by wild beasts. On the contrary, he who with faith prays in the shrine will be granted additional years of life. Whoever performs this pilgrimage zealously will have the merit of 1,000 pilgrimages to Mecca, of 1,000 martyrdoms, of 1,000 days of fasting, and of freeing 1,000 slaves. No devils or evil spirits will harm him in any way during the following year; if he should die, he will be buried by angels, and, on the Day of Resurrection, he will rise again with the followers of the Imam Husain, whom he will recognize by the flag he carries in his hand; and the Imam will escort his pilgrims straight to Paradise in triumph.

According to another tradition, all those who are buried in the shrine of the Iman, no matter what sins they may have committed, will be subjected to no examination on the Day of Resurrection, but will be tossed straight into Paradise, as it were from a sheet; and the angels will shake them by the hand in congratulation.

Thus many aged Shiites settled in Kerbela to die. Others who lived far from the holy city asked in their will for their bodies to be transported there. For centuries endless caravans of the dead have been coming into Kerbela from Persia and India, transforming the town into a vast burial ground.

Wherever Shiites live their great Festival is those days of the month of Muharram on which Husain suffered his passion. During these ten days the whole of Persia is in mourning. The King, the ministers and the officials are dressed in black or grey. Mule drivers and soldiers go about with their shirts hanging down and their chests bare, which is regarded as a sign of great grief. On the first of Muharram, which is also the beginning of the year, the festival proper begins. The passion of Husain is recounted from wooden pulpits, with as much detail and elaboration of the incidents as possible. The listeners are deeply affected; their cries of "O, Husain, O Husain!" are accompanied by groans and tears. The recitation continues throughout the day, the mullahs, or preachers, taking turns in the various pulpits. During the first nine days of the month, groups of men wander through the streets, their half-naked bodies painted red or black. They tear out their hair, wound themselves with swords, drag chains behind them and perform wild dances. Fights, resulting in bloodshed and even in death, frequently develop between them and others of a different persuasion.

On the tenth of Muharram the festival culminates in a great procession originally designed as a funerary parade to re-enact the burial of Husain.

Its centre is the coffin of Husain, carried by eight men and flanked on each side by a banner-bearer. Four horses follow behind the coffin, and some sixty blood-smeared men singing a martial song. Next comes a horse which represents Duldul, the war-horse of Husain. In the rear is usually a group of perhaps fifty men, beating two wooden staves rhythmically against each other.

The frenzy which seizes the mourning crowds during this festival is almost inconceivable. The reader will get some idea of it from the description of events in Teheran which follows later.

The real Passion Plays, in which Husain's sufferings are dramatically represented, only became an institution towards the beginning of the 19th century. Gobineau, who spent much time in Persia during the 1850s and later, has left a fascinating description of them.

The theatres were founded by rich people; to spend money on them was considered a meritorious work by which the donor "built himself a palace in paradise". The larger theatres held 2-3,000 people; in Isfahan plays were performed before an audience of 20,000. Admission was free; anyone, beggar or rich man, could walk in. The performance started at five in the morning and, before the actual Passion Play began, many hours were spent in processions, dances, sermons and singing. Refreshments were handed round, and the wealthy and respectable accounted it an honour to serve the most ragged of the spectators in person.

Two kinds of fraternities which took part on these occasions are described by Gobineau. "Men and children with torches, following a large black flag, enter the theatre in procession and walk round singing. At night these bands can be seen hurrying through the streets from one theatre to another. A few children run in front shouting shrilly 'Ay, Husain. Ay, Husain!' The brethren take up their positions in front of the pulpits of the preachers, singing and accompanying them-selves in a wild and bizarre manner. They form their right hand into a kind of shell and violently and rhythmically beat themselves with it beneath the left shoulder. A hollow sound ensues, produced by many hands simultaneously, which can be heard at a distance, and is very effective. Sometimes the blows are heavy and slow, and produce a dragging rhythm; sometimes they are quick and urgent and excite the audience. Once the fraternities have started, it rarely happens that they are not imitated by the whole theatre. At a sign from their leader all the brethren start to sing, to beat themselves and to leap from the ground, repeating a short, abrupt cry, 'Hasan, Husain!'

"A fraternity of a different kind are the Berbers. They bring their music with them, consisting of tambourines of different sizes. The upper part of their body and their feet are bare, and they wear nothing on their heads. There are men of all ages, and also children from 12 to 16 years old. Their skin is very dark. They carry iron chains and long needles; some have a wooden disk in each hand. They enter the theatre in procession and, at first rather slowly, strike up a litany consisting of these two words only 'Hasan, Husain!'

"The tambourines accompany them faster and faster; those with wooden disks beat them together in rhythm, and they all start dancing. The audience accompany them by beating their breasts in the manner described. After some time the brethren start to flagellate themselves with their chains, first gently and with obvious caution; then they become animated and hit harder and harder. Those with needles prick their arms and cheeks; blood flows; the crowd, intoxicated, starts to sob, and the excitement mounts. The leader of the brethren runs to and fro between the rows, rousing the weak and restraining the over-zealous. If the excitement mounts too high he silences the music and calls a halt. It is difficult not to be moved by such a scene; one feels pity, sympathy and horror all at the same time. Sometimes one sees flagel-lants who, the moment the dance stops, raise their arms with the chains to heaven and cry out 'Ya Allah!' ('O God') in a voice so profound and with a look so devout and compelling that one is seized with admiration, so much their whole being is, as it were, transfigured."

The fraternity might be described as an orchestra of grief; and their effect is that of a crowd crystal. The pain they inflict on themselves is the pain of Husain, which, by being exhibited, becomes the pain of the whole community. Their beating on their chests, which is taken up by the spectators, gives rise to a rhythmic crowd sustained by the emotion of the lament. Husain has been torn away from all of them, and belongs to all of them together.

But it is not only the fraternities, as crystals, who make the audience into a lamenting crowd. There are also the preachers and others who make their appearance singly, and who produce the same effect. Let us hear what Gobineau experienced as an eye-witness on such an occasion.

"The theatre is brim-full. It is the end of June, and the heat under the immense tent is stifling. The crowd is partaking of refreshments. A dervish mounts the stage and sings a song of praise. The people accompany him by beating their breasts. The man appears to be tired and his voice is not exactly entrancing. He makes no impression and the chanting begins to weary. He seems to feel it himself and stops, descends from the stage and disappears. Everything is quiet again. Then suddenly a great hefty soldier, a Turk, takes up the chant in a thundering voice, slapping himself resoundingly on the chest with ever increasing violence. A second soldier responds; he too is a Turk, though from another regiment, and is just as ragged as the first. The beating on the breast begins again with great precision. For twenty-five minutes the panting crowd is swept along by these two men, everyone beating themselves black and blue. The monotonous song with its strong rhythm intoxicates them. They beat themselves as hard as they can; the sound is hollow, deep, regular and unceasing, but this is not enough to satisfy all of them. A young negro, who looks like a porter, stands up in the middle of the crouching crowd. He throws off his cap and begins singing at the top of his voice, simultaneously beating his shaven head with both fists. He was ten paces away from me and I could follow every movement he made. His lips went pale and continued to lose colour the more animated he became. He shouted and beat on his head as if on an anvil. For about ten minutes he continued in this way. But the two soldiers were dripping with sweat and could go on no longer. Lacking their accurate and powerful voices to lead them and carry them forward, the chorus began to falter and become confused. Some of them fell silent and as though he felt the lack of physical support, the negro now closed his eyes and sank down on his neighbour. Everyone seemed to feel pity and respect for him. They put ice on his head and held water to his lips. But he had fainted and it was some time before he came to himself. When he did, he gently and politely thanked all those who had helped him.

"As soon as calm had returned, a man in a green robe mounted the stage. There was nothing unusual about him; he looked like a grocer from the bazaar. This man preached a sermon on paradise, describing its size with powerful eloquence. In order to get there it was not sufficient to read the Koran, the book of the Prophet. 'It is not enough to do everything that the Holy Book recommends; it is not enough to come every day to the theatre and weep, as you do. Your good works must be done in the name of Husain and out of love for him. It is Husain who is the gate of Paradise; it is Husain who supports the world; it is Husain through whom salvation is won. Shout out 'Hasan, Husain!'

"The whole crowd shouts 'O, Hasan, O, Husain!'

" 'Good, now once more.'

" 'O Hasan, O Husain!'

" 'Pray God that he may always keep you in the love of Husain. Now, cry to God.'

"The whole crowd in a single movement lift their arms high and give a long reverberating shout 'Ya Allah! O God!' "

The Passion Play itself, which follows this long and exciting introduction, consists of a loose sequence of forty to fifty scenes. Every event is narrated to the Prophets by the angel Gabriel, or predicted in dreams, before it happens on the stage. In any case, everything that is going to happen is known to the spectators. There is no question of dramatic tension in our sense of the word; what matters is complete participation. The sufferings of Husain, the torments of his thirst when he was cut off from water, and all the episodes of the battle and his death are depicted in a strongly realistic manner. Only Imams, Saints, Prophets and Angels *sing*. Hated figures, like the Khalif Yazid who ordered Husain's death, and Shamr, the murderer who dealt him the fatal blow, are not allowed to sing; they only recite. Sometimes they are overwhelmed by the monstrosity of their deeds. Then they burst into tears during their wicked speeches. There is no applause. The spectators weep, groan and beat themselves on the head. Their excitement reaches such a pitch that they often try to lynch the villains of the piece, the murderers of Husain. Towards the end they see the severed head of the martyr being brought to the Khalif's court. Miracle after miracle happens on the way. A lion bows down before the head, and when the cortège halts at a Christian monastery the abbot, at the sight of Husain's head, foreswears his own faith and embraces Islam.

The death of Husain was not in vain. At the Resurrection the key of Paradise is entrusted to him. God himself decrees: "The privilege of intercession is exclusively his. Husain is, by my peculiar grace, the

Mediator for all." The prophet Mohammed hands over the key of Paradise to Husain, saying, "Go thou and deliver from the flames everyone who, in his lifetime, has shed but a single tear for thee, everyone who has in any way helped thee, everyone who has performed a pilgrimage to thy shrine, or mourned for thee, everyone who has written tragic verse for thee. Bear each and all with thee to Paradise."

No faith has ever laid greater emphasis on lament. It is the highest religious duty, and many times more meritorious than any other good work. There is ample justification for speaking here of a religion of lament.

But it is not in the theatres during the performances of the Passion Plays that this crowd undergoes its paroxysm. The "Day of Blood" in the streets of Teheran, involving half a million people, has been described by an eyewitness. His account follows here. It would be hard to find anything more compelling or more frightening.

"500,000 people, seized with madness, cover their heads with ashes and beat their foreheads on the ground. They want to give themselves up to torture, to commit suicide in groups, or to mutilate themselves with a refined cruelty. The guilds follow each other in procession. Composed of men who have retained a glimmer of reason—the human instinct of self-preservation—their members are dressed in ordinary fashion.

"A great silence descends. Men in white shirts advance in hundreds, their faces turned ecstatically to heaven.

"Of these men, several will be dead by evening, and many more mutilated and disfigured; their shirts, red with blood, will be their shrouds. They are beings who have already ceased to belong to this world. Their coarsely made shirts leave only face and hands visible: faces of martyrs, hands of murderers.

"With encouraging shouts, and infecting them with their own madness, others hand them swords. Their excitement becomes murderous; they turn round and round, brandishing over their heads the weapons they have been given. Their shouts dominate the shouts of the crowd. To be able to bear what they are going to suffer they have to work themselves into a state of catalepsy. With the steps of automata they advance, retreat and move sideways in no apparent order. In time with each step they strike their heads with their jagged swords. Blood flows and their shirts become scarlet. The sight of the blood brings the confusion in the minds of these voluntary martyrs to a climax. Some of them collapse, striking themselves haphazardly with their swords. In their frenzy they have cut through veins and arteries, and they die where they fall before the police have time to carry them to an ambulance installed behind the closed shutters of a shop.

"The crowd, insensible to the blows of the police, closes over them and drags them to another part of the town where the massacre continues. As they are carried past, the raging crowd rages more and more fiercely. There is not one man who retains the balance of his mind. Those who lack the courage for massacre offer kola to others, inciting them with the drug and with curses.

"The martyrs take off their shirts, which are now regarded as blessed, and give them to those who carry them. Others, who were not at first among the voluntary victims, suddenly, in the general commotion, discover their thirst for blood. They ask for weapons, tear their clothes off, and wound themselves haphazardly.

"Sometimes there is a gap in the procession when one of the participants falls down exhausted. But the gap is only momentary. The crowd immediately closes over the wretched man and kicks him and tramples on him. No destiny is accounted more beautiful than to die on the feast-day of Ashura, when the gates of all eight paradises stand wide open for the saints, and everyone seeks to enter there.

"Soldiers on duty, who are supposed to take charge of the wounded and maintain order, are infected with the frenzy of the crowd and tear off their uniforms and join in the bloodshed.

"The madness seizes the children, even very young ones. Beside a fountain, a mother, drunk with pride, hugs a child who has just mutilated himself. Another woman comes running, shouting, 'He has gouged out an eye. In a few minutes he will put out the other.' The parents watch it with delight."

Catholicism and the Crowd

To THE UNBIASED spectator Catholicism displays *deliberation, calm,* and *spaciousness.* Its very name contains its chief claim, which is that it has room for everyone. Its expectation is that everyone will turn to it. On certain conditions, which no one can find hard, everyone is received into it. In the theory, though not in the procedure, of this reception it has preserved a last trace of equality which contrasts strongly with its otherwise strictly hierarchical character.

Catholicism owes the calm which, after its spaciousness, is for many its strongest attraction, to its great age and its aversion to anything violently crowd-like. Its suspicion of the crowd is long-standing, dating perhaps from the first heretical activities of the Montanists, who turned against the bishops with what can only be called a decided lack of respect. The threat contained in such sudden outbreaks—the ease and speed with which they spread, the difficulty of controlling them and, above all, the discharge from the burdens of distance which they procure for their participants (including specifically the distances of ecclesiastical hierarchy)—very easily decided the Church to see the open crowd as its main enemy, and to oppose it in every possible way.

The whole substance of the faith, as well as all the practical forms of its organization, is coloured by this unshakeable conviction. There has never been a state on earth capable of defending itself in so many ways against the crowd. Compared with the Church all other rulers seem poor amateurs.

First of all there is the ritual itself, the element in any religion which has the most immediate effect on an assembly of believers, and which, in this case, is of a sustained and unsurpassed deliberation. The movements of the priests in their stiff, heavy canonicals, their measured steps, the drawing-out of their words—all this is like an infinite dilution of lament, spread so evenly over the centuries that scarcely anything remains of the suddenness of death and the violence of grief. It is the temporal lament mummified.

Communication *between* the worshippers is hindered in several ways. They do not preach to each other; the word of the simple believer has no sanctity whatsoever. Everything he expects, everything which is to free him from the manifold burdens weighing on him, comes to him from a higher authority. He only understands what is explained to him. The sacred word is tendered to him carefully weighed and wrapped up; precisely because of its sanctity it is *protected* from him. Even his sins belong to the priest to whom he must confess them. Communicating them to other ordinary believers brings him no relief; nor is he allowed to keep them to himself. In all profounder questions of morality he stands alone, confronted by the whole priesthood. In exchange for the moderately contented life which they procure for him he delivers himself entirely into their hands.

Even the way in which the communion is administered separates each believer from the others who receive it with him, instead of there and then uniting them. The communicant receives a precious treasure for himself. It is for himself that he expects it, and for himself that he must guard it. If one observes those waiting for communion it is impossible not to be struck by the fact that each individual is occupied exclusively with himself. The person in front of and behind him matters even less to him than a fellow human being in ordinary life; and that is little enough. The communion links the recipient with the vast, invisible church, but it detaches him from those actually present. Among themselves the communicants feel as little one body as a group of men who have found treasure and have just divided it between them.

In the very shape of this process, which is of such cardinal importance for the faith, the church reveals its cautiousness towards anything even remotely resembling a crowd. It weakens and blurs everything which the real people who are present have in common, and replaces it with the distant prospect of something mysteriously communal, something which towers over the faithful and is independent of them, and which never really lifts the barrier between itself and them during their life-time. The permitted crowd to which Catholicism always points—that of the angels and the blessed—is not only removed into a far distant world and thus, through its very remoteness, rendered harmless; it is also, in itself, of an exemplary composure and calm. The blessed are not imagined as active; their composure resembles that of a procession. They walk about slowly and sing; they glorify God and feel their happiness. They all act in the same way; there is no mistaking the uniformity of their destinies, and no attempt to mask or disrupt the endless sameness of their existence. They are many, they are close together and they are all filled with the same bliss; but these are their only crowd-like traits. Their numbers grow, but so slowly as to be imperceptible; there is never any mention of them increasing. They have no direction, for their state is final. The heavenly court they form is immutable. There is nowhere else they want to go and nothing they can expect. This is surely the mildest and most harmless kind of crowd imaginable. It is just possible to call it a crowd, but in reality it stands on the border-line: an assembled choir, singing beautiful but not too exciting songs; and, succeeding to the uncertainty of struggle, *chosen-ness* as a settled state of eternal duration. If, of all human desires, duration were not the hardest to achieve, it would be difficult to understand what constitutes the attraction of the crowd of the blessed.

Life is never quite as serene and ordered on earth as among the blessed but, whatever the church has to show, is shown *slowly*. Processions are impressive examples of this. They are intended to be seen by as many people as possible and their progress is ordered accordingly; their movement resembles a soft shuffle. They bring the faithful together by brushing slowly and gently past them, without tempting them to any decided movement, unless it be to kneel in adoration, or to join the procession in due order—that is, at its end—without thought or wish of a more prominent position in it.

The procession always presents a picture of the ecclesiastical hierarchy. Its members walk in the robes of their full dignity and each is recognised and named according to his office. Benediction is expected from those who have the right to bestow it. It is this articulation of the parts in a procession which prevents the spectators from approaching anything like a crowd state. Their gaze is drawn to so many different levels at the same time that any levelling among themselves, any surge towards unity, is precluded. The adult spectator never sees himself as priest or bishop. These always remain separate from him and he always ranks them higher than himself. But the more devout he is, the more he will want to prove his veneration of those who are so much higher and holier than he is. This, and no more, is precisely what a procession is for. Its aim is to arouse communal *veneration* among the faithful. Other communal feelings are positively not wanted, for they might lead to outbursts of emotion and activity which would be uncontrollable. And even the veneration is graduated in that it mounts from level to level along the length of the procession, levels which are all known, expected and permanent. Thus any sting of suddenness is taken out of it. It rises slowly and steadily like the tide until it reaches its height, and then subsides again.

Considering the importance the church attaches to all forms of organization, it is not surprising that it should comprise many crowd crystals. There is nowhere, perhaps, that their function can better be studied, though it should be remembered that these particular crystals are subordinated to the general trend of the church, which is to circumvent, or rather to slow down, the formation of crowds.

Among these crowd crystals are monasteries and religious orders. These contain the true Christians, those who live for poverty, chastity and obedience. Their function is to confront the many who call themselves Christians, but who cannot live as such, with the recurring presence of those who truly do. Their garb is the most important single means to this end. It signifies renunciation of, and detachment from, the habitual bonds of family.

Their function changes completely in times of danger. The church cannot always afford its dignified restraint, its dislike of the open crowd and the prohibition it normally lays on its formation. There are times when enemies threaten it from outside and defections increase with such rapidity that they can only be fought by means of a counter-epidemic; times when the church feels driven to oppose hostile crowds with crowds of its own. In such times monks become agitators who wander about preaching, inciting the people to activities of a kind usually shunned. The most spectacular example of such conscious crowd formation on the part of the church is the Crusades.

The Holy Fire in Jerusalem

THE GREEK FESTIVAL of Easter week in Jerusalem culminates in an extraordinary event. On Easter Eve the Holy Fire descends from heaven in the Chapel of the Sepulchre. Thousands of pilgrims from all over the world gather to light their candles at the flame as it shoots forth from the grave of the Redeemer. The fire itself is not reckoned dangerous; the faithful are convinced that it will do them no harm. But the struggle to reach the fire has lost many pilgrims their lives.

Stanley, who later became Dean of Westminster, was present in the Church of the Sepulchre during the Easter Festival of 1853, and has left a detailed account of it.

"The chapel which contains the Sepulchre stands in the middle of the church, rising from a dense mass of pilgrims who sit or stand wedged round it; whilst round them, and between an equally dense mass which goes round the walls of the church itself, a lane is formed by two lines, or rather circles, of Turkish soldiers stationed to keep order. Above are galleries for the spectators. It is the morning of Easter Saturday and for the first two hours everything is tranquil. Nothing indicates what is coming, except that two or three pilgrims who have got close to the aperture in the wall of the Sepulchre keep their hands fixed in it with a clench never relaxed.

"It is about noon that the circular lane is suddenly broken through by a tangled group rushing violently round it till they are caught by one of the Turkish soldiers. It seems to be the belief of the Arab Greeks that unless they run round the sepulchre a certain number of times the fire will not come. Accordingly, the night before, and from this time forward for two hours, a succession of mad gambols takes place round and round the Holy Sepulchre. Tangled masses of twenty, thirty, fifty men start in a run, catch hold of each other, lift one of themselves on their shoulders, and rush on with him till be leaps off and someone else succeeds; some of them dressed in sheepskins, some almost naked; one usually preceding the rest as a fugleman, clapping his hands, to which they respond in like manner, adding also wild howls, of which the chief burden is—'This is the tomb of Jesus Christ—God save the Sultan'—'Jesus Christ has redeemed us.' What begins in the lesser groups soon grows in magnitude and extent till at last the whole of the circle between the troops is occupied by a race, a whirl, a torrent of these wild figures, wheeling round the sepulchre. Gradually the frenzy subsides or is checked; the course is cleared, and out of the Greek Church a long procession with embroidered banners begins to defile round the Sepulchre.

"From this moment the excitement, which has before been confined to the runners and dancers, becomes universal. Hedged in by the soldiers, the two huge masses of pilgrims still remain in their places, all joining, however, in a wild succession of yells, through which are caught from time to time strangely, almost affectingly, mingled, the chants of the procession. Thrice the procession paces round; at the third time the two lines of Turkish soldiers join and fall in behind. One great movement sways the multitude from side to side. The crisis of the day is now approaching. The presence of the Turks is believed to prevent the descent of the fire, and at this point it is that they are driven, or consent to be driven, out of the church. In a moment the confusion as of a battle and a victory, pervades the church. In every direction the raging mob bursts in upon the troops, who pour out of the church at the south-east corner—the procession is broken through, the banners stagger and waver.

"In one small but compact band the Bishop of Petra (who is on this occasion the 'Bishop of the Fire', the representative of the Patriarch) is hurried to the Chapel of the Sepulchre, and the door is closed behind him. The whole church is now one heaving sea of heads and resounds with the uproar. One vacant space alone is left: a narrow lane from the aperture on the north side of the chapel to the wall of the church. By the aperture itself stands a priest to catch the fire; on each side of the lane, so far as the eye can reach, hundreds of bare arms are stretched out like the branches of a leafless forest, quivering in some violent tempest.

"In earlier and bolder times the expectation of the Divine presence was at this juncture raised to a still higher pitch by the appearance of a dove hovering above the cupola of the chapel, to indicate the visible descent of the Holy Ghost. This extraordinary act has now been discontinued; but the belief still continues—and it is only from the knowledge of that belief that the full horror of the scene, the intense excitement of the next few moments, can be adequately conceived. At last the moment comes. A bright flame as of burning wood appears inside the hole—a light, as every educated Greek knows and acknowledges, kindled by the Bishop within—the light, as every pilgrim believes, of the descent of God himself upon the Holy Tomb. Any distinct feature or incident is lost in the universal whirl of excitement which envelopes the church, as slowly, gradually, the fire spreads from hand to hand, from taper to taper, through that vast multitude—till at last the whole edifice from gallery to gallery, and through the area below, is one wide blaze of thousands of burning candles.

"It is now that the Bishop or Patriarch is carried out of the chapel in triumph on the shoulders of the people, in a fainting state, to give the impression that he is overcome by the glory of the Almighty, from whose immediate presence he is believed to come.

"It is now that the great rush to escape from the rolling smoke and suffocating heat, and to carry the lighted tapers into the streets and houses of Jerusalem, through the one entrance to the church, leads at times to the violent pressure which in 1834 lost the lives of hundreds. For a short time the pilgrims run to and fro—rubbing their faces and breasts against the fire to attest its supposed harmlessness. But the wild enthusiasm terminates from the moment that the fire is communicated; and perhaps not the least extraordinary part of the spectacle is the rapid and total subsidence of a frenzy so intense. The furious agitation of the morning is strangely contrasted with the profound repose of the evening, when the church is once again filled and overlaid by one mass of pilgrims wrapt in deep sleep and waiting for the midnight service."

The great disaster of 1834 was also witnessed by an Englishman, Robert Curzon. The essential part of his account, terrible in its clarity, follows here.

At midnight of Good Friday Curzon went with his companions to the Church of the Holy Sepulchre to see the procession of the Greeks. Every window, every corner, every foot of space where a human being could insert himself was crammed with people, with the exception of the gallery reserved for Ibrahim Pasha, the Turkish governor of Jerusalem, and his English guests. There were said to be 17,000 pilgrims in Jerusalem and almost all had come to see the sacred fire.

Next morning the soldiers made a way through the crowd for Ibrahim Pasha and, accompanied by a kind of crazy procession, he took his place in the gallery.

"The people were by this time become furious; they were worn out with standing in such a crowd all night and as the time approached for the exhibition of the holy fire they could not contain themselves for joy. Their excitement increased until about one o'clock a magnificent procession moved out of the Greek chapel. It conducted the Patriarch three times round the tomb; after which he took off his robes of cloth of silver, and went into the sepulchre, the door of which was then closed. The agitation of the pilgrims was now extreme; they screamed aloud; and the dense mass of people shook to and fro, like a field of corn in the wind.

"There is a round hole in one part of the chapel over the sepulchre, and up to this the man who had agreed to pay the highest sum for this honour was conducted by a strong guard of soldiers. There was silence for a minute; and then a light appeared out of the tomb, and the happy pilgrim received the holy fire from the Patriarch within. It consisted of a bundle of thin wax candles, lit, and enclosed in an iron frame to prevent their being torn asunder and put out in the crowd; for a furious battle commenced immediately; everyone being so eager to obtain the holy light, that one man put out the candle of his neighbour in trying to light his own.

"This was the whole of the ceremony: no sermon, no prayers, nothing except a little chanting during the processions. Soon you saw the lights increasing in all directions, everyone having lit his candle from the holy flame: the chapels, the galleries and every corner where a candle could possibly be displayed, immediately appeared to be in a blaze. The people in their frenzy put bunches of lighted tapers to their faces, hands, and breasts, to purify themselves from their sins.

"In a short time the smoke of the candles obscured everything in the place, and I could see it rolling in great volumes out of the aperture at the top of the dome. The smell was terrible; and three unhappy people, overcome by heat and bad air, fell from the upper range of galleries, and were dashed to pieces on the heads of the people below. One poor Armenian lady, seventeen years of age, died where she sat, of heat, thirst, and fatigue.

"After a while, when he had seen all that was to be seen, Ibrahim Pasha got up and went away, his numerous guards making a line for him by main force through the dense mass of people which filled the body of the church. As the crowd was so immense, we waited for a little while, and then set out all together to return to our convent. I went first and my friends followed me, the soldiers making way for us across the church. I got as far as the place where the Virgin is said to have stood during the Crucifixion, when I saw a number of people lying one on another all about this part of the church, and as far as I could see towards the door. I made my way between them as well as I could, till they were so thick that there was actually a great heap of bodies on which I trod. It then suddenly struck me they were all dead! I had not perceived this at first, for I thought they were only very much fatigued with the ceremonies, and had lain down to rest themselves there; but when I came to so great a heap of bodies I looked down at them, and saw that sharp, hard appearance of the face which is never to be mistaken. Many of them were quite black with suffocation, and further on were others all bloody and covered with the brains and entrails of those who had been trodden to pieces by the crowd.

"At this time there was no crowd in this part of the church; but a little further on, round the corner towards the great door, the people, who were quite panic-struck, continued to press forward, and everyone was doing his utmost to escape. The guards outside, frightened at the rush from within, thought that the Christians wished to attack them, and the confusion soon grew into a battle. The soldiers with their bayonets killed numbers of fainting wretches, and the walls were spattered with blood and brains of men who had been felled, like oxen, with the butt-ends of the soldiers' muskets. Everyone struggled to defend himself or to get away, and in the mêlée all who fell were immediately trampled to death by the rest. So desperate and savage did the fight become, that even the panic-struck and frightened pilgrims appeared at last to have been more intent upon the destruction of each other than desirous to save themselves.

"For my part, as soon as I perceived the danger, I had cried out to my companions to turn back, which they had done; but I myself was carried on by the press till I came near the door, where all were fighting for their lives. Here, seeing certain destruction before me, I made every endeavour to get back. An officer of the Pasha, who by his star was a colonel, equally alarmed with myself, was also trying to return; he caught hold of my cloak and pulled me down on the body of an old man who was breathing out his last sigh. As the officer was pressing me to the ground, we wrestled together among the dying and the dead with the energy of despair. I struggled with this man till I pulled him down, and happily got again upon my legs—(I afterwards found that he never rose again).

"I stood up for a minute among the press of people, held up on the uncomfortable footing of dead bodies by the dense crowd who were squeezed together in this narrow part of the church. We all stood still for a short time, when of a sudden the crowd swayed, a cry arose, the crowd opened, and I found myself standing in the centre of a line of men, with another line opposite to me, all pale and ghastly with torn and bloody clothes, and there we stood glaring at each other; but in a moment a sudden impulse seized upon us, with a shriek that echoed in the long aisles of the Church of the Holy Sepulchre the two adverse lines dashed at each other, and I was soon engaged tearing and wrestling with a thin, half naked man, whose legs were smeared with blood. The crowd again fell back, and by desperate fighting and hard struggles, I made my way back into the body of the church, where I found my friends, and we succeeded in reaching the sacristy of the Catholics, and thence the room which had been assigned to us by the monks, but not without a fierce conflict at the door of the sacristy with a crowd of frightened pilgrims who tried to press through with us. I thanked God for my escape—I had a narrow chance.

"The dead were lying in heaps, even upon the stone of unction; and I saw full four hundred unhappy people, dead and living, heaped promiscuously one upon another, in some places about five feet high. Ibrahim Pasha had left the church only a few minutes before me, and very narrowly escaped with his life; he was so pressed upon by the crowd on all sides, and it was said attacked by several of them, that it was only by the greatest exertions of his suite, several of whom were killed, that he gained the outer court. He fainted more than once in the struggle, and I was told that some of his attendants at last had to cut a way for him with their swords through the dense ranks of the frantic pilgrims. He remained outside, giving orders for the removal of the corpses, and making his men drag out the bodies of those who appeared to be still alive from the heaps of the dead.

"After the fearful catastrophe in the Church of the Holy Sepulchre, the whole host of pilgrims seemed to have become panic-struck, and everyone was anxious to escape from the city. There was a report, too, that the plague had broken out, and we with the rest made instant preparation for our departure."

To understand what happened here one must distinguish between the normal course of the Easter festival and this panic of 1834 which Curzon witnessed.

Easter is the Feast of the Resurrection. The lamenting pack which had formed round the Cross and the grave of Christ is transformed into one of triumph, for the Resurrection is a victory and is celebrated as such. Fire works here as a crowd symbol of victory. It should be transmitted to each man, so that his soul may share in the Resurrection. Each man must, so to speak, become that fire which springs from the

Holy Ghost and this is why he must light his candle at it. When he has done so he carries the precious fire out of the church to his home.

The fraud connected with the origin of the fire is irrelevant. The essential fact is the transmutation of the pack, from one of lament to one of triumph. In gathering round the grave of the Saviour, the members of the pack participated in his death; in lighting their candles at the Easter fire, which shoots forth from the grave, they participate in his Resurrection.

Very beautiful and significant, too, is the multiplication of the lights, thousands springing suddenly from the one. This crowd of lights is the crowd of those who shall have life because they believe. It forms and grows with prodigious speed, the speed with which fire spreads, and only fire. Fire is the truest symbol of the suddenness and velocity of crowd growth.

But before this stage is reached, before the fire actually appears, it must be fought for. The Turkish soldiers in the church, who are unbelievers, must be driven out, for so long as they are there the fire cannot appear. Their retreat is part of the ritual of the Festival and takes place at its appointed moment after the procession of the Greek dignitaries. The Turks move of their own accord towards the exit, but the pilgrims press after them as though they were driving them out, and the church is suddenly full of a tumult as of fighting and victory.

The ceremony begins with two stagnating crowds, which are separated by the soldiers. Small rhythmical packs of Arab Christians move between them and incite them. These wild, fanatical packs have the function of crowd crystals and infect those waiting for the fire with their own excitement. Then the procession of the image bearers appears. This is a slow crowd, but on this occasion it is the first to attain its goal; the half-swooning Patriarch who is carried round the church after the kindling of the fire is a living testimony to its success.

The panic of 1834, with its fearful consequences, arose out of the elements of contention inherent in the ceremony. In an enclosed space the danger of panic from fire is always great, but it was increased here by the presence in the church at the beginning of the ceremony of two opposed groups: the infidel Turks and the pilgrims who wanted to expel them. Curzon's description is rich in details which clarify this aspect of the panic. In one of the many apparently totally irrational and disconnected moments of the day he suddenly finds himself standing in a line of men facing another hostile line. Without even knowing

who is on either side, the two lines fall on each other in mortal combat. Curzon speaks of the heaps of corpses on which people trod and
clambered in the attempt to save themselves. The Church of the
Sepulchre has become a battlefield. The dead and the still living lie
piled together. The Resurrection has become its contrary and is now a
universal defeat. The idea of plague, of a still larger heap of dead,
takes possession of the pilgrims, and they flee from the city of the Holy
Sepulchre.

THE CROWD IN HISTORY

National Crowd Symbols

MOST ATTEMPTS TO find out what nations really are have suffered from an intrinsic defect: they have been attempts to define the general concept of nationality. People have said that a nation is this or that, apparently believing that all that mattered was to find the right definition; once found, this would be applicable to all nations equally. They have adduced language or territory, written literature, history, form of government or so-called national feeling; and in every case the exceptions have proved more important than the rule. It has been like clutching at some adventitious garment, in the belief that the living creature within could be thus grasped.

Apart from this seemingly objective approach, there is another, more naïve one, which consists in being interested in one nation only—one's own—and indifferent to all the rest. Its components are an unshakeable belief in the superiority of this one nation; prophetic visions of unique greatness, and a peculiar mixture of moral and feral pretensions. But it must not be assumed that all these national ideologies have the same content. It is only in their importunate appetite and the claims they make that they are alike. They want the same thing, but in themselves they are different. They want aggrandisement, and substantiate their claim with the fact of their increase. There is no nation, it seems, which has not been promised the whole earth, and none which is not bound to inherit it in the course of nature. All the other nations who hear of this feel threatened, and their fear blinds them to everything except the threat. Thus people overlook the fact that the concrete contents of these national claims, the real ideologies behind them, are very different from one another. One must take the trouble to find out what is peculiar in each nation; and do it without being infected by its greed. One must stand apart, a devotee of none, but profoundly and honestly interested in all of them. One should allow each to unfold in one's mind as though one were condemned actually to belong to it for a good part of a lifetime. But one must never surrender entirely to one at the cost of all the others.

For it is idle to speak of nations as though there were not real differences between them. They wage long wars against one another and a considerable proportion of each nation takes an active part in these wars. What they are fighting *for* is proclaimed often enough, but what they fight *as* is unknown. It is true they have a name for it; they say they fight as Frenchmen or as Germans, English or Japanese. But what meaning is attached to any of these words by the person using it of himself? In what does he believe himself to be different when, as a Frenchman or a German, a Japanese or an Englishman, he goes to war? The factual differences do not matter so much. An investigation of customs, traditions, politics and literature, could be thorough and still not touch the distinctive character of a nation, that which, when it goes to war, becomes its *faith*.

Thus nations are regarded here as though they were religions; and they do in fact tend to turn into something resembling religions from time to time. The germ is always latent in them, becoming active in times of war.

We can take it for granted that no member of a nation ever sees himself as alone. As soon as he is named, or names himself, something more comprehensive moves into his consciousness, a larger unit to which he feels himself to be related. The nature of this unit is no more a matter of indifference than his relationship to it. It is not simply the geographical unit of his country, as it is found on a map; the average man is indifferent to this. Frontiers may have their tension for him, but not the whole area of a country. Nor does he think of his language, distinctly and recognisably though this may differ from that of others. Words which are familiar to him certainly affect him deeply, and especially in times of excitement. But it is not a vocabulary which stands behind him, and which he is ready to fight for. And the history of his nation means even less to the man in the street. He does not know its true course, nor the fullness of its continuity. He does not know how his nation used to live, and only a few of the names of those who lived before him. The figures and moments of which he is aware are remote from anything the proper historian understands as history.

The larger unit to which he feels himself related is always a *crowd* or a *crowd symbol*. It always has some of the characteristics of crowds or their symbols: density, growth and infinite openness; surprising, or very striking, cohesion; a common rhythm or a sudden discharge. Many of these symbols have already been treated at length, for example, sea, forest and corn. It is unnecessary to recapitulate here the qualities and functions which have made them crowd symbols. They will recur in the discussion of the conceptions and feelings nations have about themselves. But it must be stressed that these crowd symbols are never seen as naked or isolated. Every member of a nation always sees himself, or his picture of himself, in a fixed relationship to the particular symbol which has become the most important for his nation. In its periodic reappearance when the moment demands it lies the continuity of national feeling. A nation's consciousness of itself changes when, and only when, its symbol changes. It is less immutable than one supposes, a fact which offers some hope for the continued existence of mankind.

In the following pages an attempt is made to consider a few nations with reference to their symbols. In order to follow the argument without bias the reader should imagine himself back about twenty years. And it is essential that he should remember that I am here reducing things to their simplest and most general form and hence shall be saying very little about men as individuals.

The English

It is advisable to begin with a nation which, though it does not make much public parade of its identity, yet undoubtedly retains the most stable national feeling in the world today: with England. Everyone knows what the *sea* means to an Englishman; what is not sufficiently known is the precise form of the connection between his relationship to the sea and his famous individualism. The Englishman sees himself as a captain on board a ship with a small group of people, the sea around and beneath him. He is almost alone; as captain he is in many ways isolated even from his crew.

The sea is there to be ruled. This conception is decisive. Ships are as much alone on its vast surface as isolated individuals; and each is personified in its captain. His power of command is absolute and undisputed. The course he steers is a command he gives the sea. The fact that it is carried out through the medium of the crew makes people forget that it is actually the *sea* which has to obey. The captain decides on the goal and the sea, as though it were alive, carries him there, though not without storms and other manifestations of hostility. Considering the immensity of the sea, it is a matter of some importance whom it obeys most frequently. Obedience comes more easily to it when the goal is some British territory. When this is so, the sea behaves like a horse which knows the way and its rider. A ship of another nation is like an unpractised rider on a borrowed horse; the horse behaves much worse than when its master is riding it. The sea, too, is so large that the number of ships by which it is controlled is also important.

When one comes to consider the character of the sea itself one must remember how numerous and violent are the changes to which it is subject. It is more varied in its transformations than any of the animal crowds with which men have dealings; and how harmless and stable, compared to the sea, are the hunter's forests and the farmer's fields.

The Englishman's disasters have been experienced at sea; his dead he has often had to imagine lying at the bottom of the sea; and thus the sea has offered him transformation and danger.

His life at home is complementary to life at sea: security and monotony are its essential characteristics. Everyone has his place which, except to go to sea, he is not supposed to leave for the sake of any transformation; everyone is as sure of his habits as of his possessions.

The Dutch

The importance of national crowd symbols can be seen particularly clearly in the contrast between the English and the Dutch. The two peoples come of similar stock, their languages are related and the religious development of both countries is virtually the same. Both are seafaring nations and founders of maritime empires. The destiny of a Dutch sea captain on a voyage of trade and discovery differed in no way from that of an English captain. The wars they fought with each other were those of closely related rivals. And yet there is a difference between them which may appear insignificant but, in fact, is very important. It concerns their national crowd symbols.

The English conquered their island, but they did not wrest it from the sea. It is through his ships alone that the Englishman subjugates the sea; its ruler is the ship's captain. The Dutchman had to win the land he inhabits from the sea. It is so low lying that he has to protect it by dykes. The dykes are the beginning and end of his national life. The crowd of men equates itself with the dyke and together they withstand the sea. If the dykes are damaged, the land is endangered. In times of crisis the dykes are breached and the Dutch find safety from their enemies on artificial islands. Nowhere else has the feeling of a human wall opposing the sea been so strongly developed. In peacetime people rely on the dykes, but when they have to be destroyed in front of an advancing enemy, their strength is transmitted to the men who will erect them again after the war. The dyke maintains itself in their faith until it can become reality again. In a curious and unmistakable way the Dutch, in time of real danger, carry their barriers against the sea *within themselves*.

Whenever the English were attacked on their island they relied on the sea; with storms it came to their aid against their enemies. They were sure of their island and in their ships each of them felt the same security. The Dutch, on the other hand, always had danger at their back; for them the sea was never entirely subdued. It is true that they sailed upon it to the ends of the earth, but it might always turn against them at home and in times of extremity they had to turn the sea even against themselves in order to keep back the enemy who threatened them.

The Germans

The crowd symbol of the Germans was the *army*. But the army was more than just the army; it was the *marching forest*. In no other modern country has the forest-feeling remained as alive as it has in Germany. The parallel rigidity of the upright trees and their density and number fill the heart of the German with a deep and mysterious delight. To this day he loves to go deep into the forest where his forefathers lived; he feels at one with the trees.

Their orderly separation and the stress on the vertical distinguish this forest from the tropical kind where creepers grow in all directions. In tropical forests the eye loses itself in the foreground; there is a chaotic and unarticulated mass of growth, full of colour and life, which effectively precludes any sensation of order, or even of repetition. The forests of the temperate zone, on the other hand, have a conspicuous rhythm. The eye moves along lines of clearly visible trees into a uniform distance. Each individual tree is always taller than a man and goes on growing until it becomes a giant. Its steadfastness has much in common with the same virtue in a warrior. In a single tree the bark resembles a coat of mail; in a whole forest, where there are many trees of the same kind growing together, it suggests rather the uniforms of an army. For the German, without his being clearly aware of it, army and forest transfused each other in every possible way. What to others might seem the army's dreariness and barrenness kept for the German the life and glow of the forest. He was never afraid in it; he felt protected, one amongst many others. He took the rigidity and straightness of trees for his own law.

The boy who escaped into the forest from the confinement of home, thinking to be alone there and able to dream, actually anticipated his entry into the army. In the forest he found the others waiting for him, true, faithful, and upright as he himself wanted to be; each like every other, for each grows straight, and yet quite different in height and strength. The effect of this early forest romanticism on the German must never be underrated. He absorbed it from countless poems and songs and the forest which appears in these is often called "German".

The Englishman likes to imagine himself at sea, the German in a forest. It is impossible to express the difference of their national feeling more concisely.

The French

The present crowd symbol of the French is of recent date; it is their *revolution*. The Feast of Liberty is celebrated once a year and has become the special occasion of national rejoicing. On the 14th July anyone may dance in the streets with anyone. People who are just as little free, equal and fraternal as in other countries can for once behave as though they were. The Bastille is stormed and the streets are again as full as they were then. The crowd, for centuries the victim of royal justice, takes justice into its own hands. The memory of the executions of the time, a continuous sequence of mass-exaltations of the most stirring kind, contributes more to the feeling of festivity than people may care to admit. Anyone who opposed the crowd, gave it his head. He owed the crowd his head and, by giving it, he helped in his own way to maintain and increase its exaltation.

The Marseillaise dates from that time, and there is no other national hymn which has its vitality. The outbreak of freedom as a periodic event, recurring annually and expected annually, has great advantages as the crowd symbol of a nation. Like the actual Revolution, it releases forces of defence. The French armies that conquered Europe sprang from the Revolution; it found its Napoleon and reached the summit of military glory. The victories belonged to the Revolution and its general; the final defeat was the Emperor's.

Several objections could be made to this use of the Revolution as the national crowd symbol of the French. It seems too vague, having neither the concreteness of the English captain on his ship, nor the wooden order of the German army on the march. But one should not forget that to the Englishman's ship belongs the surging sea, and to the German's army the swaying forest. They are what nourish his feeling and keep it fluid. The crowd feeling of the Revolution is expressed in a movement and an object no less concrete: the storming of the Bastille.

Until one or two generations ago everyone would have added the word "French" to the word "Revolution". Their own most popular memory was also what they were known by in the world; it was their most characteristic production. Thus the Russians with their revolution made a sensible breach in the national consciousness of the French.

The Swiss

Switzerland is a state whose national cohesion is indisputable. The patriotic feeling of the Swiss is greater than that of many peoples who speak only one language. The four languages spoken in Switzerland, the diversity of the cantons, their different social structures, the division into two religious confessions, whose wars are still fresh in memory— none of this seriously weakens the national consciousness of the Swiss; but then the crowd symbol they have in common is their mountains. It is always before their eyes, unshakeable and impregnable to a degree equalled by no other national symbol.

The Swiss can see the tops of their mountains from everywhere, but there are points from which the chain appears more complete. The feeling that, from them, all the mountains can be seen together endows such places with an element of sacredness. Sometimes, on evenings which cannot be predicted in advance and over which man has no influence, the mountains begin to glow; this is their highest con- secration. The difficulty of access to them and their hardness give the Swiss a feeling of security. The peaks are divided, but below the mountains are linked like the limbs of a single gigantic body. They *are* one body, and that body is the country itself.

The Swiss plans for defence during the last two wars expressed this equation of the nation and the chain of the Alps in a curious way. In the case of an attack all the fertile land, all the cities and all the centres of production were to be left undefended. The army was to retire to the mountains and would only have fought there. People and country would appear to have been sacrificed, but Switzerland would still have been represented by the army in the mountains; the crowd symbol of the nation would have become the country itself.

It is a special kind of dyke which the Swiss have. They do not have to erect it themselves like the Dutch. They neither build it nor breach it and no sea pounds against it. The mountains stand and all the Swiss have to do is to know them thoroughly. Every section of them is climbed or travelled over. The Alps act like a magnet, attracting from all countries people who emulate the Swiss in admiring and exploring them. From whatever country they come, mountaineers are like devout Swiss; the army of them, scattered through the whole world after brief periodic terms of service in the mountains, keeps the prestige of Switzerland alive. It would be worth exploring the extent of their practical contribution to the preservation of Swiss independence.

The Spaniards

If the Englishman sees himself as a captain, the Spaniard sees himself as a matador. In place of the sea which obeys the captain, the bull-fighter has his admiring crowd. The animal which he has to kill in accordance with the noble rules of his art is the vicious old monster of myth. He must show no fear; everything depends on his self-control. His smallest movement is watched and judged by thousands. It is the Roman arena which is preserved here, but the bullfighter has changed since then and become a noble knight. He now fights alone, and his meaning and costume, and especially his prestige, were changed by the Middle Ages. Man's slave, the wild beast he has subjugated, once more rebels against him. But the hero who went out to fight it in antiquity is ready for it again. He takes up his position in the sight of the whole human race; so sure is he of his vocation that he feels able to show his audience every detail of the way he kills the monster. He knows exactly what to do; his steps are calculated and his movements as pre-scribed as those of a dance. *But he really kills.* Thousands watch the death and multiply it by their excitement.

The execution of the wild beast which no longer has a right to its wildness, which is goaded into wildness and then condemned to die for it; the execution, the blood and the immaculate knight, are doubly mirrored in the eyes of the admiring. Every man is at once the knight who slays the bull and part of the crowd which acclaims him. Across the bullfighter, who is himself, he sees himself again on the far side of the ring, as crowd. The audience is a ring, a creature closed in on itself. Wherever one looks one meets eyes; there is only one voice to be heard, and that is one's own.

Thus the Spaniard, yearning for his matador, early grows accustomed to the sight of a specific crowd. He learns to know it thoroughly, and it is so strongly alive that it precludes many more recent developments and formations which have become indispensable in other countries. The bullfighter in the ring, who represents so much for him, also becomes a national crowd symbol. Whenever he thinks of large num-bers of Spaniards together, he will also think of the place where they are most frequently together. Compared with these violent crowd-delights, those of the church are mild and harmless. This was not always so, and the crowd-economy of the Spaniard was differently ordered in the times when the church did not shrink from kindling hell-fire for heretics here in this world.

The Italians

A modern nation's consciousness of itself and its behaviour in war depends largely on its recognition of the national crowd symbol. Many peoples have had a spiteful trick played on them by history long after they have won their fight for unity. Italy may serve as an example of the difficulty a nation has in visualizing itself when all its cities are haunted by greater memories and when these memories are deliberately made use of to confuse its present.

Before Italy had won its unity, things were far clearer in the minds of its people. As soon as the parasitic enemy had been driven out, the dismembered body would be pieced together again and would feel and act as a single organism. In cases like this, where the enemy has been in the country for a long time and the sense of oppression is acute, all peoples form similar pictures of their plight. The enemy are numerous, ugly and hated; they come like a swarm of locusts to live off the good, honest soil of the natives. If they intend to stay, they will divide up this soil and weaken the links between the natives in every possible way. The reaction to this is conspiracy and, if there is a series of propitious moments, the driving out of the enemy.

This is what finally happened in Italy and she found the unity so ardently, though for long so vainly, desired by her greatest minds.

But, from this moment on, it became clear that there are dangers in allowing a city like Rome to go on existing. The crowd-buildings of ancient times still stood there, *empty*. The Coliseum was a ruin all too well preserved; it would be easy to feel poor and outcast there. The second Rome, on the other hand, the Rome of St. Peter, had kept much of its old power of attraction. The Church of St. Peter was continually filled with pilgrims from all over the world. But this second Rome was in no way suited to be the focal point of distinctive nationhood. Its appeal was still indiscriminately to all men, and its organization derived from a period before nations in the modern sense existed.

Between these two Romes the national feeling of modern Italy was, as it were, paralysed. And there was no escaping this, for Rome and the Romans had once been Italy. Fascism attempted what appeared the simplest solution, which was to dress up in the genuine antique costume. But this did not really fit; it was much too big and the movements it permitted the body inside it were so violent that every bone was broken. The Fora were excavated, but they did not fill with Romans. The Fasces aroused only the hatred of those who were beaten; neither threat nor castigation gave anyone anything to be proud of.

Fortunately for the Italians, the attempt to impose a false crowd symbol on Italy was a failure.

The Jews

No people is more difficult to understand than the Jews. Debarred from their country of origin, they have spread over the whole of the inhabited earth. Their talent for adaptation is well known, but the degree of their adaptation is immensely variable. Among them were to be found Spaniards, Indians and Chinese. They carry languages and cultures with them from one country to another and guard them more tenaciously than their possessions. Fools may tell stories of their sameness everywhere, but anyone who knows them well will be inclined to think that there are more varied types among them than among any other people. The extent of variation between Jews, both in their nature and their appearance, is one of the most extraordinary phenomena there is. The popular saying that both the best and the worst men are to be found amongst them is a naïve way of expressing this fact. Jews are different from other people, but, in reality, they are most different from each other.

The Jews have been admired for continuing to exist. They are not the only people who are found everywhere; the Armenians are certainly equally far-spread. Nor are they the oldest people; the history of the Chinese goes back much further than theirs. But, of the old peoples, they are the only one which has been wandering for so long. They have had most time in which to disappear without trace and, in spite of this, they are more here now than they ever were.

Until a few years ago, they had no territorial or linguistic unity. Most of them no longer understood Hebrew; they spoke in a hundred tongues. To millions of them their old religion had become an empty sack. Even the number of Christians amongst them was gradually increasing, especially among the intellectuals; and the number of those without any religion at all was far larger still. Speaking superficially, from the point of view of self-preservation in the vulgar sense, they should have done everything possible to let it be forgotten that they were Jews, and to forget it themselves. But they cannot forget it; nor do most of them want to. One is driven to ask in what respect these people remain Jews; what makes them into Jews; what is the ultimate nature of the bond they feel when they say "I am a Jew".

This bond has existed from the beginning of their history and has been re-formed over and over again with astounding monotony during its course: it is the Exodus from Egypt. Let us visualize the actual content of this tradition: a whole people, numbered, it is true, but none the less a multitude, wanders for forty years through the desert. Their legendary forefather had been promised progeny numerous as the sand on the shores of the sea. Now this progeny exists and wanders, sand through the sand of the desert. The sea allows them to pass, but it closes over their enemies. Their goal is a promised land, which their swords will conquer for them.

The image of this multitude moving year after year through the desert has become the crowd symbol of the Jews. It has remained to this day as distinct and comprehensible as it was then. The people see themselves together before they settled and then dispersed; they see themselves on their migration. In this state of density they received their law. If ever a crowd had a goal, they had. They had many adventures and these were common to all of them. The crowd they formed was a *naked* crowd; of all the many things which normally enmesh men in their separate lives scarcely any existed in these surroundings. Around them was nothing but sand, the barest of all crowds; nothing is more likely than the image of sand to emphasise the feeling of being alone with itself which this wandering procession must have had. Often its goal was obliterated and the crowd, threatening to disintegrate, had to be roused, gripped and held together by chastisement or exhortation. The number of people in the procession—600-700,000—was enormous, and not only by the modest standards of remote antiquity. The duration of their wanderings is of particular importance. What this crowd sustained for forty years can later be stretched to cover any period of time. This long wandering inflicted as a punishment contains all the torments of later migrations.

Germany and Versailles

IN ORDER TO clarify as much as possible some of the concepts I have formulated, I propose to add here a few words about the crowd-structure of Germany, the Germany which, in the first third of this century, astonished the world with formations and tendencies of an entirely unprecedented kind, whose deadly seriousness went completely unrealized at the time and which are only now beginning slowly to be understood.

The crowd symbol of the united German nation which formed after the Franco-Prussian War of 1870-71 was, and remained, the army.

Every German was proud of the army and it was only a few isolated individuals who were able to remain outside the influence of this symbol. It was the war which supplied even a universal thinker like Nietzsche with the stimulus for his chief work, *The Will to Power*; the sight he never forgot was that of a cavalry squadron. The point of this reference to Nietzsche is that he proves how general the importance of the army had become in Germany; how this crowd symbol had an effect even on those who haughtily detached themselves from the crowd. Bourgeois and worker, peasant and scholar, Catholic and Protestant, Prussian and Bavarian, they all saw the army as the symbol of the nation. The deeper roots of this symbol, its origin in the *forest*, have already been uncovered. For a German, forest and army are so intimately connected that either can equally well stand as the crowd symbol of the nation; in this respect they are identical.

Apart from its influence as a symbol, the army did also exist in a concrete form; and this fact was of decisive importance. A symbol lives in the minds and feelings of men, as did that curious entity, the forest-army. The actual army, on the other hand, in which every young German served, functioned as a *closed crowd*. The belief in universal military service, the conviction of its profound significance and the veneration accorded it, had a wider reach than the traditional religions, for it embraced Catholics and Protestants alike. Anyone who excluded himself was no German. I said earlier that it was only in a very limited sense that armies could be called crowds. This, however, was not so with a German; the army was by far the most important closed crowd he experienced. It was closed because those belonging to it were either young men of certain age groups only, who served for a limited period, or professional soldiers. But every young man passed through it at some time and remained inwardly linked to it for the rest of his life.

The Prussian Junker caste which provided the greater part of its officers acted as the crowd crystal of this army. It was like an order of chivalry with strict, though in this case, unwritten laws; or like a hereditary orchestra, thoroughly familiar with the music with which it has to infect its audience.

On the outbreak of the First World War the whole German people became one open crowd. The enthusiasm of those days has often been described. Many people in other countries had been counting on the internationalism of the Social Democrats and were astounded at their failure to act. They forgot that the Social Democrats, too, bore within them this forest-army symbol of their nation; that they themselves had belonged to the closed crowd of the army and that, whilst in it, they had been under the command and influence of a highly disciplined and immensely effective crowd crystal, the Junker and officer caste. Their membership of a political party carried very little weight in comparison with this.

But those first August days of 1914 were also the days in which National Socialism was begotten. Hitler himself is our authority for this. He later described how, at the outbreak of war, he fell on his knees and thanked God. It was his decisive experience, the one moment at which he himself honestly became part of a crowd. He never forgot it and his whole subsequent career was devoted to the re-creation of this moment, but *from outside*. Germany was to be again as it was then, conscious of its military striking power and exulting and united in it.

But Hitler would never have achieved his purpose had not the Treaty of Versailles disbanded the German army. The prohibition on universal military service robbed the Germans of their most essential closed crowd. The activities they were denied, the exercises, the receiving and passing on of orders, became something which they had to procure for themselves again at all costs. The prohibition on universal military service was the *birth* of National Socialism. Every closed crowd which is dissolved by force transforms itself into an open crowd to which it imparts all its own characteristics. The party came to the rescue of the army, and the party had no limits set to its recruitment from within the nation. Every single German—man, woman or child, soldier or civilian—could become a National Socialist. He was probably even more anxious to become one if he had not been a soldier before, because, by doing so, he achieved participation in activities hitherto denied him.

Hitler used the slogan *The Diktat of Versailles* with unparalleled and unwearying monotony; and many have marvelled at its effectiveness. Repetition never weakened it; on the contrary, it grew stronger with the years. What was the actual content of this slogan? What was it that Hitler passed on to his audiences by it? To a German the word "Versailles" did not so much mean the defeat, which he never really acknowledged, as the prohibition of the army; the prohibition of specific and sacrosanct practices without which he could not really imagine life. The prohibition of the army was like the prohibition of a religion. The faith of his fathers had been proscribed, and it was every man's sacred duty to re-establish it. Every time it was used, the word "Versailles" probed this wound and kept it bleeding, so that it never closed. As long as the word "Versailles" was uttered with sufficient force at mass meetings it was impossible for healing to begin.

In this connection it is important to notice that what was spoken of was always a *diktat* and never a treaty. *Diktat* belongs to the sphere of *command*. A single alien command, a command coming from the enemy and therefore dubbed *diktat* had put an end to the whole virile activity of command amongst Germans themselves, that is within the army. Anyone who heard or read the words "Diktat of Versailles" felt in his depths what had been taken away from him, which was the German army. To reconstitute it seemed the only really important goal; once it was there again, everything would be as it had been before. The army's importance as a national crowd symbol had never been shaken; the forest, which was the older and deeper-rooted part of this symbol, still stood untouched.

The choice of the word "Versailles" as his central slogan was there-fore particularly fortunate from Hitler's point of view. Not only did it remind the Germans of the latest painful event in their life as a nation, of the prohibition of general conscription and the suppression of their right to an army in which every man could serve for a few years, but it also summed up other familiar and important moments of German history.

It was at Versailles that Bismarck had founded the Second German Empire. The unity of Germany had been proclaimed there in the moment of elation and irresistible strength following a great victory. And the victory had been won over Napoleon III, who regarded him-self as the successor of the great Napoleon and the inheritor of his spirit, and who had risen to power through the veneration accorded to his legendary name. But Versailles was also the seat of Louis XIV, and had been built by him. Of all the French rulers before Napoleon, Louis XIV was the one who had most deeply humiliated the Germans. It was he who had incorporated Strasbourg with its cathedral into France and it was his troops who had devastated the castle at Heidel-berg.

Thus the proclamation of the German Empire at Versailles was a belated victory over both Louis XIV and Napoleon together; and it had been won alone, without the help of any ally. There is plenty of confirmation of the effect which the word "Versailles" had on Germans at this time, and it was inevitable that it should, for the name of Versailles was bound up with the greatest triumph of modern German history.

Every time Hitler spoke of the notorious *Diktat*, the memory of that triumph echoed in the word and was transmitted to his audience as a promise. If the former enemies of Germany had had ears to hear, they would have known it for a threat of war and defeat. With the exception of those directed against the Jews, it can be maintained without exaggeration that all the important slogans of National Socialism—"The Third Reich", the "Sieg-heil", etc.—derive directly from the words "The Diktat of Versailles". The whole content of the movement is concentrated in them: the defeat to be turned into victory; the prohibited army to be re-created for this purpose.

Perhaps one should also give a thought to the symbol of the movement, the Swastika. Its effect is a twofold one; that of the sign and that of the word. And both have something cruel about them. The sign resembles two twisted gallows; it threatens the spectator insidiously, as though it said "You wait. You will be surprised at what will hang here". In as far as the swastika has a revolving movement, this too contains menace; it recalls the limbs of the criminals who used to be broken on the wheel.

The word has absorbed the cruel and bloodthirsty elements of the Christian cross, as though it were *good* to crucify. *Haken*, the first part of the German word, recalls *hakenstellen*, an expression commonly used by boys for "tripping up". Thus it forebodes the fall of many. For some it conjures up military visions of heel clicking; the German for "heels" being *hacken*. Thus, with the threat of cruel punishment, it combines an insidious viciousness and a hidden reminder of military discipline.

Inflation and the Crowd

INFLATION IS A crowd phenomenon in the strictest and most concrete sense of the word. The confusion it wreaks on the population of whole countries is by no means confined to the actual period of the inflation. One may say that, apart from wars and revolutions, there is nothing in our modern civilizations which compares in importance to it. The upheavals caused by inflations are so profound that people prefer to hush them up and conceal them. They may also hesitate to attribute to money—the value of which is, after all, artificially fixed by man— an efficacy in forming crowds which is out of all proportion to its practical function, and which seems both contrary to reason and infinitely shaming.

At this point it is necessary to say something about the psychological qualities of money. Money can become a crowd symbol, and, in certain circumstances, the units of which it is composed may accumulate to form a crowd. But, in contrast to the other crowd symbols I have discussed, the individuality of its units is always emphatically stressed. Each coin has a clear and firm edge and its own specific weight. It can be recognized at a glance and passes freely from hand to hand, continually changing its surroundings. Often it has the head of a ruler stamped on it, from whom, especially when it is a valuable coin, it will take its name; there have been Louis d'or and Maria Theresa thalers. People like imagining a coin as an individual. The hand closes round it, feeling its planes and edges as a whole. A tenderness for the coin which can do so much for them is universal amongst men, and part of its "character". In one respect the coin is superior to a living creature. Being made of metal, its hardness secures "eternal" existence for it; except by fire, it can scarcely be destroyed at all. A coin does not attain its size through growth; it issues ready-made from the mint and should remain as it then is; it should never change.

Reliability is perhaps the most important attribute of coins. All the owner has to do is to guard them well from other people; they do not run away of their own accord like animals. They need not be watched; a use can always be found for them; and they have no moods to be considered. The status of each coin is further consolidated by its relation to other coins of different values. Their strict hierarchy makes them even more like people. One could speak of the social system of coins, the classes here being classes of value. A higher coin can always be exchanged for a lower, but never a lower for a higher.

Among most peoples a heap of coins has always been known as treasure, and treasure, as we saw, is a crowd symbol. It is felt to be a unit; one can come on it without knowing exactly how much it really contains; one can rummage in it and separate coin from coin; it is always expected to be larger than it is; and it is often hidden away, to come suddenly to light. But it is not only the man who cherishes life-long hopes of finding treasure who expects it to be greater than it is. The man who is in process of amassing it imagines it as continually growing and does everything in his power to promote this. It is certainly true that, with many men who live for their money alone, treasure takes the place of the human crowd. This is exemplified in the many stories of lonely misers. They are the successors of the mythical monsters who existed solely to guard, watch and cherish some treasure.

It may be objected that this connection between coins and treasure no longer holds for modern man; that paper money is in use everywhere; that the rich now keep their treasure in banks in an abstract and invisible form. But the importance of a gold reserve for a strong currency and the fact that there are still actual gold currencies to be found, prove that treasure has by no means entirely lost its old importance. The great majority of men, even in countries which are highly developed technically, are still paid for their work by the hour and, almost everywhere, the size of their wage still comes within the range imagined as covered by coins. Coins are still received as change for paper money, and the old feeling for them, the old attitude, is still familiar to everyone. Getting change is a daily part of the simplest and commonest processes of living, something which every child learns as early as possible.

But it is true that a new relationship to money has developed alongside the old one. In every country the monetary unit has acquired a more abstract value. This does not mean, however, that it is felt to be less of a unit. If the coins of earlier days had something of the strict hierarchical organization of a closed society, modern paper money is akin to the inhabitants of a great city.

The modern treasure is the *million*. The word has a cosmopolitan ring; it is understood all over the world and can refer to any type of currency. The interesting thing about the million is that it can be reached in leaps and bounds by clever speculation; it dangles before the eyes of all whose ambition is to make money. The millionaire has taken over some of the dazzling qualities of the old fairy-tale king. The connotation of the word million is twofold; it can refer to both money and people. This is particularly striking in political speeches. The lust of seeing numbers mount up is characteristic, for example, of Hitler's speeches. There the word usually referred to the millions of Germans living outside the Reich and still waiting for their deliverance. After his first bloodless victories and before the outbreak of his war, Hitler had a particular partiality for the mounting numbers of the populations of his empire. He contrasted them with the total numbers of all the Germans in the world. It was his confessed aim to bring all these within his sphere of influence; and in all his threats, self-congratulations and demands he used the word *million*. Other politicians use it more often of money, but the word has undoubtedly acquired some ambiguity. Through being used to express populations, and especially the populations of metropolitan cities which are invariably expressed in millions, the abstract number has become filled with a crowd-meaning contained by no other number today. Since it is counted in the same millions, money and the crowd are closer today than they have ever been.

What is it that happens in an inflation? The unit of money suddenly loses its identity. The crowd it is part of starts growing and, the larger it becomes, the smaller becomes the worth of each unit. The millions one always wanted are suddenly there in one's hand, but they are no longer millions in fact, but only in name. It is as though the process of sudden increase had deprived the thing which increases of all value. The movement has the character of a flight and, once it has started within a currency, there is no foreseeable end to it. Just as one can go on counting upwards to any figure, so money can be devalued downwards to any depth.

This process contains that urge to rapid and unlimited growth which I have characterized as one of the most important and striking psychological attributes of the crowd. But here the growth negates itself; as the crowd grows, its units become weaker and weaker. What used to be one Mark is first called 10,000, then 100,000, then a million. The identification of the individual with his mark is thus broken, for the latter is no longer fixed and stable, but changes from one moment to the next. It is no longer like a person; it has no continuity and it has less and less value. A man who has been accustomed to rely on it cannot help feeling its degradation as his own. He has identified himself with it for too long and his confidence in it has been like his confidence in himself. Not only is everything visibly shaken during an inflation, nothing remaining certain or unchanged even for an hour, but also each man, as a person, becomes less. Whatever he is or was, like the million he always wanted he becomes nothing. Everyone has a million and everyone is nothing. The process of the formation of treasure has become its opposite, and all the reliability of money is blown away by the wind. No treasure can be added to; each, on the contrary, grows less and less; every accumulation of treasure disappears. An inflation can be called a witches' sabbath of devaluation where men and the units of their money have the strangest effects on each other. The one stands for the other, men feeling themselves as "bad" as their money; and this becomes worse and worse. Together they are all at its mercy and all feel equally worthless.

Thus in an inflation something happens which was certainly never intended and which is so dangerous that anyone with any measure of public responsibility who is capable of foreseeing it must fear it. It is a double devaluation originating in a double identification. The *individual* feels depreciated because the unit on which he relied, and with which he had equated himself, starts sliding; and the *crowd* feels depreciated because the *million* is. It has been shown that the word million is ambiguous, standing for both a large sum of money and a large number of people, particularly the people inhabiting a modern city; and that one meaning passes into the other and feeds on it. All the crowds which form in times of inflation—and they form very frequently—are subject to the pressure of the depreciated million. Together people are worth as little as each is worth alone. As the millions mount up, a whole people, numbered in millions, becomes nothing.

The process throws together people whose material interests normally lie far apart. The wage-earner is hit equally with the rentier. Overnight a man can lose a large part, or all, of what he thought safe in his bank. An inflation cancels out distinctions between men which had seemed eternal and brings together in the same inflation crowd people who before would scarcely have nodded to each other in the street.

No one ever forgets a sudden depreciation of himself, for it is too painful. Unless he can thrust it on to someone else, he carries it with him for the rest of his life. And the crowd as such never forgets its depreciation. The natural tendency afterwards is to find something which is worth even less than oneself, which one can despise as one was despised oneself. It is not enough to take over an old contempt and to maintain it at the same level. What is wanted is a dynamic process of humiliation. Something must be treated in such a way that it becomes worth less and less, as the unit of money did during the inflation. And this process must be continued until its object is reduced to a state of utter worthlessness. Then one can throw it away like paper, or repulp it.

The object Hitler found for this process during the German inflation was the Jews. They seemed made for it: their long-standing connection with money, their traditional understanding of its movements and fluctuations, their skill in speculation, the way they flocked together in money markets, where their behaviour contrasted strikingly with the soldierly conduct which was the German ideal—all this, in a time of doubt, instability and hostility to money, could not but make them appear dubious and hostile. The individual Jew seemed "bad" because he was on good terms with money when others did not know how to manage it and would have preferred to have nothing more to do with it. If the inflation had led only to the depreciation of Germans as individuals, the incitement of hatred against individual Jews would have sufficed. But this was not so, for, when their millions tumbled, the Germans also felt humiliated as a crowd. Hitler saw this clearly and therefore turned his activities against the Jews as a whole.

In its treatment of the Jews National Socialism repeated the process of inflation with great precision. First they were attacked as wicked and dangerous, as enemies; then they were more and more depreciated; then, there not being enough in Germany itself, those in the conquered territories were gathered in; and finally they were treated literally as vermin, to be destroyed with impunity by the million. The world is still horrified and shaken by the fact that the Germans could go so far; that they either participated in a crime of such magnitude, or connived at it, or ignored it. It might not have been possible to get them to do so if, a few years before, they had not been through an inflation during which the Mark fell to a billionth of its former value. It was this inflation, as a crowd experience, which they shifted on to the Jews.

The Nature of the Parliamentary System

THE TWO-PARTY system of modern parliaments uses the psychological structure of opposing armies. In England in the Civil War these actually existed, although unwillingly. No one likes killing his own countrymen; the feeling of kinship always tends to restrain bloodshed and sometimes even brings civil wars to an early end. But the two factions remain; they fight on, but in a form of warfare which has renounced killing. In real fighting it is assumed that the greater number will win. The chief concern of any commander is to be stronger than his adversary at the point of conflict: to have more men there. The successful commander is the one who succeeds in concentrating superior forces at the greatest number of crucial points, even if his total forces are less.

A parliamentary vote does nothing but ascertain the relative strengths of two groups at a given time and place. Knowing them beforehand is not enough. One party may have 360 members and the other only 240, but the actual vote is decisive, as the moment in which the one is really measured against the other. It is all that is left of the original lethal clash and it is played out in many forms, with threats, abuse and physical provocation which may lead to blows or missiles. But the counting of the vote ends the battle. It is assumed that 360 men would have defeated 240. The "crowd of the dead" does not come into the question; in a parliament there are, and can be, no dead. This fact is made clear by the practice of parliamentary immunity. A member's immunity is twofold: it operates both in relation to the government and its agents and also in relation to other members. This second aspect is usually too little stressed.

Now no one has ever really believed that the majority decision is necessarily the wiser one because it has received the greater number of votes. It is will against will as in war. Each is convinced that right and reason are on his side. Conviction comes easily and the purpose of a party is, precisely, to keep this will and conviction alive. The member of an outvoted party accepts the majority decision, not because he has ceased to believe in his own case, but simply because he admits defeat. It is easy for him to do this because nothing happens to him: he is not punished in any way for his previous opposition. He would react quite differently if his life was endangered. What he anticipates, however, is future battles, and many of them; in none of them will he be killed.

All members of a parliament share in a like immunity. It is this measure of equality which makes them a crowd and there is no distinction here between the members of either party. The parliamentary system functions only so long as this immunity is preserved. It crumbles as soon as it admits anyone who allows himself to reckon on the death of any member whatsoever. Nothing is more dangerous here than to see any of the living as dead. War is war because the dead are included in the final reckoning. Parliament is parliament only so long as the dead are excluded.

The instinctive way in which the English Parliament, for example, dissociates itself from its dead, even from those who have died peacefully and outside its walls, is shown in the system of by-elections. The dead man's successor is not settled in advance and no one succeeds automatically to his place. Fresh candidates are put up and a new election is held in all its formality. The dead man has no place in Parliament; he cannot bequeath his membership and he can never know for certain who will succeed him after his death. Death with all its perilous after-effects has been successfully excluded from the English Parliament.

This interpretation of the parliamentary system may be disputed on the grounds that all continental parliaments consist of numerous parties which vary greatly in size and only sometimes cohere into two opposing groups. But this fact does not affect the significance of the vote. This, everywhere and always, is the crucial moment which determines events, and the crucial factor in it is *two figures*, the greater of which binds all who have taken part in the vote. All parliaments everywhere stand or fall by the twofold immunity of their members.

The popular election of representatives is basically similar to parliamentary procedure. The candidate who has proved himself the strongest, the victor, is reckoned to be the best. And the strongest candidate is the one who obtains the most votes. If the 17,562 who voted for him were to join battle with the 13,204 who voted for his opponent, they would win. But this conflict, too, must stop short of killing. The "immunity" of the voters is, however, less important than the "immunity" of the ballot papers on which they vote. Every method of influencing the voters is permitted up to the moment in which they finally make their choice of candidate and write down or indicate his name. The opposing candidate will be held up to every kind of popular contumely and hatred. The elector can take active part in several electoral contests. If he is politically inclined, he will vastly enjoy the ups and downs of the fight; but the moment in which he casts his vote is almost sacred; the sealed boxes which hold the ballot papers are sacred; and so is the count.

The solemnity of all these activities derives from the renunciation of death as an instrument of decision. Every single vote puts death, as it were, on one side. But the effect that killing would have had on the strength of the enemy is scrupulously put down in figures; and anyone who tampers with these figures, who destroys or falsifies them, lets death in again without knowing it. Militarists who mock the ballot only betray their own bloodthirsty proclivities. A ballot-form, like a treaty, is to them only a scrap of paper; that it has not been dipped in blood renders it contemptible in their eyes; for them the only valid decisions are those reached through blood.

The voting of a member of parliament is more concentrated than that of an elector. The widely separated moments in which the latter, as such, exists are brought close together in his representative. That is what he is there for: to vote *frequently*. But the number of those amongst whom he votes is relatively much smaller. Intensity and repetition have to supply the excitement that the electors derive from their numbers.

Distribution and Increase.
Socialism and Production

THE PROBLEM OF justice is as old as that of distribution. Whenever men went hunting together the sequel was distribution. As a pack they had been united, but when it came to the distribution of the prey they had to divide, never having developed the communal stomach which would enable them to feed as one creature. In the communion they found a rite which perhaps came nearest to such a conception. It was an approximation, though an inadequate one, to an ideal state for which they felt a need. The *isolation* which eating entails is one of the roots of that terrifying growth called power. Anyone who eats alone and in secret, must kill alone. Anyone who kills with others, must share the prey with them.

Justice begins with the recognition of the necessity of sharing. The oldest law is that which regulates it, and this is still the most important law today and, as such, has remained the basic concern of all movements which have at heart the community of human activities and of human existence in general.

Justice requires that everyone should have enough to eat. But it also requires that everyone should contribute to the production of food. The overwhelming majority of men are engaged in the production of goods of all kinds; something has gone wrong with distribution. This, reduced to the simplest terms, is the content of socialism.

But, however they are divided about the way in which goods are distributed in the modern world, the adversaries and the partisans of socialism are at one over the precondition of this problem. This is production. Both sides in the ideological conflict which has split the earth into two almost equal halves instigate and further production in every possible way. Whether goods are produced to be sold or to be shared, the actual process of production is not only not questioned by either side, but is venerated. One might almost say that, in the eyes of most people today, there is something sacred about it.

It may well be asked where this veneration derives from. Perhaps some point can be found in human history where production became sacrosanct. But a little reflection will show that there is no such point. The phenomenon is so old that any attempt to fix a historical date for it must be meaningless.

The *hubris* of production goes back to the *increase pack*. The connection may be overlooked because, in practice, it is no longer packs which devote themselves to procuring increase. These have become the enormous crowds which grow daily larger in every centre of civilization. But if we remember that no end can be seen to this growth, that there are more and more people producing more and more goods, that these goods include live animals and plants, and that the methods used to produce them can now scarcely be distinguished from those used to produce inaminate goods, then we shall have to admit that the increase pack has been man's most fruitful and successful creation. Increase ceremonies have become machines and techniques. Every factory is a unit serving the same cult. What is new is the acceleration of the process. What in former days was generation and increase of *expectancy*, directed towards rain or corn, the approach of herds of animals which could be hunted, or the growth of other animals which had been domesticated, has today become production itself. We press a few buttons, connect up various levers and everything we want, of every possible kind, is there to hand in a few hours, or even less.

It is worth pointing out that the strict and exclusive combination of proletariat and production, which has acquired such prestige during the last hundred years, re-establishes in a particularly pure form the old conception which was the core of the increase pack. The proletariat are those who increase fastest, and they do so in two ways. First they have more children than other people and thus, through their progeny, come to resemble a crowd, and secondly their numbers are increased by the influx of people from the country to the centres of production. It is exactly the same twofold growth which the readers will remember as characteristic of the primitive increase pack. People flocked to its feasts and ceremonies and there, many of them gathered together already, they gave themselves up to rites and practices designed to ensure a numerous progeny.

When the concept of a dispossessed proletariat was first advanced and began to take effect, it retained the full optimism of increase. No one supposed for a moment that, because their lives were miserable, there ought perhaps to be fewer of them. People relied on production; through its increase the proletariat too would increase. Their productivity should serve themselves. Proletariat and production should grow together. This is the very connection which invariably manifests itself in the activities of primitive increase packs. People want to become more numerous themselves, and therefore all the things on which they live must become more numerous too. The one desire cannot be separated from the other. They are so closely linked that it is often not clear what it is that should increase.

I have shown that, through transformations into animals which lived together in large numbers, man strengthened his feeling for his own increase. It might indeed be said that he *learned* it from such animals. He was confronted with shoals of fish, swarms of insects, great herds of hoofed animals, and, if he acted these creatures so well in his dances that he became them and felt like them, if he succeeded in fixing these transformations as totems and in passing them on to his descendants as a sacred tradition, he also passed on, together with them, his determination to achieve an increase far exceeding that natural to man.

Modern man's relationship to production is exactly the same. Machines today can produce more than anyone would once have dreamed of. Through them, multiplication has grown to monstrous proportions. But since, on the whole, it is objects which are multiplied and not living creatures, man's addiction to sheer numbers increases with the increase of his needs. He can find uses for more and more things and, in using them, he discovers yet further needs. It is production in this sense of unrestricted multiplication in every direction which is the most striking characteristic of "capitalist" countries. In countries where the "proletariat" is accorded a special position, and where large accumulations of capital in the hands of individuals are forbidden, the problems of equitable distribution are at least theoretically ranked equal in importance with those of increase.

The Self-Destruction of the Xosas

ONE MORNING IN May 1856 a young Xosa girl went to fetch water from the little river that ran near her home. When she came back she described how she had seen strange men by the river, quite different from any she had seen before. Her uncle, who was called Umhlakaza, went to the river to see the strangers and found them where she had said. They told him to go back to his house and perform certain ceremonies; when he had done this, he should sacrifice an ox to the spirits of the dead, and, on the fourth day, return to them again. There was in their appearance something which demanded obedience and Umhlakaza did as they ordered. On the fourth day he went again to the river. The strange people were again there and, to his astonishment, he recognized among them his brother who had died many years before. Then, for the first time, he learned who and what they were. They explained that they had come from battlefields beyond the sea to help the Xosas against the white men, their eternal enemies: through their invincible power, the English would be driven from the land. Umhlakaza must act as intermediary between them and the chiefs, to pass on the instructions they would give him. For astonishing things would come to pass, more astonishing than anything that had ever yet happened, if their proffered help was accepted. Above all, he must tell his people to abandon witchcraft against each other, and to kill fat cattle and eat.

The news of this communication from the spirit world spread rapidly among the Xosas. Kreli, the paramount chief of the tribe, greeted the message with joy. In fact it is said, although it cannot be proved, that he himself was the original author of the whole scheme. Word went round that the command of the spirits must be obeyed; the best cattle must be slaughtered and eaten. Some of the Xosas lived in British territory and messengers were sent to their Chiefs too, telling them what had happened and asking for their help. Immediately all the Xosa clans were in commotion. Most of the chiefs began slaughtering their cattle. Only one of them, Sandile, hesitated; he was a cautious man. The British High Commissioner informed Kreli that, while he could do as he pleased in his own territory, he would be punished if he went on inciting British subjects to destroy their property. But this threat did not trouble Kreli much. He was convinced that the time was near in which *he* would be the one to decree punishment.

The revelations communicated through the prophet increased rapidly. Standing in the middle of the river, in the presence of a multitude of deluded people, the girl heard beneath her feet strange unearthly sounds. The prophet, her uncle, declared that they were the voices of the spirits holding council over the affairs of men. The very first command had been to slaughter cattle, but the ghosts were insatiable in their demands. More and more cattle were killed, but still never enough. The delusion continued month after month, spreading wider every day and seizing fresh victims. The cautious Sandile succumbed to it after a while, urged passionately by his brother who, with his own eyes, had seen the spirits of two of their father's dead councillors. He had spoken to them and they had sent word to Sandile commanding him to kill his cattle unless he wanted to perish with the white man.

The final order had already been given through the prophet. Its fulfilment was to be the last act of preparation required of the Xosas before they were thought worthy of the help of the spirit host. Not a goat or an ox or a cow out of all their herds must be left living and every grain of corn in their granaries must be destroyed. A glorious future awaited those who obeyed. On the appointed day, herds of thousands upon thousands of cattle more beautiful than all they had slaughtered would rise up out of the earth and cover the pastures far and wide; great fields of millet, ripe and ready to eat, would spring from the ground in an instant. On that day the ancient heroes of the tribe, the great and the wise of years gone by, would rise again and share in the joys of the faithful. Sickness and sorrow would be no more, nor the infirmities of age; beauty and youth would return to the risen dead, as to the enfeebled living. But terrible would be the fate of those who had set themselves against the will of the spirits, or neglected to fulfil their commands. That same day which would bring so much joy to the faithful would be to them a day of ruin and destruction. The sky would fall on them and crush them, together with the half-breeds and the white men.

Missionaries and government officials strove in vain to stem this madness. The Xosas were possessed by a delirious frenzy and would neither listen to argument nor brook opposition. The whites who attempted to interfere were threatened and their lives were no longer safe. The Xosas were in the grip of a fanatical belief and many of their leaders, moreover, saw in this a favourable opportunity for war. Their intention throughout was to hurl the full force of the Xosa tribe, well armed and starving, against the British Colony. Their own excitement was too great for them to see the terrible dangers of such an undertaking.

There were some who did not believe either in the predictions of the prophet or in their chance of succeeding in such a war, but who nevertheless destroyed their last particle of food. Among them was one of Kreli's uncles. "It is the Chief's command", he said and then, when there was nothing left to eat, the old man and his favourite wife sat themselves down in an empty kraal and died. Kreli's chief councillor was also one of those who opposed the plan until he saw that words were useless. Then, saying that all he had was his chief's, he gave the order for slaughter and destruction and fled from the place, a raving madman. And thus it was with thousands: the chief commanded, and they obeyed.

In the early months of 1857 an unusual activity ruled throughout the land. Great kraals were got ready to hold the cattle which were expected to appear so soon and in such enormous numbers. Huge skin sacks were prepared to contain the milk which was soon to flow like water. Many of the people were already starving even as they worked. East of the River Kei, the prophet's order had been carried out to the letter, but the resurrection day was still postponed. Chief Sandile had been late in beginning the slaughter of the cattle and, in his territory, it was not yet complete. Some of the Xosas, therefore, were already starving while others were still engaged in destroying their resources.

The government did everything possible to protect the frontiers. Watch posts were strengthened and every available soldier was despatched there. The colonists, too, prepared to meet the shock. As soon as the defences had been seen to, provisions were laid in to save the lives of the starving.

At last the long awaited day came. All through the night the Xosas had watched in a fever of excitement. They were waiting for two blood-red suns to rise over the eastern hills; then the heavens would fall on their enemies and crush them. Half-dead with hunger, they spent the night in wild rejoicings. When, at last, there rose as usual but the one sun, their hearts sank. But they did not despair at once. Perhaps midday had been meant, when the sun was highest. When nothing happened then, they fixed their hopes on its setting. But the sun set and everything was over.

The warriors who were to have burst on the colony in a body had, by some inexplicable error, not been gathered together. And now it was too late; nor was it possible to postpone the day of the rising again. The fierce excitement of the Xosas had turned to deepest despair. It was not as warriors, but as starving beggars that they now made their way towards the colony. Brother fought against brother and father against son for scraps and shreds of the great milk sacks made so carefully in the days of hope. The old, the sick and the weak were left to their fate. People hunted for plants to eat, and even for the roots of trees. Those within reach of the sea tried to keep themselves alive on shellfish, but they were not used to this kind of food, got dysentery from it and died in hundreds. In many places, whole families sat down together to die. Fifteen or twenty skeletons were found later under a single tree: parents who had died with their children. A ceaseless stream of starving creatures poured into the colony. Mostly they were young men and women, but there were fathers and mothers among them carrying half-dead children on their backs. They squatted in front of the farmhouses, begging piteously for food.

During this year, 1857, the population of British Xosa-land fell from 105,000 to 37,000: 68,000 people died. And this was in territory where thousands of lives were saved by the stocks of food laid in by the government. In the native territories, where there were no such stocks, an even greater proportion died. The power of the Xosa tribe was utterly broken.

This story has not been told at such length without good reason. It might have been invented by someone who wanted to show with what consistency and precision events follow upon each other within a crowd. But the story is true; these things really happened in South Africa, and not in the distant past, but in the fifties of the last century. There are eyewitness accounts of them which anyone may read.

Let us try to pick out the essential points of the narrative.

The first thing which strikes one is the *aliveness* of the Xosa dead. They really share the fortunes of the living. They find ways and means of communicating with them. They promise an army to help them. As an army, and thus as a *crowd of dead warriors*, they will reinforce the army of the living Xosas in precisely the same way that one tribe would reinforce another as the result of an alliance. But this alliance is between the tribe and its own dead.

When the promised day comes, everyone shall suddenly be *equal*. The old shall be young again, the sick healthy, the careworn joyful; and the dead shall mingle with the living. The movement towards this universal equality is initiated by the first command: there must be no more witchcraft practised against each other; it is the confusion of conflicting wills which does most to mar the unity and equality of the tribe. On the promised day the crowd of the tribe, which is too weak to overcome its enemies alone, will be suddenly increased by the whole great crowd of the dead.

The direction in which this crowd will move is also foretold: it will move against the white man's colony, whose boundaries already enclose part of it. Thanks to the reinforcement of the spirits, its power will be invincible.

Further, the spirits have the same desires as the living; they like to eat meat, and cattle must be sacrificed so that they may. Presumably they also eat the grain that is destroyed. At first the sacrifices come singly and may be taken as signs of piety and devotion. But then their numbers increase; the dead demand everything. Men's passionate desire for increase, normally the increase of their corn and cattle, is transformed here into desire for the increase of the dead. It is cattle that have been *slaughtered* which must increase, and corn that has been *destroyed*: corn and cattle for the dead.

The tendency of all human crowds to become more and more—the blind, reckless, dynamic movement which sacrifices everything to itself and which is always present in a gathering crowd—this tendency is *transferable*. Hunters transfer it to their prey, which can never be numerous enough for them and whose fertility they seek to foster by ritual ceremonies. Pastoral peoples transfer it to their herds; they do everything possible to make them grow and, with skill and practice in breeding, they actually succeed in this. Agricultural peoples transfer it to their produce; their corn bears thirty or one hundredfold and the granaries in which they store it are made to be seen and admired; they are the outward and visible signs of successful increase. Men work so hard to achieve it and their transferred crowd-feeling for their corn and their cattle is so strong that they acquire from it a new sense of human dignity. Sometimes, indeed, they feel as though they had done it all themselves.

During their "self-destruction", all the human desire of the Xosas for increase of men, corn and cattle, became bound up with their idea of the dead. For their revenge on the white men who had gradually stolen their land and for success in war against those they had so often fought unsuccessfully, one thing was necessary: that their dead should rise again. As soon as they were assured of this, as soon as the dead in endless numbers had really risen, then the war could begin. And the dead, when they returned, would restore to them not only the cattle and millet that they themselves had sacrificed, but all that had ever been sacrificed to them.

The slaughtered cattle and the corn which had been destroyed had the function of crowd crystals, attracting to themselves *all* corn and cattle. (In earlier times, human beings as well would certainly have been sacrificed to the same end.) Then, on the appointed day, the pastures would teem with new herds and the millet stand ripe in the fields.

Thus the whole project turned on the reappearance of the dead, bringing with them the means of life. For this great end the living sacrificed everything, strengthened in their purpose by those among the dead whom they *knew*. The prophet's brother and the two former councillors of the old chief were guarantors of the pact with the dead. Anyone who opposed it, or hesitated over it, took from the crowd something which belonged to it and destroyed its unity. It would be better, therefore, if he were openly on the side of the enemy; with them he would go down to destruction.

If one considers the catastrophic outcome of these events in the light of the Xosas' own beliefs—the fact that on the promised day nothing happened, no fields of millet appeared, no herds and no army of the dead—then one may say that they had indeed been deceived by their dead. The dead had not meant the agreement seriously; they were not concerned with victory over the white men, but simply with their own aggrandisement. By false pretences, they got hold of, first, the grain and the cattle of the living, and then the living themselves, who died of starvation. Thus the dead *were* victorious, but in a different manner and a different war. In the end, it was they who were left as the *largest crowd*.

Also of particular importance in the behaviour of the Xosas is the rôle of *commands*. A command stands alone; there is something isolated about it. The dead from whom it comes need an intermediary to pass it on; and for this they make use throughout of the temporal hierarchy. The prophet must address himself to the chiefs and persuade them to accept the commands of the spirits. As soon as Kreli, the Paramount Chief, has declared his acceptance, everything follows the normal chain of command. Messengers are sent to all the Xosa clans including those under the "false" rule of the British. Even the unbelieving, who for a long time oppose the carrying out of the scheme—among them Kreli's uncle and his chief councillor—ultimately submit and the reason they give is: It is the chief's "Command".

The story becomes more extraordinary still when we consider the *content* of the command. What it actually refers to is the slaughter of cattle, that is, *killing*. The more insistently it is repeated, the more comprehensive its application becomes. It becomes a crowd event and anticipates war itself. Seen in its light, the cattle stand for the *enemy*. They stand for them and for *their* cattle, as the corn which is destroyed stands for *their* corn. The war begins in the aggressors' own country, but is waged as though they were already in the enemy's; the command meanwhile resumes its original character of *death sentence*, the instinctive death sentence decreed by one species upon another.

Over all the animals that man keeps captive hangs his death sentence. It is, it is true, *suspended*, and often for a long time, but it is never remitted. Thus, man with impunity inflicts on his animals the death of which he is always conscious. The span of life he allows them is as set as his own, but in their case *he* decides when it is over. Their death is easier for him when he has many of them and those to be slaughtered can be chosen out of a whole herd. Then his two aims—the increase of his herds and the killing of the individual beasts which he needs—can easily be combined. Here, as herdsman, he has more power than any hunter. His animals are all in one place and do not flee from him. The duration of their lives is in his hands. He does not have to kill them when and where he finds them. The *force* of the hunter has become the *power* of the herdsman.

Thus the command laid on the Xosas is the command in its essence. The carrying out of the death sentence on their cattle must precede the slaughter of their enemies, as though the two killings were at bottom one: they are one.

It should be noticed that the command to kill comes from the dead themselves, as though they were the final authority. And in the end, in fact, they compel everything and everyone to come over to their side. Among them are generations of chiefs, all those who gave orders in life. Their united authority is great, and would still be great even if they appeared among the living as men like themselves, not as the dead. But one cannot escape the impression that death has increased their power. The fact that, through the prophet, they can make themselves heard, that they appear at all, and speak to him, adds to their former natural authority a supernatural one; they have cheated death and are still impressively active. To circumvent death, to evade it, is one of the oldest and strongest desires of rulers. In this connection it is worth adding that Kreli survived by many years his people's death from starvation.

THE ENTRAILS OF POWER

Seizing and Incorporation

THE PSYCHOLOGY of seizing and incorporating, like that of eating in general, is still completely unexplored. We tend to take the whole process for granted and never reflect on the mysteriousness of much that occurs in the course of it. There is nothing about us which is more strongly primitive. It is something we share with animals, but even this strange fact has not so far made us pay more attention to it.

The approach, with hostile intent, of one creature to another falls into several distinct acts, each of which has its particular traditional significance. First there is the lying in wait for prey; the prey is marked down long before it is aware of our designs on it. With feelings of pleasure and approval it is contemplated, observed and kept watch over; it is seen as meat whilst it is still alive, and so intensely and irrevocably seen as meat that nothing can deflect the watcher's determination to get hold of it. Already while he is prowling round it he feels that it *belongs* to him. From the moment he selects it as his prey, he thinks of it as incorporated into himself.

This watching and lying in wait for prey is a state of such peculiar tension that it can acquire a significance of its own independent of circumstances. It is a state which one tends to prolong. Later it may be induced for its own sake, without reference to any immediate prospect of prey. But man does not lie in ambush and turn persecutor with impunity. Anything of this kind which he actively undertakes, he also experiences passively in himself, in exactly the same form, only more strongly, for his greater intelligence is aware of more dangers and doubles the torment of being persecuted.

Man is not always strong enough to obtain his prey directly. The skill and experience in pursuit which he has acquired have resulted in his developing all kinds of complicated traps. Often he makes use of the power of transformation which is his specific gift and appears disguised as the animal he is after. He acts it so well that it believes him. This manner of trapping an animal may be termed flattery. The animal is told "I am like you. I am you. You can safely let me come near you."

After the stealthy approach and the leap—treated in another context—the next thing is the first *touching* of the prey. This is perhaps what is feared most. The fingers of the attacker feel what will soon belong to his whole body. Contact through the other senses, sight, hearing and smell, is not nearly so dangerous. With them there can be space between the attacker and the victim and, as long as this space exists, nothing is finally decided and there is still some chance of escape. The sensation of touch, on the other hand, is the forerunner of tasting. The fairy-tale witch asks her victim to stretch out a finger so that she can feel whether he is fat enough to eat.

The design of one body on the other becomes concrete from the moment of touching. Even at the lowest levels of life this moment has something decisive about it. It contains the oldest terrors; we dream of it, we imagine it, and civilized life is nothing but a sustained effort to avoid it. Whether resistance is continued after this moment, or is given up completely, depends on the ratio of power between the toucher and the touched, or rather on what the latter imagines this ratio to be. Usually he will fight on to try and save his skin and only if the power confronting him appears overwhelming will he abandon the attempt. The touch to which one resigns oneself because all resistance appears hopeless—and particularly so as regards the future—has, in our society, become the *arrest*. The feel of the hand of authority on his shoulder is usually enough to make a man give himself up without having to be actually seized. He cowers and goes quietly. He maintains an appearance of composure, even though it is not everywhere that this is justified by what is likely to happen to him subsequently.

The next stage of approach is the act of seizure. The fingers of the hand form a hollow into which they try to compress part of the creature they touch. They do this without regard to the shape and organic cohesion of the prey. Whether they injure it or not at this stage is irrelevant; it is simply that some part of its body has to be got into the space thus formed as a pledge for the whole. This space within the grasping hand is the anteroom of the mouth and the stomach by which the prey is finally incorporated. With many animals it is the armed mouth itself which does the seizing, instead of hand or claw. Among men the hand which never lets go has become the very emblem of power: "He was delivered into his hands", "He was in their hands", "It is in God's hands". Similar expressions are common in all languages.

For the actual process of seizing what is really important is the *pressure* exerted by the human hand. The fingers close round the object seized; the hollow space into which this has been forced narrows. The aim is to be able to feel it with the whole inner surface of the hand, and to feel it more firmly. The original lightness and delicacy of touch is first extended to a wider area, then strengthened, and finally concentrated until that part of the body which is touched is as firmly compressed as possible. Pressure of this kind came to supersede the habit of using claws to rend the victim. It is true that in some archaic cults the victim was still clawed, but the actors were disguised as animals and what they did was deliberately bestial. For the real job, men came to rely on their teeth.

Pressure can increase until it crushes. Whether it actually reaches this point or not depends on how dangerous the prey is. If the attacker has had a hard fight to overcome it, if he has been seriously threatened by it, or enraged or injured, he will want to make it pay for this and will press harder than is necessary to make sure of it. But even more than fear or rage, it is contempt which urges him on to crush it. An insect, something so small that it scarcely counts, is crushed because one would not otherwise know what had happened to it; no human hand can form a hollow small enough for it. But, in addition to the desire to get rid of a pest and to be sure it is really disposed of, our behaviour to a gnat or a flea betrays the contempt we feel for a being which is utterly defenceless, which exists in a completely different order of size and power from us, with which we have nothing in common, into which we never transform ourselves and which we never fear except when it suddenly appears in crowds. The destruction of these tiny creatures is the only act of violence which remains unpunished even *within* us. Their blood does not stain our hands, for it does not remind us of our own. We never look into their glazing eyes. We do not eat them. They have never—at least not amongst us in the West—had the benefit of our growing, if not yet very effective, concern for life. In brief, they are outlaws. If I say to someone, "I could crush you with one hand", I am expressing the greatest possible contempt. It is as though I were saying "You are an insect. You mean nothing to me. I can do what I like with you and that won't mean anything to me either. You mean nothing to anyone. You can be destroyed with impunity without anyone noticing. It would make no difference to anyone. Certainly not to me."

The most extreme form of destruction through pressure, that is, *grinding*, cannot be achieved by the hand, for this is too soft. Grinding requires a great preponderance of weight and hard objects above and below, between which something is ground. If he wants to do this himself, man has to use his teeth. In general we do not think of something living when we speak of grinding; the process is relegated to inorganic nature, the word being most frequently used in connection with natural catastrophes such as the fall of large rocks which grind or pulverize living creatures. The word is used in a figurative sense, but is never taken quite literally. It conveys the idea of a destructive power not really proper to man himself. There is something impersonal about it. The body as such is not capable of grinding and therefore magnanimously renounces it. The most it is capable of is "an iron grip".

It is remarkable what respect this is accorded. The functions of the hand are so manifold that it is not surprising that there should be a large number of expressions connected with them. But the hand's real glory derives from the *grip*, that central and most often celebrated act of power. The moment of seizing, which is decisive amongst animals as well as amongst men, has always created the strongest impression on men, and their superstitious awe of the great cats of prey, the tiger and the lion, is based upon it. These are the great *seizers* and they do their seizing alone. With them, the lying in wait and watching, the sudden leap, the thrusting in of the claws and the mauling are all still one. The momentum of the action, its pitilessness, the assurance with which it is carried out, the never questioned superiority of the killer, the fact that he can choose whatever he wants as his prey—all this has contributed to his enormous prestige. However we look at it, this is the highest concentration of power and, as such, has made an ineradicable impression on man; all kings have wanted to be lions. It is the very act of seizing and its success which has been admired and praised. The simple exercise of superior strength has been universally regarded as courage and greatness.

The lion does not have to transform himself in order to catch his prey; he remains himself throughout. Before he goes hunting he makes himself known by his roar; he alone can afford to announce his intention loudly and audibly to every creature. This reveals an indestructible arrogance which can never be deflected and which, for this very reason, spreads even greater terror. Power at its core and its apex despises transformation. It is sufficient unto itself and wills only itself. In this form it has always seemed remarkable to man; free and absolute, it exists for nothing and no one except itself. This is the peak of its glory and, to this very day, it seems as though there were nothing which could prevent its reappearance in the same form.

There is, however, a second act of power which is not quite so glorious but no less essential. Dazzled by the grandeur of the act of seizing we tend to forget that there is something equally important which runs parallel to it, namely, to avoid being seized.

All the empty space which a man who holds power creates round himself serves this second purpose. Every man, even the least, seeks to prevent anyone else coming too near him. Every form of social life established amongst men expresses itself in distances which allay the ceaseless fear of being seized and caught. Symmetry, which is so striking a feature of many ancient civilizations, derives in part from man's attempt to create uniform distances all round himself. Within these civilizations, safety is based on distances and is also emblematically expressed by them. The ruler on whose existence that of everyone else depends stands furthest and most clearly apart; in this, and not only in his splendour, he is equated with the sun, or, as among the Chinese, with the sky itself, which is even more spacious. Access to him is made difficult, palaces with more and more rooms being built round him. Each gate and each door is heavily guarded so that it is impossible to intrude on him against his will. He, from his remote security, can have anyone seized wherever he may be. But how is anyone to seize him, protected as he is by his hundredfold separation?

The actual *incorporation* of the prey begins in the mouth. From hand to mouth is the route followed by everything which can be eaten. Among the many creatures which have no arms for grasping, the process is initiated by the mouth itself, by the teeth or by a beak protruding from it.

The most striking natural instrument of power in man and in many animals is the teeth. The way they are arranged in rows and their shining smoothness are quite different from anything else belonging to the body. One feels tempted to call them the very first manifestation of order and one so striking that it almost shouts for recognition. It is an order which operates as a threat to the world outside, not always visible, but visible whenever the mouth opens, which is often. The substance of the teeth differs from that of all the other visible parts of the body and would be impressive even if people only had two teeth. They are smooth, hard and unyielding and can be clenched without any change of shape; they make the same effect as well polished and firmly set stones.

From a very early stage man used all kinds of stones as weapons and tools, but it was a long time before he learnt to polish them to the smoothness of teeth. It is probable that his teeth served him as a model for the improvement of his tools. The teeth of all kinds of large animals had always been useful to him; he might have captured them at the risk of his life and some of the power of the animal which had threatened him still seemed to him to be contained in them. He wore them as trophies and talismans to pass on to others the terror they had once aroused in him. He proudly displayed on his body the scars they had caused; these ranked as badges of honour and were so much desired that they were often artificially produced.

Thus both his own teeth and those of alien and stronger animals affected man in a wide variety of ways. By their very nature they occupied a position midway between an actual part of the body and a tool. The fact that they could fall out, or be knocked out, made them even more like a tool.

Smoothness and *order*, the manifest attributes of the teeth, have entered into the very nature of power. They are inseparable from it and, in every manifestation of power, they are the first things to be established. The conjunction began with primitive tools, but, as power grew, these early attributes became more pronounced. The leap from stone to metal was perhaps the most striking move in the direction of increased smoothness. However much stone was polished, the sword, made first of bronze and then of iron, was smoother. The real attraction of metal lies in the fact that it is smoother than anything else. In the machines and vehicles of the contemporary world smoothness has increased and has also become smoothness of performance. Language expresses this very simply; we say "everything is going smoothly", or "functions smoothly"; and we mean by this that some process is completely and undisturbedly within our power. In modern life the bias towards smoothness has spread to fields where it formerly tended to be avoided. Houses and furniture used to be decorated, as were the limbs and bodies of men. Modes of decoration changed, but decoration always existed and was obstinately preserved even after it had lost its symbolical meaning. Today smoothness has conquered our houses, their walls and all the objects we put into them; ornament and decoration are despised and regarded as a sign of bad taste. We speak of function, clarity of line and utility, but what has really triumphed is smoothness, and the prestige of the power it conceals.

The example of modern architecture shows how difficult it is to separate smoothness from order. Their common history is old, as old as the teeth. The uniformity of the whole row of front teeth and the regular spaces between them stood as models for many different kinds of arrangements. Many of those which we take for granted today may originally have derived from them. The order of military formations, which is artificially created by man himself, is in myth connected with teeth: the soldiers of Cadmus, who sprang from the soil, were sown as dragon's teeth.

There are certainly other instances of order to be seen in nature, that of various grasses for example, and the more rigid one of trees. But man did not find these in himself as he did teeth; they were not so directly and uninterruptedly linked with his intake of food, and it was not so easy to make use of them. It was the fact that the teeth are used for biting which so emphatically drew man's attention to their order, and the fact that they fall out with unpleasant consequences which made him conscious of the importance of this order.

The teeth are the armed guardians of the mouth and the mouth is indeed a strait place, the prototype of all prisons. Whatever goes in there is lost, and much goes in whilst still alive. Large numbers of animals first kill their prey only in the mouth, and some not even then. The readiness with which the mouth opens in anticipation of prey, the ease with which, once shut, it remains shut, recall the most feared attributes of a prison. It can scarcely be wrong to assume that the mouth did in fact exert a hidden influence on prisons. Primitive man certainly knew other creatures besides whales in whose mouth there was room for him. In this terrible place nothing could thrive, even if there were time to settle there. It is barren and nothing can take root in it. When the gaping maws of dragons had been virtually extirpated, man found a symbolic substitute for them in prisons. In times when these used to be torture chambers they resembled a hostile mouth in many respects. Hell still presents the same appearance today. Prisons, on the other hand, have become puritanical. The smoothness of teeth has conquered the world; the walls of cells are all smooth and even the window opening is small. For the prisoner, freedom is the space beyond the clenched teeth, and these are now represented by the bare walls of his cell.

The narrow gorge through which everything has to pass is, for the few who live so long, the ultimate terror. Man's imagination has been continually occupied by the several stages of incorporation. The gaping jaws of the large beasts which threatened him have pursued him even into his dreams and myths. Voyages of discovery down these jaws were no less important to him than those over the sea, and certainly as dangerous. Some who had given up all hope were pulled living out of the maw of these beasts and bore the marks of their teeth on them for the rest of their lives.

The road that the prey travels through the body is a long one and on the way all its substance is sucked out of it; everything useful is abstracted from it till all that remains is refuse and stench.

This process, which stands at the end of every act of seizing, gives us a clue to the nature of power in general.

Anyone who wants to rule men first tries to humiliate them, to trick them out of their rights and their capacity for resistance, until they are as powerless before him as animals. He uses them like animals and, even if he does not tell them so, in himself he always knows quite clearly that they mean just as little to him; when he speaks to his intimates he will call them sheep or cattle. His ultimate aim is to incorporate them into himself and to suck the substance out of them. What remains of them afterwards does not matter to him. The worse he has treated them, the more he despises them. When they are no more use at all, he disposes of them as he does of his excrement, simply seeing to it that they do not poison the air of his house.

He will not dare to identify all the individual stages of this process even to himself. If he is a braggart he may admit to his familiars that he degrades to the status of animals the men he procures for himself. But, since he does not have his subjects slaughtered in slaughter-houses nor actually use them to feed his body, he will deny that he sucks them dry and digests them; on the contrary, it is he who feeds them. Thus it is easy to overlook the real nature of these processes, particularly as man has learnt to keep animals which he does not kill, or not immediately, since they are of more use to him in other ways.

But, quite apart from the person who wields power and knows how to concentrate so much in his two hands, the relation of each and every man to his own excrement belongs to the sphere of power. Nothing has been so much part of one as that which turns into excrement. The constant pressure which, during the whole of its long progress through the body, is applied to the prey which has become food; its dissolution and intimate union with the creature digesting it; the complete and final annihilation, first of all functions and then of everything which once constituted its individuality; its assimilation to something already existing, that is, to the body of the eater—all this may very well be seen as the central, if most hidden, process of power. It is so much a matter of course, so automatic and so far beyond consciousness, that one underrates its importance. One tends to see only the thousand tricks of power which are enacted above ground; but these are the least part of it. Underneath, day in, day out, is digestion and again digestion. Something alien is seized, cut up into small bits, incorporated into oneself, and assimilated. By this process alone man lives; if it ceases, he dies. So much he has always known. But it is clear that *all* the phases of this process, and not only the external and half-conscious ones, must have their correspondence in the psyche. It is not altogether easy to find these correspondences. We shall, however, come on clear traces of them in the course of our enquiry, and shall follow them up. As will be seen, the symptoms of *melancholia* are especially illuminating in this context.

The excrement, which is what remains of all this, is loaded with our whole blood guilt. By it we know what we have murdered. It is the compressed sum of all the evidence against us. It is our daily and continuing sin and, as such, it stinks and cries to heaven. It is remarkable how we isolate ourselves with it; in special rooms, set aside for the purpose, we get rid of it; our most private moment is when we withdraw there; we are alone only with our excrement. It is clear that we are ashamed of it. It is the age-old seal of that power-process of digestion, which is enacted in darkness and which, without this, would remain hidden for ever.

The Hand

THE HAND OWES its origin to life in trees. Its primary characteristic is the separation of the thumb. It is the thumb's powerful development, and the gap between it and the other fingers, which make it possible to use what was once a claw to grasp whole branches and thus make it easy and natural to move about in trees: we see from the monkeys how useful hands are in this respect. As is now generally recognized, this is the oldest function of the hand.

There is, however, a tendency to overlook the fact that the two hands have different functions in climbing; they do not do the same thing at the same time. While the one hand is reaching for a new branch, the other holds fast to the old one. This holding fast is of cardinal importance, for in rapid movement it alone prevents a fall. In no circumstances must the hand from which the weight of the body is suspended loosen its hold, and this teaches the hand a tenacity of grip which is quite different from the older grip on prey. In addition, as soon as the second hand has grasped the new branch, the first hand must loosen its grip on the old one. Unless this is done quickly the climbing creature cannot proceed. The hand thus acquires a new faculty: the ability to let go of something instantly. Prey was never reliquished except under extreme pressure and against all the habits and desires of the holder.

For each hand, therefore, the act of climbing consists of two consecutive stages: grasping, letting go; grasping, letting go. It is true that one hand does the same as the other, but a stage later. At any given moment each is doing the opposite of the other. What distinguishes monkeys from other animals is the quick succession of these two movements; grasping and letting go follow immediately on each other, and it is to this that they owe part of the marvellous nimbleness we admire in them.

The higher monkeys or apes, who have abandoned the trees for the ground, have retained this essential faculty by which the two hands, as it were, partner each other; and there is a widespread human occupation which, in the whole manner of its pursuit, clearly recalls it: this is *trading*.

The essence of trading is the giving of one object in exchange for another. The one hand tenaciously holds on to the object with which it seeks to tempt the stranger. The other hand is stretched out in demand towards the second object, which it seeks to have in exchange for its own. As soon as it touches this, the first hand lets go of its object; but not before, or it may lose both. The crudest form of cheating, when something is taken from someone without any return being made, corresponds, translated into the context of climbing, to falling from the tree. To prevent this the trader remains on his guard during the whole transaction and scrutinizes every movement of his opposite number. The profound and universal pleasure men take in trading is thus partly explained by the fact that trade is a translation into non-physical terms of one of the oldest movement patterns. In nothing else today is man so near the apes.

After this sortie into a much later time let us return to the hand itself and its origins. Among the branches of trees the hand learned a mode of grasp which was no longer solely concerned with immediate food. The route from hand to mouth, which is short and scarcely susceptible of variation, was thus interrupted. A branch which broke off in the hand was the origin of the *stick*. Enemies could be fended off with a stick and space made for the primitive creature who perhaps no more than resembled man. Seen from a tree, the stick was the weapon which lay nearest to hand. Man put his trust in it and has never abandoned it. It was a cudgel; sharpened, it became a spear; bent and the ends tied together, a bow; skilfully cut, it made arrows. But through all these transformations it remained what it had been originally: an instrument to create distance, something which kept away from men the touch and the grasp that they feared. In the same way that the upright human stance still retains a measure of grandeur, so, through all its transformations the stick has never wholly lost its magical quality; as sceptre and as sorcerer's wand it has remained the attribute of two important forms of power.

THE ENTRAILS OF POWER 213

The Patience of the Hand

It is the violent activities of the hands which are thought of as the oldest. We not only think of the act of seizing with hostile intent, which is expected to be cruel and sudden, but automatically, and in spite of their technical complexity and the remoteness of their derivation, we add to the group many movements which in fact only developed later: hitting, stabbing, thrusting, throwing, shooting. The speed and precision of these movements may be greater, but in substance and in intent they have remained the same. They are important for hunters and soldiers, but they have added nothing to the special glory of the human hand.

The hand has found other ways to perfect itself and these, in all cases, are ways which renounce predatory violence. Its true greatness lies in its *patience*. It is the quiet, prolonged activities of the hand which have created the only world in which we care to live. The potter whose hands are skilled in shaping clay stands as creator at the beginning of the Bible.

But how did the hands learn patience? How did the fingers of the hand become sensitive? One of the earliest occupations we know of is the picking over of the fur of a friend which monkeys delight in. We imagine that they are searching for something and, as they often do undoubtedly find something, we have ascribed a purely practical and far too narrow purpose to this activity. In reality they do it principally for the agreeable sensation that the individual fingers receive from the hairs of the skin. It constitutes the most primitive "finger exercises" that we know. It was through them that the hand became the delicate instrument we marvel at today.

The Finger Exercises of Monkeys

Everyone who observes monkeys is struck by their solicitous mutual examination of each other's coats. The meticulous way in which they separate and observe each individual hair leads one to suppose that they are hunting for vermin. Their posture recalls that of men looking for fleas, and their hands go carefully to their mouths as though they had found something—so frequently and productively, in fact, that it seems to prove the necessity of such a search. This, therefore, has always been the popular interpretation of it. Only recently has the proceeding been more precisely explained by zoologists.

A coherent description and analysis of this monkey habit may be

found in Zuckerman's book *The Social Life of Monkeys and Apes.*
It is so revealing that I shall quote from it an length.

" 'Flea-catching', regardless of what the sociologists may have to
say, is the most fundamental and basal form of social intercourse
between Rhesus monkeys. Monkeys, and to a lesser extent apes, spend
a great part of the day grooming one another. An animal will carefully examine a fellow's coat with its fingers, eating many of the odds
and ends that it finds. These are carried to its mouth either by hand
or sometimes, after licking a tuft of hair, by direct nibbling. The
performance implies exceedingly well co-ordinated movements of the
fingers, associated with exact accommodation and convergence of the
eyes. This behaviour is commonly misinterpreted as an attempt to
remove lice. Actually vermin are rarely found on either captive or wild
monkeys. The fruits of the search generally turn out to be small, loose,
scaly fragments of skin, particles of skin secretion, thorns and other
foreign matter. When not engaged in other pursuits, monkeys react
immediately to the presence of fur by 'picking'. The stimulus of hair
is one to which a monkey responds as soon as it is born, and one which
remains powerfully effective in all phases of its growth. In the lack of a
companion, a healthy monkey will pick through its own fur. Two,
and sometimes even three, monkeys may, as a group, pick over one of
their fellows. Usually the one being cleaned is passive, except for
movements which facilitate the investigations carried out by its grooms.
Sometimes, however, it may simultaneously be engaged in picking
through the coat of yet another animal. Monkeys do not confine their
grooming activities to their own kind. Any hairy object, animate or
inanimate, may form the subject of their investigations. They readily
pick over the hair of a human 'friend'. They may be seen in captivity,
and have been seen in the wild, picking through the fur of animals
belonging to different orders. The performance seems to have sexual
significance, not only because of its gentle stimulation of numerous
cutaneous end organs, but also because it is sometimes accompanied
by direct sexual activity. For this reason and because of its frequent
expression, it is perhaps legitimate to regard the picking reaction and
the stimulus of hair as factors involved in the maintenance of a social
group of sub-human primates."

The surprising thing in this account is Zuckerman's attribution of
sexual significance. He speaks of two or three monkeys together
picking over the fur of a companion, and he stresses the significance for
them of all kinds of fur. Later in his book he *contrasts* this "picking"
with sexual activity and points out that even in periods of sexual

inactivity when they show little sign of such interest, they still come to the bars of their cages to be scratched. He also has a good deal to say about the early significance of fur for the young monkey.

The first external phenomenon of which a monkey has any sensory experience is hair. As soon as a baby monkey or ape is born it is pulled by its mother to her breast, and its fingers immediately clutch and hold her fur. "Unaided, the young animal finds the nipple by 'trial and error'. For about the first month of its life it lives entirely on milk, and is carried by its mother wherever she goes. When the mother is sitting, the young animal is generally held close to her body, with its feet clutching at the hair of her belly and its hands buried in the fur of her chest. When she moves the baby hangs on in the same way, slung, as it were, beneath her. Usually it holds on by its own unaided efforts, but sometimes the mother clasps it with one 'arm', while she hops along on three 'legs'. When she is sitting she may embrace her baby with both arms. The baby manifests a strong interest in fur. It crawls over it's mother's fur; within a week it may scratch its own body. I once observed a monkey, a week old, vaguely exploring with its hands the fur of its father, who was sitting close to its mother. Sometimes the mother monkey behaves as though she were irritated by having her fur clutched." One monkey in the London Gardens persisted in pulling away the hands and feet of her infant wherever they clasped.

The behaviour of a nursing monkey does not alter when her baby dies. She continues to press it to her breast and carries it in her arms wherever she goes. "At first she never puts it down, picking through its fur as she did when it lived. She examines its mouth and its eyes, its nose and its ears. In a few days one notices a change in her behaviour. A slightly decomposing body now droops over her arms. Except when moving, she no longer presses it to her breast, and although she continues to groom the body and to bite at the skin, she begins to lay it on the ground more frequently. The body becomes yet more decomposed, and mummification sets in, but her investigation of the skin and fur continues. The dried-up body now begins to disintegrate. One notices a leg missing, an arm missing, and it is soon a shrivelled bit of skin. The mother is more often seen biting off pieces—it is unknown whether she swallows them. At about this stage she may abandon of her own accord what is left of the shrivelled remains."

Monkeys often retain many kinds of furry and feathery objects. Zuckerman observed a year-old baboon who seized a young kitten, killed it and kept it in her arms the whole day, picking through its fur meanwhile, and protesting vigorously when it was removed in the evening. Monkeys in the London Zoo can be seen picking through the feathers of sparrows they have killed. Also recorded is the case of a captive monkey who mothered the dead body of a rat thrown to her as elaborately as the monkey described above mothered her own dead infant.

From the evidence he collected Zuckerman deduced that there are three factors which contribute to effective maternal behaviour. The two primary ones are fundamentally of social significance: first, the mother's attraction to a small furry object, and second, the living baby's strong attraction to its mother's fur. The third factor is the sucking reflex of the young animal, whose operation relieves mammary tension in the mother.

The reaction to fur is thus a basic factor in social behaviour. Its importance is indicated by the fact that a young primate will cling to its mother's fur even after her death; but its attraction is apparently not to the specific body, since it is equally soothed by the carcase of any other dead baboon. "The fundamental nature of the reaction to fur is perhaps also indicated by its ill-defined character and by the variety of the situations in which it is evoked. Feathers, brooms, mice, kittens are all adequate stimuli. It seems very likely that the social performance of grooming develops from this innate response to fur, and that it always remains one of the fundamental bonds holding monkeys together."

It will be seen from these lengthy extracts that Zuckerman himself does not really believe in the specific sexual significance of the grooming of the coat among primates. He is quite clear that fur, in itself, and in all circumstances, has a peculiar attraction for monkeys. The pleasure which the touch of hair affords them must be of a quite particular kind, and they seek it from any source, the dead as well as the living, and strangers as well as their own kind. The size of the animal they tend does not matter. For this purpose the baby means as much to the mother as the mother to the baby. Mating couples and friends indulge in it equally and several animals may occupy themselves simultaneously with the fur of one.

The pleasure is a pleasure of the *fingers*. They can never have enough of hair; they can spend whole hours drawing their fingers through it. And these are the animals whose liveliness and inconsequent mobility are proverbial. There is an old Chinese tradition according to which monkeys have no stomachs and digest their food by leaping around. Hence the contrast to the endless patience they display in this kind of grooming is all the more striking. Through it the fingers become more and more sensitive. The feeling of many hair tips simultaneously engenders a particular sense of touch which is entirely different from the crude sensation of snatching or grasping. One is irresistibly put in mind of all those later occupations of mankind which depend on the delicacy and patience of the fingers. The as yet unknown ancestors of man, like all the apes, had a long period of such finger exercises behind them. Without these our hands would never have developed as far as they have. Various factors may originally have given rise to this grooming; perhaps the search for parasites and perhaps the early experiences of the baby ape at the hairy breast of its mother. But the process itself, in the developed state in which it can be observed in all monkeys, has a unified significance of its own. Without it we should never have learnt to *shape* anything, nor to sew, nor to *stroke*. The real specific life of the hand begins with it. As a man watched his hands at work, the changing shapes they fashioned must gradually have impressed themselves on his mind. Without this we should probably never have learnt to form symbols for things, nor, therefore, to *speak*.

The Hands and the Birth of Objects

The hand which scoops up water is the first vessel. The fingers of both hands intertwined are the first basket. The rich development of all kinds of intertwining, from the game of cat's cradle to weaving, seems to me to have its origin here. One feels that hands live their own life and their own transformations. It is not enough that this or that shape should exist in the surrounding world. Before early man could create it himself, his hands and fingers had to enact it. Empty fruit husks in the shape of cups, like coconut shells, may have existed for a long time, but were thrown away heedlessly. It was the fingers forming a hollow to scoop up water which made the cup real. One could say that objects in our sense, objects which have value because we ourselves have made them, first existed as signs made by hands. There seems to be an immensely important turning point where the nascent sign language for things first comprehends a desire to shape them oneself, long before this is actually attempted.

What man, with the help of his hands, enacted, was only *made* long afterwards, when it had been enacted often enough. *Words* and *objects* are accordingly the emanations and products of a single unified experience: *representation by means of the hands*. Everything that a man can do, everything that represents his culture, he first incorporated into himself by means of transformation. Hands and face were the instruments of these transformations and their significance, compared with the rest of the body, became increasingly great. The specific life of the hands, in this its earliest sense, still retains its pristine force in gesticulation.

Destructiveness in Monkeys and Men

Destructiveness in monkeys and men can plausibly be regarded as "hardening exercises" of the hands and fingers. Life in trees brought the hands of the climbing monkey into constant contact with a material harder than themselves. To make use of the branches of trees he had to hold on to them, but he also had to know how to break them. The testing of his "ground" was a testing of branches and twigs; one that broke easily was a false basis for progress. The exploration of the tree world was a ceaseless confrontation of hardness. It still remained necessary for him to test it even when he had acquired considerable experience of it. The stick which, to him as to men, became the earliest weapon, was the first in the long series of *hard* instruments. The hardness of the hands was measured against it, as later against stones. Fruit and the flesh of animals was soft; softest of all was fur. The grooming and picking of the coat trained the delicacy of the fingers; the breaking of whatever they held their strength.

There is thus a separate destructiveness of the hand, not immediately connected with prey and killing. It is of a purely mechanical nature and mechanical inventions are extensions of it. Precisely because of its innocence it has become particularly dangerous. It knows itself to be without any intention to kill, and thus feels free to embark on anything. What it does appears to be the concern of the hands alone, of their flexibility and skill, their harmless usefulness. It is this mechanical destructiveness of the hands, now grown to a complex system of technology, which, whenever it is linked with a real intention to kill, supplies the automatic element of the resulting process, that empty mindlessness which is so particularly disquieting. No one actually intends anything; it all happens, as it were, of itself.

Privately, and on a small scale, everyone experiences the same process in himself whenever his fingers thoughtlessly break matches or crumple paper. The multiform ramifications which this mechanical urge to destroy exhibits amongst men are closely connected with the development of his tool-using technique. It was through it that he learnt to master the hard with the hard. But, in the last resort, it is always the hands that matter. Their faculty of independent life has had tremendous consequences. In more than one respect, man's hands have been his destiny.

The Killers are always the Powerful

It is not only the whole hand which has served as a model and stimulus. The individual fingers, and particularly the extended index finger, have also acquired a significance of their own. The tip of the finger is pointed and armoured with a nail. It first provided man with the sensation of stabbing. From it developed the dagger, which is a harder and more pointed finger. The arrow is a cross between finger and bird; it was lengthened in order to penetrate further, and made more slender to fly better. Beak and thorn also influenced its composition; beaks in any case are proper to feathered objects. A pointed stick became a spear, an arm extended into a single finger.

All weapons of this kind are concentrated on a point. Man was himself stabbed by long, hard thorns and pulled them out with his fingers. The finger which detached itself from the rest of the hand and, acting like a thorn, passed on the stab is the psychological origin of this kind of weapon. The man who has been stabbed stabs back with his finger and with the artificial finger he gradually learns to make.

Not all the operations of the hand are invested with the same degree of power; their prestige varies greatly. Things which are particularly important for the practical existence of a group of men may be highly valued, but the greatest respect is always accorded to anything which has to do with killing. That which can kill is feared; that which does not directly serve killing is merely useful. All that the patient skills of the hand bring to those who confine themselves to them is subjection. It is those who devote themselves to killing who have power.

On the Psychology of Eating

EVERYTHING WHICH IS eaten is the food of power. The hungry man feels empty space within himself. He overcomes the discomfort which this causes him by filling himself with food. The fuller he is the better he feels. The man who can eat more than anyone else lies back satisfied and heavy with food; he is a champion. There are peoples who take such a champion eater for their chief. His full belly seems to them a guarantee that they themselves will never go hungry for long. It is as though he had filled it for all of them. The connection between power and digestion is obvious here.

With other forms of chiefdom the eating capacity of the ruler
becomes less significant. It is no longer necessary that his girth should
be greater than that of everyone else. But he continues to eat and drink
copiously with members of his entourage, and the food and drink he
sets before them *belongs to him*. He may not be the largest eater himself,
but he owns the largest store of food, the most corn and the most
cattle. If he wanted to, he could still always be the champion eater, but
he transfers the satisfaction of repletion to his court, to those who eat
with him, only reserving for himself the right to be offered everything
first. But the king in his character of champion eater has never wholly
disappeared. Time and again the rôle is re-enacted for the benefit of
delighted subjects. Ruling groups in general are also prone to gluttony;
the feats of the later Romans are proverbial, in this respect, and all
families whose power is securely established tend to exhibit themselves
in this way and are later imitated and surpassed by those newly arrived.

In many societies the capacity and the passion for extravagance have
gone as far as formal, ritually ordered orgies of destruction. The most
famous of these is the Potlatch of the Indians of north-western America
which consisted of great festal assemblies of the whole community,
culminating in contests of destruction among the chiefs. Each chief
boasted of the amount of property he was prepared to destroy. The
one who destroyed most was the victor and enjoyed the greatest fame.
Eating more than anyone else presupposes the destruction of animals
which belong to the eater. One has the impression that, in the Potlatch,
the destroying of other kinds of property is an extension of the destroying of eatables. Thus the chief was able to boast far more than if he
had actually had to eat everything, and in addition was spared the
physical consequences of doing so.

It may be useful to have a look at eating in general, independent of
the eater's position in the social scale. A certain esteem for each other
is clearly evident in all who eat together. This is already expressed by
the fact of their *sharing*. The food in the common dish before them
belongs to all of them together. Everyone takes some of it and sees
that others take some too. Everyone tries to be fair and not to take
advantage of anyone else. The bond between the eaters is strongest
when it is *one* animal they partake of, one body which they knew as a
living unit, or one loaf of bread. But the touch of solemnity in their
attitude cannot be explained by this alone; their mutual esteem also
means that they will not eat each other. It is true that membership of
the same group always carries a guarantee of this, but only in the
moment of eating is it convincingly expressed. People sit together,

bare their teeth and eat and, even in this critical moment, feel no desire to eat each other. They respect themselves for this, and respect their companions for an abstemiousness equal to their own.

In a *family* the husband contributes food and the wife prepares it for him. The fact that he habitually eats what she has prepared constitutes the strongest link between them. Family life is closest where its members frequently eat together. When one thinks of it, the picture one forms is that of parents and children sitting round a table. Everything else seems to be a preparation for this moment. The more often and the more regularly it recurs, the more those who thus eat together feel themselves to be a family. To be accepted at the family table amounts almost to being accepted into the family.

This may be the most appropriate place to say something about the *mother*, who is the core and very heart of this institution. A mother is one who gives her own body to be eaten. She first nourishes the child in her womb and then gives it her milk. This activity continues in a less concentrated form throughout many years; her thoughts, in so far as she is a mother, revolve round the food the growing child needs. It does not have to be her own child; a strange child may be substituted for her own, or she may adopt one. Her passion is to give food, to watch the child eating and profiting by the food it eats; its growth and increase in weight are her constant aims. Her behaviour appears selfless and is so if one regards her as a separate unit, as one single human being. But what has really happened is that she now has two stomachs instead of one, and keeps control of both. At first she is more interested in the new stomach, and in the new and undeveloped body, than in her own; pregnancy has merely been externalized. The concept which I have put forward of digestion as a central process of power holds for the mother too, but in her case the process is distributed between two bodies and is made clearer and more conscious by the fact that the new body, for whose nourishment she provides, is separated from her own. The mother's power over a young child is absolute, not only because its life depends on her, but also because she herself feels a very strong urge to exercise this power all the time. The concentration of the appetite for domination on such a small organism gives rise to a feeling of superiority greater than that obtaining in any other habitual relationship between human beings.

She is occupied day and night with this domination, and its continuity and the enormous number of details in which it is expressed give it a roundness and perfection which no other kind of power achieves. It is not confined to the giving of orders, for these could not be understood by a very young child. It means that a creature is kept prisoner, even though in this case genuinely for its own advantage; that the mother, though without knowing what is happening, can pass on to it the commands imposed on *her* decades before and which she has since retained intact in herself; that she can enforce *growth*—something to which rulers only approximate by conferring promotions in rank. For the mother, the child combines the qualities of both plants and animals. It allows her the enjoyment of sovereign rights which can otherwise only be exercised separately; like a plant, she can make it grow in accordance with her wishes and, like an animal, she can keep it prisoner and control its movements. It grows under her hands like corn and like a domestic animal it carries out those movements which she permits it; it removes from her part of the long-standing burden of commands which weighs so heavily upon every civilized being and, finally, it grows into a man or a woman, a new and complete person, for whose accession the group in which she lives is permanently indebted to her. There is no intenser form of power. That the rôle of the mother is not normally seen in this light is due to two facts: first, that what everyone chiefly remembers is the period when this power is *decreasing*, and second, that the sovereign rights of the father are superficially more striking, though in reality far less important.

The family becomes rigid and hard when it excludes others from its meals; those that must be fed provide a natural pretext for the exclusion of others. The hollowness of this pretext is revealed by families which have no children and yet make not the slightest move to share their meal with others. The "family" of two is man's most contemptible creation. But, even where there are children, we may often feel that they are used as a mere cover for naked selfishness. People save "for the sake of the children" and allow others to starve. What they are really doing is keeping everything for themselves.

Modern man likes eating in restaurants, at separate tables, with his own little group, for which *he* pays. Since everyone else in the place is doing the same thing, he eats his meal under the pleasing illusion that everyone everywhere has enough to eat. Even sensitive people do not need this illusion afterwards; those who have eaten do not mind stumbling over the hungry.

The eater increases in weight; he is and he feels heavier, and there is a boast in this: he cannot grow any more, but there, on the very spot, under everyone's eyes, he can increase in weight. This is another reason why people like eating with others; it is a contest in repletion.

The satisfaction of repletion, of the moment when nothing more can be absorbed, is part of the goal and pleasure of eating and originally no-one was ashamed of it; there might be a large quantity of game which had to be eaten up before it went bad and so everyone ate as much as he could and carried his store of food within him.

Anyone who eats alone renounces the prestige which the process would bring him in the eyes of others. He bares his teeth simply for the sake of eating, and this impresses no-one, for there is no-one there to be impressed. But when people eat together, they can all see each other's mouths opening. Everyone can watch everyone else's teeth while his own are in action at the same time. To be without teeth is contemptible and there is a touch of asceticism in refusing to show those that one has. The natural occasion on which to show off one's teeth is when eating with others. Contemporary etiquette requires the mouth to be closed while eating and thus reduces to a minimum the slight threat contained in opening it at all. But we are not yet as harmless as this makes us appear; we eat with knife and fork, that is, with two instruments which could easily be used for attack; everyone has these ready in front of him, or he may even carry them around with him. And the bit of food which we cut off and, as elegantly as possible, shove in our mouths is still called a "bite".

Laughter has been objected to as vulgar because, in laughing, the mouth is opened wide and the teeth are shown. Originally laughter contained a feeling of pleasure in prey or food which seemed certain. A human being who falls down reminds us of an animal we might have hunted and brought down ourselves. Every sudden fall which arouses laughter does so because it suggests helplessness and reminds us that the fallen can, if we want, be treated as prey. If we went further and actually ate it, we would not laugh. We laugh *instead* of eating it. Laughter is our physical reaction to the escape of potential food. As Hobbes said, laughter expresses a sudden feeling of superiority, but he did not add that it only occurs when the normal consequences of this superiority do not ensue. His conception contains only half the truth. Perhaps because animals do not laugh, he did not see that our laughter is originally an animal reaction. But neither do animals deny themselves obtainable food if they really want it. Only man has learnt to replace the final stage of incorporation by a symbolic act. It is as though the whole interior process of gulping down food could be summed up and replaced by those movements of the diaphragm which are characteristic of laughter.

The only animal to make a sound really resembling human laughter is the hyena. This sound can be induced by placing food before a captive hyena and then withdrawing it quickly before the animal has time to snatch it. Here it is worth remembering that, in freedom, the hyena's food consists of carrion. It is easy to imagine how often food must have been snatched away from under its eyes by other animals after its own appetite had been aroused.

THE SURVIVOR

The Survivor

THE MOMENT OF *survival* is the moment of power. Horror at the sight of death turns into satisfaction that it is someone else who is dead. The dead man lies on the ground while the survivor stands. It is as though there had been a fight and the one had struck down the other. In survival, each man is the enemy of every other, and all grief is insignificant measured against this elemental triumph. Whether the survivor is confronted by one dead man or by many, the essence of the situation is that he feels *unique*. He sees himself standing there alone and exults in it; and when we speak of the power which this moment gives him, we should never forget that it derives from his sense of uniqueness and from nothing else.

All man's designs on immortality contain something of this desire for survival. He does not only want to exist for always, but to exist when others are no longer there. He wants to live longer than everyone else, and to *know* it; and when he is no longer there himself, then his name must continue.

The lowest form of survival is killing. As a man kills an animal for food, and cuts bits from it as it lies defenceless on the ground and divides it for himself and his kin to devour, so also, and in the same manner, he seeks to kill anyone who stands in his way, or sets himself up against him as an enemy. He wants to strike him down so that he can feel that he still stands while the other lies prostrate. But this other must not disappear completely; his physical presence as a corpse is indispensable for the feeling of triumph. Now the victor can do whatever he wants with him, and he cannot retaliate, but must lie there, never to stand upright again. His weapon can be taken away and pieces cut from his body and kept forever as trophies. This moment of confronting the man he has killed fills the survivor with a special kind of strength. There is nothing that can be compared with it, and there is no moment which more demands repetition.

For the survivor knows of many deaths. If he has been in battle he has seen those around him fall. He went into battle with the conscious intention of maintaining his ground against the enemy. His declared aim was to despatch as many of them as possible and he can only conquer if he succeeds. Victory and survival are one and the same to him. But a victor also has a price to pay. Many of his own people lie among the dead. Friend and foe share the battlefield; their dead are heaped together and often, indeed, can no longer be distinguished; a common grave awaits them.

Fortunate and favoured, the survivor stands in the midst of the fallen. For him there is one tremendous fact: while countless others have died, many of them his comrades, he is still alive. The dead lie helpless; he stands upright amongst them, and it is as though the battle had been fought in order for him to survive it. Death has been deflected from him to those others. Not that he has avoided danger; he, with his friends, stood in the path of death. They fell; he stands exulting.

This feeling of superiority to the dead is known to everyone who has fought in a war. It may be masked by grief for comrades, but these are few and the dead are always many. The feeling of strength, of standing alone against the dead, is in the end stronger than any grief. It is a feeling of being chosen from amongst the many who manifestly shared the same fate. Simply because he is still there, the survivor feels that he is *better* than they are. He has proved himself, for he is alive. He has proved himself among many others, for the fallen are not alive. The man who achieves this often is a *hero*. He is stronger. There is more life in him. He is the favoured of the gods.

Survival and Invulnerability

MAN'S BODY IS naked and vulnerable, exposed in its softness to every assault. With care and cunning he may be able to fend off things which come near, but it is easy to reach him from a distance; spears and arrows can transfix him. He has invented shields and armour, and built walls and whole fortresses round himself; what he most desires from all these precautions is a feeling of invulnerability.

There are two different ways by which he has sought to acquire this. They are exactly opposite to each other and their results, therefore, are also quite different. At times he has sought to keep danger at a distance. He has set large spaces between danger and himself, which can be watched and guarded. He has as it were, hidden from danger; he has banished it.

But the other way is the one on which he has always prided himself. He has sought out danger and confronted it. He has allowed it to approach as closely as possible and staked everything on the issue. Out of all possible situations, he has chosen the one involving risk and then enhanced that risk. He has made an enemy and challenged him—the man may have been his enemy already, or he himself may first have chosen him as one, but here, as always, his movement is towards the greatest danger and an ineluctable decision.

This is the way of the *hero*. What does the hero really want? What. is his true aim? The glory which all peoples accord their heroes—a tough and enduring glory if their deeds offer sufficient variety in quick succession—tends to mask their deeper motives. It is assumed that glory is their sole motive, but it is more likely that they were originally seeking for something different: for the ever-growing sense of invulnerability which can be won in this way.

The concrete situation in which the hero finds himself when he has overcome a danger is that of survivor. His enemy wanted his life as he his enemy's; this was the declared and fixed intent with which they met. The enemy succumbs, but the hero comes through the fighting unhurt and, filled with the consciousness of this prodigious fact, plunges into the next fight. No harm came to him, and no harm will, for each victory, each enemy killed, makes him feel more secure; his invulnerability armours him more and more completely.

There is no other way in which this feeling can be won. The man who hides from danger, or who banishes it, simply postpones the moment of decision. The man who faces it, and truly survives it; who then faces the next one; who piles up the moments of survival—he is the man who attains the feeling of invulnerability. Only when he has attained it does he actually become a hero, able to take any risk, for by then there is nothing that he fears. We might perhaps admire him more if he acted *in spite of* fear, but that is the point of view of a spectator, of someone who stands outside events. The people want their hero invulnerable.

A hero's deeds, however, are by no means confined to single combats. He may take on a whole pack of enemies and not only escape alive from the fight, but succeed in killing them, thus, as if at one blow, establishing his conviction of invulnerability.

Genghis Khan was once asked by one of his oldest and most faithful companions: "You are the ruler and you are called a hero. What marks of conquest and victory do you carry on you?" Genghis Khan replied: "Once, before I ascended the throne, I was riding along a road and I came on six men who lay in ambush by a bridge, waiting to attempt my life. When I got near, I drew my sword and attacked them. They showered me with a hail of arrows, but the arrows all went astray and none of them touched me. I killed all the men with my sword and rode on unharmed. On my way back, I passed the place where I had killed the six men. Their horses were straying riderless and I drove them home before me."

It was his invulnerability while fighting six enemies at once that Genghis Khan considered the certain mark of victory and conquest.

Survival as a Passion

THE SATISFACTION in survival, which is a kind of pleasure, can become a dangerous and insatiable passion. It feeds on its occasions. The larger and more frequent the heaps of dead which a survivor confronts, the stronger and more insistent becomes his need for them. The careers of heroes and soldiers suggest that a kind of addiction ensues, which in the end becomes incurable. The usual explanation of this is that such men can only breathe in danger; to them an existence without danger is stale and flat; they find no savour in a peaceful life. The attraction of danger should not be underestimated, but what we tend to forget is that such men do not set out on their adventures alone. There are others with them who succumb to the danger and this affords them the continually repeated pleasure of survival, which is what they really need and what they can no longer do without.

In order to satisfy this craving it is not always necessary to expose oneself to danger. No one man can himself kill enough other men. On a battlefield, however, there are thousands all acting in the same way, and, if a man is their commander, if he controls their movements, if the very battle springs from his decision, then he can appropriate to himself all the dead bodies which result from it, for he is responsible for them. It is not for nothing that the commander in the field bears his proud title. He commands; he sends his men against the enemy, and to their death. If he is victorious, all the dead on the battlefield belong to him, both those who fought for him and those who fought against him. In victory after victory he survives them all. And this is what he wants; the triumph he celebrates later leaves no doubt of it. The significance of his victories is measured by the number of the dead. A triumph is ludicrous when the enemy has surrendered without a proper fight and there are only a few dead. It is glorious when the enemy has defended himself bravely, when the victory was strongly contested and cost many lives.

"Caesar surpassed all other commanders in the fact that he fought more battles than any of them and killed greater numbers of the enemy. For, though his campaigns in Gaul did not last for as much as ten complete years, in this time he took by storm more than 800 cities, subdued 300 nations and fought pitched battles at various times with three million men, of whom he destroyed one million in the actual fighting and took another million prisoners."

This is the opinion of Plutarch, one of the humanest spirits mankind has produced, who cannot be reproached with war-lust or blood-thirstiness. It is worth considering for that reason, and because of the exactness of the reckoning. Caesar fought three million enemies, of whom he killed one million and made another million prisoners. The numbers were surpassed by later commanders, both Mongols and non-Mongols, but this judgment is significant for the naïvety with which everything that happened is ascribed to the commander alone: the towns taken by storm, the subjugated nations, the millions fought and captured, all belong to Caesar. But it is not Plutarch who is naïve; it is history. Ever since the Pharaohs described their battles, such reports have been customary, and to this day they have scarcely altered.

Caesar was fortunate and survived many enemies. It is considered tactless in such circumstances to reckon the victor's own losses. They are known, but one does not reproach the great man with them. In Caesar's case they were not excessive compared with the number of the enemy fallen. He did, none the less, survive several thousand of his allies and fellow Romans. Here, too, he was not entirely unsuccessful.

These proud balance sheets are handed down from generation to generation and each generation contains potential warrior-heroes whose passion to survive great crowds of fellow human beings is fanned to fury by them. History seemed to vindicate their purpose even before they had achieved it. Those who are most skilled in this kind of survival have the largest and securest place in it. Their fame depends in the end less on victory or defeat than on the monstrous number of their victims. Nobody knows what Napoleon's real feelings were during the retreat from Moscow.

The Ruler as Survivor

THE PARANOIAC type of ruler may be defined as one who uses every means to keep danger away from his person. Instead of challenging and confronting it and abiding the issue of a fight which might go against him, he seeks by circumspection and cunning to block its approach to him. He creates empty space all round him which he can survey, and he observes and assesses every sign of approaching danger. He does this on all sides, for he knows that he is dealing with many who may simultaneously advance against him, and this keeps awake in him the fear of being surrounded. Danger is everywhere, not only in front of him; it threatens especially from behind, where he might not notice it quickly enough. He has eyes all round him and not the slightest sound must escape his attention, for it might conceal a hostile intent.

The essence of all danger is naturally death and it is important to discover what is his special attitude to this. The first and decisive attribute of the autocrat is his power over life and death. No-one may come near him; a messenger, or anyone who has to approach him, is searched for weapons. Death is systematically kept away from him, but he himself may and must decree it. He may decree it as and when he wills and his sentence will always be executed; it is the seal of his power, and his power is only absolute so long as his right to decree death remains uncontested.

For the autocrat's only true subject is the man who will let himself be killed by him. This is the final proof of obedience and it is always the same. His soldiers are trained in a kind of double preparedness: they are sent to kill his enemies and they are ready to die for him. But all his other subjects too, who are not soldiers, know that he can pounce on them at any time. The terror that he spreads around him is part of him; it is his right, and it is for this right that he is most honoured: in extreme cases he will be worshipped for it. God himself has suspended the sentence of death over all living men, and over all who are yet to live. *When* the sentence is carried out depends on his whim. No one thinks of opposing it, for this would be fruitless.

Earthly rulers, however, are less fortunate than God, for they do not live for ever and their subjects know that to their days, too, an end is set; and that this end, like any other, can be hastened by violence. Any man who refuses obedience to his ruler, challenges him. No ruler can be permanently certain of the obedience of his subjects. As long as they allow themselves to be killed by him he can sleep in peace, but as soon as anyone evades his sentence he is endangered.

The sense of this danger is always alert in a ruler. Later, when the nature of command is discussed, it will be shown that his fears *must* increase the more often his commands are carried out. He can only calm his fears by making an example of someone. He will order an execution for its own sake, the victim's guilt being almost irrelevant. He *needs* executions from time to time and, the more his fears increase, the more he needs them. His most dependable, one might say his truest, subjects are those he has sent to their deaths.

For, from every execution for which he is responsible, some strength accrues to him. It is the strength of *survival* which he gains from it. His victims need not actually have challenged him, but they might have, and his fear transforms them—perhaps only retrospectively—into enemies who have fought against him. He condemns them; they are struck down and he survives them. The right to pronounce sentence of death becomes in his hands a weapon like any other, only far more effective. Many barbarian and oriental rulers have set great store on this heaping up of victims round them, where they can actually see them all the time; but, even where custom has been against such accumulation, the thoughts of rulers have been busy with it. The Emperor Domitian is reported to have contrived a macabre game of this kind. The banquet he arranged, which has certainly never been repeated in the same form, gives a clear picture of the inmost nature of the paranoiac ruler. The description of it by Dio Cassius runs as follows:

"On another occasion he entertained the foremost men among the senators and knights in the following fashion. He prepared a room that was pitch black on every side, ceiling, walls and floor, and had made ready bare couches of the same colour resting on the uncovered floor; then he invited in his guests, alone at night, without their attendants. And first he set beside each of them a slab shaped like a gravestone, bearing the guest's name, and also a small lamp, such as hangs in tombs. Next comely naked boys, likewise painted black, entered like phantoms, and after encircling the guests in an awe-inspiring dance took up their stations at their feet. After this all the things that are commonly offered at the sacrifices to departed spirits were likewise set before the guests, all of them black and in dishes of similar colour. Consequently, every single one of the guests feared and trembled and was kept in constant expectation of having his throat cut the next moment, the more so as on the part of everybody except Domitian there was dead silence, as if they were already in the realms of the dead, and the emperor himself conversed only upon topics relating to death and slaughter. Finally he dismissed them; but he first removed their slaves, who had stood in the vestibule, and now gave his guests in charge of other slaves whom they did not know, to be conveyed either in carriages or litters; and by this procedure he filled them with far greater fear. And scarcely had each guest reached his home and was beginning to get his breath again, as one might say, when word was brought him that a messenger from the Augustus had come. While they were accordingly expecting to perish this time in any case, one person brought in the slab, which was of silver, and the others in turn brought in various articles, including the dishes which had been set before them at the dinner, which were constructed of very costly material; and last of all came that particular boy who had been each guest's familiar spirit, now washed and adorned. Thus, after having passed the entire night in terror, they received the gifts."

Such was the Funeral Banquet of Domitian, as people called it.

The continuous state of terror in which Domitian kept his guests rendered them speechless. He alone spoke, and he spoke of death and killing. It was as though they were all dead and he alone lived. He had gathered together at this banquet all his victims—for victims they must have seemed to themselves—and as such, though disguised as guests, he addressed them. He himself was disguised as host, but in reality was the survivor. His situation as survivor was not only re-affirmed in relation to each guest, but was also subtly enhanced. The guests are as if dead, but he is still in a position to kill them. Thus the very *process* of survival is caught. In releasing them, he pardons them; but they tremble again when he hands them over to unknown slaves. They reach their homes and he again sends messengers of death to them; but these bring gifts and, amongst them, the greatest of all—the gift of life. He is able, as it were, to despatch them from life to death and then to bring them back to life again. It was a game which gave him the most intense sensation of power imaginable and he enjoyed it to the full.

The Escape of Josephus

AMONG THE STORIES of the war between the Jews and the Romans, which took place during Domitian's youth, there is an account of an incident which perfectly illustrates the nature of the survivor. The Roman forces were commanded by Vespasian, the father of Domitian, and it was during this war that the Flavii achieved imperial power.

The Jews had been chafing under Roman rule for some time. When they finally rose against it in earnest, they appointed commanders in each district of the country, to collect troops and to prepare the defence of the towns so that there would be some chance of their being able to repel the inevitable attack of the Roman legions. Josephus, then barely thirty years old, was appointed commander in Galilee and he set to work zealously to accomplish his task. In his *History of the Jewish War* he describes the obstacles he had to contend with: dissensions among the townspeople; rivals who intrigued against him and collected troops on their own account; towns which refused to acknowledge his leadership, or later denied it again. But, with astonishing energy, he got together an army—though it was badly equipped—and fortified strongholds against the coming of the Romans.

And, in due course, they came. They were under the command of Vespasian, who had with him his son, Titus, a young man the same age as Josephus. (Nero was then still emperor in Rome.) Vespasian had distinguished himself in many theatres of war and was known as a general of long experience. He advanced into Galilee and surrounded Josephus and his army in the town of Jotapata. The Jews defended it stubbornly and bravely. Josephus was full of resource and knew how every attack should be met. The siege lasted for forty-seven days and the Romans suffered heavy losses in the course of it. When at last, and then only by treachery and at night, they succeeded in forcing their way in, the defenders were all asleep and did not realize that the Romans were among them until daybreak. Then they fell into terrible despair and many of them killed themselves.

Josephus escaped. I shall give in his own words his story of what happened to him after the capture of the town, for, as far as I know, there is in all literature no other comparable account of a survivor. With curious self-awareness and with an insight into the very nature of survival, he describes everything that he did in order to save his life. It was comparatively easy for him to be honest, for he did not write his account until later, when he already stood high in the favour of the Romans.

"After the fall of Jotapata, the Romans searched everywhere for Josephus—among the dead and in all the secret hiding places of the city—partly because the soldiers themselves were incensed against him, and partly because their commander was set on his capture, thinking that it might determine the whole course of the war. Josephus, however, as if helped by divine providence, had managed to slip through the enemy during the fighting and had jumped down into an underground cistern which opened on one side into a large cave, invisible from above. In this cave he found forty men of importance concealed, who had provided themselves with food for several days, and here he lay hid in the daytime, for the enemy were all around, but emerged at night to search for a way of escape and to see where sentries were posted. But the whole neighbourhood was so closely guarded on his account that there was no possibility of escape, and so he retreated into the cave again. For two days he eluded his pursuers in this way, but on the third day a woman who had been among those in the cave was captured, and she betrayed him. Vespasian immediately despatched two Tribunes with instructions to promise Josephus his safety and to persuade him to come out of the cave.

"The Tribunes arrived and spoke courteously to him and guaranteed his life; but to no purpose, for he knew, or thought he knew, what he had to expect in return for all the injuries the Romans had suffered at his hands. The gentle bearing of those who spoke to him in no way altered his estimate of the fate that awaited him. He could not rid himself of the fear that the Romans were only trying to entice him out of the cave in order to execute him. Finally, Vespasian sent a third messenger, the Tribune Nicanor, who was well known to Josephus; in fact, they had formerly been friends. Nicanor described the leniency with which the Romans treated their vanquished foes. He explained, too, that the generals admired Josephus for his courage more than they hated him, and that Vespasian had no intention of having him executed. If he wished, he could kill him without his leaving the cave; but, in fact, what he wanted was to save the life of a brave man. He added that it was unthinkable that Vespasian should maliciously send Josephus's friend to him to trap him, covering a breach of faith with the mask of friendship; nor would he, Nicanor, ever have lent himself to such a betrayal of friendship.

"As even Nicanor, however, failed to bring Josephus to a decision, the soldiers in their fury prepared to set fire to the cave; but Nicanor held them back, for he was determined to take Josephus alive. Surrounded thus by hostile, threatening soldiers, and with Nicanor still urging him to surrender, Josephus remembered suddenly the terrible dreams in which God had revealed to him the impending disasters of the Jewish people and the fates of the Roman Emperors; for he was skilled in the interpretation of dreams. A priest himself, and the son of a priest, he was familiar with the prophecies of the Holy Scriptures and could expound those that were obscure. At this very moment he was filled with inspiration, the terrors of those dreams rose up before him and silently he prayed to God, thus: 'Since Thou art resolved to humble the Jewish people, whom Thou didst create; since all good fortune is passed to the Romans; and since Thou hast chosen my spirit to make known the things that are to come, I yield myself to the Romans; but Thou art my witness that I go, not as a traitor, but as Thy servant.'

"After he had prayed, he told Nicanor he would go with him. When the Jews who had been with him in hiding saw that he had decided to yield to the enemy's persuasion, they crowded round him and reproached him vehemently. They reminded him of all who, on his persuasion, had died for freedom; of his own reputation for courage, which had been so great, yet now he wanted to live a slave. They asked what mercy he, supposed to be so wise, thought he would obtain from those he had fought so stubbornly. They said he had wholly forgotten himself and that his care for his own life was an outrage to God and to the Laws of their fathers. *He* might be dazzled by the good fortune of the Romans; *they* were still mindful of the honour of their people; their right hands and their swords were his to command if he died willingly as leader of the Jews; if he refused, he should die unwillingly as a traitor. They drew their swords and threatened to cut him down if he gave himself up to the Romans.

"Josephus was very frightened, but it seemed to him that he would be betraying the commands of God if he died before proclaiming them, and in his urgent need he began to reason with his companions. He said that it was indeed noble to die in war, but then it must be according to the custom of war, that is, by the hand of the victor. It was cowardly in the extreme to kill oneself. Suicide was both repugnant to the very nature of all living beings and an outrage against God the Creator. God gave men life and to God must men commit their end. Those who turned their hands against themselves were hateful to God, and he would punish both them and their descendants. To all that they had suffered in this life, they must not now add sin against their Creator. If deliverance should come, they should not refuse it. It would not be shameful in them to accept their lives, for they had sufficiently proved their courage by their deeds. But if they had to die, then they should die at the hands of their conquerors. He had no thought of going over to the Romans and so becoming a traitor himself; he hoped rather for treachery on *their* part. If, in spite of their given word they killed him, he would die joyfully. Their broken faith, which God would punish, would be to him a greater consolation than victory itself.

"Thus Josephus put forward every possible argument to dissuade his companions from suicide. But despair had made them deaf. They had long dedicated themselves to death and his words served only to increase their frenzy. They accused him of cowardice and pressed round him with drawn swords, as if ready to strike him down. In danger of his life, and torn by conflicting emotions, Josephus called one man by name, fixed another with a stare of command, took a third by the arm, pleaded with a fourth and so, in each case, succeeded in averting the sword of death. He was like a wild animal at bay, turning to face each successive assailant; and as they still, even in this last extremity, respected him as their commander, their arms were as if paralysed, their daggers slipped from their hands, and many who had drawn their swords against him sheathed them again of their own free will.

"In spite of his desperate position, Josephus's presence of mind did not fail him. On the contrary, putting his trust in God, he staked his life on a gamble and addressed his companions thus: 'Since we are resolved to die, and will not be turned from it, let us draw lots and kill each other accordingly. The first man on whom the lot falls shall be killed by the second, and he, in turn, by the third; and so on, as chance decides. In this way, all shall die, but no-one will have been compelled to take his own life, except the last man. It would be unfair if he, after the death of his companions, changed his mind and did not kill himself.'

"With this proposal Josephus won their confidence again, and when they had all declared their agreement, he drew lots with the rest and each man on whom the lot fell offered himself to be killed by the next, for each imagined that a moment later his general would die too; and death with Josephus seemed sweeter than life. At last—let us say that it was either by chance or by divine providence—only Josephus was left with one other man. Since he did not want to risk the lot falling on him, nor, supposing he escaped it, to stain his hands with the blood of a fellow Jew, he persuaded this man that they should both give themselves up to the Romans and so save their lives.

"Having thus come safely through two wars—one with the Romans and one with his own people—Josephus was brought by Nicanor before Vespasian. All the Romans crowded to see the commander of the Jews and pressed shouting round him, some exulting in his capture, some threatening him, and others thrusting their way forwards to see him close. Those at the back clamoured for his execution; those nearer him remembered his deeds and marvelled at the change in his fortunes. Among the officers, though, there were none who, in spite of their former hatred, were not moved by the sight of him. Titus, in particular, was impressed by his steadfast bearing in misfortune, and moved by fellow feeling for his youth—he was the same age as Josephus. He wanted to save his life and pleaded strenuously for him with his father. Vespasian, however, put Josephus under strict guard, proposing to send him immediately to Nero.

"When Josephus heard this, he asked to speak to Vespasian alone.

Vespasian ordered everyone to withdraw, except his son, Titus, and two close friends, and Josephus then spoke thus:

" 'You think, Vespasian, that I am simply a prisoner of war who has fallen into your hands. But you are mistaken: I stand before you as harbinger of great events. I, Josephus, am sent by God to declare this message to you. Were this not so, I would not be here, for I know the Jewish law and how a general should die. You want to send me to Nero. Why? He and his successors who will ascend the throne before you will not rule for long. You yourself, Vespasian, shall be Caesar and Emperor, you and your son here. Fetter me more securely and guard me for yourself till that time comes. For you will be Caesar and master, not only over me, but over land and sea and the whole human race. Let me be closely watched and, if I have taken the Name of God in vain, then kill me as I shall have deserved.'

"At first Vespasian did not really trust Josephus; he thought he was lying to save his life. Gradually, however, he began to believe what he said, for God Himself had already awoken in him imperial ambitions, and he had also received other signs of future power. He discovered, too, that Josephus had prophesied truly on other occasions. One of those who had been present at his private interview with Vespasian expressed surprise that he had not predicted either the fall of Jotapata or his own capture, and suggested that what he put forward now was a fable to ingratiate himself with his enemies. But Josephus replied that he had predicted to the people of Jotapata that the town would fall after forty-seven days and that he himself would be taken alive by the Romans. Vespasian had secret enquiries made among the other prisoners, and when they confirmed what Josephus had said, he began to believe the predictions about himself. It is true that he still kept Josephus fettered and in prison, but he gave him a splendid robe and other valuable presents and, from then on, thanks to Titus, treated him with kindness and consideration."

Josephus's struggle falls into three distinct acts. First, he escapes the slaughter after the fall of Jotapata. The defenders of the town either kill themselves or are killed by the Romans; a few are taken prisoner. Josephus escapes by hiding in the cave by the cistern. Here he finds forty men, whom he expressly describes as "important". They, like himself, are all survivors. They have provided themselves with food and hope to remain hidden from the Romans until some way of escape offers.

But the presence of Josephus, who is the man the Romans are actually searching for, is betrayed to them by a woman. Thereupon, the

situation changes radically and the second, and by far the most interesting act, begins; one may say that it is unique in the frankness with
which events are described by the chief actor.

The Romans promise Josephus his life. As soon as he believes them,
they cease to be enemies. It is, in the deepest sense, a question of faith.
At precisely the right moment, he remembers a prophetic dream he
once had. In it he had been warned that the Jews would be conquered. They are conquered, though at first, it is true, only in the
fortress of Jotapata which he had commanded. Fortune is on the side
of the Romans. The vision in which this had been revealed to him
came from God and God would also help him to find the way to the
Romans. He commends himself to God and turns to his new enemies,
the Jews who are with him in the cave. They want to commit suicide,
so as not to fall into the hands of the Romans. He, their leader, who had
spurred them on to fight, should be the first to welcome this form of
annihilation. But he is determined to live. He pleads with them and
with a hundred arguments seeks to take from them their desire for
death. But he does not succeed. Everything he says against death
increases their blind passion for it, and also their anger against himself,
who shuns it. He sees that he can only escape if they all kill each other
and he is the last to remain alive. He therefore makes a show of agree-
ing with them and hits upon the notion of drawing lots.

The reader will have his own ideas about the way in which these
lots were drawn; it is difficult not to suspect fraud. It is the one point
in his narrative where Josephus is obscure. He ascribes the extraordinary outcome of this gamble on death either to God or to chance, but
he also, as it were, leaves it open to the reader to guess the real course
of events. For what follows is monstrous: his companions butcher
each other before his eyes. But not simultaneously. Each killing follows
the other in due order, and between each the lots are drawn again.
Each man has with his own hand to kill one of his comrades and then
himself be killed by the next on whom the lot falls. The religious
scruples that Josephus advanced against self-murder evidently do not
apply to murder. As each man falls, his own hope of deliverance grows.
Individually and collectively, he wants them all dead. For himself he
wants nothing but to live. They die gladly, believing that their
commander dies with them. They cannot suppose that he will be the
last left alive. It is unlikely that they even envisage the possibility.
But since one of them has to be the last, Josephus forearms himself
against this thought too. He tells them that it would be very unfair if
the last man changed his mind after the death of his companions, and

so saved his life. This, precisely, is what he intends to do. What could least be done after the death of comrades is what he himself wants to do. Pretending in this last hour to be wholly with them, to be one of them, he sends them all to their deaths and, by doing so, saves his own life. They are all caught in the same fate and believe him caught too. But he stands outside it, and destines it only for them. They die so that he may live.

The deception is complete. It is the deception of all leaders. They pretend that they will be the first to die, but, in reality, they send their people to death, so that they themselves may stay alive longer. The trick is always the same. The leader wants to survive, for with each survival he grows stronger. If he has enemies, so much the better; he survives *them*. If not, he has his own people. In any event he uses both, whether successively or together. Enemies he can use openly; that is why he has enemies. His own people must be used secretly.

In Josephus's cave the trick is made manifest. Outside are the enemy, but their former threats have turned to a promise. Inside the cave are his friends. They still hold firmly to their leader's old convictions, convictions with which he himself had imbued them, and they refuse to take advantage of this new hope. Thus the cave which Josephus had intended as his refuge becomes the place of his greatest danger. He dupes the friends who want to lay violent hands both on him and on themselves, and consigns them to a common death. From the very beginning, he has had no thought of sharing it; nor does he share it when it comes. He is left in the end with one sole companion and since, as he says, he has no wish to stain his hands with the blood of a fellow Jew, he persuades this man to surrender. One man alone he can persuade to live. Forty had been too many for him. The two of them give themselves up to the Romans.

Thus he emerges safely from the war against his own people. This is precisely what he brings the Romans: the enhanced sense of his own life, feeding on the deaths of those he had led. The transmission of this newly won power to Vespasian is the third act of the struggle. It is embodied in a prophetic promise. The Romans were perfectly familiar with the Jews' stubborn belief in God. They knew that the last thing a Jew would do was to take the name of God in vain. Josephus had strong reasons for wanting to see Vespasian emperor in place of Nero. Nero, to whom Vespasian proposed sending him, had not promised him his life; Vespasian had. He knew, too, that Nero despised Vespasian, who was much older than himself, and fell asleep in public when he sang. He had often treated him harshly and had only called again on his military experience when the insurrection of the Jews had begun to assume dangerous proportions. Vespasian thus had every reason to mistrust Nero. A promise of future power must have been welcome to him.

Josephus may himself have believed that the message he gave Vespasian was from God. Prophecy was in his blood; he believed that he was a true prophet and, in prophesying, he brought the Romans something that they themselves lacked. He did not take the gods of the Romans seriously; to him they were superstition. But he knew that he had to convince Vespasian of the importance and authenticity of his message; and Vespasian, like every other Roman, despised the Jews and their religion. He was one man alone among enemies on whom he had inflicted terrible injuries, enemies who but lately had been cursing him, yet he faced them confidently, he expressed himself with force, and he believed in himself more strongly than in anything else. This belief he owed to the fact that he had survived his own people. The power which he had achieved in the underground cave he transmitted to Vespasian, so that the latter survived not only Nero, his junior by thirty years, but also no less than three of Nero's successors. Each of these died, in effect, by the hand of the other, and Vespasian became Emperor of the Romans.

The Despot's Hostility to Survivors.
Rulers and Their Successors

MUHAMMAD TUGHLAK, the Sultan of Delhi, had various schemes even more grandiose than those of Napoleon and Alexander. Among them was the conquest of China from across the Himalayas. An army of 100,000 horsemen was collected, which set out in the year 1337. Of this whole army, all but ten men perished cruelly in the mountains. These ten returned to Delhi with the news of the disaster and there, at the command of the Sultan, were all executed.

This hostility to survivors is common to despotic rulers, all of whom regard survival as their prerogative; it is their real wealth and their most precious possession. Anyone who presumes to make himself conspicuous by surviving great danger, and especially anyone who survives large numbers of other people, trespasses upon their province and their hatred is accordingly directed against him.

Wherever government was absolute and unquestioned, as in the

Islamic East for example, the rage that survivors aroused in the ruler could be shown openly. Even if he felt obliged to find pretexts for their destruction, these barely disguised the naked passion which filled him.

By secession from Delhi, another Islamic empire arose in the Deccan. One Sultan of the new dynasty, Muhammad Shah, spent his whole reign in fierce wars against the neighbouring Hindu kings. One day the Hindus succeeded in capturing the important town of Mudkal, and all its inhabitants, men, women and children, were put to the sword. *One* man only escaped and carried the news to the capital of the Sultan. "On hearing it", says the chronicler, "Muhammad Shah was seized with a transport of grief and rage, in which he commanded the unfortunate messenger to be instantly put to death; exclaiming that he could never bear in his presence a wretch who could survive the sight of the slaughter of so many brave companions".

Here it is still possible to speak of a pretext, and it is probable that the Sultan did not really know why he could not bear the sight of the only survivor. Hakim, the Khalif of Egypt who ruled about A.D. 1000, was much clearer-headed about the games which could be played with power and enjoyed them in a manner reminiscent of the Emperor Domitian. He liked to wander around at night disguised in various ways. During one of these nocturnal wanderings, on a hill near Cairo, he came across ten well-armed men, who recognised him and begged him for money. He said to them, "Divide into two groups and fight each other. The winner shall be given money." They obeyed him and fought so fiercely that nine of them were killed. To the tenth, the man who was left, Hakim threw a large number of gold coins which he had in his sleeve. But as the man stooped to pick them up, Hakim had him cut to pieces by his guards. In all this he showed a clear insight into the *process* of survival. He also enjoyed it as a kind of performance which he himself had conjured up. He finished by adding to it the pleasure of destroying the survivor.

Strangest of all is the relationship between the despotic ruler and his successor. Where succession is hereditary, the ruler being succeeded by his own son, the relationship is doubly difficult. It is natural for a ruler, as for any other man, to be survived by his son, and since in this case the son is himself a future ruler, it is natural that he too, from an early age, should have harboured a mounting passion for survival. Thus both father and son have every reason to hate each other. Their rivalry originates in the disparity of their positions and, for this very reason, is particularly acrimonious. The one who has present power knows that he will die before the other. The one who as yet has no power, feels certain that he will outlive the other. On the one side is an ardent desire for the death of an older man—one who, of all men, least wants to die, for otherwise he would not be a ruler; on the other is a determination to delay by all possible means the accession to power of a younger man. It is a conflict for which there is no real solution. History is full of the rebellions of sons against their fathers. Some succeed in bringing about their fathers' downfall; others are defeated by them and then either pardoned or killed.

It is not surprising that, with a dynasty of long-lived absolute rulers, it should become a kind of institution for sons to rebel against their fathers. The history of the Mogul emperors illustrates this point very clearly. Prince Salim, the eldest son of the Emperor Akbar, "impatient to take the reins of government into his hands, and chafing at the long life of his father, which kept him from the enjoyments of the dignities he so much desired, resolved to usurp the same, and on his own authority began to assume the name and exercise the prerogatives of a king". This statement appears in a contemporary chronicle of the Jesuits, who knew both father and son well, since they strove for the favour of both. Prince Salim formed his own court. He hired assassins who ambushed and murdered his father's most intimate friend and counsellor. His rebellion lasted for three years, during which period there was one feigned reconciliation. Finally Akbar threatened to nominate another successor to the throne and, under this pressure, Salim accepted an invitation to his father's court. He was received with apparent cordiality, then his father drew him into an inner chamber, boxed his ears and locked him into a bathroom. Then he handed him over to a physician and two servants, as though he were mad; and wine, of which he was very fond, was forbidden him. The prince was then in his 36th year. After a few days Akbar released him and reinstated him as his successor. The following year Akbar died from dysentery. It was said that he had been poisoned by his son, but there is now no means of finding out what really happened. "After the death of his father, which he had so much desired", Salim became Emperor at last, taking the name Jahangir.

Akbar ruled for forty-five years; Jahangir for twenty-two. But though the latter's reign was only half as long as his father's, exactly the same experience befell him. His favourite son, Shah Jehan, whom he himself had nominated as his successor, rebelled and fought against him for three years. Finally he was defeated and sued his father for peace. He was pardoned, but on one hard condition: he had to send his two sons as hostages to the imperial court. He himself waited for his father's death, taking good care never to appear in his presence again. Two years after the conclusion of peace Jahangir died and Shah Jehan became emperor.

Shah Jehan ruled for thirty years. What he had done to his father was now done to him, but *his* son was luckier. Aurangzeb, the younger of the two princes who had been kept as hostages at their grandfather's court, rebelled against his father and his elder brother. The famous "War of Secession" which started then was described by European eye-witnesses. It ended with the victory of Aurangzeb, who had his brother executed and kept his father prisoner for the eight years until his death.

Soon after his victory Aurangzeb made himself Emperor and reigned for half a century. His own favourite son lost patience long before the expiry of that time, and rebelled against his father. The old man, however, was much more cunning than his son and managed to estrange the latter's allies. The son had to flee to Persia and died in exile before his father.

From the dynastic history of the Mogul Empire as a whole a remarkably uniform picture emerges. Its age of splendour lasted for 150 years and, during this time, only four emperors ruled, each the son of the preceding one and each tenacious, long-lived and clinging to power with all his might. Their reigns are all strikingly long; Akbar's lasted forty-five years, his son's twenty-two, his grandson's thirty and his great-grandson's fifty. Beginning with Akbar himself, none of the sons could endure waiting; each who later became emperor rose against his father. Their rebellions ended differently. Jahangir and Shah Jehan were defeated and afterwards pardoned by their fathers; Aurangzeb took his father prisoner and then deposed him; his own son died, a failure, in exile. With Aurangzeb's death the power of the Mogul Empire came to an end.

In this long-lived dynasty each son rebelled against his father and each father waged war on his son.

The intensest feeling for power is that found in a ruler who *wants no son*. The best known case is that of Shaka, the early nineteenth century founder of the nation and empire of the Zulus in South Africa. He was a great general, who has been compared with Napoleon, and never has there been a more naked despot. He refused to marry, because he did not want a legitimate heir. Even the urgent entreaties of his mother, whom he always greatly honoured, did not move him. She wanted a grandson more than anything else, but he was obdurate. His harem consisted of hundreds of women—ultimately there were 1,200 of them—whose official title was "sisters". They were forbidden to be with child and were strictly watched. Any "sister" found pregnant was punished with death. With his own hands Shaka killed the child of one of these women which had been concealed from him. He flattered himself on his skill and self-control and therefore believed that no woman could ever become pregnant by him. Thus he avoided being put in the position of having a growing son to fear. He was murdered at the age of forty-one by two of his brothers.

If it is permissible to turn from human to divine rulers we might remember here the God of Mohammed, whose autocracy is the least disputed of any god's. He is there from the very beginning in the plenitude of his power and, unlike the God of the Old Testament, never has serious rivals to contend with. Again and again in the Koran it is vehemently affirmed that no-one begot him, and also that he begot no-one. This affirmation, and the disputatious attitude to Christianity which it expresses, derives from the sense of the unity and indivisibility of God's power.

Contrasted with this, there are cases of oriental rulers with hundreds of sons, all compelled to fight each other for the succession. One can assume that knowledge of the hostility between them does something to lessen the bitterness their father feels about the succession of any one of them.

The deeper significance of hereditary succession, its real purpose and advantage, will be discussed in another context. Here I have only wished to show that the hostility between a ruler and his successor is of a particular kind which must increase side by side with the increase of the specific passion of power, the passion for survival.

Forms of Survival

THERE ARE MANY different forms of survival and it is worth while seeing that we leave no important one out of account.

The earliest event in every man's life, occurring long before birth and of even greater importance, is his conception; and this has never yet been considered in relation to the concept of survival. We already know a great deal, and may soon know everything, about what happens once the spermatozoon has actually penetrated into the egg cell. Scarcely any thought, however, has been given to the fact that there are an overwhelming number of spermatozoa which do not reach their goal, although they play an active part in the process of generation as a whole. It is not a single spermatozoon which sets out for the egg cell, but about 200 million, all of which are all released together in *one* ejaculation and then, in a dense mass, move together towards *one* goal.

They are present in enormous numbers and, since they come into existence through partition, they are all equal; their density could not be greater, and they all have the same goal. These four traits, it will be remembered, are what I have described as the essential attributes of the crowd.

It is unnecessary to point out that a crowd of spermatozoa cannot be the same as a crowd of people. But there is undoubtedly an analogy between the two phenomena, and perhaps more than an analogy.

All the spermatozoa except one *perish*, either on the way to, or in the immediate vicinity of, the goal. One single seed alone penetrates the egg cell, and this seed can very well be called the survivor. It is, as it were, the leader of all the others and succeeds in achieving what every leader, either secretly or openly, hopes for, which is to *survive* those he leads. It is to such a survivor, one out of 200 million, that every human being owes his existence.

From this we pass on to other, more familiar forms of survival. In the preceding chapters there has been frequent mention of *killing*. A man is confronted by the enemy. It may be a single enemy, whom he can ambush or fight an open duel with; it may be a pack which he feels closing in on him; or it may be a whole crowd. In this last case he will not be fighting alone, but together with his own people. The higher his rank, however, the more he will feel that survival is his sole right: it is generals who "win". But, since many of his own people as well as of the enemy will have fallen, the heap of the dead is a mixed one, consisting of friends and enemies alike; in this respect battles are "neutral", like epidemics.

At this point we pass from *killing* to *dying*, dying on the most colossal scale known, that is, in epidemics and other natural catastrophes. In these anyone who survives, survives *all* who are mortal, friend and foe alike. All normal ties are dissolved, and dying becomes so universal that no-one even knows who it is that is being buried. Of great significance in this context are the continually recurring stories of people who come back to life in the midst of a heap of the dead, who wake amongst the dead. Such people tend to think of themselves as invulnerable, plague-heroes as it were.

The satisfaction which follows individual deaths is more moderate and more concealed. The victims may be friends or relatives and there is no question of active killing and no sense of being attacked. Nothing is done to hasten death, but it is waited for. The young survive the old; sons their fathers.

A son finds it natural that his father should die before him. Filial duty hurries him to the death-bed, to close his father's eyes and carry him to his grave. During this period, which may last for days, he has his father lying dead before him. The man who, more than anyone else, could once order him about is now reduced to silence and, helpless, must endure everything which is done to his body. And it is his son, for many years wholly at his mercy, who directs and arranges all this.

Here the satisfaction in survival results from the relationship between the two protagonists. One who was once all-powerful is now impotent, his strength extinguished and his lifeless remains at the disposal of the very being who was for many years weak, helpless and entirely in his power.

Everything the father leaves strengthens the son; the inheritance is the son's booty. He can do the opposite of everything the father would have done. If the father was thrifty, the son can be wasteful, reckless where he was prudent. It is as though a new régime had been proclaimed and the breach between the old and the new is immense and irreparable. The breach results from survival and is also the most intimate and personal expression of it.

Among people of the same age survival is very different. Since it is a question of one's own group the urge to survive is concealed by milder forms of rivalry. Young men of the same age are grouped together as a class and then, on the fulfillment of certain rites involving severe and often cruel ordeals, are promoted to the next class. It may happen that some of them perish during these ordeals, but that is the exception.

The old, that is those men who are still alive after the lapse of a certain number of years, enjoy great authority, especially among primitive peoples, who, on the whole, tend to die earlier than we do, for they undergo greater perils and are more vulnerable to disease. For them it is a real achievement to reach a certain age, and one which brings its reward. Not only do the old know more, having gained experience in a great variety of situations, but the fact that they are still alive shows that they have proved themselves. To emerge unscathed from all the dangers of war, hunting and accident they must have been lucky; and with every escape their prestige will have grown. They have trophies proving their victories over their enemies. The group they belong to is of necessity small and therefore very much aware of their long-continued membership in it. They have experienced many occasions for lament, but they are still alive and every death of a contemporary increases their prestige. The group may not be fully conscious of this and may well attach greater importance to victories over enemies, but one thing is certain: the most elementary and obvious form of success is to remain alive. The old are not only alive, but are *still* alive. Old men can take as many young wives as they want, whilst young men may have to content themselves with old ones. They have the right of deciding where the group shall migrate, whom it shall make war on and with whom ally itself. In so far as one can speak of government in such conditions, it is the old men together who govern.

The desire for a long life which plays such a large part in most cultures really means that most people want to survive their contemporaries. They know that many die early and they want a different fate for themselves. When they pray to the gods for long life they differentiate themselves from their companions. It is true that the latter are not mentioned in the prayer, but what the supplicant visualizes is himself living longer than others. The most wholesome embodiment of longevity is the *Patriarch*, one who can survey many generations of his descendants, but is always imagined alone in his own generation. It is as though a new race began with him. As long as he has grandsons and great-grandsons alive it does not matter if some of his sons have died before him. Indeed, the fact that his life has proved tougher than theirs increases his authority.

Within the class of old men there is always one who in the end is left solitary, the very oldest of them all. The Etruscans fixed the length of the century by the duration of his life. It is worth saying a little more about this.

The "century" of the Etruscans varied, being sometimes shorter and sometimes longer, its duration in each case being decided afresh. In every generation there is one man who lives to be older than the rest. The Etruscans believed that when this man died, who was the very oldest of all, the one who had survived all his contemporaries, the gods gave men certain signs, and they then adjusted the length of the century to coincide with the length of his life. If he lived to the age of 110, the century was counted as 110 years; if he died at 105, the century was that much shorter. The survivor *was* the century; the years of his life constituted it.

Each city and each people were thought to have a predestined number of such centuries, starting from the foundation of the city.

Ten were allotted to the nation of the Etruscans. If the survivor of each generation had an unusually long life, the nation as a whole lived to be so much older. The connection between the two is remarkable and, as a religious institution, unique.

Only survival at a distance in time is wholly innocent. A man cannot have killed people who lived long before him and whom he did not know; he cannot have wished for their death, nor even have waited for it. He learns of their existence only when they exist no longer. In fact, by his awareness of their lives, however insubstantial the form of survival it assists them to, he serves them more than they serve him. It can, however, be shown that they do contribute something to his own sense of survival.

We survive the ancestors we have not known personally and we also survive preceding humanity as a whole. It is in graveyards and cemeteries that the second of these experiences is brought home to us, and we see then how closely it resembles survival in epidemics. Instead of plague, it is the general epidemic of death which confronts us, whose victims over the years lie gathered together in this one place.

At this point it may be objected that the concept of survival, as I have described it, has long been known under a different name: that of the instinct of self-preservation.

But are the two really identical? Do the words express the same thing? It seems to me that they do not, and, if we ask ourselves what kind of activity we imagine when we speak of self-preservation and if we look at the word itself, the reasons for the inadequacy of the concept become apparent. First there is the stress on *self*: every human being is postulated as solitary and self-sufficient. But the second half of the word is even more important; by "preservation" we actually mean two things: first, that every creature must *eat* in order to stay alive and, second, that, in some way or other, every creature defends itself against attack. We see it before us rather as if it were a statue, with one hand reaching for food and with the other fending off its enemies. A peaceful creature indeed! Left to itself, it would eat a handful of grass and never do anyone the slightest harm.

Is there any conception less appropriate to man, more misleading and more ridiculous? It is true that man does eat, but not the same food as a cow; nor is he led to pasture. His way of procuring his prey is cunning, bloodthirsty and strenuous; there is certainly nothing passive about it. He does not mildly defend himself, but attacks his enemies as soon as he senses them in the distance; and his weapons of attack are far better developed than his weapons of defence. True, he wants to "preserve" himself, but he also simultaneously wants other things which are inseparable from this. He wants to kill so that he can survive others; he wants to stay alive so as not to have others surviving him.

If "self-preservation" included these two desires then the concept would have a meaning, but, as it is, there is no reason why we should retain it when another is so much more accurate.

All the forms of survival I have enumerated are of great antiquity and, as will be shown, are found even amongst primitive peoples.

The Survivor in Primitive Belief

MANA IS THE name given in the Pacific to a kind of supernatural and impersonal power, which can pass from one man to another. It is something which is much desired, and an individual can increase his own measure of it. A brave warrior can acquire it to a high degree, but he does not owe it to his skill in fighting or to his bodily strength; it passes into him as the *mana* of his slain enemy.

"In the Marquesas it was through personal prowess that a tribesman became a war chief. The warrior was thought to embody the *mana* of all those whom he had killed, his own *mana* increasing in proportion with his prowess. In the mind of the native, the prowess was the result, however, not the cause of his *mana*. The *mana* of the warrior's spear was likewise increased with each death he inflicted. As the sign of his assumption of his defeated enemy's power, the victor in a hand-to-hand combat assumed his slain foe's name; with a view to absorbing directly his *mana*, he ate some of his flesh; and to bind the presence of the empowering influence in battle, to insure his intimate rapport with the captured *mana*, he wore as a part of his war dress some physical relic of his vanquished foe—a bone, a dried hand, sometimes a whole skull."

The effect of victory on the survivor could not be more clearly conceived. By killing his opponent the survivor becomes stronger and the addition of *mana* makes him capable of new victories. It is a kind of blessing which he wrests from his enemy, but he only obtains it if the latter is killed. The physical presence of the enemy, first alive and then dead, is essential. There must have been fighting and killing, and the personal act of killing is crucial. The manageable parts of the corpse which the victor removes and either embodies into himself, or wears as trophies, serve as continual reminders of the increase of his power.

They make him feel stronger and he uses them to arouse terror; each new enemy he challenges trembles and sees the same fate threatening him.

The Murngin of Arnhem Land in Australia believe in a more personal but equally profitable relationship between the killer and the killed. The spirit of the slain man enters the body of the slayer, who then not only acquires double strength, but actually becomes larger. It is easy to imagine how this prospect stimulates young men in war, each of them seeking out an enemy in order to gain his strength. But this will only be achieved if the killing takes place by night, for by day the victim will see his murderer and will then be much too angry to enter his body.

This process of "entering" has been precisely described. It is so remarkable that I shall quote a large part of the description.

"When a man kills another during a feud, he returns home and does not eat cooked food until the soul of the dead man approaches him. He can hear the dead man's soul coming because the shaft of the spear which hangs from the stone head within the man drags on the ground and hits against the trees and bushes as he walks. When the spirit is very near, the killer can hear sounds coming from the dead man's wound. . . . He takes the spear, removes the spear head, and puts the spear end of the shaft between his own big toe and the toe next to it. The other end of the shaft is placed against his left shoulder. . . . The soul then enters the socket where the spear head was, and pushes its way upward into the leg of the killer, and finally into the body. It walks like an ant. It finally enters the stomach and shuts it up. The man feels sick and his abdomen becomes feverish. He rubs his stomach and calls out the proper name of the man he has killed. This cures him and he becomes normal again, for the spirit leaves the stomach and enters the heart. When the spirit enters the heart it has the same effect as if the blood of the dead man had been given to the killer. It is as though the man, before he died, had given his life's blood to the man who was to kill him.

"The slayer, grown larger and exceedingly strong, acquires all the life strength the dead man once possessed. When the slayer dreams, the soul tells him that he has food for him and gives directions where to go to find it. He says, 'Down there by the river you will find many kangaroo', or 'In that old tree there is a large honeybee's nest', or, 'Near that large sand bank you will harpoon a very large turtle and find many eggs on the beach.'

"The killer listens, and after a little time sneaks away from camp by himself and goes out in the bush, where he meets the soul of the dead man. The soul comes very close and lies down. The slayer is frightened and cries 'Who is that? Somebody is near me.' When he draws near where the spirit of the dead man was he finds a kangaroo. . . . It is unusually small. He looks at it and understands the meaning of its being there in the place where he had heard the movements of the dead man's soul. He takes sweat from under his arm and rubs it on his right arm. . . . He picks up his spear and calls out the name of the dead man and spears the animal. The animal is immediately killed, but becomes much larger while dying. The man attempts to lift it. He finds this impossible because it has grown so large. He leaves the kill and returns to camp to tell his friends. He says when he arrives, 'I have just killed the soul of the dead man. Do not let anyone hear of this because he might get angry again.' His more intimate friends and relatives go out with him to help skin the animal and prepare it for eating. When they cut it up they find fat everywhere which is considered one of the greatest delicacies. When they cook it, only very small pieces are placed on the fire at first. They are tasted with much care, and the meat always tastes unpleasant.

"Then the whole animal is cooked and a feast made with the parts more appreciated by the natives. The remainder is carried back to the main camp. The old men of the camp look and see that it is an animal of enormous size. They gather around it and someone asks, 'Where did you kill him?'

" 'Up there by the river.'

"The old men know that this is no ordinary kill because there is fat everywhere. After some little time one of the old men asks, 'Did you see somebody's soul out there in the bush?'

" 'No,' lies the young man.

"The old men then taste the flesh of the animal, but it does not taste the same as it ordinarily does. It has a slightly different flavour, it is not like a natural kangaroo.

"The old men shake their heads affirmatively and click their tongues: 'You have seen the dead man's soul all right.' "

Here the survivor procures for himself the strength and blood of his enemy. Not only does he himself swell, but his animal prey also grows fatter and larger. The gain which he derives from the enemy is personal and absolutely immediate. Thus the thoughts of young men are early directed towards war. But, since the whole business is transacted stealthily and by night, it has very little in common with our own traditional conception of the hero.

The hero we know who, fearless and alone, falls on the enemy, is found in the Fiji Islands. There is a story of a boy who is brought up by his mother, without knowing his father. With threats he forces her to tell him who his father is and, as soon as he learns that it is the sky-king, he sets out to find him. When he does, his father is disappointed because he is so small. He says he needs men, not boys, for he is fighting a war. The men sitting round the king laugh, but the boy smashes the head of one of the mockers with his club. The king is delighted and asks him to stay.

"And on the morrow, in the early morning, the foe came up to the town, shouting for war, and crying 'Come out to us, O Sky-king, for we are hungry. Come out to us, that we may eat.'

"Then the boy rose up, saying, 'Let no man follow me. Stay you all in the town'; and, taking in his hand the club which he had made, he rushed out into the midst of the enemy, striking savagely right and left, killing with every blow; till at length they fled before him, and he sat down on a heap of dead bodies, calling to the townfolk—'Come forth and drag the slain away.' So they came out, singing the Death-song, and dragged away the bodies of the slain, forty and two, while the wooden drum sounded the 'Death-roll' in the town.

"Four times afterwards did the boy smite his father's enemies, so that their souls grew small, and they came bringing peace-offerings to the Sky-king, saying, 'Pity us my lord, and let us live'; wherefore he was left without an enemy, and his rule stretched over all the sky."

Here the boy takes on all the enemy single-handed and each of his blows goes home. At the end he is seen sitting on a heap of dead bodies, and every single man in the heap was killed by him personally. It should not, however, be thought that such things happen only in stories. The Fiji Islanders have four distinct names for heroes. The killer of one man is called *Koroi*; of ten men, *Koli*; of twenty, *Visa*; and of thirty, *Wangka*. A famous chief, whose achievement was even greater, was called *Koli-Visa-Wangka*; he was the killer of 10 + 20 + 30, that is, of sixty men.

The feats of these super-heroes are perhaps even more impressive than the feats of ours, for they not only kill their enemies, but eat them afterwards. A chief who has conceived a special hatred for some man reserves the right to eat him up alone and in this case really does refuse to allow anyone else a bit of him.

But a hero, it may be said, does not only fight human enemies. In stories his chief concern is with dangerous monsters from whom he has to liberate his people. The monster is gradually devouring them

and there is no-one able to resist him. The best they are capable of is a
regulation of terror: so many victims yearly are delivered up to him.
But the hero takes pity on his people, sets out quite alone and, in face
of great dangers, slays the monster with his own hands. His people are
grateful to him and his memory is faithfully cherished. In virtue of the
invulnerability through which he manages to save others, he appears
as a figure of light.

There are, however, myths in which the connection between this
figure of light and heaps of dead bodies—and not only those of
enemies—is clearly recognized. The most concentrated of these myths
comes from a South American people, the Uitoto. It is to be found in
the important and much too little known collection of K. T. Preuss.
That part of it which is relevant to our subject follows here in an
abridged form.

"Two girls who lived with their father on a river bank saw one day
in the water a very pretty, tiny snake and tried to catch it. But it
always escaped them, until their father made a very fine sieve for them,
in which they caught the creature and brought it home. They put it
in a small pot with water and set all kinds of food before it, but it
rejected everything. But then, in a dream, the father had the idea of
feeding the snake with a special kind of starch, and it then began to
eat properly. It grew as thick as a thread and then as a finger-tip, and
the girls put it into a larger pot. The creature went on eating the starch
and grew as thick as an arm. They put it into a small lake. It continued
to eat the starch greedily and was so hungry that, with its food, it
seized and swallowed the hand and arm of the girl who was feeding it.
Soon it was as big as a tree fallen into the water. It began to go about
on land and to eat deer and other animals, but it still came when it was
called and swallowed the enormous quantities of starch which the girls
prepared for it. It made a cave for itself under the villages and tribes
and began to eat the forefathers of men, the first people in the world.
'Darling, come and eat', the girls called and the snake came out of its
hole, seized the bowl of starch which one of the girls held, and her
arm, right up to her head; and dragged her away and swallowed her.

"The other sister went away weeping to tell her father. He decided
to take revenge. He licked tobacco, as these people always do when they
decide on the death of some creature, became intoxicated and, in a
dream, hit on a way of taking revenge. He prepared starch to offer to
the snake as food and called the creature which had swallowed his
daughter and said to it, 'Swallow me!' He was prepared to suffer
anything and drank from the tobacco-box which hung round his neck

in order to kill it. The snake came at his call and seized the bowl of starch which he held out. Then the father jumped into its jaws and sat down. 'I have killed him', thought the snake and dragged and carried the father away.

"Then it ate a whole tribe and there were people rotting on top of the father's body. Then it swallowed another tribe and men rotted on his body. They rotted on top of him whilst he sat there, and he had to endure the stench. The snake swallowed all the tribes on the river and made away with them, so that no-one remained alive. The father had taken a shell with him from home, to cut open the snake's belly. But he cut and slit it only a little, whereupon the snake felt pains. Then it ate the tribes along another river. People were afraid and did not go out into the plantations, but stayed at home all the time. And indeed it was impossible to go about, for the snake had its hole in the middle of the path and, if anyone came from the fields, it seized him and dragged him away. The people wept and were afraid that the snake would eat them and did not take a step out of doors. When they so much as got out of their hammocks, they feared that the snake had its hole there and would seize and drag them away.

"People stank and rotted on the father's body. He drank tobacco juice from his box and made cuts in the middle of the snake's belly, so that it had great pains. 'What is the matter with me? I have swallowed Deihoma, the Cutting One. I feel pains,' said the snake, and cried out.

"Then it went to another tribe, came up out of the earth and seized all the people there. They could go nowhere, not even down to the river. If they went to fetch water from the river the snake seized them and dragged them away. As soon as their feet touched the floor in the morning, it seized them and dragged them away. Deihoma gashed its belly with his shell and it cried out, 'How is it that I suffer pains? I have swallowed Deihoma, the Cutting One, and that is what hurts me!'

"And his guardian spirits warned him: 'Deihoma, this is not yet the creek on the river where you live. Be careful how you cut. Your creek is still far distant.' At these words Deihoma stopped cutting and the snake went to feed among the people where it had fed before, and immediately seized them. 'It goes on eating! Where are we to live? It has destroyed our people', said the inhabitants of the villages. They wasted away. What did they have to eat?

"The people perished and rotted on Deihoma's body. Meanwhile he drank from his tobacco-box and cut into the snake's belly, and continued to sit inside it as before. For an endless time the wretched man had had nothing to eat and only tobacco-juice to drink. For what should he eat? He drank tobacco-juice and remained calm, in spite of the stench of putrefaction.

"The tribes did not exist any more. The snake had eaten the bodies of all those who lived by the river at the foot of heaven, so that now there were no more people. Deihoma's guardian spirits spoke to him: 'Deihoma, this is the creek on the river where you live. Go to it now and cut strongly. Two more windings of the river and you are at home. He cut. 'Cut, Deihoma, cut strongly', they said. Deihoma cut on, slit the snake's belly and opened it in the creek and jumped out through the opening.

"As soon as he was out he sat down. His head had peeled completely and he was hairless. The snake lay there writhing. Thus Deihoma returned after an endless time of wretchedness inside the snake. He washed himself thoroughly in the creek, went to his hut and saw his daughters again, who rejoiced over their father.'

In the full version of this myth, which has been considerably shortened here, there are no less than fifteen passages describing how the bodies of the people swallowed by the snake lay rotting on top of the hero. There is something offensive and compelling about this image; next to eating it is what recurs most frequently in the myth. By drinking tobacco-juice Deihoma keeps himself alive. His calm and imperturbability in the midst of putrefaction is characteristic of the hero. All the people in the world could lie rotting on top of him and he would still remain, alone in the midst of universal corruption, upright and intent on his goal. He is, as it were, an *innocent* hero, for none of the corpses are of his killing. But he is in the midst of the putrefaction and endures it. It does not strike him down; on the contrary, one could say it is this which keeps him upright. The concentration of this myth, where everything really important is enacted within the body of the snake, is completely authoritative; it is truth itself.

A hero is a man who survives again and again by means of killing. But the survivor need not always be a hero. He may be simply a man who finds himself in an equivalent position in respect of the crowd of his own people, all except himself having perished.

How does a man come to save his life in war, when all those to whom he belongs have been killed, and how does he feel when he is alone? There is an informative passage about this in an Indian myth, taken down by Koch-Grünberg among the Taulipang in South America.

"The enemies came and attacked. They came at night to the village, which consisted of five houses, and set fire to it from two sides, so that it should be light and the inhabitants would not be able to escape in the darkness. They killed many of them with their clubs as they were trying to flee from their houses.

"A man named Maitchaule lay down unhurt among a heap of dead and smeared his face and his body with blood to deceive the enemy. These believed that everyone was dead, and left. The man remained there alone. Then he got up, washed and went to another house not far from there. He thought there were people there, but he found no-one. They had all fled. He found only manioc-cake and cold roasted meat, and ate. Then he began to think. He went out of the house and a long way off. He sat down and thought. He thought of his father and his mother, who had been killed by the enemy, and that he now had no-one left. He said, 'I want to lie with my companions who are dead.' He returned, full of fear, to the burnt-down village. There were a great many vultures there. Maitchaule was a medicine-man and had dreamt of a beautiful girl. He chased the vultures away and lay down beside his dead companions. He had smeared himself with blood again. He held his hands over his head, so that he was ready to snatch quickly. The vultures returned and fought over the corpses. Then the daughter of the King-vulture came. What did the daughter of the King-vulture do? She settled on Maitchaule's chest. Just as she was about to rend his body he seized her. The vultures flew away. He said to the King-vulture's daughter, 'Change yourself into a woman. I am so lonely here and have no-one to help me.' He took her with him to the empty house and kept her there like a tame bird. He said to her, 'I am going fishing now. When I come back I want to find you changed into a woman.' "

First he lies down amongst the dead in order to escape, and makes himself look like one of them so as not to be found. Then he discovers that he is the only man left alive and he feels sad and full of fear. He decides to lie down again amongst his dead companions. At first he thinks of sharing their fate, but he cannot really be in earnest about this, for he has just dreamt of a beautiful girl. As he sees nothing living around him except vultures, he catches a vulture to be his wife. It should be added that, at his wish, the bird does then change into a woman.

It is remarkable how many tribes all over the world attribute their origin to one couple which alone remains alive after some great catastrophe. In the familiar case of the Biblical deluge the austerity of the myth is softened by the fact that Noah claims his whole family. He is permitted to take them with him into the ark and also one pair from each living species. But it was he himself who had found mercy in the sight of God; the quality needed for survival, in this case piety, was *his*, and it was for his sake alone that others were saved. There are more extreme examples of the same story, tales in which the whole human race perishes except for the single pair of ancestors. These stories are not always linked with the conception of a deluge. Often they are about epidemics, in which everybody dies except for one man who wanders here and there, searching, until at last he finds one single woman, or perhaps two, whom he marries and with whom he founds a new race.

It is part of the strength and glory of this ancestor that he was once left as the only human being alive. Even if not expressed in so many words, it is accounted a kind of merit in him that he did not perish with everyone else. To the prestige he enjoys as the ancestor of all those who come after him is added respect for the strength and good fortune shown in his survival. Whilst he lived amongst his fellows he may not have distinguished himself particularly; he was one man like many others. But then suddenly he is entirely alone. The period of his solitary wanderings is described in detail, most space being devoted to his search for people who may still be alive, instead of whom he finds corpses everywhere. The growing certainty that there is no-one except himself fills him with despair. But there is also a second element, which is always clearly recognizable, and that is his courage. Humanity begins again with him and is built on him alone. If he had not had the courage to start again by himself it would not exist at all.

One of the purest versions of this tradition is the story of the origin of the Kutenai which I shall now quote verbatim.

"The people were living there, and at once they had an epidemic. They died. All died. Then they went about. They told one another the news. Among all the Kutenai there was sickness. They arrived at one town, and told the news to one another. It was everywhere the same. At one town they did not see anybody. They were all dead. Only one person was left. One day the one that was left was cured. He was a man. He was alone. He thought: 'Well, let me go around the world to see if there is any place where there is any one. If there is no one left, I won't see it again. There is nobody. Nobody ever comes on a visit.' Then he started in his canoe. He went about in it. He started in his canoe, and came to the last camp of the Kutenai. When he arrived by the water where the people used to be, there was nobody; and when he went about, he saw only dead ones, no signs. He knew that nobody was left. There were no signs. After the one who was alive had left, not having seen anything, he went along in his canoe. He arrived where there had been a town. He went out, and there were only dead ones. There was nobody in the town. He started to go back. Then he came to the last place where Kutenai lived. He went to the town, and dead bodies were all piled up inside the tents. He always went about, and he knew that all the people were gone. He was crying as he went along. He thought: 'I am the only one left in this country, for the dogs also are dead.' When he came to the farthest village, he went about, and he saw some footprints of people. They had a tent. There were no dead bodies. Farther away there was the village site. He knew there must be two or three (alive). He even saw footprints, large ones and smaller ones. He did not know if there were three. He knew some one was saved. He went on in his canoe, and thought: 'I'll paddle that way. Those who lived here used to go that way. If it is a man, he might have moved.' Then he started in his canoe.

"He went along in his canoe and saw above there two black bears eating berries. He thought: 'I'll go and shoot them. If I shoot them, I'll eat them. I'll dry them. Then I'll see if anyone is left. After I have dried the meat, I'll look for them. I have seen footprints of people. They might be hungry men or women. They shall eat.' Then he started, and went there where the bears were. He arrived, and saw that they were not bears, but women. He saw one older one, and the other one a girl. He thought: 'I am glad to see people. Let me take that woman to be my wife.' Then he went and took hold of the girl. The girl spoke, and said to her mother: 'Mother, I see a man.' Her mother looked. The woman saw that her daughter was telling the truth. She saw a man taking her daughter. Then the woman and the girl and the youth cried, because they saw that all the Kutenai were dead. When they saw each other, they all cried together. The older woman said: 'Don't take my daughter. She is still small. Take me. You shall be my husband. Later on, when this my daughter is large, she shall be your wife. Then you shall have children.' Then the youth married the older woman. It was not long before the woman said: 'Now I see that my daughter is grown up. Now she may be your wife. It is good if you have children. Her body is strong now.' Then the youth took the girl for his wife. Then the Kutenai increased from there."

A third kind of catastrophe, one which sometimes follows epidemics and wars, is *mass suicide*; it, too, has its survivors. The Ba-ila, a Bantu people living in Rhodesia, have a legend which illustrates this point. It refers to a quarrel between two of their clans, the "Goats" and the "Hornets".

"Once upon a time the 'Goats' had a dispute with another clan, the 'Hornets', over a question of chieftainship; the 'Goats' having got the worst of it and being ousted from the premier position, planned to destroy themselves in the lake. They set to work to twist a very long rope—men, women, and children. Then they gathered on the lakeside and tied the rope in turn around their necks, and all plunged into the unfathomable depths. A man of another clan, the 'Lions', had married a woman of the 'Goats', and after failing to induce her to refrain from suicide, determined to die with her. They happened to be the last to be tied to the rope; they were pulled in and on the point of drowning when the man, repenting, cut the rope, and so freed himself and his wife. She struggled to escape from him, screaming 'Let me go! let me go!' but he persevered and brought her to land. This is why to this day the 'Lions' say to the 'Goats', 'It is we who saved you from extinction'."

Finally I want to draw attention to the deliberate use of survivors, especially to one historical and well-attested case. In a war of extermination between two South American Indian tribes a single man of the defeated side was left alive by the enemy and sent back to his own people. He was to tell them what he had seen and so deprive them of the courage for further fighting. Humboldt recounts the story of this messenger of horror.

"The long resistance which the Cabres, united under a brave leader, offered to the Caraibs, had ended by the year 1720 in the annihilation of the former. The Cabres had defeated their enemies at the mouth of the river; a large number of Caraibs were killed while fleeing between the cataracts and an island. The prisoners were eaten, but, with the refined cruelty and cunning typical of the peoples of South and North America, one Caraib was left alive. He was forced to climb a tree and witness all the barbarities and then was immediately sent off to recount them to the defeated. But the victorious jubilation of the Cabres' chief did not last long. The Caraibs returned in such numbers that, apart from a few miserable specimens, all the man-eating Cabres were exterminated."

This one man, left alive out of mockery, is forced to climb a tree and watch his own people being eaten. All the warriors with whom he went into battle have died fighting or, taken prisoner, have found their way into their enemies' bellies. As an enforced survivor, the horrors he has witnessed printed on his eyeballs, he is sent back to his own people. The substance of the message he takes, as his enemies imagine it, is thus: "Only one of you remains. You see how powerful we are.

Never dare to fight us again." But the impact of what this one man saw is so great and his enforced uniqueness so impressive that, on the contrary, he rouses his people to revenge. All the Caraibs everywhere mass together and make an end of the Cabres for ever.

This story, which is not the only one of its kind, proves the clarity with which primitive peoples see the survivor. They are perfectly aware of the singularity of his position and take it into account and try to make use of it for their own ends. The Caraib who was forced to climb the tree served both sides, friend and enemy alike. If we have the courage, there is an immense amount we can learn from his dual rôle.

The Resentment of the Dead

No-one who studies the original documents of any religion can fail to be amazed at the power of the dead. There are peoples whose existence is almost wholly dominated by rites connected with them.

The first thing that strikes one is the universal *fear* of the dead. They are discontented and full of envy for those they have left behind. They try to take revenge on them, sometimes for injuries done them during their life-time, but often simply because they themselves are no longer alive. It is the jealousy of the dead that the living fear most, and they try to propitiate them by flattery and by offerings of food. They provide them with everything they need for their journey to the land of the dead, so that they may go far off and never return to harm and torment the living. The spirits of the dead send disease, or bring it with them; they have power over the increase of game and of crops, and a hundred ways of meddling with life. Passionately and continually they seek to get hold of the living.

Since the dead envy the living all the objects of daily life which they themselves have had to leave behind, it was originally customary for the living to keep nothing, or as little as possible, of what had belonged to the dead. Everything was put in the grave, or burnt with them. The huts they had lived in were abandoned and never used again; or they were buried in their houses with all their property, to prove that no-one wanted to keep any of it. But even this did not wholly assuage their wrath, for the deeper envy of the dead was not directed towards objects, which could be made or acquired afresh, but to life itself.

It is certainly remarkable that the same feeling should be attributed to the dead everywhere and under the most varied conditions. The dead of all peoples, it seems, are dominated by the same emotions.

In the eyes of those who are still alive, everyone who is dead has suffered a defeat, which consists in *having been survived*. The dead cannot resign themselves to this injury which was inflicted on them, and so it is natural that they should want to inflict it on others.

Thus every dead man is someone who has been survived. Only in those vast and infrequent catastrophes where everyone, or nearly everyone, perishes together does the situation alter. In the individual, isolated death which we are considering it is *one* man who is torn from his family and his group. There are large numbers of survivors and all of them who have any right to the dead man form a lamenting pack to mourn him. They feel weakened by his death and their love for him is also still present; indeed it is often impossible to separate the one feeling from the other. They lament him passionately and there is no doubt that, at bottom, their mourning is genuine. If its manifestations appear suspect to outsiders this is because the situation is complex and, for that reason, equivocal.

For the same people who have cause to lament are also survivors. They lament their loss, but they feel a kind of satisfaction in their own survival. They will not normally admit this, even to themselves, for they regard it as improper, but they are always perfectly aware of what the dead man's feelings must be. He is bound to hate them, for they still have what he has lost, which is life. Therefore they call on his soul to return in order to convince him that they did not want his death. They remind him how good they were to him while he was amongst them. They count up the practical proofs of their having done everything he would have wanted done. His last wishes are conscientiously carried out; in many places they have the force of law. And behind all they do lies the unshakeable conviction that the dead man must hate them for having survived him.

"An Indian child in Demerara had taken to the habit of eating sand, which contributed to its early death. While the dead body of the child lay in the open coffin, which his father had procured from a Creole carpenter in the neighbourhood, and just before the interment, the grandmother of the child stood over it and in wailing tone said:

" 'My child, I always told you not to eat sand. I never gave you any, for I knew it was not good for you: you always sought it yourself. I told you that it was bad. Now see, it has killed you. Don't trouble me, for it was your own doing; some evil thing put it into your head to eat it. Look, I put your arrow and bow by your side that you may amuse yourself. I was always kind to you: be good and don't trouble me.'

"Then the mother came up crying, and said as in a chant: 'My child, I brought you into the world to see and enjoy all the good things. This breast (she held it up) nourished you as long as you were willing to take it. I made your laps and pretty skirts. I took care of you and fed you, and played with you and never beat you. You must be good and not bring evil upon me.'

"The father of the child likewise approached and said: 'My boy, when I told you that the sand would kill you, you would not listen to me, and now see, you are dead. I went out and got a beautiful coffin for you. I shall have to work to pay for it. I made your grave in a pleasant spot where you loved to play. I shall place you comfortably, and put some sand for you to eat, for now it can not harm you, and I know that you like it. You must not bring bad luck to me; but look for him who made you eat the sand.' "

Grandmother, mother and father had loved this child. But, despite their love and the fact that he is so small, they fear his resentment, for they are still alive. They protest their innocence of his death. The grandmother gives him a bow and arrows to take with him; the father has bought him an expensive coffin and puts sand in the grave for him to eat, for he knows how fond he is of it. The simple tenderness they show the child is moving and yet there is something disquieting about it, for it is permeated with fear.

With some peoples belief in the continued existence of the dead has developed into an *ancestor cult*. Wherever this has assumed a rigid form it is as though people had learnt a way of taming the dead, or, at any rate, those who matter to them. Regular offerings of what they desire, namely, praise and food, keep them contented. Looked after according to traditional rules they become allies. Whatever they were in this life they remain in the hereafter, continuing to occupy their former positions. A man who was a powerful chieftain on earth will still be one in the grave. During sacrifices and invocations he is the first to be named. His sensibilities are treated with consideration, for, if they are hurt, he can become very dangerous. He takes an interest in the welfare of his descendants and it is essential that he should be well disposed to them, for much depends on him. He likes to be near them and nothing must be done which might drive him away.

Among the Zulus in South Africa the relationship between the living and their ancestors was particularly intimate. The reports which the British missionary Callaway collected about a hundred years ago, and later published, provide the most authentic account of their ancestor cult. He lets his authorities speak for themselves, taking down their words in their own language. His book, *The Religious System of the Amazulu*, is rare and for that reason too little known. It is among the essential documents of mankind.

The ancestors of the Zulus turn into snakes and go into the ground, but they are not, as one might suppose, mythical snakes, which no-one ever sees. They are familiar species which play near the huts and often enter them. Some of these snakes resemble specific ancestors in their physical peculiarities and are recognized as such by the living.

But they are not only snakes, for they appear to the living in dreams in their human shape, and talk to them. People wait for these dreams and grow uneasy if they do not have them. They *want* to talk to their dead and to see them "bright and clear" in their dreams. Sometimes the image of the ancestors is obscured and grows dark and then certain rites must be carried out so that it becomes clear again. From time to time, but especially on important occasions, sacrifices are offered to them; goats and oxen are slaughtered and they are solemnly invited to partake of them. They are addressed in a loud voice by their "laud-giving" names, on which they set great store. They love to be honoured and are insulted if these names are forgotten or passed over in silence. The cries of the sacrificial animal must be loud, so that they can hear them. The ancestors love these cries. Sheep, who die silently, are no use as victims. The sacrifice is regarded as a meal which the dead share with the living; it is a kind of communion of the living and the dead.

If people live as their ancestors used to, if they follow the old usages and customs and keep them unchanged, and if the dead are offered their regular sacrifices, they are content, and will further the well-being of their descendants. When someone falls ill, he knows that one of his ancestors is displeased, and he will do his utmost to find out why.

For the dead are by no means always just. They were human beings whom one knew, and their faults and weaknesses are equally well remembered. When they appear in dreams it is in a way which corresponds to their character. One case, which Callaway recorded at some length, shows how, even when honoured and well-fed, the dead can on occasion be seized with rancour against their survivors, solely because they are still alive. Transposed into our own terms, the history of a grudge of this kind corresponds to the course of a dangerous illness.

An elder brother has died. His possessions and particularly his cattle, which are the wealth of these people, have passed to his younger brother. This is the normal succession and so the younger brother, having duly made the customary sacrifices, enters on his inheritance unaware of any offence against the dead man. But suddenly he falls seriously ill and his elder brother appears to him in a dream.

"I dreamed that he was beating me, and saying, 'How is it that you no longer know that I am?' I answered him, 'What can I do that you may see I know you? I know that you are my brother.' He asked, 'When you sacrifice a bullock, why do you not call upon me?' I replied, 'I do call on you, and laud you by your laud-giving names. Just tell me the bullock which I have killed without calling on you.' He answered, saying, 'I wish for meat.' I refused him, saying, 'No, my brother, I have no bullock; do you see any in the cattle-pen?' 'Though there be but one', he said, 'I demand it'. When I awoke, I had a pain in my side; when I tried to breathe, I could not; my breath was short.

"The man was obstinate, and would not agree to kill a bullock. He said, 'I am really ill, and I know the disease with which I am affected.' The people said to him, 'If you know it, why do you not get rid of it? Can a man purposely cause the disease which affects him? When he knows what it is, does he wish to die? For when the spirit is angry with a man, it destroys him.'

"He replied, 'Not so, Sirs; I have been made ill by a man. I see him in sleep, when I am lying down; because he wishes for meat, he has acted towards me with tricks, and says that, when I kill cattle, I do not call on him. So I am much surprised for my part, for I have killed so many cattle, and there is not one that I killed without calling on him. If he wished for meat, he could just tell me, 'My brother, I wish for meat.' But he says to me that I never laud him. I am angry, and say he just wants to kill me.'

"The people said, 'Do you mean to say that the spirit still understands how to speak? Where is he, that we too may take him to task? For we were present at all times when you slaughtered cattle; and you lauded him, and called upon him by the laud-giving names which he received for his bravery; and we heard. And if it could really be that that brother of yours, or any other man who is already dead, should rise again, we could take him to task, and ask, 'Why do you say such things?'

"The sick man replied, 'Eh! My brother acts in this boastful way because he is oldest, for I am younger than he. I wonder when he tells me just to destroy all the cattle. Did he die and leave none behind?'

"The people said, 'The man is dead. But we are really speaking with you, and your eyes are still really looking upon us. So we say, as regards that man, you should just speak quietly with him; and if you have a goat only, worship him with it. It is a shame in him to come and kill you. Why do you constantly see your brother in your sleep, and become ill? It were well that a man should dream of his brother, and awake with his body in health.'

"He said, 'Eh, Sirs, I will now give him the flesh he loves. He demands flesh; he kills me. He wrongs me; daily I dream of him, and then awake in suffering. I say, he is not a man; he was a wretch, who liked to fight with people. He was a man of a word and a blow. If a man spoke to him he wished at once to fight with him; and then a dispute might arise. It was caused by him, and then he would fight. And he did not see it nor say, 'The fault was committed by me; I ought not to fight with these people.' His spirit is like him; it is wicked; it is constantly angry. But I will give him his flesh which he demands of me. If I see that he leaves me and I am well, I will kill some cattle in the morning. If it is he, let me get well and breathe, and my breath no longer cut me, as it cuts me at the present time.'

"The people assented, 'Yes, yes, if in the morning you are well, then we shall see that it is indeed the spirit of your brother. But if in the morning you are still ill, we will not say it is your brother; then we will know it is only a simple disease.'

"When the sun went down he was still complaining of pain. But at the time of milking the cows, he said, 'Give me some food, that I may eat.' The food was fluid, not thick, and he was able to swallow a little. Then he said, 'Just give me some beer, I am thirsty.' His wives gave him beer, and had confidence in their hearts. They rejoiced, for they had been fearful, saying, 'Is it then that the disease is great, since he does not eat?' They did not speak out their joy, but looked at each other only. He drank the beer and said, 'Give me some snuff too, my children, let me just take a little.' They gave him some, he took it, and lay down; and sleep came.

"And in the middle of the night his brother came and said 'So then have you pointed out the cattle? Will you kill them in the morning?'

"The sleeper assented, 'Yes, yes, I will kill one. Why do you, my brother, say to me I never call on you, whilst whenever I kill cattle I call on you by your laud-giving names; for you were a brave, and stabbed in the conflict?'

"He replied, 'I say it with reason, when I wish for flesh. *I indeed died and left you with a village.* You had a large village.'

" 'Yes, yes, my brother, you left me with a village. But when you left me with it, and died, had you killed all the cattle?'

" 'No, I had not killed them all.'

" 'Well then, child of my father, do you tell *me* to destroy them all?'

" 'No, I do not tell you to destroy them all. But I tell you to kill, that your village may be great.'

"He awoke and felt that he was now well, the pain in his side being no longer there. He sat up and nudged his wife. 'Awake and light a fire.' His wife awoke and blew up the fire. She asked him how he was. He replied, 'Oh! just be quiet; on awaking my body was feeling light. I have been speaking with my brother; on awaking I was quite well.' He took some snuff, and went to sleep. The spirit of his brother came again. He said, 'See, I have cured you now. Kill the cattle in the morning.'

"In the morning he arose and went into the cattle-pen. He had some younger brothers; he called them, and they went in with him. 'I just call you, for I am now well. My brother says, he has cured me.' Then he told them to bring an ox. They brought it. 'Bring that barren cow.' They brought them both. They came to him to the upper part of the pen, and stood there. He prayed, saying:

" 'Well then, eat, ye people of our house. Let a good spirit be with us, that the very children may be well, and the people be in health! I ask, how is it that you, since you are my brother, come to me again and again in my sleep, and I dream of you, and am then sick? That spirit is good which comes to a man and tells him good news. I am always complaining that I am constantly ill. What cattle are those which their owner devours, devouring them through being ill? I say, Cease; leave off making me ill. I say, Come to me when I am asleep, and tell me a matter, and say, My brother, I wish so-and-so. You come to me for the purpose of killing me. It is clear that you were a bad fellow when you were a man: are you still a bad fellow under the ground? I used not to think that your spirit would come to me with kindness, and tell me good news. But how is it that you come with evil, you, my eldest brother, who ought to bring good to the village, that no evil might come to it, for I know that you are its owner?'

"Then he said these words about the cattle, and returned thanks: 'There are the cattle which I offer you. Here is a red ox, here is a red and white barren cow. Kill them. I say, Tell me a matter kindly, that on awakening my body may be free from pain. I say, let all the spirits of the people of our house come here together to you, you who are fond of meat.'

"And then he said, 'Stab them.' One of his brothers takes an assagai, and stabs the barren cow; it falls down. He stabs the ox; both bellow;

he kills them—they die. He tells them to skin them. So they skin them, the hides are taken off; they eat them in the cattle-pen. All the men assemble to ask for food. They take it away joint by joint. They eat and are satisfied, and give thanks, saying, 'We thank you, Son of So-and-so. When a spirit makes you ill, we shall know that it is your wretched brother. We did not know, during your very severe illness, that we should eat meat with you again. We now see it is the wretch which is killing you. We are glad because we see you are well.' "

"I am indeed dead", says the elder brother, and this sentence contains the core of the dispute, the dangerous illness and the whole sequence of events. Whatever the dead man's behaviour and demands, he is indeed dead, and this is sufficient reason for bitterness. "I left you a village" he says, and adds quickly, "You have a large village". This village is the other's life, and thus he might also have added, "I am dead and you are alive."

This is the reproach that the living man fears and by dreaming of it he acknowledges its justice: he *did* survive his brother. The magnitude of this wrong, beside which all other wrongs pale, gives the dead man power to transform his own bitterness into serious illness for the other. "He wants to kill me" says the younger brother, and adds to himself, "because he is dead". Thus he knows very well why he fears him and it is in order to propitiate him that he finally gives way about the sacrifice.

Survival, as one sees, carries with it considerable uneasiness for the survivors. Even where regular forms of honouring them have been instituted, the dead can never quite be trusted. The more powerful a man was here on earth, the greater and more dangerous is his rancour afterwards.

In the kingdom of Uganda a way was found of keeping the spirit of the dead king among his faithful subjects. He was not sent away nor allowed to vanish, but forced to remain in this world. After his death a medium, or *mandwa*, was nominated, in whom the spirit of the dead king took up its abode. This medium, who had the function of a priest, reproduced the appearance, gestures and exact language of the dead king, even, as is reliably attested in one case, to the extent of using the obsolete speech of 300 years before, when the king in question had lived. It might even happen that a medium used words which no-one, not even his colleagues, understood. For, if a *mandwa* died, the spirit of the king descended on another member of the same clan. One *mandwa* took over the office from another and thus the spirit of the king was never without a dwelling place.

It should not be imagined, however, that the medium acted the king continuously. From time to time, as the saying was, "the king took him by the head". He became possessed and embodied the dead man in every detail. In clans responsible for providing *mandwas* the characteristics of each king at the time of his death were handed down orally and mimetically. King Kigala had died at a very advanced age; his medium was quite a young man, but, when "the king took him by the head", he changed into an old man; his face became wrinkled and he limped and slavered at the mouth.

These seizures were treated with awe. It was regarded as an honour to be present at them; one was in the presence of the dead king and *recognised* him. He for his part, being able to manifest himself as he wished in the body of a man whose sole office this was, might be expected to feel less resentment at having been survived than those completely cast out from the world of the living.

It was amongst the Chinese that the most significant development of an ancestor cult took place. In order to make plain what they meant by an ancestor I must explain briefly their conception of the soul.

They believed that every man possessed two souls. One of these, *po*, originated with the sperm and thus was in existence from the moment of conception. Memory was part of this soul. The other, *hun*, originated with the air breathed in after birth, and then took form gradually. This soul had the shape of the body it animated, but was invisible. Intelligence belonged to it and grew with it. It was the superior soul.

After death the breath-soul ascended into the sky, whilst the sperm-soul remained with the corpse in the grave. It was this inferior soul which was most feared; it was malicious and jealous and sought to drag the living with it to death. As the body decayed the sperm-soul also gradually dissolved and thus ultimately lost its power to harm.

The superior breath-soul, on the other hand, continued to exist. It needed food, for it was a long journey to the world of the dead, and if it was not given food by its descendants it suffered terribly. If it lost its way it was unhappy and then became as dangerous as the sperm-soul.

Funeral rites had a double purpose. They were intended to protect the living from the activities of the dead and, at the same time, to secure survival for the souls of the dead. Communication with the dead was dangerous if it was they who initiated it, but it was auspicious if it took the form of an ancestor cult, following the demands of tradition and carried out at the proper times.

The survival of the soul depended on the physical and moral strength it had gained during life on earth. These were acquired through *food* and through *study*. Of special importance was the difference between the soul of a lord, who was a meat-eater and had been well fed all his life, and that of an ordinary, cheaply and badly fed peasant. "Only lords", says Granet, "have a soul in the proper sense of the word. And this soul is not used up with the years, but is enriched by them. A lord prepares for death by filling himself with exquisite dishes and life-giving drinks. In the course of his life he incorporates into himself a great number of essences and, the larger and more fruitful his estates, the more of these there will be. He increases the rich substance of his ancestors, who themselves had their fill of meat and game. At his death his soul does not dissolve like a common soul, but escapes, full of strength, out of his body.

"If a lord has lived according to the rules of his station, his soul after death, still further ennobled and purified by the funerary rites, will possess a sublime and shining power. It has the beneficent strength of a guardian spirit and, at the same time, retains all the traits of an enduring and sacred personality. It has become an *ancestor-soul.*"

A special cult is dedicated to it, in a particular temple. It shares in all the seasonal ceremonies and in the life of the countryside and the people. If game is plentiful it eats well; if the harvest is bad it starves. The ancestor-soul feeds on the corn, meat and game of the manorial lands which are its home. But, rich as the personality of such a soul is so long as it continues to exist in its accumulated and concentrated strength, there comes a moment when it too dissolves and is extinguished. After four or five generations the "soul-tablet" with which it was ritually linked loses its claims to a special sanctuary, and is put away in a stone chest with the tablets of all the earlier ancestors whose individual memory is already lost. The ancestor it represents and whose name it bears is no longer honoured as a lord. His forceful individuality, distinct for so long, vanishes. His course is run, his rôle as an ancestor finished. The rites dedicated to him enabled him to escape for a good many years the fate of the common dead. Now his soul joins the crowd of all the other dead and becomes anonymous as they are.

Not all ancestors survive for as long as four or five generations. It depends on their rank whether their tablet is kept in position for so long and their soul called on to accept food. But, however long or short the period, the fact that they continue to exist at all changes in some respects the character of survival.

The son no longer feels a secret triumph in being alive when his father is dead, for the latter remains present as an ancestor. The son owes him everything he has and must keep him well-disposed. He must provide food for him even after his death and carefully refrain from behaving arrogantly towards him. As long as the son is alive the ancestor-soul of his father will, in every case, exist too and will, as we have seen, retain all the traits of a distinct and recognisable person. The father, on his side, is very much concerned with being fed and venerated. For his new existence as an ancestor it is of cardinal importance that his son should be alive: without descendants there would be no-one to venerate him. He wants his son and succeeding generations to survive him. He wants them to prosper, for on their prosperity depends his own existence as an ancestor. He wants people to go on living for as long as they are prepared to remember him. There is thus a close and mutually rewarding link between the modified form of survival enjoyed by ancestors and the pride of the descendants who procure it for them.

The fact that ancestors remain separate and distinguishable individuals for some generations is also important. They are known as individuals and venerated as such, only those of the remoter past fusing into a crowd. Between every living man and this crowd stand separate and clearly defined individuals such as his father and grandfather, and the very nature of the relationship between him and them means that any feeling of triumph in his own present existence which comes to tinge his veneration will be of a very mild and moderate kind and carry no temptation to increase the number of the dead. His own death will some day increase it by one, but this he naturally wants to defer for as long as possible. Survival loses its crowd characteristics; as a driving passion it would be absurd and incomprehensible and thus it ceases to be murderous. Piety towards the dead and awareness of self have entered into an alliance. The one merges into the other, but the best of both is preserved.

If one reflects on the figure of the ideal ruler as it takes shape in Chinese history and thought one is struck by its humanity. It is probable that the absence of brutality in this image is due to the particular form of ancestor worship.

Epidemics

THE BEST DESCRIPTION of plague is that given by Thucydides, who suffered from it himself and recovered. Tersely and accurately it covers every essential aspect of the phenomenon. I propose to quote the most important parts of it, though in a slightly different order.

"People died like flies. The bodies of the dying were heaped one on top of the other, and half-dead creatures could be seen staggering about in the streets or flocking round the fountains in their desire for water. The temples in which they took up their quarters were full of the dead bodies of people who had died inside them.

"The members of some households were so overwhelmed by the weight of their calamities that they had actually given up the usual practice of making laments for the dead.

"All the funeral ceremonies which used to be observed were now disorganised, and they buried the dead as best they could. Many people, lacking the necessary means of burial because so many deaths had already occurred in their households, adopted the most shameless methods. They would arrive first at a funeral pyre that had been made by others, put their own dead upon it and set it alight, or, finding another pyre burning, they would throw the corpse that they were carrying on top of the other one and go away.

"No fear of God or law of man had a restraining influence. As for the Gods, it seemed to be the same thing whether one worshipped them or not, when one saw the good and the bad dying indiscriminately. As for offences against human law, no-one expected to live long enough to be brought to trial and punished; instead everyone felt that already a far heavier sentence had been passed on him and was hanging over him, and that before the time for its execution arrived it was only natural to get some pleasure out of life.

"The ones who felt most pity for the sick and the dying were those who had had the plague themselves and had recovered from it. They knew what it was like and at the same time felt themselves to be safe, for no-one caught the disease twice, or, if he did, the second attack was never fatal. Such people were congratulated on all sides, and they themselves were so elated at the time of their recovery that they fondly imagined that they could never die of any other disease in the future."

Among the misfortunes which have visited mankind the great epidemics have left a particularly vivid memory. Their onset is as sudden as a catastrophe of nature, but whilst an earthquake, for example, generally exhausts itself in a few short shocks, an epidemic may last for months or a whole year. An earthquake does its worst at one blow, all its victims perishing simultaneously. An epidemic of plague, on the other hand, has a cumulative effect. At first only a few people are attacked, then the number of cases grows. The dead are visible everywhere and soon there are more dead to be seen than living.

The final result of an epidemic may be the same as that of an earth-quake, but in an epidemic people *see* the advance of death; it takes place under their very eyes. They are like participants in a battle which lasts longer than all known battles. But the enemy is hidden; he is nowhere to be seen and cannot be hit. One can only wait to be hit by him. In this battle only the enemy is active; he strikes where he likes and strikes down so many that one soon comes to fear that no-one will escape.

As soon as an epidemic is acknowledged, it is felt that it can have only one end, and that is the death of everyone.

Since there is no cure for it, those it attacks expect the execution of the sentence pronounced on them. But only those seized by the con-tagion constitute a crowd. They are equal in relation to the fate await-ing them; their numbers grow with increasing speed; they are moving towards a common goal which they reach in a few days, and they end in the greatest state of density possible to human bodies, pressed together in a heap of corpses. There are those who believe that this stagnating crowd of the dead is only temporarily dead and, at a given moment, will rise again and stand in serried ranks before God, awaiting the Last Judgement. But, even if we disregard the subsequent fate of the dead—for not all religions share the same conception of it—one thing remains indisputable: an epidemic results in a crowd of the dying and the dead. "Streets and temples" are full of them. Often it is no longer possible to bury the victims singly in the proper way; in huge mass graves they are heaped one on top of the other, thousands of them together in the same grave.

There are three important and familiar phenomena which result in a heap of corpses. They are closely related and it is therefore par-ticularly important to analyse their differences. They are: battle, mass suicide and epidemic.

The aim of a battle is a heap of enemy dead. The number of living enemies is to be reduced so that the number of one's own people becomes comparatively greater. That some of these should also perish in the process is inevitable, but this is not what is desired. The goal is a heap of enemy dead and each combatant strives for it actively, with the strength of his own arm.

In mass suicide this activity is turned against one's own people. Men, women and children kill each other, until nothing remains but the heap of their own dead. Fire is used so that destruction shall be complete and nothing left to fall into the hands of the enemy.

In an epidemic the result is the same as in mass suicide, but it is not voluntary and seems to have been imposed from outside by some unknown power. The goal takes longer to reach and people live in an equality of terrible expectation, all ordinary relationships abrogated.

The element of contagion, which plays so large a part in an epidemic, has the effect of making people separate from each other. The safest thing is to keep away from everyone else, for anyone may already have the infection on him. Some flee from the town and disperse to their estates; others shut themselves up in their houses and allow no-one in. Each man shuns every other; his last hope is to keep his distance. The prospect of life, and life itself, is expressed in terms of distance from the sick. Those who catch the infection end by forming a dead mass; those who have so far escaped it keep away from everyone, even their closest relatives, their parents, husbands or wives and children. It is strange to see how the hope of survival isolates them, each becoming a single individual confronting the crowd of victims.

But in the midst of universal disaster, when everyone attacked by the disease is given up for lost, the most astounding thing happens: a few, a very few, recover. The feelings of such people can be imagined. Not only have they survived, but they also feel themselves to be invulnerable, and thus they can afford sympathy for the sick and dying by whom they are surrounded. "Such people", says Thucydides, "were so elated at the time of their recovery that they fondly imagined that they could never die of any other disease in the future."

Cemeteries

THE ATTRACTION of cemeteries and graveyards is so strong that people visit them even if no-one belonging to them is buried there. In foreign cities they make a pilgrimage to the cemetery and walk about there as though it were an amenity specially provided for them. It is not always veneration for some famous man which draws them there. Even where this is the original motive, the visit always turns into something more. A cemetery very soon induces a special state of mind. We have a pious habit of deceiving ourselves about this mood. In fact, the awe we feel, and still more the awe we exhibit, covers a secret satisfaction.

What does someone who finds himself in a graveyard actually do? How does he move and what occupies his thoughts? He wanders slowly up and down between the graves, looking at this stone and that, reading the names on them and feeling drawn to some of them. Then he begins to notice what is engraved beneath the names. He finds a couple who lived together for a long time and now lie together for always, as they should; or a child who died quite young; or a girl who just reached her eighteenth birthday. More and more it is periods of time which fascinate the visitor. Increasingly they stand out from the touching inscriptions on the headstones and become simply periods of time as such.

Here is a man who lived to be thirty-two; another, over there, died at forty-five. The visitor is older than either of them and yet they are already out of the race. He finds many who did not get as far as he has, but, unless they died particularly young, he feels no sadness for them. But there are also many who surpassed his present age, living for seventy or, now and again, for over eighty years, as he can still do himself. These arouse in him a desire to emulate them. For him everything is still open; his span of life is not yet fixed, and in this lies his superiority; with effort he may even surpass them. He has, anyway, a good chance of equalling them, for one advantage is his in any case: their goal is reached; they are no longer alive. They are there for him to compete with, but all the strength is on his side; they have no strength, but only a stated goal; and even those of them who lived longest are dead now. They cannot look him in the eyes as man to man and he draws from them the strength to become, and to remain for ever, *more* than they are. The eighty-nine-year-old who lies there acts on him like a spur. What is there to prevent *him* from living to ninety?

But this is not the only kind of calculation which occupies the man who stands between the rows of graves. He begins to notice how long it is that some of the buried have lain there. The time that separates him from their death is somehow reassuring and exhilarating: he has known the world for that much longer. In graveyards which have old memorials going back to the 17th and 18th centuries the visitor stands patiently before the half-effaced inscriptions, not moving until he has deciphered them. Chronology, which is normally only used for practical purposes, suddenly acquires a vivid and meaningful life for him. All the centuries he knows of are his. The man in the grave knows nothing of the man who stands beside it, reflecting on the span of the completed life. For him time ended with the year of his death; for the other it has continued right up to the present. What would he, long dead, not give still to be able to stand by the side of the visitor! 200 years have passed since he died; the other is, as it were, 200 years older than him. Many of the things which happened during those years are known to him; he has read about them, heard people talk and experienced some of them himself. He is in a position where it would be difficult not to feel some superiority, and the natural man does feel it.

But he feels more than this. As he walks among the graves he feels that he is alone. Side by side at his feet lie the unknown dead, and they are many. How many is not known, but the number is very great and there will be more and more of them. They cannot move, but must remain there, crowded together. He alone comes and goes as he wishes; he alone stands upright.

Immortality

CONSIDERATION OF literary or any other private immortality can best start with a man like Stendhal. It would be hard to find a man less sympathetic to religion and more completely unaffected by its promises and obligations. His thoughts and feelings were directed wholly to this life and he experienced it with exactness and depth. He gave himself up to it, enjoying what could give him pleasure; but he did not become shallow or stale in doing so, because he allowed everything that was separate to remain separate, instead of trying to construct spurious unities. He thought much, but his thoughts were never cold. He was suspicious of everything that did not move him. All that he recorded and all that he shaped remained close to the fiery moment of genesis. He loved many things and believed in some, but all of them remained miraculously concrete for him. They were all there in him and he could find them at once without resort to specious tricks of arrangement.

This man, who took nothing for granted, who wanted to discover everything for himself; who, as far as life is feeling and spirit, was life itself; who was in the heart of every situation and therefore had a right to look at it from outside; with whom word and substance were so intuitively one that it was as though he had taken it on himself to purify language single-handed—this rare and truly free man had, none the less, one article of faith, which he spoke of as simply and naturally as of a mistress.

Without pitying himself, he was content to write for a few, but he was certain that in a hundred years he would be read by many. Nowhere in modern times is a belief in literary immortality to be found in a clearer, purer and less pretentious form. What does a man mean who holds this belief? He means that he will still be here when everyone else who lived at the same time is no longer here. It is not that he feels any animosity towards the living as such; he does not try to get rid of them, nor harm them in any way. He does not even see them as opponents. He despises those who acquire false fame and would despise himself too if he fought them with their own weapons. He bears them no malice, for he knows how completely mistaken they are, but he chooses the company of those to whom he himself will one day belong, men of earlier times whose work still lives, who speak to him and *feed* him. The gratitude he feels to them is gratitude for life itself.

Killing in order to survive is meaningless to such a man, for it is not now that he wants to survive. It is only in a hundred years that he will enter the lists, when he is no longer alive and thus cannot kill. Then it will be a question of work contending against work, with nothing that he himself can do. The true rivalry, the one that matters, begins when the rivals are no longer there. Thus he cannot even watch the fight. But the *work* must be there and, if it is to be there, it must contain the greatest and purest measure of life. Not only does he abjure killing, but he takes with him into immortality all who were alive with him here, and it is then that all these, the least as well as the greatest, are most truly alive.

He is the exact opposite of those rulers whose whole entourage must die when they die, so that they may find among the dead all they have been used to on earth. In nothing is their ultimate powerlessness more terribly revealed. They kill in death as they have killed in life; a retinue of the slain accompanies them from one world to the other.

But whoever opens Stendhal will find him and also everything which surrounded him; and he finds it *here*, in this life. Thus the dead offer themselves as food to the living; their immortality profits them. It is a reversal of sacrifice to the dead, which profits both dead and living. There is no more rancour between them and the sting has been taken from survival.

ELEMENTS OF POWER

Force and Power

THE WORD "force" suggests something close and immediate in its effect, something more directly compelling than power. The phrase "physical force" is really only a more explicit expression of the same idea, for power in its lower and cruder manifestations is always better described as force; it is by force, for example, that prey is seized and carried to the mouth. When force gives itself time in which to operate it becomes power, but when the moment of crisis arrives, the moment of irrevocable decision, it reverts to being pure force. Power is more general and operates over a wider space than force; it includes much more, but is less dynamic. It is more ceremonious and even has a certain measure of patience. The distinction between force and power can be illustrated very simply by the relationship between cat and mouse.

The cat uses force to catch the mouse, to seize it, hold it in its claws and ultimately kill it. But while it is *playing* with it another factor is present. It lets it go, allows it to run about a little and even turn its back; and, during this time, the mouse is no longer subjected to force. But it is still within the power of the cat and can be caught again. If it gets right away it escapes from the cat's sphere of power; but, up to the point at which it can no longer be reached, it is still within it. The space which the cat dominates, the moments of hope it allows the mouse, while continuing however to watch it closely all the time and never relaxing its interest and intention to destroy it—all this together, space, hope, watchfulness and destructive intent, can be called the actual body of power, or, more simply, power itself.

Inherent in power, therefore, as opposed to force, is a certain extension in space and in time. I suggested earlier that the mouth was the prototype of the prison. There is in any case a relationship between the two which will serve to illustrate the relationship between force and power. Once inside his enemy's mouth the victim has no hope left, for he has neither time nor space to manœuvre in. In both these respects a prison is like an extension of the mouth. Like a mouse under the eyes of a cat the prisoner can walk up and down a little and can turn his back on his warders; he has time before him, in course of which he can hope to escape or be released. But the whole machinery of the prison, in one cell of which he is confined, seems geared to his destruction and he is conscious of it all the time, even when it is not actually in operation.

The distinction between force and power can be seen in another quite different sphere, that of the varying degrees of religious submission. Everyone who believes in God believes that he is continuously in His power and, in his own way, has come to terms with it. But there are those for whom this is not enough. They await some sharp intervention, some direct act of divine force, which they can recognize and feel as such. They live in expectation of God's commands; for them He has the cruder features of a ruler. His active will and their active and explicit submission in each particular case become the core of their religion. Religions of this kind incline to the doctrine of predestination; their adherents are always able to feel that everything which happens to them is a direct expression of God's will. Thus, all their lives, they find fresh occasions to submit. It is as though they were already in God's mouth, to be crushed in the next instant. But they have to live their whole lives in this terrible place, undaunted by it and still striving to do right.

Islam and Calvinism are the religions which exhibit this trend most strongly. Their believers yearn for God's force; His power alone does not satisfy them; it is too distant and leaves them too free. The state of continuous expectation of command, to which, early in life, they surrender themselves for good and all, marks them deeply and also has a momentous effect on their attitude to other people. It creates a soldierly type of believer, men to whom battle is the truest representation of life and who feel no fear in actual battles because for them the whole of life is a battle. I shall say more about this type of believer in connection with command.

Power and Speed

THE SPEED WHICH is relevant to power is speed in pursuit and speed of grasp. For both man took animals for his models. From wolves and other animals which run their quarry down he learned to pursue and overtake his prey. From the cat tribe he learned to spring on it; here the masters he admired and envied were the lion, the leopard and the tiger. Birds of prey combine both movements; an eagle or a falcon which flies alone, visible to all, and swoops down from a height, is a perfect expression of the dual process. They gave man the arrow, whose

speed long remained the greatest he possessed. In the form of arrows
men swooped on their prey.

Thus these creatures early became symbols of power. Sometimes
men thought of them as gods, sometimes as the ancestors of their
rulers: Genghis Khan was descended from a wolf and Horus, as a
falcon, was the God of the Egyptian Pharaohs; in the African kingdoms
lions and leopards were the sacred animals of the royal clan; and from
the flames of the pyre on which his body was burnt the soul of a Roman
emperor flew up to heaven as an eagle.

But swiftest of all was, and is, lightning. There is no defence against
it and the superstitious fear it arouses is universal. The Franciscan monk
Rubruck, who was sent by St. Louis on an embassy to the Mongols,
reported that they feared thunder and lightning above all things. In a
storm they drove any stranger out of their tents, wrapped themselves
in black felt and hid inside until it was over. The Persian historian
Rashid, who was in the service of the Mongols, tells how they avoided
the flesh of all animals killed by lightning, not daring even to go near
them. All kinds of prohibitions sprang from their attempt to propitiate
lightning; anything which might draw it down on them had to be
avoided. With other peoples lightning is the weapon of the supreme
God.

Sudden lightning in darkness is like a revelation; it both strikes and
illuminates. But it is not always the same and people study each manifestation in the hope of discovering the will of their gods: they ask
what kind of lightning it is, which quarter of the sky it is in, where it
comes from and where it disappears. Among the Etruscans its interpretation was the task of a special body of priests, whose office was
continued in the Roman *fulguratores*.

"The power of a ruler", says an old Chinese text, "is like the lightning flash, though its force is less." It is remarkable how many stories
there are of rulers being struck by lightning. These cannot all be literally true, but the connection is in itself revealing. Such stories are
particularly common among the Romans and the Mongols, both of
them peoples who believed in a supreme sky-god and had a strongly
developed feeling for power. They thought of lightning as a supernatural command and as striking where it was *intended* to strike. If a
king was struck it was by a ruler even mightier than himself. It stood
for the quickest, the most sudden and also the most public form of
punishment.

Men imitated lightning with their weapons: the flash and roar of
fire-arms, and particularly of artillery, have always terrified peoples

who did not possess them; to them they are thunder and lightning.

But, even before this, men had sought ways of increasing their own animal speed: the taming of the horse and the perfecting of mounted armies led to the great invasions from the east. In every contemporary account of the Mongols, great stress is laid on their speed: suddenly they were there, only to vanish again and appear somewhere else even more suddenly. They turned even the speed of flight to account; scarcely did their enemies believe them fled than they were again surrounded by them.

Since that time physical speed has become an even more important part of power. It is unnecessary to enlarge here on the rôle it plays in our own machine civilization.

Different from speed in grasping or seizing, though allied to it, is the sudden unmasking of an opponent. Some apparently harmless and submissive creature stands before one; one tears off its mask and reveals an enemy. To make its effect the unmasking must be sudden and swift. It is pursuit narrowed and concentrated into a small space; speed here has become drama. As we shall see later, the rapid substitution of one mask for another is an age-old method of deception. Each fresh mask is a different manifestation of power and makes its own effect. Where there are opposing protagonists the dissembling of the one is matched by that of the other. The unmasking of an opponent is the counterpart of this process. A ruler invites civil or military notables to a banquet and then suddenly, when they least expect an act of enmity, has them all butchered. The change from one form of behaviour to another exactly corresponds to a rapid change of masks. The performance is carried through with the greatest possible speed, for on this depends its whole success. A despot must always be conscious of his own sustained dissimulation and will always, therefore, expect the same from others. Any means of forestalling its effects will seem to him permissible, and indeed obligatory. The fact that in his speed he may crush the innocent does not trouble him: in the complex world of masks there must always be errors. What does disturb him profoundly is to let an enemy escape by failing to move fast enough.

Question and Answer

ALL QUESTIONING is a forcible intrusion. When used as an instrument of power it is like a knife cutting into the flesh of the victim. The questioner knows what there is to find, but he wants actually to touch

it and bring it to light. He sets to work on the internal organs with the
sureness of a surgeon. But he is a special kind of surgeon, one who keeps
his victim alive in order to find out more about him and, instead of
anaesthetizing, deliberately stimulates pain in certain organs in order
to find out what he wants to know about the rest of the body.

Questions are intended to be answered; those which are not answered are like arrows shot into the air. The most innocuous questions
are those which remain isolated and do not lead on to others. We stop
some one in the street, ask him what a certain building is, are told and
go on our way satisfied. For a moment we had the stranger fast and
compelled his attention. The clearer and more convincing his answer,
the quicker we let him go. He has provided what was wanted and
need never see us again.

Sometimes, however, the questioner is not content with this and
will put further questions. If these continue the person they are
addressed to soon becomes annoyed: not only is he physically detained,
but, with every answer, he is forced to reveal more of himself. What
he reveals may be something quite superficial and unimportant, but it
is a stranger who has got it from him, and it may also be connected
with other things, which lie deeper in him and are far more important.
Thus his annoyance soon turns to suspicion.

On the questioner the effect is an enhanced feeling of power. He
enjoys this and consequently asks more and more questions; every
answer he receives is an act of submission. Personal freedom consists
largely in having a defence against questions. The most blatant tyranny
is the one which asks the most blatant questions.

It is possible to find answers which prevent further questions. Altern-
atively, anyone whose position allows it can counter with questions of
his own: among equals this is an established method of self-defence.
Anyone to whom this course is not open must either give a full and
serious answer to the question—which is what his interlocutor wants—
or, by cunning, must stop him wanting to probe further. If, for
example, he acknowledges the other's real superiority by flattering
him, he may feel no need to demonstrate it himself; or he may deflect
him towards other people, whom he will find more interesting or
profitable to question. If he can blur his real identity by skilful dissimulation he can treat the question as though it were aimed at someone else and so outside his competence to answer.

The final purpose of questioning is to dissect, but it begins by
probing gently at a succession of points and then, wherever resistance
seems weak, forcing an entrance. Its findings may not all be used at

once, but can be put on one side for later, when the particular thing for which it is searching has been found. Behind every real question there is always a deliberate aim; purposeless questions like those of a child or a fool can easily be turned aside.

The situation is most dangerous for the person questioned when short, concise answers are demanded; it is difficult, if not impossible, to dissemble convincingly in a few words. The crudest form of defence is to pretend to be deaf or not to have understood; but this only serves between equals. When there is disparity of strength the question can be translated into other terms or put in writing; and any answer given will then be much more binding, since the questioner can keep it for reference.

Anyone who is externally defenceless can retreat and arm himself inwardly. The inner armour against questions is possession of a secret, a secret being like a second body encased within the first, and better defended. Anyone who comes near it is liable to receive an unpleasant surprise. A secret is something denser than the matter surrounding it, not continuous with it and kept in almost impenetrable darkness. Whatever its contents a secret is always dangerous. The most important thing about it is its density, that is, its effectiveness as a defence against questions.

A question met with silence is like a weapon rebounding from shield or armour. Silence is an extreme form of defence, whose advantages and disadvantages are almost equally balanced. It is true that a man who refuses to speak does not give himself away, but on the other hand he may appear more dangerous than he is; his silence is taken to mean that he must have much to hide, more than he may in fact have, and this makes it seem all the more important not to let him go. Persistent silence leads to cross-examination and to torture.

But always, even in normal circumstances, an answer restricts the movements of the person who gives it; he has to abide by it; it forces him to take up a fixed position and to remain there, whereas his questioner can shoot at him from anywhere, changing his position as it suits him. He can circle round him, take him by surprise and so throw him into confusion. The ability to change his ground gives him a freedom which the other is denied. He probes his defences with questions and, when he succeeds in piercing them, that is, in forcing him to answer, he has him pinned down and unable to move. "Who are you?" "I am so and so". From this time on he must be himself, or his lies will entangle him. He is no longer able to escape by transforming himself. If the questioning continues for any length of time he ends up in fetters.

The first question concerns identity, the second is about place. Since both presuppose speech, one is led to ask whether there was an original situation which preceded this verbal questioning and corresponded to it. If there was, place and identity must have coincided in it, for one without the other would be meaningless. Such a situation existed, and still exists; it is the hesitant examination of prey. "Who are you? Are you good to eat?" An animal, which is continually in search of food, touches and sniffs at everything it finds, and sticks its nose into everything: "What is this? Is it something to eat? What does it taste like?" The answer is a smell and either a movement or a lifeless rigidity. The strange body is simultaneously also a place; by smelling and touching it the animal makes itself at home with and in it; translated into our terms, it names it.

Early childhood is characterized by two different but connected series of events, which follow each other with increasing rapidity. On the one side is the stream of commands which issues from the parents; on the other, the innumerable questions of the child. The first questions of children are like a cry for food, though already in a more developed form. They are harmless, for they never procure for the child the full knowledge possessed by its parents, whose superiority thus remains immense.

What are the questions with which children begin? Among the earliest are those referring to place: "Where is . . . ?" Other early questions are, "What is . . . ?" "Who is . . . ?" The part played by place and identity is already apparent. These are the first things a child asks about. Only later, towards the end of the third year, do its questions begin with "Why?"; and much later still with "When?" and "How long?", the questions about time. It is a long while before a child has any real conception of time.

The original question, as we have seen, is a hesitant touching, but it soon seeks to penetrate further. It cuts like a knife; and this is why, for example, small children so much dislike disjunctive questions. Asked which it would rather have, an apple or a pear, a child will either not answer, or will say "pear", simply because that was the last word it heard. A real decision, one which would involve separating apple from pear, is too hard for it, for at heart it wants both.

A question cuts most sharply when only one or other of the two simplest answers is possible: yes or no. Since these are exact contraries, excluding everything intermediate, the separation entailed is felt to be particularly final and significant.

Often we do not know what we think until a question is put to us.

As long as it is polite it leaves us free to decide for or against, but it forces us to come down on one side *or* the other.

In Plato's dialogues Socrates appears as the supreme master of the question. He despised all the ordinary forms of power and sedulously avoided everything resembling them. The wisdom which constituted his superiority was at the service of anyone who wanted it, but his normal method of sharing it was not by giving elaborate lectures, but by asking questions. The *Dialogues* are full of questions and most of them come from Socrates, including all the more important ones. He is shown pinning his hearers down and compelling them to make choices of every possible kind. He dominated them exclusively through questions.

Questions are to some extent restricted by the forms of civilization. There are certain things, for instance, which one does not ask a stranger. If one does, it is like coming too close to him; it is an intrusion and he has reason to feel offended. Restraint, on the other hand, is intended to convince him of the respect one feels for him. A stranger is treated as though he were the stronger—a form of flattery he is expected to reciprocate. Only in this way, maintaining a certain distance between each other, free from the threat of questions and behaving as though all were not only strong but equally strong, do men feel secure and able to leave each other in peace.

Perhaps the most important question of all is about the future; certainly it is one charged with tremendous urgency. But the gods to whom it is directed are not obliged to answer and hence, the more urgent the question, the more despairing it is. The gods never commit themselves, never stand to be questioned; no force can penetrate their intentions. Their utterances are ambiguous and defy analysis. Questions asked of them never lead anywhere, for only one answer is ever given. This answer may often only be a sign and great numbers of such omens have been recorded by the priests of many nations; thousands have come down to us from the Babylonians, for example. But these do not form a system; there is no inner connection between any of them, but each stands isolated by itself. Collected together they form lists, nothing more, and even someone who knew them all would only be able to relate them individually to disconnected fragments of the future.

Cross-examination is the exact opposite of this. It deals with the past, recreating it in the fulness of its actuality, and it is directed at someone weaker than the questioner. But before considering the significance of trials I want to say something about a procedure which is established in most countries today, that is, the system of police registration. A group of questions has taken shape, which is everywhere the same and whose basic purpose is to serve security and order. The state wants to know as much as possible about each person, so as to be able to deal with him if and when he becomes dangerous. The first official question a man is asked is his name, the second his address. These, as we have seen, are the two oldest questions, those concerning identity and place. Occupation, which is the next question, reveals the field of his activity and the probable extent of his possessions; from that and from his age his prestige and influence can be deduced—how he should be treated, in fact. His replies also cover his human possessions: he has to state whether he has a wife and children. Place of birth and nationality indicate his probable beliefs and, in an age of fanatical nationalism, are more revealing than his religion, which is no longer as significant as it used to be. With all this, including photograph and signature, much is already established.

His answers to these questions are accepted; for the time being they arouse no suspicion. Only in a cross-examination conducted with a particular purpose do questions become loaded with suspicion. Each by itself could be evaded, but together they form a framework which controls the answers. The man on trial stands in a relation of hostility to his examiner and, as he is much the weaker, he will escape only if he succeeds in convincing him that he is not an enemy.

In judicial examinations the questioning gives the questioner, who is already the more powerful, a retrospective omniscience. The comings and goings of the suspect, the rooms he entered, how he spent this or that hour, all that at the time seemed free and unpersecuted, are suddenly subject to scrutiny. He must come and go again as he did then, re-enter every room and re-live every hour, until as little as possible remains of his former freedom. Before he can deliver judgement the judge requires innumerable facts; his power is specifically grounded in omniscience. To this end he has the right to ask questions: "Where were you?" "When were you there?" "What were you doing?" The suspect establishes an alibi, if he can, by setting place against place, identity against identity: "At that time I was not there, but somewhere else. It was not I who did that, but another man."

"Once upon a time", runs an old Wendish legend, "there was a peasant girl of Dehsa who lay down on the grass at midday and slept. Her betrothed sat by her. He was thinking how he could get rid of his bride. Then the noon-woman came and questioned him. Each time he answered her she put fresh questions to him. As the clock struck one his heart stopped beating. The noon-woman had questioned him to death."

Secrecy

SECRECY LIES at the very core of power. The act of lying in wait for prey is essentially secret. Hiding, or taking on the colour of its surroundings and betraying itself by no movement, the lurking creature disappears entirely, covering itself with secrecy as with a second skin. This state, which can last for a long time, is characterized by a peculiar blend of patience and impatience and, the longer it lasts, the fiercer becomes the anticipation of the moment of success. But in order to achieve success in the end the watcher must be capable of endless patience. If this breaks a moment too soon everything will have been in vain and, weighed down with disappointment, he must start again from the beginning.

The final seizing of the prey is open, for terror is part of its intended effect, but from the moment of incorporation onwards, everything happens in the dark again. The mouth is dark and the stomach and bowels still darker. No-one knows and no-one thinks about what goes on inside him. Of this absolutely fundamental process of incorporation by far the larger part remains secret. It begins with the active and deliberate secrecy of lying in wait and ends as something unknown and involuntary in the secret recesses of the body. Only the intervening moment of seizure flashes out, like lightning illuminating its own brief passage.

The profoundest secret is that which is enacted within the body. A medicine-man who works from his knowledge of bodily processes has to undergo special operations on his own body before he is allowed to practise his profession. Among the Aranda in Australia a man who wants to become a medicine-man wanders away to the mouth of the cave where the spirits dwell. Here, first of all, his tongue is perforated by a lance thrown at him by one of the spirits. He is quite alone and it is part of his initiation that he should feel great fear of the spirits. The courage to endure loneliness, and this in a place of particular danger, is one of the qualifications of his profession. Later, as he believes, a second spear pierces his head from ear to ear. He falls dead and is carried by the spirits into the cave where they live. As far as our world is concerned he is unconscious, but in that other world all his internal

organs are removed and replaced with a completely new and presumably better set, either invulnerable or, at any rate, less susceptible
to the assaults of magic. In this way he is strengthened for his rôle,
but from *within*; his new power originates in his intestines. He must
have been dead before he can begin to exercise it, for death makes
possible the complete penetration and exploration of his body.
His secret is known only to him and to the spirits; it lies within his
body.

A peculiar feature is that the young medicine-man is provided by
the spirits with a supply of small crystals. These are indispensable for
his profession and he is thought to carry them around in his body.
The treatment of any sick person involves great play with these crystals.
The magician gives them to his patient and then draws them out again
from the afflicted parts of the latter's body: hard particles of foreign
matter in the patient's body have caused his illness. They are like a
peculiar currency of disease, the exchange rate of which is known only
to magicians.

But except for this close-range treatment of the sick, magic always
operates at a distance. All kinds of "pointing-sticks" are secretly
prepared and then, from a long way off, trained on the victim,
who, all unsuspecting, succumbs to the terrible power of sorcery:
this exemplifies the secretiveness of lying in wait. Or small spears are
thrown with hostile intent, some appearing in the sky as comets.
Here the act itself is quick, though it may be some time before its
effect is felt.

Any Aranda can use sorcery to harm individuals, but only a
medicine-man can ward off evil; through initiation and practice they
are better protected than others. Certain very old medicine-men can
bring down disease not only on individuals, but on whole groups of
men and women. There are thus three degrees of power, the most
powerful man being he who can bring disease to many people
simultaneously.

The magic of strangers who live far off is greatly dreaded. They are
probably feared more than one's own people because the antidotes to
their sorcery are not so well known. In addition, the perpetrators will
not feel the same sense of responsibility as for evil deeds committed
within their own group.

In the protection against evil and in the treatment of sickness the
power of the medicine-man is regarded as good, but it is also coupled
with the perpetration of evil on a large scale. Nothing bad happens of
itself; everything is always caused by a malevolent human being or

spirit. What we would call *cause* is to them *guilt*. Every death is a murder and must be revenged as murder.

All this is astonishingly close to the world of the paranoiac. In the two chapters on the Schreber case at the end of this book we shall see this more clearly. There we find even the attack on the internal organs described in detail. After their complete destruction and after long sufferings they are regenerated and are then invulnerable.

Secrecy retains its dual character in all the higher manifestations of power. It is only a step from the primitive medicine-man to the paranoiac, and from both of them to the despot of history. In him secrecy is primarily active. He is thoroughly familiar with it and knows how to assess its value and use it on any given occasion. When he lies in wait he knows what he is watching for and knows, too, which of his creatures he can use to help him. He has many secrets, for he has many desires; and he organizes these secrets so that they guard one another. He reveals one thing to one man and another to a second, and sees to it that they have no chance of combining them.

Everyone who knows something is watched by a second person who, however, is never told precisely what he is watching for. He has to record each word and movement, and by full and frequent reports, enable the ruler to assess the loyalty of the suspect. But this watcher is himself watched and his report corrected by that of yet another. Thus the ruler is always currently informed on the capacity and reliability of the vessels to which he has confided his secrets and can judge which of them is likely to crack or overflow. He has a filing system of secrets to which he alone keeps the key. He would feel endangered if he entrusted it entirely to anyone else.

Power is impenetrable. The man who has it sees through other men, but does not allow them to see through him. He must be more reticent than anyone; no-one must know his opinions or intentions.

A classic example is Filippo Maria, the last of the Visconti Dukes of Milan, who were a great power in 15th-century Italy. He was unequalled in his capacity to disguise his thoughts. He never said openly what he wanted, but veiled everything by his peculiar way of expressing it. He would, for example, continue to praise a man he no longer liked, or, if he distinguished someone with honours and presents, he would accuse him at the same time of violence or stupidity and make him feel that he was unworthy of his good fortune. If he wanted to have someone at his court he would make lengthy advances to him, fill him with false hopes and then drop him. As soon as the man believed he was forgotten, he would recall him. When he bestowed a favour on someone who deserved well of him he had a peculiarly cunning way of questioning other people about it as though he himself knew nothing of it. As a general rule he always gave something different from what he was asked for, or not in the way it was wanted. If he intended to bestow some present or honour he would interrogate the man for days beforehand on all kinds of indifferent topics, so that the latter had no notion of what was in his mind. In order to conceal his intentions he often complained about the conferring of favours he himself had decreed, or about the execution of death sentences he himself had imposed.

In this last case it looks almost as though he were wanting to keep secrets even from himself. They lose their conscious and active character and merge into that other, more passive form, transacted in the dark cavities of our body, hidden safe where they can never be known, and forgotten even by ourselves.

"It is the privilege of kings to keep their secrets from father, mother, brothers, wives and friends." Thus it is written in the Arabic *Book of the Crown*, which records many of the old traditions of the Sassanid kings of Persia.

Chosroes II, the Victorious, invented special ways of testing the discretion of men he wanted to use. If he knew that two of his courtiers were close friends and stood together against all comers he closeted himself with one of them, told him as a secret that he had decided to have the other executed and forbade him under threat of punishment to reveal this to him. From then on he watched the behaviour of the threatened man as he came and went in the palace, the colour of his face and his demeanour as he stood before him. If he saw that his behaviour was in no way changed he knew that the first man had not betrayed the secret and he then took him even more into his confidence, treated him with special distinction, advanced him in rank and generally let him feel his approbation. Alone with him later he would say "I had intended to have that man executed, because of certain news which had reached me concerning him; but, on closer investigation, it has turned out to be false." But if he saw that the threatened man was afraid and kept apart, or turned his face away, then he knew that his secret had been betrayed and thrust the offender from his favour, degraded him in rank and treated him harshly, meanwhile giving the original suspect to understand that he had only wanted to test his friend by confiding a secret to him.

Thus he only trusted the discretion of a courtier if he was able to force him to a fatal betrayal of his best friend; the highest discretion was reserved for his own service. "A man who does not know how to serve the king" he said "is no use to himself either, and a man who is no use to himself is no use to anyone."

The power of remaining silent is always highly valued. It means being able to resist the innumerable provocations to speech, treating questions as though they had never been put and never letting it be seen whether what others say has caused pleasure or the reverse. It is voluntary dumbness; and it is not deaf. The stoic virtue of imperturbability, if carried to the extreme, would lead to silence.

The man who maintains a deliberate silence knows exactly what should be left unspoken. Since, in practice, no-one can remain silent forever, he has to decide what can be said and what cannot. It is the latter which he really knows. It is more precise and is also more precious. Silence not only guards it, but gives it greater concentration. He is forced to think about it every time he has to protect it. A man who says very little in any case always *appears* more concentrated than others; his silence leads one to suppose that he has much to conceal, that he is thinking of something secret.

The secret concealed in silence should never be forgotten. Its possessor is respected for not surrendering it, even though it grows in him and burns him more and more fiercely.

Silence isolates. A man who remains silent is more alone than those who talk. Thus the power of self-sufficiency is attributed to him. He is the guardian of a treasure and the treasure is within himself.

Silence inhibits self-transformation. A man who will not speak can dissemble, but only in a rigid way; he can wear a mask, but he has to keep a firm hold of it. The *fluidity* of transformation is denied him; its result is too uncertain; he cannot know where it would take him if he surrendered to it. People become silent when they fear transformation. Silence prevents them responding to occasions for transformation. All men's movements are played out in speech; silence is motionless.

The taciturn person has the advantage that people wait for his utterances and attach special importance to them. When they come they are terse and isolated and sound like commands.

The man-made distinction between those who give orders and those who have to obey them implies that they have no common language between them. They are supposed to behave as though they could not talk to, nor understand, each other; and, apart from orders, this fiction is maintained in all circumstances. Even within their own sphere commanders tend to be sparing of words and thus one comes to expect of other taciturn men, when they do speak, utterances which sound like commands.

The misgivings people feel about the relatively free forms of government, often mounting to a kind of contempt, as though they could not possibly function properly, are due to their lack of secrecy. Parliamentary debates are conducted in front of hundreds of people; publicity is of their essence. Completely contrary opinions are openly declared and measured against each other. Even so-called secret sessions do not always remain entirely so, since the professional curiosity of the press, or the financial interests of some group, lead to frequent indiscretions.

It is assumed that only a single individual, or a very small group of his creatures, is capable of keeping a secret and that deliberation is thus best confined to quite small groups, formed with secrecy in view and with very heavy penalties attached to indiscretion. The decision, it is said, should lie with one person; even he cannot know it before he has taken it and, once taken, it is quickly carried out as a command.

A large part of the prestige of dictatorships is due to the fact that they are credited with the concentrated power of secrecy. In democracies a secret is dispersed among many people and its power thus weakened. People say scornfully that everything is talked to pieces; that everyone has his say and can interfere and that nothing ever happens because everything is known about in advance. Superficially these complaints refer to lack of decisiveness, but in reality to lack of secrecy.

People will endure a great deal as long as it is new and exciting and authoritatively presented to them. If one is nothing oneself, there is a peculiar kind of servile gratification to be got from ending in the belly of power. People do not know what will happen, nor when; others may have precedence with the monster. They wait submissive and trembling and hope to be the chosen victim. This attitude leads to the glorification of the secret. Everything is subordinated to its apotheosis. It does not so much matter *what* happens, as long as it happens with the fiery suddenness of a volcano, unexpected and irresistible.

But, in the long run, all secrets which are confined to one faction, or, still more, to one man must bring disaster, not only to the possessor, which in itself might not matter, but also to all they concern; and that is of tremendous importance. Every secret is explosive, expanding with its own inner heat.

It is only today that we fully realize how dangerous secrecy can become. In different, but only apparently independent spheres, it has become loaded with more and more power. Scarcely was the human dictator dead whom the whole world had united to fight, than the secret turned up again in the shape of the atomic bomb, more dangerous than ever and potentially more dangerous still in its derivatives.

Let us define the *concentration* of a secret as the ratio between the number of those it concerns and the number of those who possess it. From this definition it can easily be seen that modern technical secrets are the most concentrated and dangerous that have ever existed. They concern *everyone*, but only a tiny number of people have real knowledge of them and their actual use depends on a handful of men.

Judgement and Condemnation

Let us start with something familiar to all of us: the pleasure of pronouncing an unfavourable verdict. "A bad book", someone says, or "a bad picture"; and he appears to be saying something objective. His face, however, betrays his enjoyment of his words. The first version of his statement is misleading and it very soon becomes more personal. "A bad writer" or "a bad painter" is what he says next and it sounds as though he were saying "a bad man". We constantly catch friends, strangers, or ourselves at this business of judgement, and the pleasure in an unfavourable verdict is always unmistakable.

It is a cruel pleasure, and one which never allows itself to be cheated of its object. The verdict is only a verdict if pronounced with almost unnatural assurance. There is no mercy in it and no caution and it accords best with its real nature when it is reached without reflection. The passion it conceals is betrayed by its speed. It is quick, unconditional judgements which excite the pleasure visible in the face of their author.

In what does this pleasure consist? It consists in relegating something to an inferior group, while presupposing a higher group to which we ourselves belong. We exalt ourselves by abasing others. The existence of two opposing kinds, different in value, is assumed to be natural and inevitable. Whatever the good is, it is there to be contrasted with the bad. We ourselves decide what belongs to each.

It is the power of a judge which we arrogate to ourselves here.

For it is only in appearance that a judge stands *between* the two camps, on the borderline dividing good from evil. In fact, he invariably reckons himself among the good; his chief claim to his office is his unshakeable allegiance to the kingdom of the good, as though he had been borne a native of it. His decision is binding. The things he judges are quite definite and factual; his vast knowledge of good and bad derives from long practical experience. But judgement is also continually usurped by those who are not judges, whom no-one has appointed, and no-one in his senses *would* appoint to such an office. No special knowledge is thought necessary; those who have the capacity to abstain from judgement can be counted on the fingers of one hand. Judgement is a disease and one of the most widespread; hardly anyone is immune from it. Let us try to discover its roots.

Man has a profound need to arrange and re-arrange in groups all the human beings he knows or can imagine; by dividing that loose, amorphous mass into two opposing groups he gives it a kind of density. He draws up these groups as though in battle array; he makes them exclusive and fills them with enmity for each other. As he imagines them and wishes them to be, they *can* only be hostile. Judgements of good and bad are an age-old instrument of dualistic classification, but one which is never wholly conceptual, nor wholly peaceful. What matters is the tension between the groups, and this is created and continually renewed by the act of judgement.

At the root of the process lies the urge to form hostile packs, which, in the end, leads inevitably to actual war packs. Through being applied to many different spheres, the process becomes diluted, but even if this means that it operates peacefully, apparently resulting only in verbal judgements, the urge to push it to its conclusion, to the active and bloody hostility of two packs, is always there in an embryonic form.

Anyone who is enmeshed in the thousand relationships of life belongs to innumerable groups of the "good" which stand opposed to as many groups of the "bad". It depends entirely on circumstances whether one or the other of these groups engenders enough inner heat to become a pack and attack the opposing group before this does the same. Ostensibly peaceful judgements then become death sentences on enemies. The frontiers of goodness are marked out exactly and woe to any of the bad who cross them. They have no business among the good and must be destroyed.

The Power of Pardon. Mercy

THE POWER OF pardoning someone who offends him is one which every individual reserves for himself, and one which we all possess. It would be fascinating to construct a whole life from the acts of forgiveness a man had permitted himself. A person of paranoid structure might be described as one who never forgives, or only with great difficulty; who takes a long time considering it; who never forgets where there is something to forgive and who invents hostile acts against himself in order not to forgive them. The strongest inner resistance such people feel is to any kind of forgiveness. If they achieve power and, at times, *have* to pardon in order to maintain it, this is done merely for show: a despot never really forgives. Each sign of hostility to him is precisely recorded, and hidden and stored up for later. Sometimes this record is, as it were, expunged in return for genuine submission: the apparent magnanimity of despots has no other meaning. They so ardently desire the subjection of everything which opposes them that they often pay a very inflated price for it.

A man who himself has no power and to whom the despot appears immensely strong, does not realize how important it is to the latter that literally everyone should submit to him. All he can evaluate—if he has any feeling for it at all—is real increases of power; he can never understand what the obeisance of the lowest and meanest of his subjects means to a king in his glory. The interest in every single soul evinced by the God of the Bible, the tenacity with which he remembers and cares for each, may be taken as the model of all who wield power. His, too, is the intricate traffic in pardons: the sinner who submits to him receives mercy. But he watches him carefully and, in his omniscience, can easily see if he deceives him.

There can be no doubt that many prohibitions exist only to enhance the power of those who can punish or pardon their transgression. An act of mercy is a very high and concentrated expression of power, for it presupposes condemnation. There can be no mercy unless there has first been condemnation. Mercy also entails *election*: pardons are usually granted only to a limited number of the condemned. The person who imposes punishment will be wary of too much lenience and, even if he manages to give the impression that he shrinks from the severity of execution, he will find a plausible excuse for it in the sacred duty of punishment, and this is what will determine his actions. But he will always leave the door to mercy open, sometimes granting a pardon himself and sometimes recommending it to the higher authority, if such there be, whose prerogative it is.

The supreme manifestation of power is the granting of a pardon at the last moment. When the execution of the death sentence is imminent, on the gallows, or in front of the firing squad, a pardon has the appearance of new life. The limitation of power is its inability to bring the dead back to life; in acts of mercy long withheld, the mighty can imagine themselves as having overcome this limitation.

THE COMMAND

The Command. Flight and Sting

"AN ORDER IS an order." Commands are by their nature final and categorical, and this may be the reason why so little thought has been given to the subject. They seem to us as natural as they are necessary and we accept them as something which has always existed. From childhood onwards we are accustomed to commands; they make up a good part of what we call education and the whole of our adult life is permeated with them, whether in the sphere of work, of war, or of religion. Thus the question has scarcely ever been raised of what a command actually is: whether it is really as simple as it appears; whether, in spite of the ease and promptness with which it normally achieves its object—that is obedience—it does not in fact mark the person who obeys it, even to the point of arousing feelings of hostility in him.

Commands are older than speech. If this were not so, dogs could not understand them. Animals can be trained because they can be taught to understand what is required of them without understanding speech. The trainer makes his will known to them in short, clear commands, no different in essence from those addressed to human beings; and they also obey his prohibitions. There is thus every reason to seek very ancient roots for the command. At the least it is clear that, in one form or another, it exists outside human society.

The original command results in *flight*. Flight is dictated to one animal by another stronger animal, by something *outside* itself. Flight only appears spontaneous; danger always has a shape and no animal flees unless it discerns it.

Disparity of strength between the two animals involved is inherent in the nature of flight. The stronger proclaims its intention to hunt and to eat the other, and thus flight is a matter of life and death. Whether in fact it is pursued or not, the weaker is compelled by the "command" to flee. It flees from the threat alone, from the eyes, the voice, the whole terrifying shape.

All command derives from this *flight-command*, as I propose to call it. In its original form the command is something enacted between two animals of different species, one of which threatens the other. The great difference in strength between the two, the fact that one of them is habitually preyed on by the other, the unalterable nature of the relationship, which is felt to have existed for ever—all this makes what happens seem absolute and irrevocable. Flight is the final and only appeal against a death sentence. For the roar of a lion *is* a death sentence. It is the one sound in its language which all its victims understand; this threat may be the only thing they have in common, widely different as they otherwise are. The oldest command—and it is far older than man—is a death sentence, and it compels the victim to flee. We should remember this when we come to discuss human commands. Beneath *all* commands glints the harshness of the death sentence. Amongst men they have become so systematized that death is normally avoided, but the threat and the fear of it is always contained in them; and the continued pronouncement and execution of real death sentences keeps alive the fear of every individual command and of commands in general.

Let us, however, forget for the moment what we have learned about the origin of commands and look at them without preconceptions, as though for the first time.

The first thing that strikes one about a command is that it initiates action. An extended finger, pointing in a certain direction, can have the effect of a command: all that seems to be involved is initiation of some definite action, with movement in one given direction. The determination of direction is especially important; reversal or deflection should be felt as equally inadmissible.

It is the nature of a command to admit of no contradiction. It should be neither discussed, nor explained, nor questioned. It is terse and clear because it must be instantly understood. Any delay in understanding it detracts from its force and, with every repetition which is not followed by performance, it loses part of its vitality until it finally becomes exhausted and powerless; it is better then not to attempt to revive it. The action initiated by a command is tied to a definite moment. It can be fixed for later, but the time of its performance must be determined, either in so many words, or as an unmistakable part of the substance of the command.

An action performed as the result of a command is different from all other actions. It is experienced and remembered as something alien, something not really our own. The speed of execution which an order demands may be part of the reason why we remember our action as alien, but it is not the whole reason. An important aspect of commands is that they come from *outside*; they are one of the constituents of life which are imposed on us, not something which develops out of ourselves. Even those solitaries who appear from time to time and, with a whole arsenal of commands, seek to found new religions and regenerate old ones, still retain the appearance of men on whom an alien burden has been laid. It is never in their own name that they speak; what they demand of others is what they have been told to demand and, whatever other lies they may tell, they are honest in this: they believe that they have been sent.

The source of a command is thus something alien; but it must also be something recognized as stronger than ourselves. We submit because we see no hope of fighting; it is prospective victors who give commands. The power behind a command must not be open to doubt; if it has fallen into abeyance it must be ready to prove itself again by force. But it is astonishing how seldom fresh proofs are called for, how long the original proof suffices. Success in conflict is perpetuated by commands; every command obeyed is an old victory won again.

The power of those who give commands appears to grow all the time. Every command, however trivial, adds something to it, not only because in practice it generally benefits the person who gives it, but because, by the very nature of commands—their knife-edged precision and the recognition they exact in the whole sphere they traverse—it tends in every way to augment and secure his power. Power discharges commands like a hail of magical arrows; those who are hit must surrender themselves. The command wounds them and also summons and guides them to the seat of power.

But the simplicity and homogeneity of the command, which at first sight seems absolute and unquestionable, is seen on closer inspection to be only apparent. A command can be taken to pieces, and *must* be if it is to be really understood.

Every command consists of *momentum* and *sting*. The momentum forces the recipient to act, and to act in accordance with the content of the command; the sting remains behind in him. When a command functions normally and as one expects, there is nothing to be seen of the sting; it is hidden and unsuspected and may only reveal its existence by some faint, scarcely perceptible recalcitrance before the command is obeyed.

But the sting sinks deep into the person who has carried out the command and remains in him unchanged. In the whole psychological structure of man there is nothing less subject to change. The content of the command—its force, range and definition—was fixed for ever in that moment in which it was first promulgated, and this, or rather its exact image in miniature, is stored up in the recipient for ever and may remain submerged for years and decades before it comes to light again. But it is never lost, and it is essential to realize this. The fulfilment of a command is not the end; it remains stored up for ever.

Those most beset by commands are children. It is a miracle that they ever survive the pressure and do not collapse under the burden of the commands laid on them by their parents and teachers. That they in turn, and in an equally cruel form, should give identical commands to their children is as natural as mastication or speech. What is surprising is the way in which commands are retained intact and unaltered from earliest childhood, ready to be used again as soon as the next generation provides victims. Not by one iota do they change; it might be only an hour, though in reality it is twenty or thirty years since they were first pronounced. The depth of the impression which commands make on children and the tenacity and fidelity with which they are preserved owe nothing to the qualities of the individual child; intelligence or exceptional gifts have nothing to do with it. No child, not even the most ordinary, forgets or forgives a single one of the commands inflicted on it.

A man's appearance, the carriage of his head, the expression of his mouth, the way he looks at one—everything that makes him recognizable—will change sooner than the shape of the command which has lodged in him as a sting and which is preserved unaltered until he himself produces it again. But the occasion must be there; the new situation which releases the command must be the exact replica of the situation in which it was received. This reproduction of earlier situations, but *in reverse*, is one of the chief sources of energy. What spurs men on to achievement is the deep urge to be rid of the commands once laid on them.

Only commands which have been carried out leave their sting lodged in the obeyer. Commands which have been evaded need not be stored; the "free" man is not the man who rids himself of commands after he has received them, but the man who knows how to evade them in the first place. But the man who takes longest to rid himself of them, or who never achieves it, is undoubtedly the least free.

No normal man feels less free because he obeys his own impulses. Even when they are strongest and their satisfaction is positively dangerous, he feels that his actions spring from himself. But there is no man who does not turn against a command imposed on him from outside; in this case everyone speaks of pressure and reserves the right to vengeance or rebellion.

The Domestication of the Command

THE FLIGHT-COMMAND, which contains a threat of death, presupposes a great difference in power between the protagonists: the one who puts the other to flight could kill him. The basic situation in nature arises from the fact that many animals feed on other animals. Those they feed on belong, however, to species different from their own and thus most animals feel threatened by creatures of a different kind; it is strangers and enemies who command them to flee.

What we normally call a command, however, is something which happens between human beings: a master gives commands to his slaves, a mother to her child. The command as we know it, has developed a long way from its biological origins; it has, as it were, been domesticated. It is part of our general social structure and also of all the more intimate human relationships; it is as important to the family as to the state. It usually looks quite different from what we described as the flight-command. A master calls his slave and the latter comes although he knows he will receive an order. A mother calls her child and it does not invariably run away; although she rains orders of all kinds on it, it continues on the whole to trust her; it stays near her and keeps running to her. The same is true of a dog: it stays near its master and comes at once when he whistles.

How was this domestication of the command brought about? What made the threat of death seem harmless? The explanation of this development lies in the fact that in the three basic relationships I have cited a kind of bribery is practised: a master feeds his slave or his dog and a mother her child. A creature which is subject to another habitually receives its food only from that other. No-one but their master feeds slaves or dogs; no-one else is under any obligation to feed them and actually no-one else *ought* to feed them. (A child, of course, *cannot* feed itself and *must* cling to its mother's breast.)

Thus a close link grows up between commands and the giving of food. This is obvious in the training of animals: when a horse has done what it is supposed to do, its trainer gives it a lump of sugar. Domesticating the command means linking it with a promise of food. Instead of being threatened with death and thus put to flight, some creature is promised what all creatures most want; and this promise is strictly kept. Instead of serving its master as food, it is itself given food to eat.

This adulteration of the original flight-command trains men and animals for all kinds and degrees of voluntary captivity, but it does not entirely change the nature of commands in general. Every command still contains the same threat. It is a modified threat, but there are stated penalties for non-compliance and these can be very heavy. The heaviest of all is the original penalty, which is death.

The Recoil. The Anxiety of Command

A COMMAND IS like an arrow. It is shot from the bow and hits a target. The man who gives a command takes aim before he shoots; like an arrow his command is intended for a definite person. An arrow remains sticking in the flesh of the man it hits and he has to pull it out in order to free himself of the threat it carries. When a command is passed on it is as though a man pulled out an arrow which had hit him, fitted that same arrow to his bow and shot it again. The wound in his body heals, but it leaves a scar. Every scar has a story; it is the mark of a particular arrow.

The man who *gives* the command, who shoots the arrow, feels a slight recoil from it. Here the analogy with an arrow ends, for the real recoil is psychological, and the marksman only feels it when he sees that he has hit his target. It is all the more important to find out exactly what happens.

The satisfaction which follows a successful command is deceptive and covers a great deal else. There is always some sensation of a recoil behind it, for a command marks not only its victim, but also its giver. An accumulation of such recoils engenders a special kind of anxiety, which I call the *anxiety of command*. It is slight in the man who only passes on commands, increasing with nearness to the real source of authority.

It is not difficult to understand how this anxiety of command accumulates. A shot which kills an isolated creature leaves no danger behind it: a creature which is dead can do no harm to anyone. A command which threatens death and then does not kill leaves the memory of the threat. Some threats miss their target, but others find it and it is these which are never forgotten; anyone who has fled from a threat, or given in to it, will invariably revenge himself when the moment comes. The man who threatens is always conscious of this and will do everything he can to make such a reversal impossible.

He feels that all those to whom he has given commands, all those he has threatened with death, are still alive and still remember. He is always conscious of the danger he would be in if they all united 'against him and this fear, which is both fully justified and yet vague and inherently unlimited—for he never knows when memory will be translated into action, nor by how many—this endless torturing awareness of danger is what I call the anxiety of command.

It is strongest in the mightiest. The concentration of anxiety is greatest in one who is a source of commands, who creates orders and receives them from no-one above him. A ruler can keep it hidden, or under control, for a long time, but, in the course of a life, it can increase until, as with certain of the Roman emperors, it suddenly manifests itself as madness.

Commands addressed to More than One Individual

THERE IS A distinction to be made between commands addressed to single individuals and those addressed to many. This distinction is already apparent in the original biological command. Some animals live singly and react singly to the threat of their enemies; others live in herds, which are collectively threatened. In the first case the animal flees or hides alone; in the second the whole herd does so. An animal which normally lives in a herd, but which is accidentally surprised alone by an enemy, will try to flee to its herd. Individual flight and mass flight are fundamentally different. The collective fear of a herd in flight is the oldest and perhaps the commonest example of a crowd state.

It seems very likely that *sacrifice* originated in this state of crowd fear. A lion pursuing a herd of gazelles, all fleeing together in fear of him, desists from pursuit as soon as he succeeds in seizing one of them. This animal, his victim, is a kind of sacrifice which procures a respite for its companions in the herd. As soon as the other gazelles see that the lion has got what it wants their fear abates. From mass flight they revert to the normal state of a herd, each animal grazing on its own and doing as it pleases. If gazelles had a religion and the lion was their god they could, in order to appease his appetite, voluntarily surrender one of their number to him. This is exactly what happens among men: religious sacrifice springs from a state of crowd fear. It serves to halt the pursuit and, for a while, still the hunger of the hostile power.

When in a state of fear a crowd wants to stay together; its members feel that their only protection in acute danger is the proximity of their fellows. They are a crowd particularly in virtue of the identical direction of their flight. An animal which happens to make a leap in a different direction is in more danger than the others; and it feels in even more danger than it is; because it is alone its fear is greater. One might call the common direction of animals fleeing together their "conviction". It is this which keeps them together and urges them forwards. They do not panic as long as they do not feel alone, as long as each animal does the same as the next, all executing exactly the same movements. In virtue of the parallel movements of head, neck and legs, this mass flight resembles what, in men, I have called the *throbbing* or *rhythmic* crowd.

But as soon as the fleeing animals are surrounded the picture changes. A common direction of flight is no longer possible and the mass flight turns into a panic: each animal tries to flee separately and each gets in the way of the rest. The circle around them tightens. During the slaughter that ensues each animal is its fellow's enemy, blocking its way to safety.

But let us now return to the command. I have said that commands addressed to single individuals are different from those addressed to numbers. Before establishing the general truth of this statement I ought to mention the most important exception to it.

An army is an artificial gathering of men and its very nature entails the abrogation of this distinction. In it the effect of a command is the same, whether it is addressed to one man, to several, or to many. An army can only exist so long as all commands have equal validity. They all come from above and each remains intact and isolated in itself. Thus an army should never be a crowd.

In a crowd a command spreads horizontally. It may originally strike a single individual from above, but, since others like himself stand near him, he immediately passes it on to them. In his fear he moves closer to them and in a second they are all affected by it. First a few of them start to move, then more, and finally all. The instantaneous spread of the same command turns them into a crowd and soon they are all in flight together.

Since the command is immediately diffused, no sting is formed. There is no time for this; what would otherwise have become permanent is instantaneously dissolved. A command to a crowd leaves no sting behind. A threat which initiates a crowd flight is dissolved in that same flight.

It is only commands that remain isolated which lead to the formation of stings. The threat contained in such commands *cannot* be completely dissolved. Anyone who has carried out an order as an individual keeps his original resistance as a sting, a hard crystal of resentment. This he can only get rid of by himself giving the same order to some one else. The sting is nothing but the hidden replica of the command he once received and could not immediately pass on. Only in this identical form can he free himself from the command.

A command addressed to a large number of people thus has a very special character. It is intended to make a crowd of them and, in as far as it succeeds in this, it does not arouse fear. The slogan of a demogogue, impelling people in a certain direction, has exactly the same function; it can be regarded as a command addressed to large numbers. From the point of view of the crowd, which wants to come into existence quickly and to maintain itself as a unit, such slogans are useful and indeed indispensable. The art of a speaker consists in compressing all his aims into slogans. By hammering them home he then engenders a crowd and helps to keep it in existence. He creates the crowd and keeps it alive by a comprehensive command from above. Once he has achieved this it scarcely matters what he demands. A speaker can insult and threaten an assemblage of people in the most terrible way and they will still love him if, by doing so, he succeeds in forming them into a crowd.

The Expectation of Commands

A SOLDIER ON DUTY acts only in accordance with commands. He may feel tempted to do various things but, since he is a soldier, his inclinations do not count and he must forgo them. He can never stand at a cross-roads, for, even if he did, it is not he who decides which road to take. His activity is completely circumscribed. What he does, he does in common with all his fellow soldiers; and he does what he is ordered to do. The blocking of all the actions which other men perform, as they believe, of their own free will, leaves him hungry for those he *has* to perform.

A sentry standing motionless on guard for hours is the best expression of a soldier's psychic state. He must not go away, nor fall asleep, nor make any movement except such exactly defined ones as may be prescribed to him. His real achievement is to resist all temptations to leave his post, in whatever shape they may appear. This *negativism*, as one may call it, is the soldier's backbone. He suppresses in himself all the fleeting impulses to activity, such as desire, fear or restlessness, of which human life mainly consists; and he fights them best by not admitting them even to himself.

Every action he performs must be sanctioned by a command and, since it is difficult for a human being to remain inactive, expectation of what he *is* allowed to do grows and accumulates in him; his desire for action mounts up continually. But since all his actions are preceded by commands, it is on these that his expectation is focussed: a good soldier is always in a state of conscious *expectation of commands.* This is increased in every possible way by his training and is also clearly expressed in military attitudes and formulae. The quintessential moment of a soldier's life is when he stands to attention before his superior, awaiting his orders. Whether the situation is put into words, as with the German formula *Zu Befehl,* or left unspoken, it is clear what causes his extreme tension and receptiveness.

A soldier's training begins with the prohibition of many things permitted to ordinary people; and heavy penalties are attached to the smallest transgression. Everyone is made aware in early childhood of a sphere of prohibited things, but the soldier's is immensely larger. Wall after wall is erected round him; they are illuminated for him, so that he sees them growing. They are as high and strong as they are clearly outlined. They are continually spoken of, so that he cannot pretend not to know them. He begins to move as though he always felt them around him. The angularity of his body is like an echo of their hardness and smoothness; he comes to resemble a stereometric figure. A soldier is like a prisoner who has adapted himself to the walls enclosing him, one who does not mind being a prisoner and fights against his confinement so little that the prison walls actually affect his shape. Whilst other prisoners have only one thought, which is to climb these walls or somehow break through them, he accepts them as part of nature, natural surroundings to which he adapts himself and which in the end become part of him.

No-one can truly be called a soldier until he has intensively incorporated into himself this whole body of prohibitions and, in the full routine of a day, and of many days, has proved that he knows exactly how to avoid everything which is prohibited. For such a person a command has a special value. It is like a sortie from a fortress where one has lain too long, or like lightning breaching the wall of prohibitions—lightning which only sometimes kills. In the vast desert of prohibitions surrounding the soldier a command comes as salvation: the stereometric figure comes to life and starts moving.

It is part of a soldier's training to learn to respond to two kinds of command: to act alone or to act jointly with others. Drill is the means of accustoming him to the latter. Here each soldier has to execute the same movements in exactly the same way and at the same time as the rest. What matters is a kind of precision better learnt by imitation of others than alone. Through it he becomes like them. An equality is established which can on occasion be used to transform a body of soldiers into a crowd. But what is generally aimed at is the opposite of this, namely a uniformity as complete as possible *without* the soldiers being a crowd.

When they are functioning as a unit, they react jointly to commands given them jointly; but it should also always be possible to split them up, to detach one or two of them, or half, or as many as their superior wishes. That they march or drill together should be only of superficial importance. A military unit is useful largely because it is fissile; a command must be able to strike any desired number of the men composing it, whether it is one, or twenty, or the whole unit. Its effectiveness should be independent of the number of people it is addressed to. It is a *constant* and remains the same whether it concerns one or all of them. This quality is of the greatest importance. It is what renders a command immune to crowd influence.

Anyone who has to give commands in an army must be able to keep himself free of all crowds, whether actual or remembered. It is his training in the expectation of command which teaches him how to do this.

Expectation of Command among the Pilgrims at Arafat

THE MOST IMPORTANT moment of the pilgrimage to Mecca, and its real climax, is the *Wukuf*, or "standing upon Arafat", which takes place some hours' journey from Mecca. An enormous number of pilgrims—sometimes as many as 6-700,000—are gathered there, "standing before Allah", on this plain surrounded by bare hills; and all of them press towards the "Mount of Mercy", which stands in the middle of the plain. From the summit of this hill, where the Prophet himself once stood, a preacher delivers a solemn discourse.

The crowd responds with the cry *"Labbeika ya Rabbi, labbeika"*: "We wait for your commands, O Lord, we wait for your commands". This cry is repeated continuously throughout the day, mounting to frenzy. Then, in a kind of sudden crowd-fear, called *Ifadha*, or torrent, everyone flees as though possessed, until they come to the next place, Mozdalifa, where they spend the night, setting out from there the following morning for Mina. People run headlong, pushing and trampling on each other; generally several lose their lives. At Mina a large number of animals is slaughtered in sacrifice and their flesh immediately shared and eaten. The ground is drenched with their blood and covered with the scattered remains.

This "Standing upon Arafat" is the moment when the *expectation of command* evinced by a religious crowd reaches its greatest intensity. "We wait for your commands, O Lord. We wait for your commands." This formula, repeated over and over again by the crowd, and a crowd of such density, expresses the situation clearly. Islam, the "surrender to God", is here reduced to its simplest form, a state in which people think of nothing but the Lord's commands and beg for them passionately. For the sudden fear which overcomes them at the given signal, there is a cogent explanation, namely that here the original character of the command—the compulsion to flee—breaks through, although without the faithful being consciously aware of it. The intensity of their collective expectation increases the effect of the divine command to such an extent that it reverts to what all command originally was: a command to flee. God's command puts men to flight. The fact that the flight is continued on the following day, after the pilgrims have spent the night in Mozdalifa, shows that the effect of the command is still not exhausted.

According to Islamic belief it is by the direct command of God that death comes to men. This death the pilgrims try to escape by passing it on to the animals they slaughter in Mina at the end of their flight. These animals perish instead of men, a substitution familiar from many religions: we remember Abraham and Isaac. Thus the pilgrims escape the slaughter God intended for them. They have surrendered themselves to his command, so much so that they have fled before him, but they have not denied him the blood he wanted: the ground is drenched with the blood of slaughtered animals.

There is no other religious usage which so forcefully illustrates the nature of a command as this *Wukuf*, the "Standing upon Arafat", with the ensuing *Ifadha*, or mass-flight. Islam is in any case a religion whose ordinances retain much of the original immediacy of commands, but in the *Wukuf* and *Ifadha* expectation of a command and the command in general find their purest expression.

Discipline and the Sting of Command

DISCIPLINE IS WHAT makes an army. But there are two kinds of discipline, the open and the secret. The open discipline is that of commands. I have shown how the narrowing down of the source of commands leads to the formation of that most curious creature, or stereometric figure rather, the soldier. The most characteristic thing about a soldier is that he lives in a permanent state of expectation of commands, which is expressed in his bearing and his very shape. When he steps out of it he ceases to be a soldier and his uniform becomes merely a façade. A real soldier is easily recognized; nothing could be more public than his state.

But this manifest discipline is not all. There is in addition a secret discipline, which the soldier does not speak of and which is not meant to be seen. Duller men may only occasionally be conscious of it, but, although hidden, it remains awake in most soldiers, particularly those of our own time. It is the discipline of promotion.

It may seem odd that something as universally familiar as promotion should be called secret. But promotion is only the public manifestation of something more profound which remains secret, if only because the way it functions is never understood by more than a very few. Promotion is the outward manifestation of the hidden workings of the stings of command.

It is obvious that, in a soldier, these stings must accumulate to a monstrous degree. Everything he does is done in response to a command; he does, and must do, nothing else. This is what the open discipline of the army demands of him. All his spontaneous impulses are suppressed. He swallows order after order and, whatever he feels about it, must go on doing so. Each command he carries out—and they are innumerable—leaves a sting behind in him.

These stings accumulate rapidly. If he is a common soldier, on the lowest step of the military hierarchy, all opportunity to get rid of them is denied him, for he himself can give no orders. He can only do what he is told to do. He obeys and, in doing so, grows more and more rigid.

A change in this enforced condition can only come about through promotion. As soon as a soldier is promoted he himself has to give orders and, in doing so, begins to rid himself of some of his stings. His position—though to a very limited degree—has turned into its opposite. He has to demand of others things which were formerly demanded of him. The situation as a whole remains exactly the same; all that has changed is his place in it. His stings come into the open as commands. He now gives to others the commands his immediate superior once gave to him. He is not left to choose how to get rid of his stings, but is put in the one position where it is inevitable: he *must* give orders. His men stand facing him in his own former attitude. They hear from him the same phrases that he heard, spoken in the same tone and charged with the same force. The duplication of the situation is almost uncanny; it is as though it had been invented for the needs of his stings of command. He strikes others with what formerly struck *him*.

But though he has reached a position where his stings of command not only can but must declare themselves, he continues himself to receive commands from above. The process now assumes a dual character: in getting rid of the old stings he accumulates new ones. These are easier to bear than the first, for he knows that fresh promotion will give them wings; he has a justified hope of getting rid of them.

To sum up we can say that the open discipline of an army manifests itself in the actual giving of commands; the secret discipline operates by using the stored up stings of command.

The Mongols. The Horse and the Arrow

ONE OF THE most striking things about the history of the Mongols is the closeness with which command is linked to the horse and the arrow. One of the main reasons for the sudden and rapid rise of their power is to be found in this combination. It is essential for us to consider it briefly.

Commands, as we have seen, have their biological origin in the flight-command. Like all similar hoofed animals the horse is built for flight. Flight, one might almost say, was its original mode of being. It lived in herds and these herds were accustomed to *fleeing together*. The command to flee was given them by the dangerous animals which preyed on their life. Mass flight was one of the commonest experiences of the horse and came to be part of its nature. As soon as the danger was past, or seemed past, it reverted to the care-free state of herd-life, each animal doing again as it pleased.

By taking possession of the horse and taming it, man formed a new unit with it. He trained it by a series of operations which can very well be regarded as commands. A few of these are sounds, but most are movements—of pressure or of pulling—which transmit to the horse the will of its rider. The horse understands the rider's wishes and obeys them. Among equestrian peoples the horse is so necessary and so close to its master that a very personal relationship grows up between them; it is subjection, but of an intimacy only possible in these circumstances.

In it the physical distance normal between the giver and the recipient of an order, including for example, that between master and dog, is obliterated. It is the rider's body which gives directions to the horse's body. The *space* of command is thus reduced to a minimum. The distant, alien quality which is part of the original character of command disappears. Command is domesticated in a quite special way and a new actor introduced into the history of relationships between creatures— the riding-animal, a servant on which one sits, which is exposed to the physical weight of its master and responds to the pressure of his body.

How does this relationship to his horse affect the command-economy of the horseman? The first thing to be said is that a rider can pass on to his horse commands he himself has received from a superior. If a goal is set him he does not reach it by running himself, but by making his horse run. Since he does this immediately, the order does not leave any sting in him; he avoids this by passing the order on to his horse. He gets rid of the particular constraint which the order would have imposed on him before he has properly felt it. The sooner he carries out his task, the quicker he mounts and the faster he rides, the less the sting remains in him. The real art of horsemen, as soon as they take on a military character, consists in being able to train another larger crowd of recipients of commands, to whom they can directly pass on everything they receive from their own superiors.

The armies of the Mongols were characterized by their very strict discipline. To the peoples they fell upon and conquered, and who were forced to observe them from close quarters, this discipline seemed the most formidable and astonishing thing they had ever encountered. Whether they were Persians, Arabs, Chinese, Russians or the Franciscan monks sent by the Pope, they all found it equally inconceivable that men should be able to obey so absolutely. But the Mongols, or Tartars, as they were generally called, bore this discipline easily, for the reason that the section of their people which carried the main burden of it was the *horses*.

Children of only two or three years old were set on horseback by the Mongols and taught to ride. We spoke earlier of how, from the very start of his upbringing, a child is crammed full of the stings of command: first, and foremost, by his mother, but later and from a rather greater distance by his father, by those to whom his education is entrusted and, in fact, by every adult or older person in his environment. None of these can rest content unless imposing ceaseless directions, commands and prohibitions on the child. From his earliest days stings of all kinds accumulate in him and it is round these that there form the compulsions and pressures of his later life. He is driven to search for other creatures on whom to unload his stings. His life becomes one long endeavour to get rid of them; he *has* to get rid of them. They are what drive him towards this or that otherwise inexplicable deed or meaningless relationship.

Compared with the child of higher, sedentary civilizations the Mongol or Kirghiz child, who learns to ride so early, enjoys a freedom of a special kind. As soon as he can manage a horse he can pass on to it everything he himself is ordered to do. He can very early discharge the stings which, although to a much smaller degree, are part of his upbringing too. A horse does the child's will long before any human being. He grows used to receiving this obedience and his life is easier for it, but he later expects of men he has conquered the same absolute physical submission.

This relationship to the horse plays a decisive part in the command-economy of man, but among the Mongols there is another important factor. This is the *arrow*, the exact image of the original, non-domesticated command.

An arrow is hostile; it is meant to kill. It travels straight through space It can be evaded, but if a man does not succeed in this it will lodge in him. It can be pulled out, but, even if it does not break, leaving the head behind, the wound remains. (The *Secret History of the Mongols* contains many stories of arrow-wounds.) The number of arrows which can be shot is unlimited. It was the Mongols' main weapon. They killed from a distance, and they also killed while moving, from the backs of their horses. We have seen that every command retains from its biological origin something of the character of a death sentence. Anything which does not flee is caught and anything which is caught is torn to pieces.

With the Mongols commands retained the character of a death sentence in the highest possible degree. They slaughtered men as they slaughtered animals. Killing was third nature to them, as riding was second. Their massacres of men were battues; down to the last detail they resembled their massacres of animals. When not going to war they went hunting; hunts to them were manœuvres. They must have been astonished when, in the course of their wide-ranging expeditions, they came on Buddhists or Christians whose priests spoke to them of the sanctity of all life. Scarcely ever has there been a greater contrast: the masters of the naked command, instinctive embodiments of it, confronted with those who seek, through their faith, so to weaken or transform it that it loses its deadliness and becomes humane.

Religious Emasculation. The Skoptsy

AMONG RELIGIOUS cults celebrated with particular intensity there are several described as leading to castrations. In antiquity the priests of the Great Mother, Cybele, were well known for this. There were thousands who, in an access of frenzy, had castrated themselves in honour of their goddess. Ten thousand of them served in her famous sanctuary at Comana in Pontus. It was not only men who dedicated themselves in this way. Women who wanted to express their adoration cut off their breasts and served the goddess. Lucian in his essay *On the Syrian Goddess* describes the frenzy which broke loose at gatherings of her believers and how one of these, when his turn came to testify, castrated himself. It was a sacrifice offered to the goddess, a proof, once and for all, of devotion to her, excluding every other love for the remainder of life.

The same operation is reported of the Russian sect of the Skoptsy the "White Doves", whose founder, Selivanov, created a sensation in the time of Catherine II with the success of his preaching. Under his influence hundreds and perhaps thousands of men castrated themselves and women cut off their breasts for the sake of their faith. An historical link between these two religious movements is scarcely possible. The latter sect sprang from Russian Christianity, a full 1500 years after the excesses of the Phrygian and Syrian priests had come to an end.

The Skoptsy were distinguished by their concentration on a very few commands and prohibitions and also by having only small groups of believers, all of whom knew each other well. All their discipline was directed towards the recognition and adoration of a living Christ among them.

They feared the distraction of books and scarcely ever read. To very few passages even of the Bible did they attach significance.

Theirs was a very close community, protected by many secret oaths.

They attached the greatest importance to secrecy and everything hinged on it. Their religious life was enacted by night, separate and hidden from the outer world. The centre of their life, what they had above all to keep secret, namely the act of castration, they called "the making-white".

This particular operation was supposed to make them pure and white and like angels. They lived as though they were already in heaven. The ceremonious veneration they showed each other, their obeisances, and their acts of praise and worship were such as angels might use among themselves.

The mutilation to which they submitted had the sharp character of a command. It was a command from on high which they derived from certain words of Jesus in the Gospels and from words spoken by God to the prophet Isaiah.

This command struck them with tremendous force and they had to pass it on with the same force. Our theory of the sting could very well be applied to them. Here the command is carried out on the recipient himself. Whatever else he might do as well, the main thing he had to do was to castrate himself. In order to understand this we must examine some commands of a special kind.

Since, with the Skoptsy, commands are given within the framework of a strict discipline, they can be compared to military commands. The soldier, too, is trained to expose himself to danger. The final purpose of all his drill is to train him to stand firm in face of the enemy when he is ordered to do so, even though the latter threaten him with death. His capacity to stand firm is just as important as his efforts to kill his enemy. Without the one he would never be capable of the other.

The soldier, like the Skopets, offers himself as a victim. Both hope to survive, but are resigned to wounds, pain, blood and mutilation. By fighting the soldier hopes to become the victor; by castrating himself the Skopets becomes an angel, with a claim to heaven. Because he has done this, he is, in fact, already there.

But the command we are here concerned with, operating within the discipline of the sect, is a secret one, and thus the position of the believer resembles that of a man under military discipline who has to carry out a secret order by himself, without anyone knowing anything about it. To do this he must not be recognizable by a uniform, but must disguise himself. The Skopets' uniform, that which makes him equal with his companions, is his castration, and this by its very nature remains hidden and never to be disclosed.

One might say that the Skopets resembles a member of the dreaded sect of Assassins, entrusted by his chief with a murder he must never divulge. Even when he has succeeded in carrying it out and has himself been apprehended no-one must ever know exactly what happened. The command he receives contains his own death sentence and is thus very close to its biological origin. He believes he is being sent to certtain death, but this is never even mentioned. For his own death, which he freely accepts, is made use of to strike down another—the named victim. The command here is thus a *double* death sentence. One death remains unexpressed, although expected; the other is fully and clearly purposed. Thus the sting in the first man, which will perish with him, is made use of before he dies to kill another.

The Mongols have a graphic expression for this hurried killing of another before one is killed oneself. The heroes in their *Secret History* say of an enemy they want to kill in their own last moment, "I shall take him with me as my pillow".

But though this glance at the Assassins has taught us something about the Skopets, his real position is still unexplained. For it is *himself* the Skopets has to strike or mutilate. The command he has accepted must be carried out on his own body and only when this has been done does he become a full member of his secret army.

The fact that the operation is generally performed by someone else should not mislead us. Its significance is that the man surrenders himself. Once he has declared his willingness it does not very much matter how it is done. In any case, since he receives the command from outside, his sting will be the same and he will want to pass it on later.

Even if, as seems likely, the mutilations started with one man, who castrated himself, he too acted on a supposed command—the command from heaven. Of this he will have been firmly convinced. He himself was first converted by the passages in the Bible which he then uses to convert others; what he passes on is only what he has received.

The sting here is visible and takes the form of a physical scar. It is less secret than the sting of command usually is, but it remains a secret from all except those who belong to the sect.

Negativism in Schizophrenia

A MAN CAN EVADE commands by not hearing them; and he can evade them by not carrying them out. The sting—and this can never be too emphatically stated—only results from the *carrying out* of a command. It is the action itself, performed as a result of external, alien pressure, which leads to the formation of a sting in human beings. A command carried out impresses its exact shape on the performer. How deeply and firmly this is imprinted depends on the force with which the command is given, its phrasing, the extent of the giver's superiority, and also, of course, on its actual content. In every case something remains, and remains as discrete and isolated as the original command. It is this that I have called the sting. We can see now how inevitable it is that each man should come in the end to carry within himself a multitude of stings. Their persistence is remarkable; nothing sinks so deep into human beings and nothing is so indissoluble. A man can become so completely riddled with them that he has no interest left for anything else and, except for them, can feel nothing.

His defence against new commands then becomes a matter of life and death. He tries not to hear them so as not to have to accept them. If he cannot help hearing them he refuses to understand them. If he is made to understand, he evades them flagrantly, by doing the opposite of what he is asked to do: when told to step forward he steps back and when told to step back he steps forward. In doing so he cannot be said to be free of the command. His is a clumsy and impotent reaction, still, in its own way, determined by the content of the command. This reaction, which, in psychiatry, is called *negativism* plays a specially important part in Schizophrenia.

The most striking thing about schizophrenics is their lack of *contact*; they are much more isolated than other people. They often give the appearance of being paralysed within themselves, as though there could be no connection between them and other people; as though they could not understand and did not want to either. In their obstinacy they resemble statues; and there is no attitude in which they may not petrify. But these same people, in other phases of their illness, suddenly behave in exactly the opposite way. They exhibit a suggestibility which can reach fantastic proportions. They do what one shows them or demands of them so quickly and so perfectly that it is as though one was in them and did it for them. They are overcome by sudden fits of servility, "suggestion-slavery" as one of them called it himself. From statues they turn into officious slaves, exaggerating their performance of whatever is asked of them in a manner that often appears ridiculous.

The contrast between these two attitudes is so great that it is difficult to understand. If, however, we provisionally leave out of account how they may appear to the schizophrenic himself and consider them, as it were, from outside, we have to admit that "normal" people frequently exhibit them too. But with them they serve a specific purpose and their manifestations are less extreme.

A soldier who resists all provocations, who remains rigid and upright where he was put, who never leaves his post, whom nothing can tempt to do what he normally likes doing and often has done—a well trained soldier on duty is in an artificial state of negativism. It is true that he can sometimes act, namely at the command of his superior; but never otherwise. In order to make him act only on commands, he has been trained to a state of negativism. But it is a negativism which is open to manipulation, for his superior can, if he chooses, transpose him into the exactly opposite state. As soon as a soldier is ordered to do something by the proper authority he behaves in a manner as officiously compliant as the schizophrenic in *his* alternative state.

We should add that the soldier knows perfectly well why he acts as he does. He obeys because he is threatened with death. I described in an earlier chapter how he gradually grows accustomed to his state and how his own nature comes to correspond with it. Here I only want to stress one thing: the unmistakable external resemblance between the soldier on duty and the schizophrenic.

But here another and very different idea obtrudes itself, which seems to me no less important. A schizophrenic in a state of extreme suggestibility behaves as a member of a crowd would. He is just as impressionable and yields just as much to every impulse reaching him from outside. But we cannot think of him as one because he is *alone*. Since no crowd can be seen round him it does not occur to anyone that he, from his own point of view, may feel as though he were in one. He is a fragment broken from a crowd. This contention can be proved only by looking at schizophrenics' own imaginings. Innumerable examples of these might be quoted. One woman claimed to have "all human beings in her body"; another to hear "the mosquitoes talking". A man "heard 729,000 girls"; another "the whispering voices of the whole of humanity". Under many different guises all kinds of crowds appear in the imaginings of schizophrenics. It would be possible to make them the starting point for an enquiry into the nature of crowds. I propose to consider the crowd-conceptions of schizophrenics elsewhere. Classification would show how extraordinarily complete they are.

It will be asked why the two contrary states which have been described here are necessary to the schizophrenic. In order to understand this we must recall what happens to an individual when he becomes part of a crowd. I have described his liberation from the burdens of distance and called this the discharge. I should now add that part of these burdens of distance is made up of the stings of command accumulated in every individual. Within a crowd all are equal; no-one has a right to give commands to anyone else; or, one might say, everyone gives commands to everyone. Not only are no new stings formed, but all the old ones are got rid of for the time being. It is as though people had slipped out of their houses, leaving their stings piled in the cellars. This *stepping out of* everything which binds, encloses and burdens them is the real reason for the elation which people feel in a crowd. Nowhere does the individual feel more free and if he desperately tries to remain part of a crowd, it is because he knows what awaits him afterwards. When he returns to his house, to *himself*, he finds them all there again, boundaries, burdens and stings.

The schizophrenic, overburdened with stings, so much so that at times he is paralysed by them, this cactus of torment and helplessness, succumbs to the illusion of the opposite state, that of being in a crowd. As long as he remains in it he does not feel his stings. He has, or so he thinks, stepped out of himself and, though the way in which this happened is obscure and questionable, he seems to derive from it at least a temporary relief from the torment of stings; he has a sense of being linked with others again. To be sure, this deliverance is an illusion, for, just at that point where he enters on his freedom, new and stronger compulsions await him. But we are not concerned here with all the aspects of schizophrenia. Let us content ourselves with one conclusion: no-one is more in need of the crowd than the schizophrenic, who is crammed with stings and feels suffocated by them. He cannot find the crowd outside and so he surrenders to one within him.

The Reversal

"For whatever food a man eats in this world, by that food he is eaten in the next world." This mysterious and startling sentence comes from the *Shatapatha-Brahmana*, an ancient Indian treatise on sacrifices. There is a story in this same book which is even stranger, the story of the wanderings of the Seer Bhrigu in the other world.

Bhrigu was a saint and the son of the god Varuna. He had acquired great Brahminical knowledge, which had gone to his head. His pride became over-weening and he set himself above his own divine father. The latter, in order to show his son how little he knew, recommended him to wander successively to the four quarters of the heavens, east, south, west, and north. There he should look carefully at everything there was to see and, on his return, report what he had seen.

"First, in the east, Bhrigu saw men chopping off the limbs of other men and dividing the pieces among themselves, saying, 'This is for you and this for me'. When Bhrigu saw this he was horrified. The people who were cutting others in pieces explained to him, 'Thus they did to us in the other world and so we do it to them in this world.'

"Then Bhrigu wandered to the south and saw men chopping off the limbs of other men and dividing them with the words, 'This is for you and this for me'. On questioning them he again received the same answer: 'Thus they did to us in the other world, and so we do it to them in this world'. In the west Bhrigu saw people silently eating other people and those who were being eaten kept silence too. 'Thus', he was told 'did they do to us in the other world and so we do it to them in this world'. But, in the north, he saw people who screamed loudly as they ate others, and those who were being eaten were screaming too. The same thing had been done to them in the other world."

On his return Bhrigu was asked by his father Varuna to recite his lesson, like a pupil. But Bhrigu said, "What shall I recite? There is nothing". The things he had seen were so terrible that everything seemed as nothing to him.

Then Varuna knew that Bhrigu had seen these things and he explained: The people in the east chopping off other people's limbs were the trees. The people in the south chopping off other people's limbs were the cattle. The people in the west silently eating silent people were the plants. The people in the north screaming aloud and devouring screaming people were the waters.

In all these cases Varuna knew of remedies. By certain sacrifices, which he indicated to his son, it was possible to escape the consequences of one's deeds in the other world.

In another treatise on sacrifice, the *Jaiminiya-Brahmana*, the same story about Bhrigu appears in a somewhat different form. He does not wander into the four quarters of the heavens, but from one world into another. Instead of four pictures there are only three. First Bhrigu sees trees who in this other world have assumed human shape and are now cutting men into pieces and eating them. Then he sees a man eating another man, who is screaming. This is explained to him: cattle which were slaughtered and eaten there have here assumed human shape and do to man what he once did to cattle. The third thing he saw was a man eating another man, who kept silence. Rice and barley have taken human shape and in this way repay their sufferings.

In this version, too, certain sacrifices are prescribed. Anyone who performs them properly will escape being eaten in the other world by trees or cattle, or rice and barley. But what we are interested in here is not the ways of avoiding this fate, but the folk-concept hidden beneath the priestly disguise. Whatever a man does in this world will be done to him in another. No special servants of justice are nominated to mete out punishment, but everyone is punished by his own victim. The only kind of deed, however, for which punishment is exacted is the eating of something else. "Just as, in this world, men eat animals, so, in the other world, animals eat men."

This sentence, which comes from another *Brahmana*, similar to the one quoted at the beginning of the chapter, finds a curious confirmation in the *Laws of Manu*. It is stated there that eating meat is no sin, for it is natural to all creatures; but for anyone who abstains from it there is a special reward. The Sanskrit word for flesh, which is *Mamsa*, is explained when we split it into its two syllables: *mam* is "me" and *sa* is "he". Thus mamsa means "me-he": "Me he (mam sa) will devour in the next world whose flesh I eat in this life. This, the wise, declare, is the real meaning of the word 'flesh'."

Here the reversal is conceived in terms of flesh and reduced to the concisest possible formula: I eat him, he me. The word for the second part of the process, the consequences of what one has done, is the actual word for flesh. The animal which was eaten remembers who ate it. Its death is not the end of it. Its soul goes on living and turns into a man in the next world and there waits patiently for its devourer. As soon as the latter dies and arrives in the other world the original situation is reversed: the victim finds his devourer, seizes him, cuts him in pieces and eats him.

The connection with our concept of a command and the sting it leaves behind should be quite evident. But here the thing is carried to such extremes and made so concrete that at first it only terrifies us. Instead of happening in this life the reversal is deferred till the next. Instead of a command simply threatening death and, in this way, compelling services of various kinds, what we are dealing with here is killing in its most extreme form, when the creature killed is eaten.

Man in the end is completely ruled by his stings. He may not succeed in bringing about a reversal, but he never ceases to strive for it. Whether he obtains deliverance or not, his stings shape him; they are his destiny. Since, however, we no longer seriously entertain the notion of another life, we think of the sting implanted by a threat of death as existing only so long as the victim is alive. According to the Indian conception, with its certainty of another life, the sting, as the hard core of the soul, continues to exist after death, and reversal happens in every case; it becomes the main business of life in the other world. There each creature does exactly what was done to him here, and does it with his own hands.

The fact that change of shape does not hinder the reversal is particularly significant. It is not the actual animal I have eaten which seizes me in the other world and cuts me up and eats me; it is a man with the soul of that animal. The outward shape of the creature has changed completely, but the sting remains the same. In all the scenes of horror Bhrigu meets on his wanderings, the sting appears as the main concern of the soul. One might even say that the soul consists of it. The true nature of the sting, about which so much has been said in the course of this enquiry into command—its absolute immutability and the exactness of the reversal it strives for—finds its most compelling expression in this Indian concept of the eaten feeding on the eaters.

The Dissolution of the Sting

THE STING FORMS *during* the carrying out of the command. It detaches itself from the command and, as an exact image of this, imprints itself on the performer. It is small, hidden and unrecognized; its most essential characteristic, as we have already seen, is immutability. It remains isolated within the person concerned, a foreign body lodged in his flesh. However deep it may lie hidden, however incapsulated, it always remains a burden.

It is very difficult to get rid of the sting. It must in fact dislodge itself and can only do so if and when it reacquires force equal to that with which it originally penetrated. For this to happen there must be an exact repetition of the original command-situation, but in *reverse*. This is what the sting waits for through months, years and decades. It is as though each sting had a memory of its own, but of one thing only: the situation in which it was implanted. When this situation recurs, the sting cannot fail to recognize it, for this is its sole content, the only thing it *can* recognize. Suddenly everything is as it was before; only the rôles of the actors are reversed. When this moment comes, the sting seizes its opportunity and hastens to fall on its victim. The reversal has at last taken place.

This is what one may call the pure case, but it not the only possible one. The same command can be given several times over by the same speaker to the same victim so that numbers of identical stings form. These do not remain isolated, but fuse into each other to form a new entity, which grows palpably and which can never be forgotten by the person it is lodged in. It is always there, it sticks up and continually obtrudes itself.

It may also happen, however, that a person receives one and the same command from several different sources. If this occurs often enough and order follows pitilessly close upon order, then the sting loses its clear outline and develops into a monster which endangers life. It grows until it forms the main substance of its host. He can never forget it and carries it around, seeking any opportunity to get rid of it. He finds innumerable situations which seem like the original one and thus suitable for reversal. But they are not. The command has been repeated so often and from so many different angles that the original situation has been obscured and he can no longer find the key to it. One memory has overlaid another, as one sting another sting. His burden can no longer be broken up into its elements. Whatever he attempts his general situation remains the same. Alone he is no longer capable of freeing himself from his burden.

The emphasis is on *alone*, for liberation can be found from all stings, including the most monstrous and the most complex; it can be found within a crowd. We have often mentioned the *reversal crowd*, but it was not really possible to explain its nature until we had studied the way in which commands operate.

A reversal crowd comes into existence for the joint liberation of a large number of people from the stings of command they cannot hope to get rid of alone. They unite to turn on some group of other people whom they see as the originators of all the commands they have borne so long. If they are soldiers, any officer can stand for those under whose command they actually were; if they are workers, any employer can take the place of those they have actually been working for. In such moments class and caste cease to be mere concepts and become reality, operating as though they were actually composed of equals. The lower class, which is in revolt, forms a single, cohesive crowd; the higher one, which is threatened and outnumbered and surrounded, forms a series of frightened packs, bent on flight.

In those who now form the crowd every individual sting, complex as it is and built up on many separate occasions, has a number of possible culprits before it. The people the crowd are attacking are there in front of them, either separate or pressed together, and they know perfectly well why they should be afraid. They need not be the actual sources of any particular sting, but, whether they are or not, they stand for them and will certainly be treated as though they were. The reversal here is directed against many people simultaneously and can therefore dissolve the most oppressive sting.

What the crowd experiences is clearest in the most concentrated case of this kind: when it is a single individual such as a king that the revolt is directed against. Here the ultimate scource of *all* commands has been the king, his officials and nobles being agents for the transmission and execution of his orders. The individuals who form the rebellious crowd have for long years been kept at a distance by threats and their obedience enforced by sanctions. Now, by a kind of unwinding process, they obliterate this distance, forcing their way into the palace which was formerly forbidden them. From as close as possible they see all it contains: rooms, furniture and inhabitants. The flight which was imposed on them by royal commands turns into intimate familiarity. If the king, from fear, deliberately allows this to happen, things may stop there for the moment; but not for long. Once the process of getting rid of stings has started, it continues inexorably. One must remember how much will have been done to these people to keep them obedient; how many stings will have accumulated in them in the course of years.

The real threat which hung continually over all their heads was death. It was renewed from time to time in executions and its authenticity proved beyond all doubt. There is only one way in which they can obtain redress for this threat, that is, by beheading the king who could formerly behead them. In this way the greatest sting, the most inclusive, the one which seems to contain all other stings, is removed from those who have jointly had to bear it.

It is not always possible to see so clearly what a reversal means. Nor is it always carried through to so extreme a conclusion. When a revolt miscarries and people do not finally get rid of their stings, they none the less remember the time when they were a crowd. For that period at any rate they were free of stings and so will always look back to it with nostalgia.

The Command and the Execution.
The Contented Executioner

ONE SPECIAL CASE has so far been purposely omitted from this enquiry. A command has been shown to be a threat of death and we
have said that it derives originally from the flight-command. The
domesticated commands we know combine reward with this threat.
The promise of food enhances the effect of the threat, but does not
otherwise change its character. The threat is never forgotten by the
person it is addressed to. He retains it in its original form until opportunity arises to get rid of it by passing it on to someone else.

But a command can also be a commission to kill. When this is so
its result is an execution; what is otherwise only threatened actually
happens. But the action is distributed between two people: one receives
the command and the second is executed.

The executioner is in the same position as anyone who submits to an
order under the threat of death. But he becomes free himself from this
threat by himself killing. He immediately passes on his own possible
fate and so anticipates the ultimate penalty which hangs over himself.
He is told to kill, and he kills. He is not in a position to resist such a
command, for it is given him by someone whose superior strength he
acknowledges. It has to be carried out quickly; generally at once, in
fact. There is no time for a sting to form.

But, even if there were time, there is no reason why a sting *should*
form. An executioner passes on exactly what has been imposed on
him. He has nothing to fear and so nothing remains behind in him.
In his case, and in his only, the account balances; the essential nature
of the command coincides with the action it brings about. Its fulfilment,
moreover, is made easy for him; no obstacles are put in its way and it
is unlikely that the victim will escape. All these circumstances are
known to the executioner from the start. Thus he can regard the
command with equanimity; he can trust it. He knows that carrying it
out will change nothing in himself. It passes, as it were, straight through
him, without damaging him at all. Of all men the executioner is the
most contented, the least affected by stings.

It is a monstrous situation and one which has never really been faced.
It can only be understood if one remembers the real nature of commands. Each of them stands or falls by the threat of death; from that

their whole force derives. This force is almost invariably in excess of what need be used to bring about the desired action and this is the real reason why a command leads to the formation of a sting. Of all commands those which really involve killing, which intend it, and actually lead to it, leave the fewest traces in the recipient.

An executioner is a man threatened with death in order to make him kill, though only those he is told to kill. If he keeps strictly to his orders nothing can happen to him. It is true that he may allow the way he carries them out to be affected by other threats which have been used against him at different times: he naturally comes to his task with any stings he has accumulated from elsewhere. But the basic mechanism of his job remains the same: killing others he frees himself from death. To him it is a clean business, with nothing shocking or unnatural about it. He cannot find in himself any of the horror he awakens in others. It is important to be quite clear about this: official killers are contented in proportion as the commands they are given lead directly to death. A prison warder's life is far more difficult than an executioner's. It is true that society penalises the latter for the gratification he derives from his job by making him a kind of outlaw; but even this is not without some advantage for him. In fact he is nothing but a tool, but still he does survive his victims and so some of the prestige of the survivor accrues to him and compensates for his outlawry. He finds himself a wife, has children and leads a normal family life.

Commands and Irresponsibility

IT IS WELL KNOWN that men who are acting under orders are capable of the most appalling deeds. When the source of their orders is blocked and they are forced to look back on what they have done, they do not recognize themselves. They say, "I never did that", and it is by no means always clear in their minds that they are lying. When they are faced with witnesses and begin to waver, they still say, "I'm not like that. I couldn't have done it". They search themselves for traces of the deed and cannot find them. It is astonishing how unaffected by it they seem. The life they lead afterwards really *is* another life, in no way coloured by their previous actions. They do not repent and do not even feel guilty. What they have done never really comes home to them.

They are people who are otherwise perfectly capable of judging their actions. What they do of their own volition leaves in them the traces one would expect. They would be ashamed to kill an unknown, defenceless creature which had not provoked them and it would disgust them to torture anyone. They are no better than most of those amongst whom they live, but they are also no worse. People who know them well in everyday life are prepared to swear on oath that they are unjustly accused.

When the long line of witnesses comes forward, however—the victims, those who know exactly what they are talking about—when, one after another, these recognize the accused and recall in minute detail his behaviour, so that it becomes absurd to doubt his guilt, then one seems faced with an insoluble riddle.

But for us it is no longer a riddle, for we know how commands work. Every command that is carried out leaves a sting in the man who does it. But this, though *in* him, remains as alien to him as the command itself was in the moment when it was given. However long it lodges in him, it is never assimilated, but remains a foreign body. It is indeed possible, as I have already shown, for several stings to fuse together and form a new conglomerate entity, but this, too, remains quite distinct from its surroundings. The sting is an interloper who never settles, an undesirable one wants to get rid of. *It is what one has done* and has, as we have seen, the exact shape of the command given to one. It lives within its host as an alien, not subject to his authority, and thus does not cause him any feeling of guilt. He does not accuse himself, but the sting; this is the true culprit, whom he carries with him everywhere. The more foreign to his nature the original command, the less guilt he feels about what it made him do; the more autonomous and separate the existence of the sting. It is his permanent witness that it was not he himself who perpetrated a given wrong. He sees himself as its victim and thus has no feeling left for the real victim.

It is true, therefore, that people who have acted on orders can feel entirely guiltless. If they are capable of really facing their subsequent situation they probably feel something like astonishment at the fact that they were once so completely at the mercy of commands. But even this stirring of insight is worthless, for it comes only when everything is long over and it relates only to the past. What happened then can still happen again; it is no assurance that they will not again behave in the same way, even when the new situation they are faced with exactly resembles the old. They remain just as defenceless as before in face of commands, only obscurely conscious of their danger.

Few, fortunately, carry this to its logical conclusion: with them the command becomes destiny and they make it their pride to surrender to it blindly, as though it were particularly manly to blind oneself.

From whatever aspect we consider the command, we can now see that, as we know it today, in the compact and perfected form it has acquired in the course of its long history, it is the most dangerous single element in the social life of mankind. We must have the courage to stand against it and break its tyranny. The full weight of its pressure must be removed; it must not be allowed to go more than skin-deep. The stings that man suffers must become burrs which can be removed with a touch.

TRANSFORMATION

Presentiment and Transformation
among the Bushmen

THE TALENT FOR transformation which has given man so much power over all other creatures has as yet scarcely been considered or begun to be understood. Though everyone possesses it, uses it and takes it for granted, yet it is one of the great mysteries and few are aware that to it they owe what is best in themselves. It is extremely difficult to understand the true nature of transformation. The most hopeful course is to approach it from several different angles.

There is a book on Bushman folklore which I regard as our most valuable record of early humanity and which has never yet been fully used, though Bleek collected the material a hundred years ago and the book has been in print for fifty. It contains a section on the presentiments of the Bushmen which throws considerable light on the subject of transformation. These presentiments are, as we shall see, the initial stages of transformations of a very simple kind. The Bushmen feel the distant approach of people whom they can neither hear nor see. They also feel when game is near and will describe the signs on their own bodies by which they recognize its approach. Some examples of this follow, given in their own terms.

"The one man feels the other man who comes. He says to his children, 'Look ye around, for your grandfather seems to be coming. This is why I feel the place of his body's old wound'. The children look around. They perceive the man coming and they say to their father, 'A man is coming yonder'. Their father says to them, 'grandfather comes yonder; he would come to me. He was the one whose coming I felt at the place of his old wound. I wanted you to see that he is really coming. For ye contradict my presentiment, which speaks truly'."

What happens here is of a marvellous simplicity. The old man, the grandfather of these children, has obviously been a long way away. He has on his body the scar of an old wound, the exact position of which is well known to his grown-up son, the children's father. It is the kind of scar which hurts from time to time and the old man has often been heard speaking of it. It is what might be called his distinctive mark. When the son thinks of his father he thinks of his old wound, but it is more than just thinking. Not only does he visualise it exactly, but he *feels* it at the corresponding place on his own body. As soon as he feels it he knows that his father, whom he has not seen for some time, is approaching; he assumes that he is coming because he feels the old wound. He tells his children, who, apparently, do not quite believe him: they may not yet have learnt to trust such presentiments. He tells them to keep watch for someone coming and soon they see a man. This can only be their grandfather, and, in fact, it is he. Their father was right; the sensation in his body did not deceive him.

A woman leaves her hut, carrying a child by a leather thong slung from her shoulder. The man remains quietly sitting there. The woman is away a long time. Suddenly the man feels her thong on his shoulder. He has the sensation of it there. It feels as though he were carrying the child himself. As soon as he feels the thong he knows that his wife is on her way back with the child.

There are presentiments of the same kind relating to animals, at least those he hunts and feeds on, which are as important to the Bushman as his nearest relations, and might almost be called his "nearest animals".

An ostrich walks about in the warm sun. A black insect, called by the Bushmen an ostrich-louse, bites it on the back of the neck and the ostrich scratches the place with its foot. The Bushman feels something in the lower part of the back of his own neck, at the same place where the ostrich is scratching itself. He feels a tapping, and it tells him that there is an ostrich near.

The springbok is a particularly important animal for the Bushman and there are many kinds of presentiments about it, which refer to its various characteristics and movements.

"We have a sensation in our feet. We feel the feet of the springbok rustling in the bushes." This sensation in the feet means that the springbok are coming. It is not that the Bushmen hear them, for they are still too far off, but with their own feet they feel the rustling the springbok make in the distance. But this is not the only thing transmitted from the animal to the man. The Bushmen say, "We have a sensation in our face on account of the blackness of the stripe on the face of the springbok." This black stripe runs down the centre of the forehead and finishes at the tip of the nose. The Bushman feels it on his own face. They also say, "We have a sensation in our eyes on account of the black marks on the eyes of the springbok."

A man feels a tapping on his ribs and says to his children, "The springbok seem to be coming, for I feel the black hair on the sides of the springbok. Climb ye the kop standing yonder that ye may look around at all places, for I feel the springbok sensation." The springbok has black hair on its flanks and for the Bushman the tapping at his own ribs indicates the black hair on the animal's flanks.

A second man will agree with the speaker. He too senses springbok, but not in the same way; he feels the blood of the slain animal. "I feel a sensation in the calves of my legs, when the springbok's blood is going to run down them. I always feel blood when I am about to kill a springbok. I sit feeling a sensation behind my back which the blood is wont to run down when I am carrying a springbok. The springbok hair lies behind my back." Again, "We have a sensation in our heads when we are about to chop the springbok's horns." And again, "The things which are numerous are used to come first when we are lying in the shade of the hut. They think we are probably lying asleep in the noonday sleep. For we really lie down to sleep the noonday sleep. But we do not lie like this when we have felt the things coming as they walk, moving their legs." "We feel a sensation in the hollows under our knees, upon which blood drops as we go along carrying the game."

From these Bushmen utterances we can see the importance they attach to such presentiments or precognitions. They feel in their bodies that certain events are going to happen. There is a kind of beating of the flesh which tells them things. Their letters, as they say, are in their bodies. These letters speak and move and make their bodies move. A man orders the others to be silent and is quite still himself when he feels that his body is tapping inside. "The presentiment speaks the truth." "Those who are stupid do not understand these teachings; they disobey them and get into trouble, such as being killed by a lion. These beatings tell those who understand them which way they are not to go and which arrow they had better not use, and also warn them when many people are coming to the house on a wagon. They inform people where they can find the person of whom they are in search, which way they must go to seek him successfully."

We are not concerned here with whether or not these presentiments are true. It may be that the Bushmen have developed, and practise in their daily lives, faculties which we have lost, or that they have reasons for continuing to believe in their presentiments, even though these sometimes deceive them. However this may be, their descriptions of the way in which these presentiments announce themselves are among the most valuable material we have on the nature of transformation; there is nothing comparable to them, for, whatever myths and fairy stores can teach us about the subject, they are all open to the

objection that they are something "invented", whereas here we learn
what an actual Bushman in real life feels when he thinks of an ostrich
or a springbok in the distance, what then happens to him, what it
really means to him to think of a creature other than himself.

The signs by which the Bushmen recognize the approach of an
animal or of another human being are in their own bodies. Their presentiments, as I have said, are the initial stages of transformations. If
they are to have any value for the analysis of transformation, we must
be careful to leave them as simple and as concrete as they are and not
to import anything alien into the Bushman's world. Let us lift them
out of the the context of our quotations and look at them one by one:

1. A son feels his father's old wound in exactly the same place on
   his own body.
2. A man feels on his own shoulders the thong his wife uses to carry
   a child.
3. An ostrich scratches the back of its neck where an insect has bitten
   it. Although he cannot see the ostrich, the Bushman feels something at the corresponding point on his own neck.
4. A man feels in his own feet the rustling of the springbok in the
   bushes. He feels on his own face the black stripe running from
   the forehead to the nose of the springbok. He feels in his own
   eyes the black marks on the eyes of the springbok. The black
   hair on the animal's flanks gives him a sensation round his own
   ribs.
5. A man feels blood on his calves and back. It is the blood of the
   springbok he will kill and carry on his back. He has a sensation
   in his head when he is going to cut off a springbok's horns. He
   feels blood in the hollow of his knees where it will drip as he
   carries home the game.

Everything under the last heading relates to the dead animal and the
desire for its blood determines the character of the transformation.
It is less simple than in the other cases and it is better, therefore, to start
by considering them separately. The most elementary thing about all
of them is that *one body is equated with another*. The body of the son *is*
the body of his father and so he feels the same wound in the same
place. The husband's body is that of his wife and so the thong by which
she carries her child presses on his shoulder too. The body of the
Bushman is the body of the ostrich. The insect "bites" him at the same
place on his neck and he scratches himself there.

In each of these cases the equation of the two bodies is through a single particular, each different in kind from the others: the wound is an old peculiarity of the body which reasserts itself from time to time; the pressure of the thong is something constant and external; the scratching is one isolated movement.

But most interesting of all is the case of the springbok. Here four or five traits are combined and make the equation of the two bodies something very complete. We have first the movement of the feet, then the black hair on the ribs, the black stripe down the forehead and nose and finally, the place on the head where the horns grow, as though the Bushman carried horns himself. Thus to movement—here movement of the feet instead of scratching as in the case of the ostrich—is added something which resembles a complete mask. The most striking thing about the animal's head, that is, its horns, combines with the black parts—the stripe down the nose and the marks in the eyes—to form the simplest possible mask. It is the Bushman's own head and yet an animal's at the same time. The man feels the black hair on his ribs as though he were wearing the animal's skin; but it is his own skin.

The body of one and the same Bushman can become in turn the body of his father, of his wife, of an ostrich and of a springbok. The fact that he can at different times be all of them and then become himself again is of the highest significance. The successive transformations are provoked by external causes. They are *clean* transformations; each creature whose coming the Bushman feels remains itself; he keeps it separate and apart, for otherwise the presentiment would be meaningless: the father with the wound is not the woman with the thong, nor the ostrich the springbok. The individual identity which the Bushman gives up is preserved in the transformation. He can become this or that, but "this" and "that" remain separate from each other, for between transformations he always becomes himself again.

The isolated, very simple traits which determine each transformation could be called its nodes. The father's old wound, the wife's leather thong and the black stripe on the springbok's head are such nodes. They are what is most striking about the other creature, characteristics which are often talked about and always easily recognized. They are what one watches for when expecting the creature's approach.

An animal which is hunted as game is, however, a special case. What the hunter really wants is its flesh and blood. His state of mind when he has killed it and is carrying it home is a particularly happy one. The carcass, slung on his back as booty, is more important to him than the body of the living animal. He feels the blood running down his calves, in the hollow under his knees and on his back, and there he also feels its hair. The dead body he carries is not his own, and cannot be, for he wants to eat it.

Thus the Bushman's presentiments about springbok are divided into two different phases. In the ways I have described he feels the living animal, his body becomes its body, moving and watching as it does. But he also feels the dead animal, as an alien body pressed to his own and in a state in which it can no longer escape him. The two phases are interchangeable. One man may imagine himself first in the earlier one, another in the later; or they can follow immediately on each other. Together they contain the Bushman's whole relation to the animal and the entire process of the hunt, from the rustling to the blood.

Flight Transformations. Hysteria, Mania and Melancholia

TRANSFORMATION FOR flight, that is, in order to escape an enemy, is universal, being found in myths and fairy stories all over the world. I propose to give four examples to illustrate the different forms which this transformation can take.

The two main forms can be described as the *linear* and the *circular*. The linear is that manifested in the *hunt*, and is very common. One creature is pursuing another, the distance between them diminishing all the time until, at the very moment when the quarry is about to be seized, it escapes by transforming itself into something different. The hunt continues, or rather, starts afresh. The danger to the quarry mounts again and its pursuer may even succeed in getting hold of it, but, at the very last moment, it transforms itself into yet another shape and thus escapes again. The same process can be repeated as many times as new metamorphoses can be found. These must be unexpected in order to take the pursuer by surprise. He is hunting a specific and familiar quarry. He knows its manner of flight, he knows its shape and knows how and when it can be seized. The moment of transformation throws him into confusion; he has to think of a new manner of hunting to match the change in his quarry; he has to transform himself. Theoretically there need be no end to the sequence of transformations and in fairy tales the process is repeated as often as possible, sympathy being generally on the side of the pursued and the preferred ending the defeat or destruction of the pursuer.

The Australian myth of the Loritja provides an apparently simple case of linear flight transformation. The "eternal uncreated ones", the *Tukutitas*, the ancestors of the totems, spring from the earth in human shape. They remain human until, one day, a monstrous black and white dog appears, who has designs upon them and pursues them. They flee, but fear that they are not swift enough. In order to remedy this they transform themselves into all kinds of creatures—kangaroos, emus and eagles being specially mentioned. It should be remarked, however, that each of them changes into one kind of creature only and retains that shape during the whole period of his flight. Two more ancestors appear, similar to the first, but either stronger or braver. They pursue the dog and kill it, whereupon, the danger being past, most of the other *Tukutitas* resume their human shape. But they retain the faculty of transforming themselves at will into the animals whose names they bear, the animals which they were during their flight.

The limitation to a single animal metamorphosis is the very essence of these double figures, the totem ancestors. I shall discuss them at length in another context; here I only want to point out that the transformation they experience, and which they can always repeat, first comes about during flight.

Linear transformations in abundance are found in the Georgian tale, *The Master and His Apprentice*. The wicked master, who is the Devil himself, has taken the boy as an apprentice and has taught him all kinds of magic. He does not want to let him go, but to keep him in his service for ever. The boy escapes, but his master catches him again and locks him into a dark stable. There he dreams of escaping, but cannot think how. Time passes and he grows sadder and sadder.

One day he notices a ray of sunlight in the stable. He watches it carefully and finds the crack in the door by which it enters. Quickly he changes himself into a mouse and slips out through the crack. His master notices that he is gone, changes himself into a cat and runs after the mouse.

Then follows a wild sequence of transformations. The cat opens its jaws in order to kill the mouse, but the mouse turns into a fish and jumps into water. Instantly the master turns into a net, and swims after the fish. He has almost caught it when it changes into a pheasant. This the master chases as a falcon. His claws are already on its body when the pheasant turns into a red-cheeked apple which drops straight into the king's lap. The master turns into a knife in the king's hand. The king is about to cut the apple in pieces, but it is gone and in its place is a small heap of millet. A hen and her chicks stand before it—the master again. They peck up the grains until there is only one left. This, in the very last moment, becomes a needle. The hen and its chicks turn into a thread in the needle's eye. The needle bursts into flame and the thread is burnt up. The master is dead. The needle changes back into the boy, who goes home to his father.

The sequence of paired metamorphoses is as follows: mouse and cat, fish and net, pheasant and falcon, apple and knife, millet and hen with chicks, needle and thread. In each pair, the one half is always congruent to the other, whether this is a living creature or an object. The one which represents the master is always in pursuit of the one which represents the boy, who always escapes at the last moment by transforming himself. It is a mad hunt, and, because of the nature of the metamorphoses chosen, a spasmodic one. Its location changes as often as its figures.

Turning to the *circular* form we remember the classical story of Proteus, as it is found in the Odyssey. Proteus, the wise Old Man of the Sea, is the master of the seals and, like them, comes once a day to dry land. First the seals come, then Proteus. He counts them all carefully, for they are his herd, and then lies down amongst them to sleep. Menelaus, on his way home from Troy, has been driven off his course by adverse winds and cast with his companions on the coast of Egypt where Proteus lives. Years pass by and still they cannot sail, and Menelaus is in despair. Proteus' daughter takes pity on him and tells him what he must do to seize her father, who can prophesy, and force him to speak. She provides Menelaus and three of his companions with the skins of seals, scoops out holes in the sand for them to hide in and covers them with the seal skins. There, in spite of the stench, they wait patiently until the seals arrive and then continue to lie amongst them in their innocent-seeming disguise. Proteus emerges from the sea, counts his herd and, having reassured himself, lies down to sleep. This is the moment for Menelaus and his companions to leap upon him, seize him and hold him fast. Proteus tries to escape from them by assuming all kinds of shapes. First he turns into a lion, then into a snake; but they still keep hold of him. He becomes a panther and then a giant boar; but they do not let go. He turns into water and then a tree in full leaf; but still they hold him fast. All the transformations by which he tries to escape take place within the grasp of their hands. In the end he tires, resumes his own shape, that of Proteus, the Old Man of the Sea, asks them what they want and answers their questions.

The reason for describing this kind of transformation flight as circular is evident. Everything happens on one spot. Each transformation is an attempt to break out in another shape, in a different direction, as it were; but each is fruitless and ends where it began, in the grip of Menelaus and his friends. There is no longer any question of a hunt; the hunt is over, the prey seized and the transformations are a series of frustrated attempts to escape on the part of the prisoner. In the end he has to accept his fate and do what is demanded of him.

Lastly I want to quote the story of Peleus and Thetis, who later became famous as the parents of Achilles. Peleus is a mortal, Thetis a goddess, and she resists union with him, regarding him as unworthy of her. He surprises her sleeping in a cave, seizes her and holds her fast. Like Proteus she tries all kinds of metamorphoses; she turns into fire and water, into a lion and a snake; but he still holds her. She changes into an enormous, slippery cuttle-fish and squirts ink at him. But it is all useless; she has to give in to him and later, after various attempts to get rid of his unborn child, she becomes the mother of Achilles.

Like Proteus, Thetis finds herself a captive, held fast by an assailant who never lets go, and the transformations she undergoes are very similar to his. Each of them is an attempt to find a direction in which she can escape. She moves within a circle trying to find a point of release. But nowhere does she succeed in breaking out of the circle and so she remains a prisoner and finally surrenders in her own person, as Thetis herself, the centre of all the transformations.

The story of Thetis does not really add anything new to that of Proteus. I have quoted it here because of its erotic colouring. In this respect it reminds one of an affliction which is widespread and well known, namely hysteria. Major attacks of hysteria are nothing but a series of violent transformations for flight. The sufferer feels seized by a superior power. In the case of a woman it may be a man she wants to escape—a man who has possessed her or who, like Peleus, wants to possess her. It may be a priest who keeps someone prisoner in the name of a god; it may be a spirit, or an actual god. What is important in each case is the victim's feeling of the physical proximity of the superior power, its immediate grip on him. Everything he does, and especially every metamorphosis he achieves, has as its aim the loosening of the grip. An amazing number of transformations are attempted, though many are not carried beyond the initial stage. One of the most common is the transformation into a dead creature: this is well known and attested in the case of animals. The pursued hopes to be given up as dead, to be left lying on the ground while his enemy goes away. This transformation is the one which is nearest to the centre of the circle, the point which is still. The subject renounces all movement, as though he were actually dead, until the other creature goes away. It is easy to see how useful it would have been for Thetis and Proteus to be able to feign death; she could not have been loved, nor he forced to prophesy. But they were both known to be gods and thus immortal. However skilfully they dissembled, their death was the one thing no-one would have believed of them.

It is this circularity of flight-transformations which gives hysteria its characteristic colour. It also explains one of its most striking features, namely the frequency of the transition from processes of an erotic to those of a religious nature. Any kind of seizure can initiate any kind of flight-transformation, the attempt to escape being always equally fruitless if the assailant has the strength to hold on.

The reverse of flight-transformation is found in the attacks of *Shamans*. They too remain on one spot during a whole séance, surrounded by a circle of people watching them. Whatever may happen to them in spirit, their body should remain where it is. Sometimes they ask to be bound, fearing that their body might wander with their spirit. The circular nature of their performance is emphasized both by the necessity of remaining rooted to an earthly centre and by the presence of the watching circle of believers. The transformations follow each other at great speed and achieve great and cumulative intensity. But—and this is the essential difference between them and normal attacks of hysteria—they are in no sense intended to assist flight. The Shaman transforms himself in order to be able to seek out auxiliary spirits who obey him. He seizes them and forces them to help him in his undertakings. He is *active*, his transformations serving the increase of his own power, not flight from someone more powerful than himself. On the journeys his spirit undertakes whilst his body lies there apparently unconscious, he penetrates to the most distant parts of heaven and the underworld. He flies, ascending as high as he wishes, flapping wings like a bird; he dives, descending as deep as he wishes, till he comes to the bottom of the sea, where he forces his way into the house of a goddess, of whom he has an urgent request to make. But always he returns to his centre, where his followers wait anxiously for his tidings. It may sometimes happen that he is put to flight or forced to use transformation in order to escape, but the general character of his activity is expansive and masterful and resembles that of Proteus and Thetis only in the circularity of the multiple transformation process.

At this point it is worth returning to the linear type of transformation exhibited in the Georgian tale of the master and his apprentice. The reader will remember that the master turned into a cat in order to catch the boy who had escaped as a mouse. Later he turns into a net, a falcon, a knife and a hen with chicks. Each of these metamorphoses makes possible a new kind of hunt. As far as he is concerned, what happens is a quick succession of aggressive transformations and of changes, not only in the way the hunt is followed, but also in its location. The events are sudden and disconnected and widely dispersed in space, and this, taken in connection with the fact that they spring from a hostile intention, gives them a striking affinity to the processes of another mental illness, namely *Mania*. The manic's transformations have a tremendous ease about them; they share the linear and roving character of the hunter's and also the disconnectedness of his aims, which change each time he fails to attain what he wants, though he nevertheless persists with the hunt. The manic also resembles the hunter in his elation; wherever he may find himself, his mood is always intense and determined; he always has *an* aim. The boy in the story stands for the changing prey, which can be anything, but whose essence is to be simply prey. Mania is a paroxysm of desire for prey. What matters to it is to sight, overtake and seize the quarry; the incorporation, that is the eating of the victim, is not so important. The hunt in the story depends on the boy having escaped from the stable. It would come to an end—the attack of mania would, as it were, be over—if the master succeeded in recapturing the boy.

It was in the dark stable that we first met the boy. "He dreams of escaping, but cannot think how. Time passes and he grows sadder and sadder." He is experiencing the onset of that state which is the complement of mania, that is melancholia. As I have been discussing the one I ought, perhaps, to say something about the other. Melancholia begins when flight-transformations are abandoned because they are all felt to be useless. A person in a state of melancholia feels that pursuit is over and he has already been captured. He cannot escape; he cannot find fresh metamorphoses. Everything he attempted has been in vain; he is resigned to his fate and sees himself as prey; first as prey, then as food, and finally as carrion or excrement. The process of depreciation, which makes his own person seem more and more worthless, is figuratively expressed as feelings of guilt. Guilt was originally the same as debt (in German there is still only one word for them both). If one is in debt to someone one is to that extent in his power. Feeling guilty and thinking of oneself as prey are thus basically the same. The melancholic does not want to eat and, as a reason for his refusal, may say that he does not deserve to. But the real reason is that he sees himself as being eaten and, if forced to eat, is reminded of this. His own mouth turns against him; it is as though a mirror were held before him and he saw a mouth in it and saw that something was being eaten. But this something is himself. The terrible penalty for always having eaten is suddenly and ineluctably there before him. This transformation into something which is eaten is the last, the transformation which ends all flight. It is to avoid it that, in whatever shape offers, everything living flees.

Self-Increase and Self-Consumption. The Double Figure of the Totem

Of the myths which the younger Strehlow recorded among the Northern Aranda in Central Australia two are of special interest to us. The first of them is the Bandicoot myth:

"In the very beginning everything was resting in perpetual darkness: night oppressed all the earth like an impenetrable thicket. The ancestor—his name was Karora—was lying asleep, in everlasting night, at the very bottom of the soak of Ilbalintja; as yet there was no water in it, but all was dry ground. Over him the soil was red with flowers and overgrown with many grasses; and a great pole was swaying above him. This pole had sprung from the midst of the bed of purple flowers which grew over the soak of Ilbalintja. At its root rested the head of Karora himself: from thence the pole mounted up towards the sky as though it would strike the very vault of the heavens. It was a living creature, covered with a smooth skin like the skin of a man.

"And Karora's head lay at the root of the great pole: he had rested thus ever from the beginning.

"And Karora was thinking, and wishes and desires flashed through his mind. Bandicoots began to come out from his navel and from his arm-pits. They burst through the sod above and sprang into life.

"And now dawn was beginning to break. From all quarters men saw a new light appearing: the sun itself began to rise, and flooded everything with its light. Then the ancestor was minded to rise, now that the sun was mounting higher. He burst through the crust that had covered him; and the gaping hole that he left behind became the Ilbalintja Soak, filled with the sweet dark juice of the honeysuckle buds. The ancestor rose, feeling hungry, since magical powers had gone out from his body.

"As yet he feels dazed; slowly his eyelids begin to flutter; then he opens them a little. He gropes about in his dazed state; he feels a moving mass of bandicoots all around him. He is now standing more firmly on his feet. He thinks, he desires. In his great hunger he seizes two young bandicoots; he cooks them some little distance away, close to the spot where the sun is standing, in the white-hot soil heated by the sun: the sun's fingers alone provide him with fire and hot ashes.

"His hunger satisfied, his thoughts turn towards a helpmate. But now evening is approaching over the earth; the sun hides his face with a veil of hair-string, covers his body with hair-string pendants, vanishes from the sight of men. And Karora falls asleep, stretching his arms out on both sides.

"While he is asleep, something emerges from underneath his armpit in the shape of a bull-roarer. It takes on human form, and grows in one night to a full-grown young man: this is his first-born son. That night Karora wakes up, because he feels that his arm is being oppressed with the weight of something heavy: he sees his first-born son lying at his side, his head resting on his father's shoulder.

"Dawn breaks. Karora rises; he sounds a loud vibrating call. The son is thereby stirred into life. He rises; he dances the ceremonial dance around his father, who is sitting adorned with full ceremonial designs worked in blood and feather-down. The son totters and stumbles; he is still only half-awake. The father puts his body and chest into a violent quiver; then the son places his hands upon him. The first ceremony has come to an end.

"The son is now sent by his father to kill some more of the bandicoots which are playing peacefully about nearby in the shade. The son brings them back to his father, who cooks them in the sun-glowing soil, as before, and shares the cooked meat with his son. Evening has come again, and soon both are asleep. Two more sons are born that night to the father, from out of his arm-pits; these he calls into life on the following morning by the loud vibrating call as before.

This process is repeated for many days and nights. The sons do the hunting; and the father brings into life an increasing number of sons each night—as many as fifty on some nights. But the end cannot be delayed overlong: soon father and sons have succeeded in devouring all the bandicoots which had originally sprung from Karora's body. In their hunger the father sends his sons away on a three-days' hunt, to scour the great Plain. For hours they search patiently among the tall white grass, in the half-light of the almost limitless expanse of mulga trees. But the vast mulga thicket is devoid of bandicoots, and they have to return.

"It is the third day. The sons are returning hungry and tired, through the great stillness. Suddenly a sound comes to their ears, a sound like that of a whirling bull-roarer. They listen; they proceed to search for the man who may be swinging it. They search and search and search. They stab with their sticks into all bandicoot nests and resting places. Suddenly something dark and hairy darts up and is gone. A shout goes up—'There goes a sandhill wallaby'. They hurl their sticks after it and break its leg. And then they hear the words of a song coming from the injured animal:

> " 'I, Tjenterama, have now grown lame,
>   Yes, lame; and the purple everlastings are
>   clinging to me.

'I am a man as you are; I am not a bandicoot.' With these words the lame Tjenterama limps away.

"The astonished brothers continue on their way home to their father. Soon they see him approaching. He leads them back to the soak. They sit on its edge in circles, one circle around the other, ever widening out like ripples in disturbed water. And then the great flood of sweet honey from the honeysuckle buds comes from the east and engulfs them; it swirls them back into the Ilbalintja Soak.

"Here the aged Karora remains; but the sons are carried by the flood under the ground to a spot in the thicket. Here they rejoin the great Tjenterama, whose leg they had unwittingly broken with their sticks. He becomes their new chief. Karora remains behind: he is lying in eternal sleep at the bottom of the Ilbalintja Soak."

The second is the Lukara myth:

"At Lukara the famous, on the brink of the great waterhole, in the very beginning, an old man was lying in a deep sleep at the foot of a Witchetty bush. Ages had passed over him; he had been lying here undisturbed, like a man who is in a perpetual state of half-dream. He had not stirred ever since the beginning, he had not moved; he had always reclined on his right arm. Ages had rolled over him, in his everlasting sleep.

"As he was nodding in perpetual slumber, the white grubs were crawling over him. They had always been on his body. The old man did not move, neither did he wake up; he lay there in a deep dream. The grubs moved over his whole body like a swarm of ants; and the old man now and then brushed a few of them off gently without waking from his slumber. They returned, however; they crept over his body, they bored their way in; he did not awaken; the ages rolled on.

"And then, one night, as the old man slept, reclining on his right arm, something fell out from under his right arm-pit, something shaped like a witchetty grub. It fell to the ground and took on human shape and grew apace; and when morning broke, the old man opened his eyes and gazed with astonishment upon his first-born son."

The myth goes on to tell how a great host of grub men was 'born' in the same way. Their father never stirred: the only sign of consciousness that he ever gave was to open his eyes; he even refused all food which his sons offered to him. The sons, however, busily proceeded to dig out witchetty grubs from the bushes nearby; and they roasted and ate them. They themselves sometimes felt the desire to become grubs again; then they would chant a spell and so transform themselves into grubs, and re-enter the roots of witchetty bushes. Thence they would emerge again to the surface and assume human form once more.

"One day, however, a stranger came from far-off Mboringka. The stranger beheld the great bundle of fat and juicy grubs which had been collected by the brothers of Lukara, and he lusted after them. The stranger offered his own bundle of grubs in exchange for the juicy Lukara grubs. But the stranger's grubs were all long and thin and poor creatures. Scornfully the Lukara men thrust the proffered bundle aside with their digging sticks; they spoke no word. The visitor was offended; he boldly snatched up the bundle of the Lukara men, and rushed away in flight before they could prevent him.

"In dismay the Lukara men returned to their sleeping father. The latter had sensed the loss of their bundle even before they arrived: he felt a sharp pain in his body when the robber snatched the grubs away. Slowly he arose, and moved after the thief with tottering steps. But he did not recover the bundle; the thief carried them off to far-distant Mboringka. The father sank down, his body turned into a living tjurunga (a sacred object of stone or wood); the sons all became tjurunga; and the bundle of stolen grubs also turned into tjurunga."

These two myths deal with two entirely different ancestors, one of whom is the father of the bandicoots, the other of the witchetty grubs. Both are important totems of the Aranda, who continued to celebrate their rites down to the very day when the legends were recorded. I want to point out some striking traits common to both myths.

Karora, the father of the bandicoots, is first alone for a long time. He lies in perpetual darkness, sleeping under the crust at the bottom of the soak. He is unconscious and, as yet, has done nothing. Suddenly a large number of bandicoots form in his body and emerge from his navel and his arm-pits. The sun appears and its light causes him to break through the crust. He is hungry, but still feels dazed. In this dazed state he gropes about him and the first thing he feels is *a living mass of bandicoots all round him.*

In the other myth the father of the grubs is lying asleep at the foot of a witchetty bush. His sleep has lasted for ever. The white grubs crawl over his whole body. They are everywhere, like a swarm of ants. From time to time he brushes a few of them off without waking. They return, however, and bore their way into his body. He continues to sleep under their swarming mass.

Both myths begin with sleep and in both the first awareness of other creatures is through a crowd-sensation, and that the densest and most direct possible, namely one felt on the skin. Karora feels the bandicoots when, half-awake, he first stretches out his arms. The old man feels the grubs on his skin as he sleeps, and brushes them away, but without being able to get rid of them, for they come back and bore their way into his body.

The sensation of being covered with enormous swarms of small insects is, of course, universally known. It is not an agreeable feeling. It occurs commonly in hallucinations, those of *delirium tremens*, for example; if not insects, the creatures are rats or mice. The tickling on the skin, or the gnawing at it, is imagined as caused by insects or small rodents. In the next chapter it is dealt with more fully, and the expression "crowd-sensation on the skin" is explained and justified. But there is one important difference between the cases we are dealing with here and those others. The sensation in the Aranda myths is a pleasant one; what the ancestor feels is something which springs from himself, not something hostile attacking him from outside.

In the first myth the bandicoots come out of the navel or arm-pits of the ancestor. He is a very strange being indeed. More than a father, he is, as it were, a mother of crowds. Innumerable creatures spring simultaneously from his body, though from parts not normally associated with birth; he is like a termite queen, but one which produces her eggs from quite different parts of her body. In the second myth the grubs are said always to have been there. There is at first no mention of their having sprung from the ancestor's body; either they crawl on it or they bore their way into it. But as the story proceeds we come on things which lead us to suspect that the grubs spring originally from him, or that he actually consists entirely of them.

These births are not only remarkable in that it is a father who gives birth, and gives birth to crowds, but also in that the process eventually results in something quite different being born.

After Karora, the father of the bandicoots, has satisfied his hunger, night falls and he sleeps again. From his arm-pit a bull-roarer emerges; it takes on human shape and, in one night, grows into a young man. Karora feels something heavy weighing on his arm; he awakes and sees his first-born son at his side. During the following night two more sons are born to him out of his arm-pits. The process is repeated for many nights and, each time, more sons are born; in some nights he produces fifty. The whole process could, in the most literal sense of the word, be called the self-increase of Karora.

Something very similar happens in the second myth. The old man still sleeps, reclining on his right arm, when suddenly one night something shaped like a witchetty grub falls from his right arm-pit. It falls to the ground, takes on human shape and grows rapidly. When morning breaks the old man opens his eyes and gazes with astonishment at his first-born son. The process repeats itself until a large number of "grub-men" have been born in the same way. It is important to point out that these men can, when they so desire, transform themselves into witchetty grubs and then back again into men.

Thus, in both myths, we have self-increase and in both two kinds of birth, two kinds of beings, sprung from the same ancestor. The bandicoot father first brings forth a large number of bandicoots and then a large number of men, both propagated in the same way. They necessarily regard themselves as closely related, for they have the same father. They both call themselves bandicoots. As a totem-name this signifies that the men belonging to it are the younger brothers of the bandicoots who were born first.

Exactly the same holds for the ancestor of the witchetty grubs. He is the father, first of these grubs and then also of men, the men being the grubs' younger brothers. Together they are the visible embodiment of the fertility of the great ancestor of the totem. Strehlow, to whom we owe a great deal of gratitude for his recording of these important myths, puts this well. "The ancestor", he says, "represents the sum total of the living essence of all the witchetty grubs, both animal and human, regarded as a whole. If we may be allowed to express it thus, every cell in the body of the original ancestor is either a living animal or a living human being. When the ancestor is a 'grub-man' then every cell in his body is potentially either a separate living witchetty grub or a separate living man of the witchetty grub totem."

This dual aspect of the totem manifests itself very clearly in the fact that the human sons sometimes feel a desire to become grubs again. Then they chant a spell, transform themselves into grubs and creep back among the roots of the witchetty bushes where these grubs usually live. Thence they can emerge again and resume human shape when they wish. The separate forms remain entirely distinct, being either grubs or men, but able to transform themselves into the other. The restriction to a single metamorphosis—for, after all, innumerable others would be possible—is what constitutes the nature of a totem. The ancestor who brought forth these two kinds of creature has nothing to do with any other. He personifies one age-old kinship to the exclusion of any others there may be. His sons feel a desire to assume one or other of two shapes. By recourse to a spell they can gratify their desire and practise this their unique and inborn transformation.

It is impossible to overemphasize the importance of the double figure of the totem. In it transformation, or rather one particular instance of it, is crystallized, and thus can be handed on to posterity. In important ceremonies, designed to serve the increase of the totem, this handing on is represented dramatically, which means that the metamorphosis which the totem embodies is also represented. The desire of grubs to turn into men, and the desire of men to turn into grubs, has been handed on as an inheritance from the ancestors to the living members of the totem clan, who regard it as their sacred duty to satisfy this desire by their dramatic ceremonies. For the increase rites to be successful it is essential that this special transformation should be properly enacted, always in exactly the same way. When events in the lives of grubs are represented each participant knows exactly who it is he enacts or watches being enacted. He is named after the grub, but can also *become* it; as long as he bears its name he will practise the traditional transformation. Its value for him is immense: the increase of the grubs depends on it, and also his own increase, for the one cannot be separated from the other. Every aspect of the life of his clan is determined by his hold on the transformation.

There is another very important element in these legends, which I should like to call *self-consumption*. The ancestor of the bandicoots and his sons feed on bandicoots; the sons of the grub-ancestor feed on grubs. It is as though there were no other sort of food, or, at least, as though they were not interested in any other. What is eaten is determined by the particular form of transformation undergone. Both processes involve the same object. The ancestor who contains in his body both bandicoot and human sons thus feeds, as it were, on himself.

Let us examine the process more closely. After Karora has brought forth the bandicoots and the sun has begun to shine, he breaks through the crust above him, stands up and feels hunger. Hungry and half-dazed he gropes about, and this is the moment when he feels the moving mass of bandicoots all round him. Then he begins to stand more firmly on his feet. He thinks, he desires. In his great hunger he seizes two young bandicoots and cooks them a little way off in the white-hot soil heated by the sun. His hunger satisfied, and only then, his thoughts turn towards a helpmate.

The bandicoots he feels as a mass all round him have sprung from him; they are part of his own body, flesh of his own flesh. In his hunger he sees them as food. He seizes two of them—said to be young ones—and cooks them. It is as though he ate two young sons of his own.

During the following night he produces his first-born human son. In the morning he sounds a loud vibrating call which infuses life into his son and sets him on his feet. Together they enact a ceremony in which their relationship as father and son is established. Immediately afterwards the father sends the son to kill more bandicoots. They are his other children, born earlier, and are playing peacefully in the shade nearby. The son brings back those he has killed to his father, who cooks them in the sun, as he did those of the previous day, and shares the meat with his son. What the son eats is the flesh of his brothers and, in fact, of his father; and it was his father himself who taught him how to kill and cook it. It is the son's first food, as it was his father's. There is, in the whole legend, no mention of any other kind of food.

During the next night two more human sons are born to Karora. In the morning he calls them to life and sends all three sons out to hunt bandicoots. They bring back the game and the father cooks it and shares it with them. The number of human sons increases, more being born each night and, in one night, fifty of them. They are all sent out hunting. But, while the number of human sons goes on increasing, Karora produces no more bandicoots. These all came into existence simultaneously at the beginning. Thus the time comes when they have all been consumed; the father and his human sons have eaten them all. Now they are hungry and the father sends the sons away on a three-days' hunt. They search patiently everywhere, always only for bandicoots, but they cannot find any. On their way back they break the leg of a creature which they mistake for an animal. Suddenly they hear it sing, "I am a man, as you are. I am no bandicoot." Then it limps away and the brothers, of whom there must by now be a great many, return to their father. The hunt is over.

Thus the father first brings forth a distinct kind of food for himself and his later-born sons; this food is the bandicoots. It is a unique act, never repeated in the legend. Then, gradually, his human sons come into the world and, together with their father, eat up this food until there is none left. He does not teach them to catch other creatures, nor indicate any other possible food. We get the impression that he wants to nourish them only with his own flesh, with the bandicoots sprung from himself. In the way in which everything else is disregarded, is almost kept away from himself and his sons, something like jealousy can be discerned. The only other being who appears in the legend is the creature at the end, whose leg the sons injure, who is also a man and himself a great ancestor, to whom the sons finally turn.

In the second myth about the father of the grubs the connection between food and progeny is similar, though not identical. The first son falls from the father's armpit as a grub, which takes on human shape as soon as it touches the ground. The father does not stir, but remains quite still. He demands nothing of the son and teaches him nothing. Many other sons follow in the same way and all the father does is to open his eyes and watch them. He refuses the food they offer him. They, however, busy themselves with digging out witchetty grubs from the roots of nearby bushes; these they roast and eat. But the strange thing is that they sometimes feel a desire to transform themselves into the same kind of grubs as those on which they feed. They change into them and creep into the roots of the bushes and live there as grubs. They are sometimes one creature, sometimes the other; now men, now grubs. But as men they feed on these grubs only, no other kind of food being mentioned.

What we have here is self-consumption on the part of the sons. The old man refuses to eat the grubs, whose father he feels himself to be, for they are his own flesh. The sons find this self-consumption easy. We get the impression that to them food and transformation are closely allied; their desire to turn into grubs appears to spring from their pleasure in eating them. They dig for them, roast and eat them and then themselves turn into grubs again. After a while they re-emerge and resume human shape. When they then eat grubs it is as though they were eating themselves.

To these two stories, that of the bandicoot-father and the grub-sons, a third should be added, which also deals with self-consumption, but in a rather different form. Strehlow gives only a short résumé of this legend.

It is the story of another grub-ancestor from Mboringka who sallies out regularly to kill grub-men who are his own sons: they are expressly said to possess human shape. He roasts and devours them with relish, delighting in their sweet flesh. One day, however, their flesh turns to grubs in his bowels. These start to eat their father from within and so he is finally devoured by his own slaughtered sons.

This case of self-consumption has a curious climax: *The thing which is eaten eats back.* The father eats his sons and these same sons eat him whilst he is still in the process of digesting them; it is a double and mutual cannibalism. But the most extraordinary thing about it is that the riposte comes from *within*, from the father's bowels. For this to be possible a transformation of the sons is necessary; they are eaten by their father as men, but it is as grubs they eat him. It is an extreme and, in its way, very complete case. Here cannibalism and transformation have entered into a close alliance. The food remains alive to the very end and itself still wants to eat. Its transformation into grubs in the father's bowels is a kind of return to life, which makes possible the satisfaction of its desire for the father's flesh.

The transformations which link man with the animals he eats are as strong as chains. Without transforming himself into animals he would never have learnt to feed himself. Each of these myths deals with an essential experience: the control of a distinct species of animal which then serves as food; the origin of a special type of food through transformation; consumption of food and the transformation of what remains after this into new life. In later societies the memory of the way in which food was originally gained, that is, through transformation, is still preserved in sacred communions. The flesh which is communally eaten is not what it seems to be; it stands for some other flesh and *becomes* it whilst it is being eaten.

It should, however, be said that the self-consumption we have been discussing, though common in the ancestor legends of the Aranda, does not occur in their real life. The actual relationship of the members of a totem clan to the animal whose name they bear is quite different from that in the legends. It is precisely the members of a clan who do not feed on their totem animal; they are prohibited from killing or eating it and should regard it as their elder brother. Only during the ceremonies which serve the totem's increase, when the old myths are enacted and the clan members appear as their own ancestors, is a small piece of the totem's flesh solemnly offered to them and eaten. They are told that they may only have very little of it; it is especially they who must abstain from it as solid nourishment. If the animal falls into their hands, they must not shed its blood; they must hand it over to such members of their family or their horde who belong to *other* totems; these are allowed to eat it.

Thus, in the period which followed the age of the ancestors and which from the point of view of living Aranda, can be described as today, self-consumption is replaced by what is essentially a principle of avoidance. Men eat the animals closely related to them as little as they would eat their own people; the period of what can be called totem-cannibalism is over: only people belonging to another clan are allowed to eat one's animal relatives, just as they allow one to eat theirs. In fact, it is more than permission that each clan gives; it facilitates the process by furthering the increase of its own totem animal. The rites serving this increase are handed down by tradition and it is a duty to perform them. Animals which have been hunted too much tend to wander away or to die out. We remember the moment in the first legend when all the bandicoots far and near had disappeared; they had been so effectively hunted by the innumerable sons of Karora that none were to be found within the space of a three-days' journey. In this moment of starvation fresh bandicoots should have been brought forth. Self-consumption had been carried too far; all the elder brothers, Karora's first sons, had been eaten up. Self-consumption should now have reverted to the self-increase with which the whole process started.

It is precisely this reversal which we find in the later rites for the increase of the totem animal. A man's kinship with his own totem animal is so close that its increase cannot really be separated from his own. The representation of the ancestors who were both, sometimes a human being and sometimes the specific animal, is an essential and recurring part of the rites. The ancestors transform themselves as they wish from the one into the other and they can only be dramatically represented if the transformation has been mastered. They appear as double figures and the process of transformation is an essential part of their representation. As long as this is properly enacted, the kinship remains real and the animal which is oneself can be made to increase.

Crowds and Transformation in Delirium Tremens

THE HALLUCINATIONS of alcoholics provide us with an opportunity to study crowds as they appear in the minds of individuals. It is true that the phenomena are due to a form of poisoning, but anyone can experience them and up to a certain point they can be artificially induced. Their universality is undeniable; the hallucinations of men of the most diverse origin and disposition all share certain fundamental characteristics. They reach their greatest force and density in Delirium

Tremens. Study of this state is doubly productive, leading towards increased understanding both of crowd-processes and of the processes of transformation, but in it the two are so curiously interwoven that it is difficult to separate the one from the other. As we learn about transformation we find that we are learning just as much about crowds and so come in the end to the conclusion that it is best not to separate the two, or, at least, as little as possible.

In order to give the reader an idea of the nature of these hallucinations I shall start by quoting the description given by Kräpelin, followed by that of Bleuler. Their points of view are not quite the same, so that what they have in common is all the more convincing.

"Among the hallucinations of Delirium Tremens", says Kräpelin, "those of sight tend to predominate. The delusions are mostly of a clearly perceptible distinctness and only rarely shadowy and indefinite. They are often terrifying and unpleasant in content. Sometimes the sufferers regard them as reality, sometimes as artifice—a magic lantern or cinematographic show meant to amuse or to frighten them. Frequently they see *crowds* of small or large objects, dust, flock, coins, spirit-glasses, bottles, rods. Almost always the apparitions are in more or less lively motion . . . ; double vision is also found. The unsteadiness of the hallucinations perhaps explains the frequency with which gliding or creeping creatures are seen. They throng between the sufferer's legs, whir through the air and cover his food; everything swarms with 'golden-winged' spiders, beetles, bugs, snakes, vermin with long stings, rats, dogs, beasts of prey . . . Great crowds of people, gendarmes or enemy horsemen, some even 'on stilts', rush on the sufferer or march past him in long strangely grouped processions; he sees single bogymen, monstrous abortions, manikins, devils and "fire-rowdies"; ghosts put their heads through the door, skim over the furniture and climb up ladders. On rarer occasions there are laughing, painted girls, lascivious scenes, carnival-jokes, theatrical performances. . . .

"From various peculiar sensations on his skin the sufferer gets the idea that ants, toads or spiders are creeping over him. . . . He feels as though he were caught in a web of delicate threads, squirted with water, bitten, stung, or shot at. He collects money which he sees lying around in heaps and has the distinct feel of it in his hands, but it disappears like quicksilver. Whatever he touches vanishes, coalesces with something else or grows to monstrous proportions, to fall to pieces again, or roll or glide away.

"Small knots or irregularities of texture in his bedclothes appear as fleas, and cracks in a table as needles; secret doors open in the walls. . . .

"The sufferer is utterly incapable of any ordered activity; he is entirely preoccupied with his hallucinations. He seldom lets them simply pass by; generally they arouse lively reactions in him. He does not stay in bed, but thrusts his way out of the room, for the time for his execution has come and everyone is waiting for him. The strange animals amuse him, he recoils from the whirring birds, tries to wipe away the vermin and squash the beetles; he snatches at the fleas with outspread fingers, gathers up the money lying about everywhere, tries to break the web of threads enclosing him and, with scrupulous care, hops over the wires stretched across the floor."

"Delirium Tremens", says Kräpelin, summing up elsewhere, "is remarkable for the masses of homogeneous hallucinations and their multiple, lively motion, appearing, disappearing and melting into each other."

Bleuler's description of delirium tremens is equally striking:

"Hallucinations of a quite distinctive character predominate. These involve primarily *sight* and *touch*. The visions are *multiple* in motion, generally colourless and have a tendency towards diminutions. In addition, the hallucinations of both touch and vision very often have the character of wires, threads, sprays of water and other elongated things. Elemental visions, as of sparks and shadows, are frequent. If auditory hallucinations are present the patient usually hears music (especially with a very decided beat), which is very rare in other psychoses. During the entire course of the disease delirious patients can establish visual relationships with hundreds of hallucinated persons, all of whom are speechless. . . .

"Small moving and multiple things are in real life usually small animals like mice and insects; hence these are among the most frequent hallucinations of alcoholics. Besides these there are often other animal visions of the most varied kinds; pigs, horses, lions and camels may appear, either diminished or life-size. Sometimes there are animals 'that do not exist', fantastic combined creatures. In exactly the same way, I have strikingly often heard of processions of all kinds of animals projected onto an imaginary board fixed to the wall. These are usually large animals, but in some cases diminished to about the size of a cat; these the patient enjoys. People, too, are frequently reduced in size, but may also appear as large as in life.

"The hallucinations of the different senses combine readily. Mice and insects are not only seen, but are touched when the patient grabs them or they crawl over his body; money is gathered up and put in a hallucinated pocket; the patient sees passing soldiers and hears their band; he sees and hears someone shooting at him; he fights with hallucinated assailants whom he hears speak and, more rarely, touches."

In the course of a few days "the hallucinations gradually become more and more blurred and less numerous. Often, however, they first lose the property of reality; the birds are no longer alive, but stuffed; the scenes are specially performed and finally become only visual projections, like those thrown by a magic lantern."

About themselves "all pure cases of delirium remain fully orientated. They know who they are, what position in the world they occupy, what family they have and where they live."

These descriptions are a condensed summary of many individually observed cases. The first important point I want to stress is the connection between *tactile* and *visual* hallucinations. The itching and prickling on the skin is felt to be caused by large numbers of very small creatures simultaneously. We are not here interested in the physiological explanation of this; what matters is that the alcoholic thinks of insects— of ants, for example—and imagines his skin being assailed by thousands of these little creatures. They swarm over him in vast armies and, since he feels them moving on himself, he tends to assume their presence everywhere. Whatever he touches they are there; the floor at his feet and the air around him are thick with them, or with anything which can be felt as multiple.

This sensation of a crowd on the skin is not peculiar to delirium tremens; everyone has experienced it with insects or some kind of irritation. Among certain African peoples it is inflicted as the traditional penalty for particular types of crime, naked men being buried alive in ant-heaps and left there until they are dead. During delirium the sensation can become more violent than mere prickling; when the attack on the skin grows more insistent, covers larger areas of the body and penetrates deeper, prickling turns into *gnawing*. It feels then as though innumerable small teeth were at work on one's body; insects have changed into the rodents of which alcoholics chiefly speak. The sensation combines their nimbleness of movement with the way they are known to use their teeth: it also includes the concept of their fertility: they are known to appear in great numbers.

In delirium due to cocaine poisoning, where tactile hallucinations are much more prominent, these are localized *in* the skin and the sufferer wants to cut them out. The visual hallucinations often become "microscopic"; innumerable tiny details are registered—animalcules, holes in the walls, dots. A patient is reported to have seen "cats, mice and rats jumping round his cell and nibbling at his legs; he leapt up and

down, screaming that he felt their teeth in him. It was spiritism; they
had come through the wall by hypnosis". One assumes that the rats or
mice attract the cats and then themselves move faster as a result of their
presence.

This crowd-sensation on the skin is what comes first; it seems in
fact to provoke some of the visual hallucinations. The second point to
notice, which is perhaps linked with the first, is the frequency of
diminution. Not only is everything perceived and felt which actually
is small; not only is a world formed in which things known to be small
predominate, but also large things are diminished in order to be able
to enter this world. Men are seen as manikins and large animals from
the Zoo are reduced to the size of cats. Everything is multiplied and
everything is reduced in size. But the sufferer himself keeps his normal
size and, even in delirium, knows who and what he is. He himself
remains the same while his surroundings undergo a radical change.
The monstrous flux they are suddenly caught up in is one of masses of
tiny things, most of which he sees as alive. In every possible way there
is *more life* around him, but it affects him as though he were a giant.
It is precisely the Lilliput effect; but the world into which this Gulliver
is transplanted is much denser, more populous and more fluid.

These changed proportions are not as astonishing as they may appear
at first sight: one should remember how numerous and how small are
the cells of which the human body is composed. These cells are of very
different kinds and act on each other continuously. They are attacked
by hosts of bacteria and other minute creatures which settle among
them and which, being alive, are always active in their own way.
One cannot entirely dismiss the suspicion that the hallucinations of
alcoholics express an obscure awareness of this fundamental condition
of the body. During their delirium alcoholics are almost wholly
detached from their surroundings; they are orientated towards themselves and filled with the most peculiar sensations. Dissociative sensations of the body are well known in other diseases. The constant trend
of delirium tremens towards the concrete and the small (in cocaine-
delirium, often the microscopically small) has some resemblance to
a dissociation of the body into its component cells.

The cinematic character of the hallucinations has, as we have seen,
often been stressed. I would like to add something about their *content*.
What the alcoholic sees is the relationships and processes of his own
body, and principally the crowd-phenomena of all its minute component parts, transposed into concepts with which he is already familiar.
This is, of course, only a guess, but it is worth remembering that there

are moments when the whole life of the "giant" man, all his qualities and all his inheritance, is concentrated in minute individual cells, massed together and moving as a crowd: the animalcules of the sperm.

Whatever we may think of this interpretation, the basic situation of the delirium—that is, a single large individual seeing himself in opposition to a numberless host of tiny aggressors—does exist and in the course of human history has become increasingly marked. It begins with the peculiar feeling about vermin, by which all mammals (to speak only of them) are plagued. Whether these are mosquitoes or lice, locusts or ants, they have always occupied men's imaginations. Their threat lies in the fact that they appear in great crowds and very suddenly. They have often stood as symbols for crowds. It is very probable that it was they who first brought man to *think* in terms of great crowds; perhaps his earliest "thousands" and "millions" were insects.

Man's power and the conception he had of himself had already expanded enormously when he stumbled upon the bacillus. This discovery made the contrast immeasurably greater. Man, with his enhanced opinion of himself, increasingly seeing himself as an individual detached from his fellow-creatures, was suddenly confronted with entities much smaller even than vermin, multiplying even more rapidly and invisible to the naked eye. On the one hand was himself, greater and more isolated than before, and on the other a crowd, larger than any he had previously imagined, of infinitesimal creatures.

It is impossible to overrate the importance of this concept. Its formation is one of the central myths in the history of human thought. It is the exact model of the dynamics of power. Man easily persuaded himself to see as vermin everything which opposed him; as such he regarded and treated all animals which he could not use. And the despot who reduces men to animals and only manages to rule them by regarding them as belonging to a lower species, reduces to vermin all who do not qualify even to be ruled and ends by destroying them by the million.

The third important point about alcoholic hallucinations is the character of the transformations found in them. The hallucinations are always outside the patient; even when he experiences them as reality, they do not transform *him*. He preferably watches them from a distance. As long as they do not threaten him, and thus force him to define his position in relation to them, he enjoys their fluidity and ease of movement. But sometimes they reach a point where even a semblance of orientation becomes impossible; when *everything* round him is fluid and transitory he naturally begins to feel very uncomfortable himself.

Two very different kinds of transformation can be observed: first, there are crowds which transform themselves into other crowds—ants into beetles and beetles into coins which, when collected, run into each other like drops of quicksilver. (Examples of this process, where something multiple changes into something different, but equally multiple, will be given later.) The second kind of transformation gives rise to monstrous hybrids. A single creature combines with another to form something new, as though two things had been photographed one on top of the other. In the processions of animals of which we heard were creatures "that do not exist, fantastic combined creatures". Aborted monstrosities and "fire-rowdies" recall the Temptation of St. Anthony as painted by Grünewald, or the creatures which populate the pictures of Hieronymus Bosch.

In order to form a clearer picture of the transformations we shall have to follow the whole course of one or two cases. Only then shall we see exactly what changes into what and even be able to conjecture how and why it happens. Study of the complete course of a delirium can also, as our second example makes particularly clear, lead to deeper insight into the nature of crowd-processes.

The first case is that of an innkeeper treated by Kräpelin. Here is a summary of the contents of his delirium, which lasted for about six days:

"He felt that it was a special day, with the devil about. Suddenly he ran into a marble pillar with his head. He wanted to dodge it, but there was an enormous marble slab opposite him across the narrow street, and one like it when he wanted to turn back. Both slabs collapsed, threatening him. Two insolent characters took him on a cart to the Ox Inn and laid him on his death-bed. A master of ceremonies directed hot rays on to his mouth with a pair of red-hot scissors, so that his vital strength gradually vanished. At his request he was given a glass of red wine; a second glass was refused with a grin by Satan himself. He then, with all kinds of pious exhortations, said goodbye to the people standing round and expired; simultaneously the corpses of his three daughters were laid beside him. In the next world he was punished by means of the sins he had committed on earth; he continually felt a terrible thirst, but as soon as he grasped a tankard or glass this disappeared out of his hand.

"The next morning he was alive again, lying on his bier in the Ox; his children were also there in the shape of white hares. There was a procession of Catholics taking place and, during it, whilst they were singing their chants, he had to press on innumerable pairs of golden spectacles lying on the floor in the backroom of the Crown Inn; each time he did this there was a shot. Those taking part in the procession then discussed whether he should simply be beaten, or be beaten to death. The landlady of the Crown was for the first, on condition that he always lodged with her. But he wanted to get away because he was not given any beer. Then a police sergeant came to liberate him. The landlord of the Crown shot at him with a revolver and was taken to prison.

"Another evening the whole Protestant community was gathered in Church for a special service. In the centre was a member of the student corps, who, before the service began, gave a kind of circus perform-ance with fifty fellow-students on small horses. Later the patient saw his wife go into a pew with one of her relatives; he himself was hidden behind the organ with a Sister of Charity and from there watched these two desecrating the Sanctuary. After that he found himself locked into the Church; eventually a glazier cut a hole in the window, so that at least some beer could be passed through to him. When he dressed himself the sleeves and all the apertures in his clothes had been blocked; they were sewn up. The pockets were unstitched. In the bath he saw himself surrounded by seven hares, floating under water, who con-tinually splashed and nibbled him."

The patient's new, real-life surroundings of which, during his delirium, he knows nothing, and against which he really knocks his head, translate themselves for him into marble. In his hallucinated state he enjoys finding himself amongst large numbers of people, as the object of their attention and even their threats. On his death-bed in the Ox he is slowly deprived of his vital strength. It is like a long-drawn-out execution, which he makes use of to collect spectators around him, keeping them there with his pious exhortations. Thirst represents all his personal desires; he suffers in the next world the punishment of Tantalus. His three daughters, laid out beside him as corpses, come to life again the next morning as he himself does, but as white hares. This expresses their innocence, but also contains the pangs of conscience he feels on their account and which gnaw at his drunkard's heart.

The procession of the Catholics is the first actual crowd-event. He is forced to play a part, but without really becoming one of the crowd. The pairs of golden spectacles lying on the floor in the back room where he finds himself are as innumerable as the participants in the procession. Each time he presses them there is a shot; this may have been intended as a salute of guns to heighten the general festivity, but,

confirmed sinner that he is, he feels as though he were shooting down
Catholics. The members of the procession see him for what he is and
hold a kind of meeting to consider his punishment. It is an extension
of the death-bed situation, this time with a larger number of people
sitting in judgment on him. One might suppose that he has a low
opinion of Catholics, but he treats the Protestant congregation assembled for their special service on another evening with scarcely more
respect: he links it with a circus performance. Here we have a striking
example of the transition of one kind of crowd into another: the
congregation transforms itself into a circus. The student, who perhaps
stands for the clergyman, has no fewer than fifty fellow-students with
him; the horses, as was to be expected, are reduced in size. It is possible
that the patient feels their hoof-beats.

The way in which the attitude in delirium tends towards that of an
observer is clearly brought out by the way he watches his wife commit
her offence. Very peculiar is his relationship to his clothes; they too
are transformed, the sleeves and all the apertures being sewn up and
the pockets unstitched. The clothes have turned into deformed monsters, their organs no longer functioning as they should. A menagerie
of transformed clothes is certainly possible in a delirium and would
not be so remote from one of animals either. Finally, the seven hares
in the bath have a fair number of teeth between them and gnaw him
quite effectively.

The second case I want to quote at some length was treated by
Bleuler. The patient, a schizophrenic, gave a description, 36 pages long,
of his experiences during an attack of delirium tremens. It may be
objected that this patient was not typical, nor, therefore his delirium.
But it seems to me, on the contrary, that it is from this particular case
that we can learn most about crowd-concepts in this kind of delirium.
The hallucinations here are somewhat less disconnected and the transformations rather less agitated. Actually the whole description has the
character of a poetic utterance; even in the short extracts given here
something of this can be felt.

"What I had suddenly to see there made my hair stand on end.
Forests, rivers and oceans with every kind of dreadful animal and human
figure, such as no human eye ever saw before, whirled by incessantly,
alternating with the workshops of every trade, in which horrible
spirit figures were working. On both sides the walls were nothing but
a single ocean with *thousands of little ships* on it; the passengers were all
naked men and women, who indulged their lust in time to music. Each
time a pair had taken their pleasure a figure stabbed them from behind

with a long spear, so that the ocean was coloured red with blood. But there were always fresh multitudes to succeed them. . . .

"A train from which many people alighted. Among them I heard the voices of my father and my sister K., who came to deliver me. I plainly heard them converse with each other. Then I heard my sister whispering with an old woman. I called to her for dear life to deliver me. She called back that she would do it, but the old woman would not let her go, warning my sister that, if she did, she would bring misfortune on the whole household and that nothing was happening to me. . . . With prayers and tears I awaited my death. A dead silence prevailed and *droves of spirit figures* surrounded me. At last one of the spirits came and held his watch at a certain distance in front of my eyes, indicating by signs that it was not yet three o'clock, for none of the figures were permitted to speak."

Then there were long negotiations between the various relatives of the patient who wanted to ransom him, some with smaller sums and some with larger. Other voices debated how they should make away with the patient. Then the relatives were induced to climb ladders, whence they were thrown into the moat, where they were heard crying out and choking. The wife of the jailer came and cut off the patient's flesh piece by piece, beginning with his feet and going up to his breast, and fried and ate it. She poured salt on his wounds. On a wildly swaying scaffold he was drawn up into the various heavens, as high as the eighth, past choirs of trumpets who proclaimed his fame. At last, by some mistake, he was returned to earth. . . . People sat at a table and ate and drank things which had the most marvellous aroma, but, when a glass was handed to him, it disappeared into nothing and he suffered great thirst. Thereupon he had to count and reckon out loud for hours. In a little flask divine drink was handed to him, but, as he took it, it broke and the contents flowed between his fingers like threads of glue. Later a great battle was fought between his tormentors and his relatives, of which he saw nothing, but heard the blows and the groans.

The "forests, rivers and oceans" which appear here are already known to us as crowd symbols, but, as though they were here only in the process of *becoming* symbols, they are not yet quite detached from the crowds for which they often come to stand later. They are still alive "with every kind of dreadful animal and human figure, which no human eye ever saw before". The propagation of new creatures, and in such numbers, by the combination of existing ones is the work of transformation. Again, the delirious patient is not himself drawn into these transformations; all the more marked, therefore, are the combinations and permutations in his world; and all these new creatures are immediately present in vast numbers. It is remarkable how this particular patient makes the familiar entities of the forest, river and ocean, in which new life has a natural origin, alternate with the "workshops of every trade". He equates production with transformation, a notion which many primitive peoples share with him. The various trades are as separate as different species, but all their products are immediately present in huge numbers; one cannot help feeling that the workshops are actually only there in order to bring into existence vast masses of things in the quickest possible way. It is the processes of work as abstractions that we see here, together with their results; they are carried out by obscure spirit-figures.

Then the walls return, as a single ocean; but now it is alive with thousands of small ships instead of with animal and human figures. The passengers are naked men and women, all, except for the differences of sex, identical in their nakedness and identical also in their dependence on the beat of the music. The crowd here is a crowd of copulating couples. They are stabbed as couples, and the blood of all of them flows into the sea and colours it red. But there are always fresh multitudes to succeed them.

The "train from which many people alight" needs more explanation. In a train one imagines a large number of people together, who have been travelling in the same direction for a long distance, separated, it is true, by the walls of their compartments, but unable to part company entirely except at stations. The terminus is a goal which was common to all of them, even though they may have started from different places. Just before they arrive, when they feel they are near their journey's end, they get up, press into the corridor and station themselves by the windows. At this point they exhibit a very mild form of crowd excitement; at least they have reached their goal together. When they alight and, on foot, cover the last stage of their journey, the length of the platform to the exit, the movement, their brief march together, is the last manifestation of this mild crowd.

On the spectator the emptying of a train, following immediately after the sight of many unknown faces, pressed closely to windows and doors, makes a crowd-effect very different from that felt by the traveller. Among all these strange faces he has to find the one or two familiar ones he has been waiting for. The "train from which many people alight" is thus actually *made* for the "watching" of delirium, which is one of the things we have been discussing here. It is also significant that one visualizes the incident as taking place in a large station where many lines meet.

The word "death" which comes a little later is followed by "dead silence". But whilst *we* only take this to mean an especially profound silence, for the *patient* the "dead" detach themselves from the word and surround him as droves of spirit-figures.

As he is drawn up into the heavens he passes choirs of trumpets who proclaim his fame. Nothing expresses the nature of fame better. The man who desires fame wants exactly this: choirs of creatures which do nothing but acclaim him. Preferably, of course, they should be human. This, too, is in some sense a mild crowd. Once in position, the choir remains there and, however much noise it makes, it comes no nearer to its object than his name.

Through the whole sequence runs a quarrel between two hostile groups: on the one side are the relatives of the patient who want to ransom and free him, on the other the enemies who want to kill him; he, or rather his *body*, is the object they fight over. First come long drawn out negotiations, his relatives offering small and then larger sums for him; he becomes more and more valuable to them. By a stratagem his party are thrown into the castle moat, where he hears them crying out and choking (we learned about the heap of the dying and the dead during our discussion of war). As a prisoner the patient is tortured and eaten in the manner of cannibals. The conflict between his torturers and his relatives leads to a great battle; he hears the blows and hears again the groans of the wounded. Thus, in addition to everything else, this delirium contains the familiar double crowd and its discharge in war. The events out of which the battle develops remind one strongly of the corresponding phases in primitive warfare.

Scarcely any of the crowd-phenomena we have discussed are missing from this account. They are not often found assembled in such distinctness and concentration.

Imitation and Simulation

IMITATION AND transformation might seem to be the same, but it is advisable to keep the two apart, for they mean different things and to distinguish them accurately may, in itself, help to elucidate the actual process of transformation.

Imitation relates to externals; there must be something before one's eyes, which is copied. Imitation of sounds means no more than the reproduction of the sounds which are heard; nothing is revealed about the inner state of the imitator. Monkeys and parrots imitate, but, as far as we know, they do not change *within* themselves in the process. One might say that they do not know what it is they are imitating; they have never experienced it from inside. Although they can jump from one thing to another, the order in which they do so has no meaning for them. Their lack of persistence makes imitation easier, for this is usually focussed on a single trait. Since, in the nature of things, it is likely to be a particularly striking trait, imitation is often mistaken for "characterization", when, in fact, this is entirely absent.

A person can be recognized by certain formulae which he uses often, and a parrot who imitates them may superficially remind one of him. But these formulae are not necessarily ones which are really characteristic of him, and may even be phrases he uses only to the parrot. In this case the parrot is imitating something quite unimportant, by which no-one who has not heard the particular phrase would recognize him.

Imitation, in a word, is nothing but a first step in the direction of transformation, a movement which immediately stops short. Such movements can occur in rapid sequence and relate to the most incongruous succession of objects. Monkeys provide a good example of this; the very ease with which they imitate something precludes a real grasp of it. Transformation, on the other hand, is like a solid body set beside the two-dimensional structure of imitation.

There is also a transitional stage, which consists in deliberately remaining midway between imitation and transformation. This I propose to call *simulation*. When the stress is on concealing what one is, rather than on pretending to be what one is not, the common term is, of course, *dis*simulation; but in practice they can generally not be separated.

To approach someone in the guise of a friend, but really with hostile intent, is an early and important kind of transformation and one which has become part of all later forms of power. It is superficial and relates to external appearances alone, to skin, horns, voice and movement. Underneath, unmoved and immovable in his deadly purpose, hides the hunter; here appearance and reality are as different from each other as they can be. This cleavage attains its perfection in the mask. Any hunter has control over himself and his weapon. But a masked hunter also controls the figure of the animal he represents; he has power over both which he exercises continuously. He is, as it were, two creatures simultaneously and keeps a firm hold on both until he has achieved his purpose. The flux of transformations of which he is capable is arrested; he stands on two sharply circumscribed sites, the one *within* the other. Both are clearly demarcated, but it is essential that the outer one should completely and consistently cover the inner. The harmless and friendly creature is outside; the hostile and deadly one inside, revealing itself only in the final act.

This duplicity is the extreme form of dissimulation. In its strict meaning the word could not be more expressive, but it has so often been used in a more trivial connection that it has lost much of its force. I want to limit it again to its narrower meaning and use it for the hiding of a hostile figure within a friendly one.

"A washerman had a donkey which could carry extraordinary burdens. In order to feed him the washerman covered him with a tiger skin and took him at nightfall to other people's corn; and the donkey enjoyed other people's corn to his heart's content. Nobody dared come near him and chase him away, for everyone took him for a tiger. But one day a watchman lay in wait for him. He had covered himself with a dust-grey cloak and held his bow in readiness to kill the beast of prey. When the donkey saw him from far-off, love stirred in him and he took the man for a she-donkey. So he cried out and ran to him. The watchman recognized the donkey by his voice and killed him."

This brief Indian tale of the donkey in the tiger's skin contains a whole small textbook of dissimulation. No-one else has yet succeeded in saying so much about it in so few words. It must be admitted that it deals only with its applications, not its origins, but these are not always as far apart as one might think.

It all starts with a washerman, someone whose job it is to wash clothes; and clothes are men's second skin. He is a good washerman and has found a donkey who can carry heavy burdens for him. (We can assume that the donkey carries the washing his master has done and also, perhaps, that the tiger skin which is essential to the story was found among the clothes the washerman had to deal with in his job.)

The donkey who works so well gets hungry and needs a great deal of food. His master clothes him in the tiger skin and leads him to other people's corn. There the donkey can eat to his heart's content, for the people are afraid of him, taking him for a tiger. Here a harmless creature is clothed in the skin of a very dangerous one. But the donkey does not know what has been done to him; the terror he arouses is beyond his understanding. He eats peacefully and to his heart's content. The people who are afraid to approach him do not even know what he is doing. The dread they feel is that of a more powerful being; it contains an element of religious awe. This keeps them from unmasking the tiger as a donkey. They keep away from him and, as long as he remains silent, he can go on eating. But now a watchman appears who is no ordinary man; he has the courage of a hunter and holds his bow in readiness to kill the tiger. In order to lure it nearer he disguises himself as prey which might interest a tiger. He puts on a dust-grey cloak; it may or may not be the skin of a donkey, but, in any case, he wants to be taken for a donkey by the supposed tiger. His dissimulation is that of a dangerous creature pretending to be harmless. It is one of the methods used by the earliest hunters to get close to their prey.

Now comes the point of the story. The donkey, having satisfied his hunger, feels lonely. Directly he sees something in the distance which looks like another donkey, he wants it to be a *she*-donkey. He brays and gallops up to this supposed she-donkey. He is recognized as a donkey by his voice and is killed by the watchman. Instead of making the effect of prey which a tiger would want to eat the watchman had, though unwittingly, made the effect of a she-donkey. Instead of the love he wanted the donkey found death.

The story is built up as a sequence of deceptions. By simulating some creature which one is not, one tries to deceive other creatures. The action consists in each simulation being rapidly followed by an effect different from the one intended. It is only man who makes deliberate use of simulation. He can disguise himself, as did the watchman, for example, and he can also disguise another creature, as the washerman did his donkey. But an animal can only be a passive subject of disguise. In this story the separation between men and animals is complete. The age of myth is past, when men really acted as true animals and animals spoke like men. Precisely through these mythical experiences man has learnt to make use of almost any animal as it suits him; his transformations have become dissimulations. Under the masks and skins with which he disguises himself he remains clearly aware of his own purposes; he remains himself, the lord of the animals. Those he cannot subjugate, like the tiger, he venerates. But some men of outstanding courage try to deal with even the tiger by means of dissimulation; the watchman by his ruse might have succeeded in killing a real tiger.

It is extraordinary that one short story should express so many essential relationships. It is not unimportant that it begins with a washerman, someone who handles clothes—the lifeless successors, as it were, of the animal skins which, in myths, are so often the means to transformation. The tiger skin the washerman uses to trick people puts life into his normally harmless bundles of washing.

Simulation, this limited form of transformation, has always been, and still remains, the only form which a ruler can safely permit himself; and a despot *cannot* carry transformation further. He is only a despot so long as he remains conscious of his inner hostility to others. This is his core, or, as it might better be called, his real shape. He is limited to transformations which keep it always and perfectly intact. His real shape is terror; it may suit him sometimes to disguise it and he can use a variety of masks for this purpose. But he will only put them on for a time and they can never effect the slightest change in the inner shape which is his true nature.

The Figure and the Mask

THE PRODUCT OF transformation is something which I propose to call the *figure*. This is an entity which is not susceptible of further transformation and which manifests itself only after transformation has been completed. Its shape is clear and limited in every respect. It is not a natural object, but a creation of man; it is his escape from the ceaseless flux of transformation. (It should not, incidentally, be confused with the "kinds" or "species" of modern science.)

We shall come nearest to understanding its nature by visualizing the divine images of ancient religions, those of the Egyptian gods, for example. The goddess Sechmet is a woman with the head of a lioness; Anubis a man with that of a jackal; Thot a man with the head of an ibis; the goddess Hathor has the head of a cow and the god Horus that of a falcon. These figures, in their clear, immutable shapes, which are twofold—the shape of an animal *and* a human being—dominated the religious conceptions of the Egyptians for thousands of years. In these forms they were depicted everywhere, and in these forms were worshipped. Their stability is particularly striking, but, even before any such rigid systems of divinities had evolved, dual animal-human figures were to be found all over the earth amongst peoples quite unconnected with each other.

The mythical ancestors of the Australian aborigines are man and animal simultaneously, or sometimes man and plant. These figures, as we know already, are called totems: there is a kangaroo, an oppossum and an emu totem. Each of these is man and animal at the same time; it acts both as a man and as a particular animal, and is regarded as the ancestor of both.

What are we to make of these archaic figures? What actually is it that they represent? If we are to understand them we must remember that they are regarded as beings belonging to an age of myth, a period in which metamorphosis was the common gift of all creatures and constantly practised. It has often been pointed out how *fluid* the world was then. Not only could a man transform himself into anything, but he also had the power to transform others. In the universal flux certain figures stand out, which are nothing but particular metamorphoses fixed and made permanent. The figure which men cling to, which becomes a life-giving tradition enacted and spoken of over and over again, is not the abstraction of an animal species, not Kangaroo or Emu, but a kangaroo who is also a man, or a man who at will can become an emu.

Thus these earliest figures are representations of the *process* of transformation. From the unending flux of innumerable possible transformations, *one* is picked out and given permanent form. The very process of transformation, or rather a particular instance of it, is secured for ever and thus, in comparison with all those which are excluded, is filled with special significance. The unchanging double figure of the totem, which contains and affirms the metamorphosis from man into kangaroo and from kangaroo into man, is the earliest and most important of all figures, their prototype.

It is what one may call a *free* figure. Its two aspects are equal in importance; neither is ranked higher than the other and neither is hidden behind the other. It reaches back into the remote past, but is so profoundly imaginative that it still affects the present. It is accessible to men; by enacting the myths in which it occurs they can share in it.

For us, too, insight into this earliest kind of figure is important. We must realize that the *figure* originates, not as something simple, but as something which to us seems complex and is thus quite different from our modern conception of a figure. Originally it expressed both the process of transformation *and* its result.

The *mask* is distinguished from all the other end-states of transformation by its rigidity. In place of the varying and continuous movement of the face it presents the exact opposite: a perfect fixity and sameness. Man's perpetual readiness for transformation is clearly expressed in the mobility of his face. The play of his features is far richer and more varied than that of any animal and he has, too, the richest experience of transformation. It is inconceivable how many changes a face can undergo in the course of a single hour. If one had time to study all the movements and moods which pass over it one would be astonished at the number of seminal transformations it reveals.

People's attitude to this play of the features varies. In some civilizations the freedom of the face is largely restricted; it is thought improper to show pain and pleasure openly; a man shuts them away inside himself and his face remains calm. The real reason for this attitude is the desire for personal autonomy: no intrusion on oneself is permitted, nor does one intrude on anyone else. A man is supposed to have the strength to stand alone and also the strength to remain himself. The two things go hand in hand, for it is the influence of one man upon another which stimulates the unending succession of transformations. They are expressed in gestures and the movements of the face and, where these are suppressed, all transformation becomes difficult and, in the end, impossible.

A little experience of the inflexibility of such unnatural "stoics" soon leads one to understand the general significance of the mask: it is a *conclusion*; into it flows all the ferment of the as yet unclear and uncompleted metamorphoses which the natural human face so miraculously expresses, and there it ends. Once the mask is in position there can be no more *beginnings*, no groping towards something new. The mask is clear-cut; it expresses something which is quite definite, and neither more nor less than this. It is *fixed*; the thing it expresses cannot change.

It is true that behind one mask there can be another: there is nothing to prevent an actor wearing a second mask under his first. Special double masks are found among many peoples. As soon as one mask opens another is seen beneath it. But this too is a mask, a separate *conclusion*. It is reached by a leap: whatever might lie between one mask and the other is eliminated; there is no preparation for the transition as there is in a face. The new, the different thing is suddenly *there*, as clear and fixed as the other was. Anything can be effected by a change of masks, but it always happens in a leap, in one sudden, concentrated movement.

The working of the mask is mainly outwards; it creates a *figure*. The mask is inviolable and sets a distance between itself and the spectator. It may come nearer to him, as sometimes in a dance, but he must always stay where he is. To fixity of form is added fixity of distance. What gives the mask its interdictory quality is the fact that it never changes.

Everything behind the mask is mysterious. When the mask is taken seriously, as in the cases we are discussing here, no-one must know what lies behind it. A mask expresses much, but hides even more. Above all it *separates*. Charged with a menace which must not be precisely known —one element of which, indeed, is the fact that it *cannot* be known—

it comes close to the spectator, but, in spite of this proximity, remains clearly separated from him. It threatens him with the secret dammed up behind it. Unlike a face, there are no passing changes in it which can be interpreted, and so he suspects and fears the unknown that it conceals.

Transposed into terms of sounds, this is an experience familiar to all of us. One arrives in a country knowing nothing of the language and is surrounded by people talking. The less one understands the more one imagines; one attributes all sorts of things to them, one suspects hostility and is incredulous, relieved and even a little disappointed when their words are translated into a familiar language. How harmless, how innocent it all was! Every completely unknown language is a kind of acoustic mask; as soon as one learns it, it becomes a *face*, understandable and soon familiar.

The true mask is something which never changes, but remains permanently and unmistakably itself, a constant in the continual flux of metamorphosis. Part of the strength of its effect is due to the fact that it reveals nothing of what is behind it. The mask is perfect because it stands alone, leaving everything behind it in shadow; the more distinct it is, the darker everything else. No-one knows what may not burst forth from behind the mask. The tension created by the contrast between its appearance and the secret it hides can become extreme. This is the real reason for the terror the mask inspires. "I am exactly what you see" it proclaims "and everything you fear is behind me." The mask fascinates and, at the same time, enforces distance. No-one dares to lay violent hands on it; if anyone but the wearer tears it off he is punished by death. While it is in action it cannot be touched; it is inviolable and sacred. The mask is clear and certain, but is loaded with the terror of uncertainty. Its power derives from the fact that it is itself known, while what it covers is never known. The mask is only known from outside or, as it were, from in front.

The real use of the mask is not in isolation, but in ceremonies and if it then behaves in a familiar and expected manner it can also have a reassuring effect. Here it stands between the dangerous power which is behind it and the spectator. If properly treated it can keep this power away from him. It can gather the danger into itself and contain it, only allowing it to overflow in one manner—the manner corresponding to its own shape. Once the spectator has established a relationship with the mask, he can behave in an appropriate way. It is a figure with its own idiosyncrasies of behaviour. Once these have been learnt, once one knows how much distance it demands, it acts as a protection against the dangerous power contained within itself.

There is much more that should be said about the mask which has become a *figure*: drama begins with it and cannot exist without it. But here we are only concerned with the mask itself. We must now look at it from the other side, for it does not only operate outwards, affecting those who do not know what it contains; a mask is something worn by a man and he is *inside* it.

The wearer knows perfectly well who he really is; but his task is to *act* the mask. While doing so he must remain within certain limits, corresponding to the nature of the mask he wears.

The mask is something put on, something external. As a physical object it remains quite distinct from the man who wears it. He feels it on him as something foreign, something which never wholly becomes part of himself; it hinders and constricts him. As long as he wears it he is two things, himself and the mask. The more often he has worn it and the better he knows it, the more of himself will flow into the figure it represents. But there is always one part of him which necessarily remains separate from it: the part that fears discovery, the part which knows that the terror he spreads is not his due. The secret he represents to those who see the mask from outside must also have an effect on himself inside it, but it clearly cannot be the same effect. *They* are afraid of the unknown; *he* is afraid of being unmasked. It is this fear which prevents him abandoning himself completely to the mask. His transformation can go a very long way, but it is never complete. The mask is a limit set to transformation. Because it can be torn away, its wearer is bound to fear for it. He must take care that he does not lose it; it must never be dropped and must never open. He feels every kind of anxiety about what may happen to it. Besides playing a part in his transformation, the mask is also a weapon or a tool which its wearer has to handle. He must manipulate it, remaining his everyday self, and, at the same time, must change into it as a performer. While he wears the mask he is thus two people and must remain two during the whole of his performance.

The Power of Unmasking

A DESPOT IS ALWAYS aware of his inner malevolence and therefore must dissimulate. But he cannot deceive everyone in this way. There are always others who also desire power and who do not acknowledge his claims, but regard themselves as his rivals. Against these he is always on his guard, for they are a potential danger to him. He waits for the right moment "to tear the mask from their faces"; behind it he finds the malevolence he knows so well in himself. Once they are unmasked, he can render them harmless. If it suits his purpose he may spare their lives for the time being, but he will see to it that they do not get away with any fresh dissimulation; he keeps their true shape clearly in his mind's eye.

He dislikes all transformations in others which he has not enforced on them himself. He may advance men he finds useful, but the social transformation thus accomplished must be absolutely distinct; it must stop there and be entirely within his power. Whether raising men up or abasing them *he* determines their place; no-one must dare to move on his own.

A ruler wages continuous warfare against spontaneous and uncontrolled transformation. The weapon he uses in this fight is the process of *unmasking*, the exact opposite of transformation. It is a process the reader has already met: Menelaus unmasked Proteus, the old man of the sea, when he refused to be frightened by any of the forms he adopted to escape, and held him fast until he became Proteus again.

It is part of the nature of this process of unmasking that the perpetrator always knows exactly what he will find. He goes for it with a terrible assurance, despising all the metamorphoses he penetrates as irrelevancies. This can happen on one occasion, as with Menelaus who simply wanted Proteus' counsel, or it can be repeated until, in the end, unmasking becomes a passion.

If it is practised often the whole world shrinks. The wealth of appearances comes to mean nothing; all variety is suspect. All the leaves on all the trees are the same, and all dry as dust; every ray of light is extinguished in a night of suspicion.

In the mental disease whose processes most closely resemble the workings of power the urge to unmask appearances becomes a kind of tyranny. This disease is Paranoia and there are two characteristics by which, among others, it is particularly distinguished; one of these, in psychiatry, is called *dissimulation*. I have been using the same term with exactly the same meaning: paranoiacs are so skilful at dissembling that many of them are never identified as such. The other characteristic is a continual urge to unmask enemies. These the paranoiac sees everywhere, in the most peaceful and harmless disguises: he has the gift of seeing through appearances and knows exactly what is behind them. He tears the mask from every face and what he then finds is always essentially the same enemy. He is addicted to the routine of unmasking, and in this he behaves exactly like a despot, but in a vacuum. The position he imagines he occupies and the importance he arrogates to himself are certainly fictitious as far as others are concerned, but he will none the less defend them by constantly applying the two linked processes of dissimulation and unmasking.

A precise and valid examination of the workings of the unmasking process is possible only in the context of an actual individual case of paranoia. The reader will find it in the last chapters of this book which deal with the case of Schreber.

Prohibitions on Transformation

PROHIBITIONS ON transformation are a social and religious phenomenon of the greatest importance, which has never been properly considered and certainly never understood. What follows is only a tentative approach to the subject.

Among the Aranda only a member of the totem has the right to take part in the totem ceremonies. Transformation into the double figure of the mythical ancestor is a prerogative reserved to certain persons; only those with a right to it can share in the metamorphosis which is handed down as an inheritance. It is as closely guarded as the words and sounds of the sacred songs connected with it. The absolutely precise and definite form which the figure has evolved makes it easy to protect. The prohibition on usurping it is strictly enforced with full religious sanctions. Only after a long and complicated initiation is a young man received into the group of those to whom the transformation is, on certain occasions, permitted. For women and children the prohibition is permanent and absolute. As an act of particular courtesy it is sometimes lifted for initiates of other totems, but this is a special occasion and, once it is over, the prohibition regains all its old force.

It is a long way from this religion to Christianity, in which the *Devil* is a prohibited figure to everyone alike. The fact that he is dangerous is stressed in every possible way; there are innumerable cautionary stories of what happens to people who have dealings with him and the eternal torments of their souls in hell are depicted in every terrifying detail. The force of this prohibition is tremendous and is most striking where people feel a compulsion to act against it. There are many stories of those who became possessed and suddenly acted as if the Devil, or even several devils, were in them. Some of them left their confessions, among the most famous of which are those of Jeanne des Anges, the prioress of the Ursuline convent at Loudun, and of Father Surin who exorcized her until the Devil entered into *him*. These were people who had devoted their lives to the service of God; any approach to the Devil, let alone transformation into him, was even more emphatically forbidden to them than to laymen, and yet they were possessed by him; the prohibited metamorphosis completely overpowered them. We can scarcely be wrong if we relate the strength of the urge towards a transformation to the strength of the prohibition laid on it.

The sexual aspect of prohibitions on transformation can be seen in the notion of witches. The real sin of witches was supposed to be sexual union with the Devil. Whatever they might do besides, the culmination of their secret existence was the orgies which the Devil shared. They were witches because they kept company with the Devil; an essential part of their metamorphosis was their sexual surrender to him.

The concept of transformation through copulation is very old indeed. Since each creature normally copulates only with the other sex of its own kind, it is possible that any deviation from this rule was felt as a transformation. If this were so, early marriage laws could be regarded as forms of prohibition on all transformations except those laid down as permitted and desirable. This sexual aspect of transformation ought to be explored in detail. It might well lead to very important conclusions.

Perhaps the most important of all prohibitions on transformation are the social. No hierarchy can be maintained without prohibitions which make it impossible for members of one class to feel equal or related to members of a higher class. This is true even of the *age*-classes of primitive societies. Once divisions have evolved they tend to become more and more strongly marked and the rise from a lower to a higher class correspondingly difficult. It can be achieved only by undergoing a special initiation, and this is experienced as a transformation in the literal sense of the word. Often the candidate is thought of as dying in the lower class, to be brought back to life in the higher: death itself divides class from class. Transformation becomes a long and dangerous journey during which the novice has to undergo every kind of ordeal and terror; he is spared none of them. But everything that he suffers as a boy he can later, as a member of the higher class, inflict on the novices *he* then tests. The higher class is thus conceived as something with a clear identity of its own and its own complete life. The knowledge of sacred songs and myths is linked with it and sometimes there is a special language. The members of lower classes and the women, who are permanently excluded from all higher classes, are kept in fear and obedience by terrifying masks and weird sounds.

The division into classes is most rigid in a caste system. As in India, membership of a caste absolutely precludes social transformation of any kind. There is a meticulous separation both from what is above and what is below; contact with anyone lower is strictly prohibited. People marry only within their own caste and all members of a caste follow the same profession, so that it is not even possible to achieve transformation through the kind of work one does. The consistency with which this system is applied is so amazing that study of it alone would reveal all the different kinds of social transformation possible; since all have to be avoided they are all carefully listed, described and analyzed. If one took any such complete system of prohibitions and reversed it, substituting positives for its negatives, one would know exactly what transformation from a lower into a higher class was thought to entail. An essay on castes in relation to transformation would be invaluable, but has not yet been written.

But there is also a type of prohibition on transformation which is *limited*, that is, imposed only on the single individual who stands at the head of society. This is found in early forms of kingship. Surprising though it may seem, the two best articulated forms of power known to the older civilizations are primarily differentiated by their contrasting relationships with transformation.

At one pole stands the *master transformer* who can assume any shape at will, whether those of animals, animal-spirits or the spirits of the dead: the trickster who takes everyone in is a familiar figure in North American Indian myth. His power depends on the countless shapes he can assume. Whatever he does is surprising; he appears and disappears unexpectedly, he snatches things or gets hold of them in extraordinary ways and only lets himself be caught if he knows he can escape again. The essential faculty which enables him to perform his astounding feats is transformation.

The master transformer achieves real power as a *Shaman*. In his séance the Shaman summons up spirits, whom he makes subject to him; he speaks their language, becomes like one of themselves and can command them in a way they understand. When he journeys up to heaven he becomes a bird, when he dives to the bottom of the sea some marine creature; anything is possible to him. His paroxysms result from the rapid sequence of transformations which continue to shake him until he selects from among them the one he needs for his purpose.

The master transformer is the one to whom the largest number of transformations is open. If we compare him with the figure of the divine king, who is subject to a hundred restrictions, who has to remain in one place and be always the same, whom no-one can approach and who very often must not even be seen, then we see that the essential difference between the two lies in their exactly opposite relationship to transformation. With one, the Shaman, transformation, is carried to its extreme and made full use of; with the other, the king, it is prohibited and prevented until he is, as it were, completely paralyzed. He has to remain so much the same that he is not even supposed to age, but must always be a man in the full maturity of health and strength. Indeed as soon as the first traces of age show—grey hairs or a decrease in virility—he is often killed.

The static quality of this type of king, to whom all *self*-transformation is forbidden, though he is a continual fount of commands which transform others, has become part of the essence of power and has had a decisive influence on our whole modern conception of power. The non-transformer has been set on a pedestal at a fixed height in a fixed and permanent place. He must never descend from this height, never come half way to meet anyone and never forget his dignity. He can, however, raise others by appointing them to this or that higher position; he can transform them both by raising them up and by abasing them. It is his function to do to others what no-one, even himself, may do to him. The man who is himself denied all transformation can transform others as he pleases.

Even this brief enumeration of a few instances of prohibition on transformation, which leaves almost everything still to be said, forces one to ask what this prohibition really signifies. Why does man want it? What deep need repeatedly drives him to impose it on himself and others? We can only approach this question tentatively.

It seems as though early man was made uneasy by the increasing fluidity of his nature, by his very gift for transformation in fact, and that this was what made him seek for some fixed and immovable barriers. There were so many sensations which he experienced as something alien operating within his body—we remember the tappings of the Bushmen—that he felt as though he had been given over to it and *forced* to become it. Without transformation he could not have obtained his food, but it was also something imposed on him, and which continued to be imposed even after he had satisfied his hunger. He felt as though there was nothing but movement everywhere and that his own being was in a state of continual flux; and this inevitably aroused in him a desire for solidity and permanence only to be satisfied through prohibitions on transformations.

We should perhaps remember in this context the significance which the Australian aborigines attach to rocks and stones. Everything that their ancestors did or experienced, all their wanderings and everything that happened in them, have become part of the landscape—permanent, unchanging landmarks. There is scarcely a rock which does not signify that some particular creature once lived and did great deeds there. In addition to these monumental features of the landscape, which are immovable, there are smaller stones which the aborigines own as objects and keep in their sacred places. These are handed down from one generation to another and to each of them is attached some definite significance. The stone is the tangible manifestation of the legend; as long as the stone remains the same the legend does not change. This concentration on the permanence of stone, something by no means wholly unknown among ourselves, seems to me to express the same profound desire, the same need, as that which leads to prohibitions on transformation.

Slavery

A SLAVE IS NOT property in the sense that a lifeless thing is property, but as cattle are. He has roughly the same kind of freedom as an animal which is allowed to graze and, on occasion, to beget or bear its young.

A *thing* is essentially impenetrable. It can be pushed or pulled about, but it cannot receive or store up commands. A slave may legally be accounted a *thing* which is owned, but this is misleading; a slave is an *animal* which is owned. A single slave can best be compared to a domesticated dog. The dog has been detached from its pack; it is isolated and under the orders of its master. When its own pursuits conflict with these orders it is made to give them up, in return for which it is fed by its master.

For both the slave and the dog, commands and food come from the same source, and in this they resemble a young child. Where they are essentially different from a child is in relation to transformations. In its play the child practises all the transformations it may be able to use later and its parents help it with these and continually encourage it to acquire fresh ones. It continues to grow in many different ways and when it has mastered its transformations it is rewarded by being promoted to adult status.

This is the opposite of what happens to a slave. Just as its master does not allow a dog to chase whatever it wants, but confines its hunting to his own needs or wishes, so the slave's master puts out of his reach one metamorphosis after another. The slave must not do this and must not do that, but *some* things he must do over and over again; and the simpler and more limited these are, the more likely his master is to require them of him. Differentiation of functions need not damage the balance of transformation in a man as long as he is still allowed to carry out a variety of operations, but, as soon as he is restricted to one operation only and, in addition, is expected to get as much as possible done in the shortest possible time—that is, to be "productive"—he becomes what we cannot help describing as a slave.

From the very beginning there must have been two distinct types of slave: the single slave, linked to his master as a dog is, and numbers of slaves together, like cattle in a field, who were, indeed, the earliest of man's slaves.

The desire to turn men into animals was the principal motive for the development of slavery. It is as difficult to over-estimate its strength as that of the opposite desire: to turn animals into men. (To this latter we owe not only major intellectual structures such as Darwinism and the doctrine of metempsychosis, but also popular amusements like the public exhibition of performing animals.)

Once men had succeeded in collecting large numbers of slaves, as they collected animals in their herds, the foundations for the tyranny of the state were laid. Nor is there the slightest doubt that a ruler's desire to own a whole people like slaves or animals grows stronger as their numbers increase.

ASPECTS OF POWER

Human Postures and Their Relation to Power

MAN, WHO PRIDES himself on standing upright, can also, while remaining in the same place, sit, lie, squat or kneel. All these postures, and particularly the change from one to another, have their own special significance. Rank and power are traditionally connected with certain postures and from the way in which men group themselves we can deduce the amount of authority which each enjoys. We know what it means when one man sits raised up while everyone round him stands; when one man stands and everyone else sits; when everyone in a room gets up as someone comes in; when one man falls on his knees before another; when a new arrival is not asked to sit down. Even a haphazard enumeration like this shows how many silent configurations of power there are. For our purpose it is necessary to look at them more closely and to attempt to determine their individual significance.

Every new posture a man adopts is related to the one which precedes it and can be properly understood only if this is known. A standing man may just have jumped out of bed, or he may, on the other hand, have risen from a chair. In the first case he may have suspected danger; in the second he may have wished to show respect to someone. All changes of position are relatively sudden. They may be familiar, expected, and in accordance with the customs of the particular community, but there is always the possibility of a change of position which is unexpected and therefore all the more significant. During a church service there is a good deal of kneeling; people are accustomed to it and even those who like it do not attach undue significance to it. But if, in the street, someone suddenly kneels to a man who may himself just have been kneeling in church, then the effect is tremendous.

In spite of their multifarious meanings there is, none the less, an indubitable tendency to fix and "monumentalize" human postures. A sitting or a standing man makes an effect *as such*, irrespective of his spatial or temporal circumstances. In monumental sculpture some of these postures have become so empty and banal that we hardly pay any attention to them, but they are still effective and meaningful when we see them in daily life.

Standing
Our pride in standing consists in feeling independent and needing no support. Whether the memory of the first time one stood alone as a

child contributes to this, or the sense of our superiority to animals, hardly any of whom by nature stand unsupported on two legs, the fact remains that a man who is standing feels confident and self-sufficient. When someone gets up from a sitting or lying position his standing is the result of a specific effort by which he makes himself as tall as he possibly can. Someone who has been standing for a long time expresses a capacity for endurance and resistance, either because, like a tree, he stands firmly in the one place, or because he allows all of himself to be seen without fear or concealment. The stiller he stands, the less often he turns and looks about him, the more impressive he is. He shows that he does not even fear an attack from behind, where he cannot see.

If there is a space between the standing man and those around him the effect he makes is enhanced. Particularly impressive is a man who stands isolated by himself, facing many others, but somehow detached from them. It is as though he, in his single person, *stood for* them all. If he draws closer to them, he will take care to stand higher than they do; and, if he comes right amongst them, they re-establish his superiority by hoisting him on their shoulders and carrying him. He has lost his independence, but he now, as it were, *sits on* them all.

People normally stand before they begin to walk or run, and because standing is thus the antecedent of all motion, a standing man creates an impression of energy which is as yet unused. Standing is the central position, from which every other position can be directly reached and any movement initiated. We tend, therefore, to ascribe a relatively high degree of tension to any one who is standing, even when he himself does not in fact feel it. (He may, for instance, be about to lie down and sleep.) We always overrate the man who stands.

When two men are introduced to each other there is always an element of solemnity in the occasion. Standing they exchange names and, standing, shake hands. By standing each shows his respect for the other, but also measures himself against him. However their relationship develops their first real contact takes place standing.

In those countries where personal independence is most highly prized, people stand more frequently and for longer periods than elsewhere. The English, for example, are particularly attached to their public-houses, where most of the drinking takes place standing up. The drinker can leave at any time and without any fuss. A small and inconspicuous movement releases him from his companions and thus he feels less constrained than if he had formally to get up from a table. Getting up would be tantamount to announcing his intention to leave, and to have to do that would limit his freedom. Even at private parties the English like to stand, indicating that they do not propose to stay long. They move about freely in the room and, since they are standing, are able to leave one person in order to talk to another with the minimum of formality. There is nothing unusual in this and so no-one is offended by it. Equality within a social group, one of the most important and useful fictions in English life, is particularly stressed on occasions when all alike have, or can have, the advantage of standing. No-one "sits above" anyone else. Everyone is free to seek out those he wants to meet.

Sitting

When we sit we make use of extraneous legs to replace the two we relinquished in order to stand upright. The chair, as we know it today, derives from the throne, and the throne presupposes subject animals or human beings, whose function it is to carry the weight of the ruler. The four legs of the chair represent the legs of an animal—a horse, an ox, or an elephant—and sitting in this way, on a raised seat, must be clearly distinguished from sitting or squatting on the ground, which means something quite different. To sit on a chair was originally a mark of distinction. The man who sat rested on other men, who were his subjects or slaves. While he might sit, they had to stand. Their fatigue did not matter so long as he was comfortable. It was he who was important and his sacred strength which must be saved, for on him depended the well-being of everyone else.

Sitting always involves a downward pressure on something which is defenceless and incapable of exerting counter-pressure. This aspect of it derives from riding, but there it is disguised, because the motion involved makes it appear that the aim is simply to reach some objective quicker than would otherwise be possible, and not pressure as such. When the element of motion is removed and riding becomes sitting, the relationship between the sitter and what he sits on acquires an independent existence of its own and it is as though the point of sitting were precisely to express this relationship. The thing sat on is no longer even animate. Its function is settled for ever and it has less volition even than a slave; its state is the quintessence of slavery. Its user is free to do exactly as he likes with it. He can come and sit down and remain sitting for as long as he pleases, or he can get up and go away without giving it a thought.

The dignity of sitting is a dignity of duration. A standing man may do anything, and our respect for him derives partly from the fact that so many possibilities are open to him, that he is alert and able to move at any moment. But we expect someone who is sitting to *remain* sitting. The downward pressure of his weight confirms his authority and the longer he makes it felt the more secure he appears. There is hardly a single human institution which has not made use of this fact to preserve and strengthen its position.

When a man sits it is physical weight which he displays, and, if this is to make its full effect, he needs to sit on something raised above the ground. In relation to the legs of a chair he actually *is* heavy. If he sat on the ground he would make an entirely different impression, for the earth is so much heavier and more solid than any of its creatures that the pressure they can exert is insignificant in comparison. The simplest form of power is that derived from a man's own body and he can express it either in terms of height—in which case he must stand—or in terms of weight—in which case he must exert visible pressure. To stand up from a sitting position is to do both. The most striking instance of this is when a judge, who has remained seated and motionless throughout the hearing of a trial, rises to his feet to deliver judgement.

The various ways of sitting are basically all ways of exerting pressure. An upholstered chair is not only soft, but also obscurely gives the sitter the feeling that he is sitting on something *living*. The give of the cushions, their springiness and tension, has something of the quality of living flesh and this may conceivably be the cause both of the aversion which many people feel for chairs that are too soft, and of the extraordinary importance which others, not generally self-indulgent, attach to this form of comfort. The latter are people to whom the exercise of power has become second nature; sitting is a daily recurring way of enjoying the process in a symbolic and attenuated form.

Lying

A man lying down is a man disarmed. All the things over which he normally takes so much trouble and which, when he stands upright, make him what he is—his bearing, his habits and all his activities— are laid aside like his clothes; it is as though they ceased to be part of him. This outward process mirrors the inward process of going to sleep, for in sleep, too, we are stripped of much that seems indispensable when we are awake—the fixed, compulsive ways of thought which are the clothes of the mind. Anyone who lies down disarms himself so completely that it is impossible to understand how men have managed to survive sleep. It is true that in their primitive state they lived, when they could, in caves, but even there they were not secure; and the miserable shelters of leaves and twigs with which many had to content themselves gave no protection at all. The marvel is that there are still men in existence. One would expect them to have been exterminated long ago, when they were many fewer, long before they reached the point of lining up for reciprocal annihilation. This one fact of sleep—defenceless, recurrent, and prolonged—shows the inadequacy of all the theories of adaptation to environment which are put forward as explanations of so much that is inexplicable.

But we are not concerned here with the more profound and difficult question of how men have managed to survive sleep, but simply with lying down and how it relates to power as compared with the other postures of the human body. At one extreme, as we saw, there is standing, which expresses power through height and independence, and sitting, which expresses it through weight and continuance. Lying is the other extreme, expressing complete impotence, especially, of course, when it is combined with sleep. But it is not an active, struggling impotence. A man who lies down gives up all relationships with his fellows and withdraws into himself. There is nothing dramatic about his state; indeed it is only by being inconspicuous that he obtains a meagre measure of security. All he wants is to have something under him. He lies at full length and, as far as possible, sees that his whole body is in contact with something which supports or protects it. A standing man is free and independent of support; a sitting man uses his weight to exert pressure on something. A recumbent man is certainly not independent, for he uses anything and everything to support him; nor can he really be said to exert pressure, for his weight is so spread that he is scarcely conscious of it.

The contrast between lying and standing is so great that there is always a temptation to startle others by switching suddenly from the one position to the other. A man who can leap up from the ground or from his bed straight to his full height proves how much alive he is, how little mastered by sleep, how, even when asleep, he hears and notices everything that matters, so that he can never be taken by surprise. Many rulers have known this and have deliberately had reports spread of the lightning speed with which they could achieve the transition. Part of the impression it makes is certainly due to desire for the continued physical growth which is denied us after a certain age. All rulers would at heart like to be taller than they are, or, better still, to have the capacity to become taller when they wanted. They would like to be able to grow suddenly and unexpectedly, so as to terrify and dominate other men, and then, without anyone seeing them do it, to shrink again, so as to be able to repeat the performance on the next suitable occasion. A man who at one moment is asleep, curled up as though in his mother's womb, and who then, on waking, springs out of bed, repeats in this sudden movement the whole process of his growth. Though, to his regret, he cannot make himself taller than he is, at least he makes himself as tall as he can.

People lie down in order to rest, but there are also those who *cannot* stand, who are injured or wounded and have to remain lying down however little they want to. Such people have the misfortune to remind those who *can* stand of a wounded animal. They are marked. They have taken a long step downhill towards death. A stricken creature is given the *coup de grâce*. If it was dangerous when alive it becomes an object of hatred when it is dead. People tread on it and push it to one side, for it cannot defend itself. It is blamed for still being in everyone's way when dead; it ought not to exist at all, not even as the empty husk of a body.

A man has further to fall than an animal and, therefore, when he does fall, arouses even more contempt and repugnance. Actually, the sight of a striken man arouses two feelings at once: there is the instinctive and habitual feeling of triumph over a hunted-down animal and also uneasiness at the fall of a fellow-man. We are discussing here what a man who can still stand really feels when he sees someone down, not what he *should* feel, and there is no doubt that the element of triumph is always there and, in certain circumstances will become very strong. The sight of large numbers of prostrate and lifeless bodies has a terrible effect on anyone who experiences it: he comes to feel as though he himself had struck them all down and his sense of power increases rapidly and uncontrollably. He appropriates to himself the whole heap of dying or dead; he alone is alive and everything around him is his booty. No feeling of triumph is more dangerous than this. A man who has once given way to it will do anything to repeat it.

Of great importance in this connection is the numerical disparity between the standing and the lying; the circumstances of their confrontation are also significant. War and battle, for example (which have already been discussed as crowd events), have their own ritual and, in them, the impulse I have described is permitted to run its course. There are no sanctions attached to the death of an enemy; in relation to him everyone can indulge his brute instinct.

In time of peace anyone who falls down in a crowded place and is unable to rise has a different effect on the many who see him. In their

own time and fashion, and to differing degrees, they all identify themselves with him. One, though perhaps with a bad conscience, will pass
him by; another will take the trouble to help him. If he manages to
get to his feet fairly quickly all the onlookers will feel pleased that this
man, who is themselves, is on his feet again. If he fails he is handed
over to the care of the appropriate institution and there is always, even
amongst civilized people, a faint feeling of contempt for anyone to
whom this happens. They procure him the help he needs, but in doing
so expel him from the society of the erect. For a time, he is not considered fully adult.

Sitting on the Ground

Sitting or squatting on the ground denotes an absence of needs, a
turning in on oneself. The body is rounded and compact as though
expecting nothing from the world. Every activity which might require
reciprocity is renounced. Since nothing is done, there is nothing for
anyone to react to. A man who sits in this attitude appears peaceful and
contented; no one fears violence from him. He is contented, either
because he has all he needs, or because he makes do with what he has,
however little. The squatting beggar proclaims his readiness to accept
whatever he may be given; he makes no distinctions and is content
with anything.

In oriental countries it is not only the poor who sit on the ground,
but also the rich when they have company; and then it expresses
something of their peculiar attitude to property. They behave as
though they carried it within themselves and were completely sure of
it. By remaining in this position they show that they feel no worry or
anxiety about being robbed of it, or losing it in any other way. They
allow themselves to be waited on, but it is as though it were their
wealth which was tended. Thus the usual severity of the relationship
between master and servant is mitigated. Unlike those who use chairs,
the oriental, when he sits, does not parade the fact that he could, if he
wished, be sitting on his fellow-creatures. He is like a beautifully clothed
sack; everything he owns is inside the sack, and it is this sack that his
servants wait on.

But squatting or sitting on the ground also implies acceptance of
everything which may happen. If he were a beggar, the rich man
would continue to sit in the same way and, in doing so, would say in
effect that he was still the same man. The posture contains both wealth
and poverty, and this, together with what we said about the absence of
needs, is why it has become the posture of contemplation, familiar to

all who know the East. The man who adopts it has freed himself from the world. He reposes in himself and burdens no-one.

Kneeling

As well as the passivity of lying down, there is another form of powerlessness, which is active. It confronts a present power and expresses itself in ways which magnify this power. Kneeling is a gesture of supplication. The condemned man offers his neck for the blow; he has accepted the fact that he will die and does nothing to prevent it, but, by the position of his body assists the fulfillment of the other's will. But he raises his joined hands and, even in this last moment, begs for mercy. Kneeling is always in some sense a prelude to a last moment. It is a form of flattery, and extreme because it has to attract attention. A man who appears resigned to being killed ascribes to him before whom he kneels the greatest possible power, the power over life and death. One so great must have it in his power to grant great things; his mercy should equal the defencelessness of his suppliant. The gulf between them is made to seem so immense that only his greatness can bridge it. If he does not, he will forever afterwards appear smaller in his own eyes than he was in the moment when his suppliant knelt to him.

The Orchestral Conductor

THERE IS NO more obvious expression of power than the performance of a conductor. Every detail of his public behaviour throws light on the nature of power. Someone who knew nothing about power could discover all its attributes, one after another, by careful observation of a conductor. The reason why this has never been done is obvious: the music the conductor evokes is thought to be the only thing that counts; people take it for granted that they go to concerts to hear symphonies and no-one is more convinced of this than the conductor himself. He believes that his business is to serve music and to interpret it faithfully.

A conductor ranks himself first among the servants of music. He is so full of it that the idea of his activity having another, non-musical meaning never enters his head. No-one would be more astonished than he at the following interpretation of it.

The conductor *stands*: ancient memories of what it meant when man first stood upright still play an important part in any representations of power. Then, he is the only person who stands. In front of him sits the orchestra and behind him the audience. He stands on a dais and can be seen both from in front and from behind. In front his movements act on the orchestra and behind on the audience. In giving his actual directions he uses only his hands, or his hands and a baton. Quite small movements are all he needs to wake this or that instrument to life or to silence it at will. He has the power of life and death over the voices of the instruments; one long silent will speak again at his command. Their diversity stands for the diversity of mankind; an orchestra is like an assemblage of different types of men. The willingness of its members to obey him makes it possible for the conductor to transform them into a unit, which he then embodies.

The complexity of the work he performs means that he must be alert. Presence of mind is among his essential attributes; law-breakers must be curbed instantly. The code of laws, in the form of the score, is in his hands. There are others who have it too and can check the way it is carried out, but the conductor alone decides what the law is and summarily punishes any breach of it. That all this happens in public and is visible in every detail gives the conductor a special kind of self-assurance. He grows accustomed to being seen and becomes less and less able to do without it.

The immobility of the audience is as much part of the conductor's design as the obedience of the orchestra. They are under a compulsion to keep still. Until he appears they move about and talk freely among themselves. The presence of the players disturbs no-one; indeed they are scarcely noticed. Then the conductor appears and everyone becomes still. He mounts the rostrum, clears his throat and raises his baton; silence falls. While he is conducting no-one may move and as soon as he finishes they must applaud. All their desire for movement, stimulated and heightened by the music, must be banked up until the end of the work and must then break loose. The conductor bows to the clapping hands; for them he returns to the rostrum again and again, as often as they want him to. To them, and to them alone, he surrenders; it is for them that he really lives. The applause he receives is the ancient salute to the victor, and the magnitude of his victory is measured by its volume. Victory and defeat become the framework within which his spiritual economy is ordered. Apart from these nothing counts; everything that the lives of other men contain is for him transformed into victory or defeat.

During a concert, and for the people gathered together in the hall, the conductor is a leader. He stands at their head with his back to them. It is him they follow, for it is he who goes first. But, instead of his feet, it is his hands which lead them. The movement of the music, which his hands bring about, represents the path his feet would be the first to tread. The crowd in the hall is carried forward by him. During the whole performance of a work they never see his face. He is merciless: there are no intervals for rest. They see his back always in front of them, as though it were their goal. If he turned round even once the spell would be broken. The road they were travelling would suddenly cease to exist and there would be nothing but a hall full of disillusioned people without movement or impetus. But the conductor can be relied on not to turn round, for, while the audience follows him behind, in front he is faced by a small army of professional players, which he must control. For this purpose, too, he uses his hands, but here they not only point the way, as they do for those behind him, but they also give orders.

His eyes hold the whole orchestra. Every player feels that the conductor sees him personally, and, still more, hears him. The voices of the instruments are opinions and convictions on which he keeps a close watch. He is omniscient, for, while the players have only their own parts in front of them, he has the whole score in his head, or on his desk. At any given moment he knows precisely what each player should be doing. His attention is everywhere at once, and it is to this that he owes a large part of his authority. He is inside the mind of every player. He knows not only what each *should* be doing, but also what he *is* doing. He is the living embodiment of law, both positive and negative. His hands decree and prohibit. His ears search out profanation.

Thus for the orchestra the conductor literally embodies the work they are playing, the simultaneity of the sounds as well as their sequence; and since, during the performance, nothing is supposed to exist except this work, for so long is the conductor the ruler of the world.

Fame

FAME IS NOT fastidious about the lips which spread it. So long as there are mouths to reiterate the one name, it does not matter whose they are. The fact that to the seeker after fame they are indistinguishable from each other and are all counted as equal shows that this passion has its origin in the experience of crowd manipulation. Names collect their own crowds. They are greedy and live their own separate lives, scarcely connected with the real natures of the men who bear them.

The crowd which the seeker after fame envisages consists of shadows, that is, of creatures who do not even have to be alive so long as they are capable of one thing, which is to repeat his name. He wants them to repeat it often, and to repeat it in front of others, so that as many as possible may hear it and learn how to say it themselves. But what these shadows are apart from this—their height, their appearance, how they live and work—is a matter of total indifference to the man whose fame they spread. As long as anyone continues to concern himself with the individuals to whom these mouths belong, as long as he woos, bribes, entices or whips them on, he is not really famous. All he is doing is to train the cadres of his future army of shadows. Only when he can afford to omit all this has he achieved fame.

The difference between a rich man, a ruler and a celebrity is something like this:

A rich man collects cattle and hoards of grain, or the money which stands for them. He does not worry about men; it is enough that he can buy them.

A ruler collects men. Grain and cattle, or money, mean nothing to him except in as far as he needs them to get hold of men. He wants, moreover, *living* men, whom he can make die before him, or take with him when he dies. He is only indirectly concerned with those who lived before his time or who are born after it.

A celebrity collects a chorus of voices. All he wants is to hear them repeat his name. As long as there are enough of them and they are versed in his name it does not matter whether these voices belong to the dead, to the living, or to the as yet unborn.

The Regulation of Time

No POLITICAL structure of any size can dispense with order, and one of the fundamental applications of order is to time, for no communal human activity can take place without it. Indeed one might say that the regulation of time is the primary attribute of all government. A new power which wants to assert itself must also enforce a new chronology; it must make it seem as though time had begun with it. Even more important to such a power is that it should endure. Its own estimate of its greatness can be deduced from the stretch of future time it lays claim to: Hitler's Reich was to last 1,000 years. The Julian calendar endured longer than this and, even today, the month called after Julius Caesar is known by his name. Of historical figures only Augustus succeeded in attaching his name uninterruptedly to a month. Others tried it, but their names have crumbled with their effigies.

The most impressive mark on the reckoning of time is that made by Christ. Here he surpassed even God himself, from whose creation of the world Jewish chronology began. The Romans counted time from the foundation of their city, a method which they took over from the Etruscans and which certainly played a not inconsiderable part in the world's picture of Rome's mighty destiny. Some conquerors content themselves with inserting their names somewhere in the calendar: Napoleon is said to have had hopes of August 15th. There is an irresistible attraction in the idea of linking one's name with a regularly recurring date. That the vast majority of people are ignorant of the origins of such designations seems to have not the slightest effect on the desire of rulers to immortalize themselves in this way. No one man has succeeded in attaching his name to a season, although there are whole centuries which are known by the name of a dynasty. Chinese history, indeed, is reckoned in dynasties; one speaks of the Han or the Tang period. Even short-lived and inglorious dynasties, which would be better forgotten, get the benefit of this. Among the Chinese it has become the usual method of reckoning large stretches of time, but it is families rather than individuals which it immortalizes.

A ruler's relationship with time, however, is not exhausted by the vanity of his name. He is concerned with the regulation of time and not only with giving his name to existing units. Chinese history begins in this way. The prestige of the Chinese legendary rulers derives in great part from the effective regulation of time which is ascribed to them. Special officials were appointed to watch over this and were punished if they neglected their duties. It was when they achieved a uniform calendar that the Chinese first became a nation.

Civilizations are perhaps best distinguished by their arrangement of time. They prove themselves by their continued capacity to organize their traditions and they disintegrate when they cease to do this. A civilization comes to an end when a people no longer takes its own chronology seriously. At this one point an analogy with the life of an individual is permissible. A man who no longer knows or cares how old he is has finished with life; he might as well be dead, when he *cannot* know. For a civilization, as for an individual, periods when the awareness of time is lost are periods of shame, which are forgotten as soon as possible.

There are obvious practical reasons for the overwhelming importance which the regulation of time has acquired. It binds together large groups of men who may live far apart and not be able to meet face to face. In a small group of perhaps fifty people everyone knows what everyone else is doing. It is easy for them to join in common activity. The rhythm of their lives is beaten out within the pack. They *dance* the continuity of the group, as they dance so many other things. The time gap between one pack activity and another does not matter, for since people live in close proximity they can always alert each other when they need to. Every expansion of the physical milieu makes it more important to do something about time. Drum and smoke signals, which bridge distance, serve this purpose.

A different kind of unity was given to large groups of people by the lives of single individuals: Kings embodied the whole period of their reign. Their death, whether it came with the decline of their strength or, as later, coincided with their natural span of life, indicated a break in time. They *were* time. Between one king and the next, time stood still. There was a gap in it—an interregnum—which people sought to keep as short as possible.

The Court

A COURT IS THOUGHT of first and foremost as a centre, a point round which people orientate themselves. The tendency to move round and round a central point is very old and, indeed, can be observed even in chimpanzees. Originally this central point was itself mobile; it could exist anywhere; it moved with the wanderings of the people who moved around it. Only gradually did its location become fixed. Rocks and trees are the prototypes of everything permanent, and it was with rocks and trees that buildings intended to endure were first built. In the course of time more and more stress was laid on the element of permanence. The difficulty of building such a centre, of moving blocks of stone for large distances, the number of men engaged in the work, and even the time it took to complete, all helped to increase the prestige it owed to its permanence.

But this fixed centre of a diminutive world, to which it gave a kind of order, was not yet a court. A court entails the existence of a body of men whose connection with it is as organic and as closely defined as that of actual parts of the building. Their duties are precisely and exhaustively laid down; they must do exactly so much, but never more. And from time to time they must assemble and, without relinquishing their identity or forgetting their position, and fully conscious of the restrictions on it, they must unite in homage to the ruler.

Their homage consists in *being there*, their faces turned towards the ruler, gathered round him, but not approaching him too close, dazzled by him, fearing him and looking to him as the source of all things. In this unique atmosphere, in which splendour, terror and hope of favour are equally blended, they spend their lives. Nothing, or almost nothing, else exists for them. They have, as it were, colonized the sun; they show other men that it is habitable.

Courtiers keep their eyes fixed on the ruler as though they were spell-bound. There is nothing else which is common to them all, but, from the highest to the lowest, they are alike in this. In the unvarying and identical direction of their gaze they have a certain crowd-like quality, but it is only a very rudimentary one, for what they look at puts each of them in mind of his particular function, that which differentiates him from all the rest.

The bearing and behaviour of a courtier infects, and is intended to infect, the ruler's other subjects. What the courtier does all the time, they should be at pains to do periodically, and certainly on various special occasions. When, for instance, the king enters a city, all its inhabitants should attend on him, as his courtiers habitually do in his palace; and their homage should be all the more enthusiastic because it has been owing for so long. The presence of the court should draw all the ruler's subjects to the capital, where they group themselves in large, concentric circles round the inner circle of courtiers. The capital is built round the court; its houses are a standing act of homage. The king, as is proper, generously repays this by the splendour of his state buildings.

A court is a good example of a *crowd crystal*. The people who compose it all have their own separate functions and, to each other, seem to be quite different. But to the rest of the world they—the courtiers— appear as identical parts of a single unit, radiating the loyalty they have in common.

The Rising Throne of the Emperor of Byzantium

SUDDEN GROWTH has always made a powerful impression on men. Size in itself is a source of wonder, and so is a man's ability to attain his full height instantaneously from a sitting or lying position, but even greater astonishment is caused by something small which suddenly becomes gigantic under the eyes of the beholder. Such figures occur frequently, of course, in the myths and fairy stories of many peoples, but it is in 10th-century Byzantium that we find change of size used consciously for the purposes of power. Liudprand of Cremona, the ambassador of Otto I, left the following account of his reception by the Byzantine Emperor.

"Before the emperor's seat stood a tree, made of bronze gilded over, whose branches were filled with birds, also made of gilded bronze, which uttered different cries, each according to its varying species. The throne itself was so marvellously fashioned that at one moment it seemed a low structure, and at another it rose high into the air. It was of immense size and was guarded by lions, made either of bronze or of wood covered over with gold, who beat the ground with their tails and gave a dreadful roar with open mouth and quivering tongue. Leaning upon the shoulders of two eunuchs I was brought into the emperor's presence. At my approach the lions began to roar and the birds to cry out, each according to its kind; but I was neither terrified nor surprised, for I had previously made enquiry about all these things, from people who were well acquainted with them. So after I had three times made obeisance to the emperor with my face upon the ground, I lifted my head, and behold! the man whom just before I had seen sitting on a moderately elevated seat had now changed his raiment and was sitting on the level of the ceiling. How it was done I could not imagine, unless perhaps he was lifted up by some such sort of device as we use for raising the timbers of a wine-press. On that occasion he did not address me personally, since, even if he had wished to do so, the wide distance between us would have rendered conversation unseemly, but by the intermediary of a secretary he enquired about my master's doings and asked after his health. I made a fitting reply and then, at a nod from the interpreter, left his presence and retired to my lodging."

While the ambassador prostrated himself, with his forehead touching the ground, the emperor's throne *grew upwards*. The abasement of the one was used for the elevation of the other. The distance between the two, which had been diminished by the fact of the ambassador's reception, was thus re-established vertically. Artificial birds which sang and lions which roared were succeeded and surpassed by the contrivance of a throne which grew. It symbolized the urge to increase inherent in all power. Exhibited to the emissary of a foreign power its threat was unmistakable.

General Paralytics and Their Notions of Greatness

WHAT DO WE actually understand by "greatness"? The word is used in so many different ways that one might despair of ever attaching a clear meaning to it. What is there that has not been called "great"? Side by side with achievements without which no existence worthy of men can be imagined we find the ludicrous and the monstrous. It is precisely in this confusion that the concept of greatness represents something men cannot live without. We must try to grasp it in its full ambiguity, and perhaps the best chance of doing so lies in approaching it in the minds of men who are not specially gifted, where it appears in its most comprehensible and prosaic form.

A common disease which has been exhaustively studied offers a particularly good opportunity. There are different forms of general paralysis, the classical form in particular being distinguished by a proliferation of notions of greatness following each other in the wildest variety and confusion and easily aroused by external events. There are also, it is true, depressive forms of the disease, in which these ideas are replaced by delusions of unworthiness and littleness. There are also cases in which both are present together. But we are not concerned here with the disease as such. What we are interested in is the concrete accumulation of notions of greatness in particular, fully documented instances. It is precisely in their profusion, their naïvety and the ease with which they can be aroused (which is what makes them seem so strange to normal people) that they throw such an astonishing light on "greatness". The reader must be patient with the long enumerations which follow. Their real significance cannot be understood unless they are given more or less complete. I should add that the two cases discussed here both lived in imperial Germany, a circumstance which affected many of their ideas.

A middle-aged business man who had been brought to Kräpelin's clinic gave the following account of himself:

"He had been driven mad by fatigue and persecution. He was now quite recovered mentally and only a little nervous. His capacity for work had increased with the care taken of him in the clinic, so that he was now fit for anything and had in fact brilliant prospects. On his release, which was due shortly, he proposed to establish a large paper-mill; a friend was to give him the necessary money. In addition, Krupp, whom this same friend knew well, had put a property near

Metz at his disposal and this he proposed to use for large-scale horti-
culture; the district was also very well suited to vineyards. There would
be fourteen horses for the work of cultivation and also a large saw-mill,
which was certain to bring him a sizeable profit. If it was pointed out
that things might not go so smoothly and that all these businesses
required substantial capital, he replied confidently that a man of his
capacity for work would know how to overcome difficulties and
that, with his excellent prospects of profits, he would never be short
of money. At the same time he casually let it be known that the Kaiser
took an interest in him and had re-established him in the noble rank
which his grandfather had relinquished because he had not the means
to keep it up; as a matter of fact he was already entitled to use it. All
this information was given in a quiet, matter-of-fact tone of voice,
and his behaviour throughout was quite normal."

It was easy to get him to extend his plans. "If someone suggested
that poultry-keeping might be profitable, he immediately assured him
that of course he was going to keep turkeys, guinea-fowl, peacocks and
pigeons, fatten geese and breed pheasants."

It was through these grandiose schemes and purchases that his illness
first became apparent. When he came to the clinic "he felt stimulated
to work and physically and mentally better than he had ever been.
Everything about the clinic pleased him and he wanted to write poetry
there, which he could do better than Goethe, Schiller or Heine. . . .
He wanted to invent countless new machines, to surround the clinic
with new buildings, to build a cathedral higher than that in Cologne
and to cover the whole clinic with an armour of glass. He was a genius,
who spoke all the languages in the world. He was going to build a
church made of cast steel, procure the highest decorations from the
Kaiser, discover a way of controlling lunatics and give the library of
the institute a thousand books, mostly philosophical works. All his
thoughts were god-like. These delusions of greatness changed continually, springing up in an instant, quickly to be superseded by fresh
ones. . . . He spoke, wrote and drew incessantly, ordered on the spot
everything he saw advertised in the newspapers—food, houses, clothes
and furniture alike. He was soon a count and soon a lieutenant-general.
He presented the Kaiser with a whole regiment of field artillery. He
offered to transfer the clinic to the top of a mountain."

Let us try to arrange this motley confusion in a provisional order.
First of all there is the preoccupation with height. He wants to build a
cathedral higher than that of Cologne and to transplant the clinic to
the top of a mountain. The elevation he brings about then comes to

him in his own person, translated into terms of rank: his grandfather was a nobleman and he himself is a count and, in the military hierarchy, a lieutenant-general; the Kaiser is interested in him and takes his advice about the distribution of honours; finally, he *gives* the Kaiser a whole regiment, implying that he wants to be higher even than his emperor.

The same urge finds expression in the sphere of the mind. Because he is a genius, he speaks all the languages of the world; it is as though he were their ruler and they his subjects; he surpasses Goethe, Schiller and Heine, the greatest poets he knows of. One gets the impression that this craving for height is not concerned with the *state* of being high up, but with the *process* of getting there quickly. The ascent must be made again and again, suddenly and quickly, whenever opportunity offers. It appears that heights hitherto thought the greatest attainable can, in fact, easily be surpassed and new records established. One is driven to suspect that the real field of competition is *growth*.

His second and no less striking trait is acquisitiveness. He speaks of a paper-mill, a market garden, horses, vineyards and a saw-mill. But the way in which he takes up the suggestion of poultry-keeping shows that, in him, acquisitiveness still retains its primitive characteristics. It means desire for every kind of increase, but particularly the increase of living creatures, whose own nature it is to want it. Turkeys, guinea-fowl, peacocks, pigeons, geese and pheasants are all counted as separate species and, in every case, the idea is that they should breed and therefore multiply and become uncountable. Acquisitiveness here is what it originally was: the encouragement of increase in natural crowds, from which increase one will oneself then benefit.

The third trait is prodigality. He orders everything advertised in the newspapers—food, clothes, houses and furniture. If he were at liberty and really had the money, he would actually buy all these things. But this does not mean that he would hoard them. He would quite certainly be as liberal with them as he is with his money and would give them away to anyone he could find. Hoarding is no more part of his nature than ownership. It is true that he sees the things he would like to buy in heaps, as it were, before him; but only so long as he has not got them. The movement of wealth matters to him more than wealth itself. He appears to have *two* typical gestures, grabbing and throwing away in handfuls; but in reality these are *one*. It is a gesture of greatness.

Let us now turn to the second case, also a middle-aged business man, but suffering from a much more agitated form of paralysis. With him, too, the whole thing began with grandiose plans. Without any financial backing, he suddenly bought a bathing establishment for 35,000 marks, and ordered champagne and white wine to the value of 14,000 and 16,000 marks respectively, to start a restaurant. While in the clinic he boasted continually: "He wants to have himself made bigger until he weighs 32 stone, have steel rods inserted into his arms and wear iron decorations weighing 2 cwt. He has an iron machine, with which he is going to make himself 50 Negresses and he will always remain 42 years old; he will marry a 16-year-old countess with a dowry of 600 million marks, who has received the rose of chastity from the Pope. He has horses who eat no oats and a hundred golden castles with swans and with whales made of bullet-proof armour. He is a great inventor and has built a castle costing 100 million marks for the Kaiser, with whom he is on Christian name terms. He has received 124 decorations from the Grand-duke and gives every beggar in the country half a million marks. At the same time he has delusions of persecution. There have been five attempts on his life and every night two buckets of blood are drawn from his buttocks, which is why he is going to behead the attendants and have them torn to pieces by dogs; he is also constructing a steam-guillotine."

In his case everything is much cruder and more obvious. His concern is with growth, the naked process itself, measured by the 32 stone he is going to weigh; with strength: he has steel rods inserted in his arms; with distinction: he is able to wear insignia weighing 2 cwt., made of the heaviest and most durable metal; and finally with potency and the ability to arrest time: to his 50 Negresses he will always remain 42 years old and only the youngest, richest and most virtuous bride is good enough for him. Oats are too commonplace for his horses; the swans in his 100 golden castles are probably women as well, and provide him with a contrast to his Negresses. He has whales, as the largest of all creatures. He also wants to be invulnerable: as well as the mention of bullet proof armour in connection with the whales there is much talk of metals. The 100 millions he controls is the cost of the castle he gives the Kaiser. In virtue of these millions he is on Christian name terms with him. There are millions of poor beggars. These, as it were, are only half-men and this is probably why he gives them half a million each. In his exalted position he naturally has enemies, but one attempt on his life is not sufficient for so important a person. The attendants who draw his blood do so from behind to show their inferiority and he has the right to behead them for their misdeeds and have them torn to pieces by dogs. But this is a slow, old-fashioned method and so he constructs a steam-guillotine for mass executions.

The more expensive a thing is, the higher the price demanded for it and the more talk of thousands there is in connection with it, the more it attracts him. Money regains its original crowd characteristics, increasing compulsively by leaps and bounds until the figures run into millions, from which point onwards it is these millions which play the decisive rôle. The concept is ambiguous, referring to men as well as to units of money, and it is clear that, in this case, money has taken over from the human crowd that urge to increase which is its most important attribute. A great man is one who disposes of millions.

Acquisition and squandering are, as we have seen already, two aspects of a single movement; buying and giving away, like everything else this man does, are means to his own expansion. His concern here is with what one might call lateral growth, as compared with the preoccupation with height we spoke of earlier. He makes no distinction between buying and giving away. With his millions he engulfs objects and makes them his; with both money and objects he engulfs men, that is, wins them over.

We find here in a naïve and therefore particularly convincing form that munificence which we know from fairy tales and history to be one of the ancient, traditional attributes of kingship: there is an account of a West African Negro King who, while on pilgrimage to Mecca, bought up the whole city of Cairo, an exploit which has never been forgotten. Ostentatious buying is still widespread today, and ostentatious spending equally so. The least resented manifestation of greatness in our own barely acknowledged money-kings is their gigantic public gifts: the madman scatters castles worth 100 million marks and finds a willing recipient in the Kaiser.

His notions of greatness change continually, but one does not get the impression that he changes with them. He always remains himself, even when his weight reaches 32 stone, or he marries his chaste countess, or addresses the Kaiser by his Christian name. On the contrary, everything which reaches him from outside is turned to his own purposes. He is the fixed and stable centre of the universe. He conquers it in that he eats and grows, but he always remains the same person. He feeds on the proliferation of his delusions and their variety is certainly important to him (for he wants to grow in every conceivable way), but it is deceptive, being basically only a variety of diet, which proves the omnivorousness of his appetite.

The multiplicity of his ideas of greatness is only possible because no *one* need be persisted in; each is fulfilled as soon as it comes into his head and can thus be discarded for another. Why is it, however, that he never envisages any opposition to his ideas? A word has only to be mentioned for him to believe that all the potentialities of power, riches and personal aggrandizement it contains are actual and within his grasp. This belief seems to be connected with the feeling that the crowd is always on his side. In each of its manifestations, whether as the 600 million marks of his bride's dowry, the hundred golden castles or the fifty Negresses he makes with his machine, the crowd is *for* him. Even when he is annoyed about something, for instance, the attendants in the clinic, he can immediately summon up a pack of dogs, who, at his command, fall on them and tear them to pieces. As soon as the idea of executions comes into his head he invents a steam-guillotine which deals with them wholesale. The crowd is always with him and never against him. The only hostile crowd we hear of consists of severed heads.

We saw in the earlier case how all the patient's projects were ready to flourish for him and particularly those connected with agriculture. Birds of all kinds were only waiting to increase and multiply for his sake, and when he suddenly wanted to do something for the library of the institution he immediately found a thousand books ready to hand. With both patients, whether they were buying or giving away, all kinds of thousands and millions stood ready at their disposal.

It is important to stress the active and friendly rôle assumed by the crowd in the delusions of the general paralytic. It never opposes him, but provides the willing material for his plans, realizing for him every desire that comes into his head. He can never desire too much, for the crowd's capacity for growth is as limitless as his own. No ruler has ever had subjects so loyal and so compliant. With paranoiacs, as we shall see, the crowd is quite different and is positively hostile. The greatness they imagine is always under attack and their notions also tend to become more and more rigid. When the hostile crowd gets the upper hand, these turn into delusions of persecution.

Summarizing what we have learnt from megalomania in paralytics, we can say that their notions of greatness centre on growth, either continuous or repeatedly starting afresh; and this growth is of two kinds. On the one hand there is the growth of the individual who wants his body to become bigger and heavier, cannot accept the fact that he has reached his physical limit, and also wants every particular kind of strength with which he is endowed to grow as well. On the other hand there is the growth of *crowds*, to which anything may belong which has a compulsive tendency to increase in numbers until the fabled million is reached. Coming or going, these millions flow through the hands of the "great man"; it is him they obey.

The greatness of which men dream contains both individual biological growth and the compulsive increase which characterizes crowds. The *kind* of crowd is not specified, for its composition does not really matter; any crowd serves the purpose.

RULERS AND PARANOIACS

African Kings

IN THE African Kings who are the subjects of this chapter we see in combination many of the aspects and elements of power which we have so far discussed separately. Everything about these Kings seems so strange and unfamiliar that one is at first tempted to dismiss them as exotic curiosities, or, if one lingers over accounts of them such as those which follow, to give way to a feeling of superiority. But one is well advised to show a little patience and humility and wait until one knows more about them. It is not for a European of the 20th century to regard himself as above savagery. His despots may use more effective means, but their ends often differ in nothing from those of these African Kings.

The following is the description given by Du Chaillu of the death of an old king in Gaboon and the election of his successor.

"While I was in the Gaboon old King Glass died. The tribe had grown tired of their King. They thought, indeed, that he was a most potent and evil-disposed wizard, and, though the matter was not openly talked about, there were few natives who would pass his house after night. When he became ill at last everybody seemed very sorry; but several of my friends told me in confidence that the whole town hoped he would die; and die he did. I was awakened one morning early by mournful cries and wails. All the town seemed lost in tears; the mourning and wailing lasted six days. On the second the old King was secretly buried by a few of the most trustworthy men of the tribe in a spot which they only knew of, and which is for ever hidden from all others. During the days of mourning the old men of the village busied themselves in choosing a new King. This also is a secret operation. The choice is made in private, and communicated to the populace only on the seventh day, when the new King is to be crowned. But the King himself is kept ignorant of his good fortune to the last.

"It happened that Njogoni, a good friend of my own, was elected. The choice fell on him, in part because he came of a good family, but chiefly because he was a favourite of the people and could get the most votes. I do not think that Njogoni had the slightest suspicion of his elevation. As he was walking on the shore on the morning of the seventh day he was suddenly set upon by the entire populace, who proceeded to a ceremony which is preliminary to the crowning, and which must deter any but the most ambitious men from aspiring to the crown. They surrounded him in a dense crowd, and then began to heap upon him every manner of abuse that the worst of mobs could imagine. Some spat in his face; some beat him with their fists; some kicked him; others threw disgusting objects at him; while those unlucky ones who stood on the outside, and could reach the poor fellow only with their voices, assiduously cursed him, his father, his mother, his sisters and brothers, and all his ancestors to the remotest generation. A stranger would not have given a cent for the life of him who was presently to be crowned.

"Amid all the noise and struggle, I caught the words which explained all this to me; for every few minutes some fellow, administering an especially severe blow or kick, would shout out, 'You are not our King yet; for a little while we will do what we please with you. By-and-by we shall have to do your will.'

"Njogoni bore himself like a man and a prospective King. He kept his temper, and took all the abuse with a smiling face. When it had lasted about half an hour, they took him to the house of the old king. Here he was seated, and became again for a little while the victim of his people's curses.

"Then all became silent; and the elders of the people rose and said, solemnly (the people repeating after them), 'Now we choose you for our king; we engage to listen to you and to obey you.'

"A silence followed, and presently the silk hat, which is the emblem of royalty, was brought in and placed on Njogoni's head. He was then dressed in a red gown, and received the greatest marks of respect from all who had just now abused him.

"Now followed a six days' festival, during which the poor king, who had taken with the office also the name of his predecessor, was obliged to receive his subjects in his own house, and was not allowed to stir out; six days of indescribable gorging of food and bad rum—of beastly drunkenness and uproarious festivity. Numbers of strangers came in from surrounding villages to pay their respects; and all brought more rum, more palm wine, and more food. Everything that tended toward festivity was given away, and all who came were welcome.

"Old King Glass, for whom for six days no end of tears had been shed, was now forgotten; and *new* King Glass, poor fellow, was sick with exhaustion, for day and night he had to be ready to receive and be civil to all who came.

"Finally, all the rum was drunk up, the allotted days were expired, and quiet once more began to reign. Now, for the first time, his new majesty was permitted to walk out and view his domains."

The sequence of crowd events is particularly important here. The whole thing begins with the *lamenting pack*, mourning the dead king. This lasts for six days. Then, on the seventh day, quite suddenly, comes the assault on the man selected as the new king. The hostility aroused by the dead king is only let loose on his successor. The *baiting crowd* which forms round the latter is also a *reversal crowd*; but it is directed, not against him, but against the dead king; it is the people freeing themselves from their hatred for the man who ruled too long and whom they came in the end only to fear. The new régime starts with the situation which every ruler fears most: that of being surrounded by rebellious subjects closing in on him. But, in spite of this, Njogoni remains calm, for he knows that it is all *transferred* hostility; in as far as it is directed against his own person, it is only acted. The painful beginning of his rule will nevertheless stick in his memory as an intimation of what may at any time actually happen to him. The king here takes up his office in the middle of a revolution, but it is a posthumous revolution, directed against a king who is already dead and not, as appears, against his successor.

The third crucial event is the feast, which, like the mourning, lasts for six days. The distribution and uninhibited general enjoyment of food and drink expresses the *increase* the new ruler is expected to bring about. If now, at the start of his reign, his land flows with rum and palm wine, so, too, it shall later; then as now, everyone shall have more to eat than he needs. It is in order to achieve such increase that the new king is installed. The feast crowd as the start of a new reign guarantees future increase.

Du Chaillu's report is a hundred years old. It has the merit of describing things from outside without too much confusing detail, but, since we now know much more about African kings, it may be useful to look at one of the more recent accounts as well.

The king of Jukun in Nigeria was regarded as a divine being and his whole life was bounded by strictly observed limitations. It was not his task to lead his people in battle nor to distinguish himself by administering his country wisely. He was not expected to be a great personality, but was regarded rather as a living reservoir of those forces which make the earth fertile and seed flourish and thus bring life and well-being to men. The conservation of these forces was ensured by ceremonies determining the course of the king's days and years.

The king rarely appeared in public. His naked foot must never touch the ground, for, if it did, the crops would be blasted; he was also forbidden to pick up anything from the ground. If he fell off his horse he was, in earlier times, promptly put to death. It might never be said that he was ill; if he did contract any serious illness he was quietly strangled, on the grounds that "it would cause confusion among the people if the groans of the king in illness were overheard". Sneezing was permissible: when the king sneezed all present slapped their thighs respectfully. It was not proper to refer to his body or to imply that he had an ordinary human body at all. A special word was used instead, signifying the kingly personality. The same word was used for any action of his. Its real meaning was a royal fiat or word issuing from the king's mouth.

When he was about to take his meal special officials uttered loud shouts, whilst others slapped their thighs twelve times. There had to be complete silence throughout the royal enclosure, and, indeed, throughout the whole town; all conversation stopped and all domestic work. The king's food was considered sacred and was set before him with elaborate cremonial, as before a divinity. When he had finished fresh shouts and thigh-slappings, taken up by officials in the outer court, announced that work and conversation were permitted again.

It was disastrous for the king to fly into a rage, point his finger at a man, or strike the ground in wrath. If he did, the whole land would be affected by blight and so all possible means had to be used to calm him in time. His spittle was sacred and he himself preserved his hair and nail-clippings in a bag which was buried with him when he died. Referring to his powers of fertility he was solemnly addressed as "Our guinea-corn! Our ground-nuts! Our beans!" He was believed to be able to control the rain and the winds. A succession of droughts and bad harvests indicated the waning of his strength and he was secretly strangled by night.

A newly elected king was made to run three times round a mound and, while doing so, was well buffeted by the dignitaries. On a later occasion he had to kill a slave, or sometimes only to wound him, in which case someone else would kill the man with the king's spear and knife.

At his coronation the leader of the royal clan would say to him, "Today we have given you the house of your father. The whole world is yours. You are our guinea-corn and our beans, our spirits and our gods. Henceforth you have no father or mother. But you are the father and mother of all. Follow in the footsteps of your forefathers and do evil to no-one, that your people may abide with you and that you may come to the end of your reign in health." All then fell down before the new king and threw dust on their heads, saying, "Our crops, our rain, our health, and our wealth."

The king had absolute power, but there were safeguards against excessive tyranny. He was compelled to consider the advice of his counsellors, a patrician caste headed by the Abo, or permanent prime minister. If the ruler's excesses threatened to harm the country, or if bad harvests or any other national calamity occurred, it was always possible to discover some breach of taboo committed in the course of his innumerable ritual duties and thus check his presumption. The Abo always had access to the king; he could admonish him and was in a position to embarrass him considerably if he chose to absent himself from the court for any longer period.

The king did not usually accompany warlike expeditions, but all spoils were theoretically his property. In practice, however, he returned half or a third of any spoils to the man who had obtained them, as a mark of esteem and an expression of his hope that the latter would acquit himself equally well on future occasions.

If a king proved his worth he would, in earlier times, rule for seven years and then be killed at the harvest festival.

In his *History of Africa*, the first serious undertaking of this kind, Westermann speaks of "the amazing similarity of structure and institutions among these kingdoms" and lists the features which they have in common. I propose to cite the most important of these, reduced to their bare essentials, and to try to interpret them in the light of the general conclusions we have reached in this book.

"The king possesses powers which give fertility to the soil; whether the crops thrive depends on him. He is also often the rain-maker." Here the king appears as the *increaser*; this is his cardinal quality. Indeed, one might say that it was for the sake of this quality that the institution of kingship was evolved. Commands of all kinds issue from the king, but the most characteristic is this enforcing of growth. "You are the father and mother of all" say the people of Jukun and this does not only mean that he feeds them all, but also that it is he who makes them and everything else grow. Here his power is that of the *increase pack*. The whole purpose and substance of that composite entity is transferred to a single individual, who just because he is single, can ensure continuity in a way that the pack cannot; being made up of many individuals it must frequently disperse. The king is a living vessel, containing within himself all the forces of increase. It is his sacred duty not to allow them to escape. It is in virtue of this that he also has the following characteristics.

"In order to preserve his powers of inducing growth and to keep him from harm his person is hedged in by a great number of regulations and taboos, which sometimes render him virtually incapable of action." The preciousness of the king's person is actually the preciousness of what he contains, and it is this which leads to his immobility. He is a vessel which is very full, from which nothing must be spilled.

"He is never visible, or only at certain times. He must never leave his palace enclosure, or only at night or on special occasions. He is never seen to eat or drink." His isolation protects him from anything which might harm him. The rarity of his appearances means that he only exists for very special purposes. Eating and drinking may be thought unsuitable because they lessen what he is supposed to increase: he should be able to live by the forces within him alone.

The crucial thing about the king is his uniqueness: a people which may have many gods has only one king. As we have seen it is important that he should be isolated. An artificial distance is created between him and his subjects and is maintained by all possible means. He shows himself rarely, or not at all, or in some sort of disguise which conceals his person either wholly or to a large extent. His preciousness is stressed in every possible way, first by covering or surrounding him with precious things and then by the rarity of his appearances. He is protected by a guard blindly devoted to him and also by ever wider spaces. The enlargement of the royal enclosure and the construction of bigger rooms within it serve to establish distance as well as to protect him.

Uniqueness, isolation, distance and preciousness thus form an important group of attributes which can be recognized at sight.

"Physical manifestations, such as coughing, sneezing, or blowing the nose, are imitated or applauded." Whatever good or bad traits a king of Monomotapa possessed, whatever his vices, virtues, faults or bodily defects, his companions and servants were at pains to imitate them; if the king was lame his companions limped. We know from Strabo and Diodorus that if one of the ancient kings of Ethiopia were maimed in any part of his body all his courtiers had to suffer the same mutilation. An Arab traveller who visited the court of Darfur at the beginning of the last century reported the courtiers' duties as follows: when the Sultan coughs as though about to speak, everyone makes the sound 'ts, ts', as nurses do to quiet little children; when he sneezes the whole assembly imitates the cry of the gecko, which resembles that of a man urging on his horse. If the Sultan happens to fall off his horse while riding, all his followers must do likewise. Anyone who remains in his saddle is laid on the ground and beaten, however high his rank. At the court of Uganda, if the king laughed, everyone laughed; if he sneezed, everyone sneezed; if he had a cold, everyone else said he had one; if he had his hair cut so did they. This imitation of the king is not confined to Africa. "At the court of Boni in Celebes it is a rule that whatever the king does all the courtiers must do too; if he stands, they must stand; if he sits, they sit; if he falls off his horse, they must fall off likewise; if he bathes, they bathe and passers-by as well must enter the water in whatever clothes, good or bad, they happen to be wearing." In China, as was reported by a French missionary, "when the emperor laughs the mandarins in attendance laugh too; when he stops laughing, they stop. When he is sad their faces fall. One would think that their faces were on springs which the emperor could touch and set in motion at his pleasure."

This taking the king as a model is universal. Sometimes it results only in admiration and veneration: nothing he does is unimportant or meaningless. But sometimes it goes further than this and people regard his every movement and utterance as a *command*: for him to sneeze means "Sneeze!"; for him to fall off his horse means "Fall off your horses!" He is so full of the force of command that everything he does must be an expression of it. Abandoning words, commands become actions again; in this case actions compelling imitation. In addition, since the whole purpose of his existence is increase, his own movements and physical peculiarities will tend to undergo the same process of multiplication. One might say that when his courtiers imitate him they become a kind of increase pack. Even if they do not feel themselves to be one, they certainly behave like one. Everyone does the same thing, namely what the king does first. The court which had become a crowd crystal returns to its origin, which is an increase pack.

Acclamation and applause can also be regarded as expressions of the will to increase. The movements and utterances which are taken as models are, as it were, strengthened by applause and the likelihood of their repetition thus enhanced. Few can withstand the compulsion of a thousand hands clapping in concert; an action which is applauded is bound to be repeated.

"If the king begins to age his magical strength is threatened; it may grow weaker, or disappear, or evil powers may turn it into its opposite. Therefore the ageing king's life must be taken and his magical strength transferred to his successor." The king's person is of importance only so long as it is undamaged: only as an intact vessel is it capable of containing the forces of increase. The smallest defect renders the king suspect to his subjects, for it means he may lose some of the substance entrusted to him and so endanger the welfare of his people. The constitution of these kingdoms is the physical constitution of the king himself. He is sworn in on condition, as it were, of his strength and health. A king who shows grey hairs, whose eyesight deteriorates, who loses his teeth, or becomes impotent, is killed, or must commit suicide; he takes poison or is strangled. These are the usual forms of death, for the shedding of his blood is forbidden. Sometimes the length of his reign is fixed from the start: the kings of Jukun, as we saw, originally ruled for seven years. Among the Bambara the newly elected king traditionally determined the length of his own reign. "A strip of cotton was put round his neck and two men pulled the ends in opposite directions whilst he himself took out of a calabash as many pebbles as he could grasp in his hand. These indicated the number of years he would reign, on the expiration of which he would be strangled."

But the artificial shortening of the king's life serves a second purpose as well as the safe-guarding of his precious increase-substance. By it his passion for survival, which might otherwise grow to dangerous proportions during the course of his reign, is blunted and checked from the very start. The king knows when he will die, and this is sooner than many of his subjects. He has the moment of his death always clearly in sight and in this respect must feel substantially inferior to those he rules. He makes a kind of pact with them. He is a ruler who, in accepting office, renounces the despot's claim to survive at all costs. The dignity he succeeds to is truly a burden. He declares his readiness to surrender his life after the lapse of a certain period of time.

The insults and blows he is subjected to before entering on his office are an intimation of what awaits him in the end. As he submits to them, so he will submit to his ultimate fate. His death is anticipated. Either by threatening him with it as a recurring possibility or by regarding it as something virtually pre-determined, the baiting crowd which forms round him makes it painfully clear to him that it is not for his own sake that he will rule. Prospective kings of the Yoruba are said to have been beaten first and anyone who did not endure the pain calmly was rejected. It might happen that the choice had fallen on one of the poorer princes who was quietly pursuing his own life and had no designs at all on the throne. He would be ordered to appear and then, to his amazement, would be brutally maltreated. His counterpart in Sierra Leone would be loaded with chains and well thrashed before being proclaimed king. The reader will remember Du Chaillu's description of a royal election in Gaboon.

Between the death of a king and the installation of a new one a period of lawlessness intervened. This, as we saw, found meaningful expression in the maltreatment of the king-elect. But the same lawlessness might also be turned against the weak and helpless. Among the Mosi of Wagadugu all criminals were released from prison after the death of a king. Murder and robbery and every kind of license were allowed. In Ashanti it was the members of the royal clan who profited from the period of anarchy; they were permitted to kill and rob any commoner. In Uganda the death of the king was at first kept secret. Then, after perhaps two days, the sacred fire burning at the entrance to the royal enclosure was extinguished and a great wailing began. The drums beat the death rhythm, so that the people knew what had happened. But no-one was allowed to speak of death; what they said was, "the fire is extinguished". A wild period of anarchy followed. Everyone tried to rob everyone else and only chiefs with a strong band of followers were able to feel safe. Lesser chiefs went in danger of being killed by the stronger ones, who did as they pleased during the short interregnum. In such circumstances it was obviously the weak and helpless who suffered most. Order returned with the new king; he actually embodied it in his own person.

The succession was not always clearly settled and, even when it was, people only recognized it when forced to do so. A peculiar concept of succession existed in the Hima states. This has been lucidly expounded by Oberg in his excellent study of the kingdom of Ankole.

Here, too, the king had to take poison as soon as his wives and followers saw signs of weakness in him. Very great stress was laid on his strength and this also determined the choice of his successor. To the ruling Hima minority it was a matter of considerable importance that the strongest of the king's many sons should succeed him. The test of strength could only be fighting. A war of succession was thus inevitable, but the kingdom could not remain without a king while it took place. Therefore, after the mourning ceremonies for the dead ruler, a mock battle took place in his kraal between common herdsmen, the winner of which was declared the mock king. The legitimate royal brothers watched this battle and after it had been decided each gathered his own followers together and went to look for the royal drums. If one met another on the way they fought and each tried to kill each other. "If one brother had fewer followers than the other he generally got killed or fled to another country. On the other hand, strategy often made up for lack of followers. The brothers spied upon one another in order to creep up during the night and get the other unawares. They put poison into the other's food or stabbed him in his sleep. Magic and the help of foreign allies were both resorted to. Each son was aided by his mother and his sister, who practised magic against his enemies and protected him from the spirits of his slain enemies." The old king's favourite son, his own choice as his successor, remained in hiding during the fight.

The war of succession might last for several months, during which period the whole country was in a state of chaos. "Every man resorted to his kinsmen for protection. It is said that there was much cattle stealing and people who had a grievance took advantage of the chaotic condition of the country to take revenge upon their enemies. But the great chiefs who guarded the borders of Ankole did not take part in the accession war. They endeavoured to keep as much internal order as possible and to guard the country from foreign invaders.

"One by one the princes were either killed or driven into exile until only one remained. The hidden son, the late king's favourite, then came out of his hiding-place and fought with the victor among his brothers for the possession of the royal drums. He did not always win, but he usually had the most powerful magicians on his side and a large following." When all his brothers were dead the survivor, with the royal drums and his mother and sister, returned to the royal kraal. The mock king was killed and the victorious brother proclaimed as the new king.

All his rivals had been exterminated. The survivor, as victor, was considered to be the strongest and was acclaimed by everyone. It can be assumed that in the other Hima states, where wars of succession were also the rule, the same principle lay at their roots. People wanted the *survivor* as their king; the fact that he had killed so many enemies endowed him in their eyes with the power they wanted him to possess.

But the actual contest for the succession was not the only means of imbuing the new king with the strength of a survivor. In the kingdom of Kitara on the northern borders of Ankole the fight for the succession was recapitulated in an amazing rite which formed part of the coronation ceremonies of the new king. The last time it was performed was at the accession of King Kabarega in 1871. The following is a description of what happened then.

Among the princes there were always some who were boys too young to take part in the fighting. Thus they were still alive when their elder brothers, apart from the victor, had exterminated each other.

One of these younger brothers was taken aside by the chief who was acting as a kind of regent and told that he had been chosen king. All the chiefs who were there assented. The boy, however, knew what was intended and said, "Do not try to deceive me. I am not king and you only want to kill me." But he had to submit and was placed on the throne. The chiefs came, brought him presents and did homage to him. With them came Kabarega, the victor, whose coronation it really was. He was dressed as a simple prince and brought a cow with him as his present. The regent asked him, "where is my cow?", to which Kabarega replied, "I have brought it to the lawful person, the king." The regent appeared to take this as an insult to himself and struck Kabarega on the arm with a cord, whereupon the latter went away wrathfully, collected his warriors and then returned. When the regent saw them coming he said to the boy on the throne, "Kabarega has come to fight". At this the boy wanted to run away, but the regent caught hold of him, took him to the back of the throne-room and strangled him. He was buried in the building.

The quarrel between the regent and the new ruler was feigned. The boy king's fate was pre-determined: a boy king was always chosen during the coronation ceremonies and killed "that death might be deceived". The war had been fought and decided; his rivals were all dead and yet, even during his coronation, the new king had to survive a brother, and the victim was buried in the innermost room of the royal enclosure, where the throne and the royal drums were.

In this same kingdom of Kitara the royal *bow* possessed symbolic significance; it had to be re-strung at each coronation. A man was chosen to supply the sinews for this from his own body. He regarded it as an honour and himself directed the removal of the sinews from his right side; it was said that he always died soon after the operation. The newly strung bow was handed to the king with four arrows, which he then shot, one to each of the four quarters of the earth, saying, "I shoot the nations to overcome them", and adding, as he shot each arrow, the names of the nations who lived in that direction. The arrows were searched for, brought back and kept to be used again. At the beginning of every year the king repeated this "shooting of the nations".

The most powerful of the neighbouring kingdoms, and always at war with Kitara, was Uganda. There, when the king came to the throne, it was said that he had "eaten Uganda" or had "eaten the drums". Possession of the drums was the sign of office and authority. There were royal drums and chiefs' drums and each office could be

recognized by the beat of its drums. During the coronation ceremonies the king said, "I am the king of Uganda. I am the king to live
longer than my ancestors, to rule the nations and put down rebellion."

The new king's first duty was mourning for his predecessor. At the
end of the mourning period he had the drums beaten and the next day
a hunt took place. A gazelle was brought and set free, which the king
had to pursue. Then two men were caught, casual passers-by on the
road; one of them was strangled and the other granted his life. The
same evening the king mounted the old royal stool and a high dignitary
administered the oath to him. Two strong men then carried him on
their shoulders through the whole enclosure for the people to do homage to him.

Then two blindfolded men were brought before the king. One of
them he wounded slightly with an arrow and sent as a kind of scapegoat to the enemy of Kitara. The other man was set free and appointed
overseer to the king's inner court and guardian of his wives. Together
with eight prisoners the new overseer was led to a place of sacrifice.
Here he was blindfolded again and seven of the prisoners were killed
with clubs in his presence; he was allowed to watch the death of the
eighth. These deaths were supposed to give strength to the king; they
certainly gave strength and loyalty to the overseer.

When the king had ruled for two or three years two men were
again brought before him; one of these he wounded and the other
was granted his life. The wounded one was killed outside the main
entrance to the enclosure; the other was appointed assistant to the
overseer and his first duty was to take the corpse of the man who had
been killed and throw it into the nearest river.

These two men were also killed to strengthen the king. There was
killing to show that he had entered on his reign and, repeatedly, there
was fresh killing so that, again and again, he might be a survivor. It
was the actual process of survival which gave him power. Striking
here, and perhaps peculiar to Uganda, is the presentation of victims in
pairs, one of whom dies while the other is granted his life. The king
exercises his two rights simultaneously. He draws strength from the
death of the one man, but he also profits by his pardoning of the
other. For this man is a witness of his companion's fate; he himself is
strengthened by being a survivor and, as one chosen for mercy, becomes all the more faithful a servant of the king.

After all this it is surprising that a king of Uganda should ever have
died. There were many of these occasions on which lives were sacrificed to him. The idea that the king could increase in power through

survival led to the introduction of regular human sacrifices. But these were a religious institution, independent of the private appetites of this or that king. Each would have his own moods and whims and it was part of his nature that these should be dangerous.

One of the main attributes of an African king was his absolute power over life and death. The terror that he spread was tremendous. "You are now Ata, you have power over life and death. Kill everyone who says he does not fear you": thus the formula of investiture of the king of Igara. He killed as he pleased and gave no reason. His wish was sufficient; he did not have to account for it. In many cases he was not allowed to shed blood himself, but the executioner who did it for him was the one indispensable official of his court. Whether the man who started by occupying that office ultimately became Prime Minister, as in Dahomey, or whether there were hundreds of executioners who formed a kind of caste, as in Ashanti; whether executions were frequent or were limited to occasional cases, the pronouncement of death sentences was always the undisputed right of the king and if he let any considerable time pass without exercising it the terror essential to his power was lost; he was no longer feared, but was held in contempt.

The king was regarded as a lion or a leopard, whether because the animal was thought to be his ancestor, or simply that he shared its qualities without being directly descended from it. His lion- or leopard-nature meant that he, like these animals, had to kill. It was right and proper for him to kill, to spread terror as these animals did; his propensity for killing was inborn.

The king of Uganda ate alone and no-one was allowed to see him eat. One of his wives had to hand him his food and then turn her back while he ate. "The lion eats alone", it was said. If the food was not to his liking, or was not brought quickly enough, he would call for the offender and spear him to death. If the wife who was waiting on him coughed during his meal, she, too, was killed. He had two spears always at hand. If someone happened to enter and surprise the king eating he was transfixed on the spot. Then the people said, "when the lion was eating he killed so-and-so". No human being was permitted to touch any food left by the king. It was given to his favourite dogs.

The king of Kitara was fed by his cook. The cook brought the meal, stuck a fork into a piece of meat and put it into the king's mouth. He did this four times and if he accidentally touched the king's teeth with the fork he was put to death.

Every morning, after the milking of the cows, the king of Kitara sat on the throne and heard the cases which were brought before him. If there was talking when he was in court and required silence, he took his two-edged sword which was always carried by a page in attendance on him. The page wore a lion skin over his right shoulder, the head hanging down in front and concealing the sword. When the king wanted it he simply held out his hand, the page put the sword into it and the king then struck down someone in the court. There were also other occasions on which he executed summary justice. When he walked within the royal enclosure he was always accompanied by the page carrying the sword and, if anything displeased him, he held out his hand, the sword was put into it and he struck the offender down on the spot.

All his commands had to be obeyed absolutely; to disregard any of them meant death. Here the command manifests itself in its oldest and purest form, as the death sentence with which the lion threatens all weaker animals. If these were enemies, they had, as it were, to be permanently in flight before the king; if subjects, they were forced to serve him. He ordered his people about as he liked and, as long as they obeyed him, granted them their lives. But essentially he was always a lion; when he wanted to, he struck.

A Sultan of Delhi: Muhammad Tughlak

THANKS TO A fortunate chance we have a picture of this Sultan far clearer and more detailed than those we have of most oriental rulers. Ibn Batuta, a famous Arab traveller who visited the whole Islamic world of his time from Morocco to China, spent seven years at his court and in his service and left a lively description of it and of the Sultan himself and his mode of government. He both enjoyed the Sultan's favour for a considerable time and then later, when he had fallen into disgrace, learnt what it was to live in deadly fear of him. As often happened then, he succeeded in ingratiating himself for a time and then had to try to save himself from the Sultan's wrath by leading the life of an ascetic.

"This king is of all men the fondest of making gifts and of shedding blood." At this court Ibn Batuta learnt to recognize the two faces of power; he knew, as few have ever known, both its prodigality and its murderousness. The psychological accuracy of his account is beyond doubt, for there is a second account, independent of his, which can be compared with it. Not long after Muhammad's death, the history of

his times was written in Persian by Ziau-d din Barani, a high official
who had lived at his court for more than seventeen years. This, which
is among the best works of its kind, contains, with much else, accounts
of three conversations which the author had with the Sultan, in which
the latter revealed his thoughts about government and about his subjects. The following account is based on these sources and makes full
and often verbatim use of them.

Muhammad Tughlak was the most highly cultured prince of his
time. His letters, both in Arabic and Persian, continued to be admired
for their elegance long after his death. Like his style, his calligraphy left
the most accomplished professors of this art far behind. He had considerable imagination and was adept in the use of metaphors; he was
well-versed in Persian poetry and, thanks to his extraordinary memory,
knew many poems by heart and quoted them both frequently and
aptly. He also had a thorough knowledge of the rest of Persian literature. Mathematics, physics, logic and Greek philosophy fascinated him
equally. "The dogmas of philosophers, which are productive of indifference and hardness of heart, had a powerful influence over him."
But he also had a physician's curiosity and would nurse sick people
himself if they had unusual symptoms which interested him. Even in
the discussion of his own special subject there was no scholar, scribe,
poet or physician who could, or would dare to, stand against the
Sultan. He was pious, adhered strictly to the precepts of his religion
and abstained from wine. His courtiers found it advisable to respect the
times for prayer; those who did not were severely punished. He set
great store by justice; and he took not only the ritual, but also the
moral precepts of Islam seriously and expected others to do the same.
In war he distinguished himself by his courage and initiative; the
exploits he performed when still under the command of his father
and his father's predecessor were universally famed. It is important
to point out the complexity of his nature. Sharply contrasting with all
the traits which made him terrible and incomprehensible to his contemporaries were these other brilliant qualities which they admired in
him and which he retained to the end.

What did the court of this just and highly accomplished prince look
like? To reach the interior of the palace one had to pass through three
doors. Outside the first door were a number of guards and also trump-
eters and flute-players. When an amir or any other person of note
arrived these sounded their instruments and said "So-and-so has come.
So-and-so has come." Outside this door there were also the platforms
where the executioners sat: when the Sultan ordered a man to be

executed the sentence was carried out here and the body left lying for three days and nights. Thus anyone approaching the palace would come first on corpses; heaps and mounds of them were always lying there; the sweepers and executioners who had to drag out the condemned and put them to death were worn out with the heavy and endless labour. Between the second and third door was a large audience hall for the general public. Outside the third door were platforms where "the scribes of the door" sat. No-one was allowed to pass this door without special permission from the Sultan. When anyone came the scribes wrote down "So-and-so came at the first hour", or the second or third as the case might be. This report was given to the Sultan after the evening prayer. Anyone who had absented himself from the palace, with or without excuse, for three days or more, was not allowed to enter it thereafter without express permission from the Sultan. If he had been ill or had some other excuse he presented the Sultan with a gift suitable to his rank. Behind the third door was an immense audience hall called "A thousand pillars"; the pillars supported a wooden roof, marvellously carved and painted.

The audiences were usually held in the afternoon, but sometimes also in the early morning. The Sultan sat cross-legged on his throne on a dais carpeted in white; he had a large cushion behind him and two others as arm-rests. The wazir stood in front of him, behind the wazir the secretaries, then the chamberlains and so on, in order of precedence. "As the Sultan sits down the chamberlains and secretaries say in their loudest voice 'Bismillah!' ('in the name of God'). A hundred armour-bearers stand on the right, and a like number on the left, carrying shields, swords and bows. The other functionaries and notables stand along the hall to right and left, where the Sultan can see them. Then they bring in sixty horses with the royal banners, half of which are ranged on the right and half on the left, where the Sultan can see them. Next fifty elephants are brought in, which are adorned with silken cloths and have their tusks shod with iron for greater efficiency in killing criminals. On the neck of each elephant is its mahout, who carries a sort of iron axe with which he punishes it and directs it to do what is required of it. Each elephant has on its back a sort of large chest capable of holding twenty warriors, or more or less, according to the size of the beast. These elephants are trained to make obeisance to the Sultan and incline their heads, and when they do the chamberlains cry in a loud voice 'Bismillah!'. They also are arranged half on the right and half on the left behind the persons standing. As each person enters who has an appointed place of standing on the right or left, he makes obeisance on reaching the station of the chamberlains, and the chamberlains say 'Bismillah', regulating the loudness of their utterance by the rank of the person concerned, who then retires to his appointed place, beyond which he never passes. If it is one of the infidel Hindus who makes obeisance the chamberlains say to him, 'God guide thee'."

From Ibn Batuta we also have a graphic description of the Sultan's entry into his capital.

"When the Sultan returns from a journey the elephants are decorated, and on sixteen of them are placed sixteen parasols, some brocaded and some set with jewels. Wooden pavilions are built several storeys high and covered with silk cloths, and in each storey there are singing girls wearing magnificent dresses and ornaments, with dancing girls amongst them. In the centre of each pavilion is a large tank made of skins and filled with syrup-water, from which all the people, natives or strangers, may drink, receiving at the same time betel leaves and areca nuts. The space between the pavilions is carpeted with silk cloths, on which the Sultan's horse treads. The walls of the street along which he passes from the gate of the city to the gate of the palace are hung with silk cloths. In front of him march footmen from his own slaves, several thousands in numbers, and behind come the mob and the soldiers. On one of his entries into the capital I saw three or four small catapults placed on elephants throwing gold and silver coins amongst the people from the moment he entered the city until he reached the palace."

Muhammad was especially open-handed with foreigners. His intelligence service gave him immediate information about anyone arriving at one of the frontier towns of his empire. His courier service was exemplary; a distance which travellers took fifty days to cover was covered in five by his couriers; every third of a mile a fresh one took over. It was not only his letters which were carried in this way; special fruits from Khorassan arrived fresh on his table and state criminals were bound, placed on a stretcher which the runners carried on their heads and brought to him as quickly as letters and fruit. The reports on foreigners who crossed the frontiers were very minute. With the utmost care they described each stranger's appearance and dress, the numbers in his party, his slaves, servants and beasts, his behaviour both in action and while resting and all his doings, omitting nothing. The Sultan studied these reports carefully. Every foreigner had to wait in the capital of the frontier province until an order had come from the Sultan respecting his further journey and the degree of honour that was to be accorded him. Each was judged entirely on his behaviour, for nothing could be known of his family or lineage in distant India. Muhammad was particularly interested in foreigners and made a practice of bestowing governorships and high dignities of state upon them: the majority of his courtiers, palace officials, ministers and judges were foreigners. By a special decree they were all given the title of "Honourable"; he paid out large sums for their maintenance and gave them magnificent gifts. They spread the fame of his generosity throughout the world.

But even more famous was his severity. "He punished small faults and great, without respect of persons, whether men of learning, piety or high station. Every day hundreds of people, chained, pinioned and fettered, are brought to his hall, and those who are for execution are executed, those for torture tortured, and those for beating beaten. It is his custom that every day all persons who are in his prison are brought to his hall, except only on Friday; this is a day of respite for them on which they clean themselves and remain at ease."

One of the gravest charges against the Sultan was that he had compelled the inhabitants of Delhi to leave their city. He had, as he thought, good reason for punishing them. They were in the habit of writing letters to him in which they insulted and reviled him. These they sealed up and addressed "To the Master of the World. None but he may read this", and then threw them into the audience hall at night. When the Sultan broke the seal he found nothing but insults and abuse. Finally he decided to lay Delhi in ruins. He paid the inhabitants the full value of their houses and dwelling places and ordered them to move to Daulatabad which he wanted to make his capital. "They refused, and his herald was sent to proclaim that no person should remain in the city after three nights. The majority complied with the order, but some of them hid in the houses. The Sultan ordered a search to be made for any persons remaining in the town, and his slaves found two men in the streets, one a cripple and the other blind. They were brought before him and he gave orders that the cripple should be flung from a mangonel and the blind man dragged from Delhi to Daulatabad, a distance of forty days' journey. He fell to pieces on the road and all of him that reached Daulatabad was his leg. When the Sultan did this, every person left the town, abandoning furniture and possessions, and the city remained utterly deserted. A person in whom I have confidence told me that the Sultan mounted one night to the roof of his palace and looked out over Delhi, where there was neither fire nor smoke nor lamp, and said 'Now my mind is tranquil and my wrath appeased'. Afterwards, he wrote to the inhabitants of the other cities commanding them to move to Delhi and repopulate it. The result was only to ruin their cities and leave Dehli still unpopulated, because of its immensity, for it is one of the greatest cities in the world. It was in this state that we found it on our arrival, empty and unpopulated, save for a few inhabitants."

The Sultan's exasperation with his subjects was not the result of having ruled for a long time. (The order to evacuate Delhi was issued in the second year of his reign.) From the very beginning there was tension between them and it grew with the passage of time. One can now only guess at the contents of the letters thrown into his audience hall, but there are grounds for believing that they referred to the way in which he had come to the throne. Muhammad's father, Tughlak Shah, lost his life in an accident when he had reigned for only four years and, though none but the initiated few could have known what really happened, suspicion was inevitable. On his return from an expedition the old Sultan ordered his son to prepare a pavilion for his reception. It was ready in three days, made, as usual, of wood, but constructed in such a way that a push at a certain point would cause it to collapse instantly. When the Sultan, with his younger and favourite son, was installed in the pavilion Muhammad asked permission for an elephant parade. This was granted him and the elephants were then paraded in such a way that, in passing under the wooden structure, they pushed against it at the sensitive spot. The pavilion collapsed and buried the Sultan and his favourite son. Muhammad delayed the rescue operations until it was too late. When the victims were at last found they were both dead, or rather, as was alleged by some, the Sultan, bent over his son, was still breathing and had, as it were, to be murdered a second time. Muhammad ascended the throne without opposition, but it was not in his power to silence talk. From the very beginning of his reign he was suspected of being his father's murderer.

The Sultanate of Delhi attained its maximum size under Muhammad Tughlak. Over two hundred years passed before—under Akbar—so much of India was again united under one rule. But Muhammad was far from being content with the roughly two dozen provinces ascribed to him. He wanted to bring the whole habitable world under his rule and nursed various ambitious schemes for the realization of this project. None of his friends or advisers were let into the secret of these schemes; he kept them to himself, as he had conceived them by himself. Any idea of his own pleased him. He never doubted himself or his goal; to him it seemed self-evident and the means he used to attain it the only proper ones.

The most ambitious of his plans of conquest were for an attack on Khorassan and Iraq and another on China. For the former an army of 370,000 horsemen was collected and the dignitaries of the threatened cities were bribed with enormous sums. But the attack was never mounted, or came to grief in its initial stages, and the army dispersed. Sums of money which, even for Muhammad, must have been considered enormous, had been entirely wasted. The other plan, the conquest of China, was to be implemented by crossing the Himalayas. 100,000 horsemen were sent into the highest mountains, thence to subdue the whole massif and its savage inhabitants and secure the passes into China. Except for ten men this whole army perished. The ten who got back to Delhi were executed by the Sultan in his disappointment.

The conquest of the world called for colossal armies and these in turn called for more and more money. It is true that Muhammad's revenues were immense. The tribute of the subject Hindu kings flowed in from all sides and from his father he had inherited, among other things, a reservoir filled with a solid mass of molten gold. But, in spite of all this, he was soon in need of money and typically sought some method of supplying the deficiency at a single stroke. He had heard about the paper money of the Chinese and conceived the idea of doing something similar with copper. He had a large number of copper coins struck, arbitrarily fixed their value at that of silver coins and ordered them to be used instead of gold and silver. Soon everything was bought and sold for copper. The result of this edict was that the house of every Hindu became a private mint; in every province copper coins were made in millions and with these people paid their tribute and bought horses and all manner of agreeable things. Princes, village chiefs and landowners grew rich by means of this copper money, and the state grew poor. Soon the value of the new money fell rapidly, while the old coins, being very rare, came to be worth four or five times their former value. In the end copper coins were worth no more than pebbles. People held back their goods and trade came to a standstill. When the Sultan realized the result of his edict he revoked it in great anger and ordered all copper to be brought to the treasury where it would be exchanged for money of the old type. So, from all the corners where it had been thrown in contempt, thousands fetched out their copper and thronged to the treasury where they were given gold and silver in exchange. Mountains of copper piled up in Tughlakabad; the treasury lost large sums and the shortage of money grew acute. As soon as the Sultan was able to assess what the copper had cost his treasury he turned against his subjects even more.

Another way of finding money was taxation. Already under his predecessors taxes had been very high and now they were raised and collected with relentless cruelty. The peasants were beggared. Any Hindu who owned land left it and fled to the jungle to join the rebels, larger or smaller bands of whom were everywhere. The land lay untilled; less and less corn was grown; there was famine in the central provinces, which, after one particularly long drought, spread throughout the empire. It lasted for several years, families were torn apart, whole towns starved and thousands of people perished.

It was possibly this famine which brought about the real change in the fortunes of the empire. Revolts became more frequent and one province after another broke away from Delhi. Muhammad was continually in the field, crushing rebellion. His cruelty grew. He laid waste whole regions; the jungles were surrounded and anyone—man, woman or child—captured there was slaughtered. The terror he spread was so great that, wherever he appeared, people prostrated themselves —if they had not already fled. But no sooner had he enforced a peace or created a desert than revolt broke out again in another part of the country. Governors of provinces who broke away from him he had skinned; the skins were stuffed with straw and the gruesome puppets carried through the countryside to arouse terror.

Muhammad felt no remorse for his cruelty; he was firmly convinced that all his measures were justified. The conversations he had on this subject with Zia Barani, the historian, are so illuminating that they deserve quotation:

"You see", said the Sultan to Barani, "how many revolts spring up. I have no pleasure in them, although men will say that they have all been caused by my excessive severity. But I am not to be turned aside from capital punishment by talk, or by revolts. You have read many histories. Have you found that kings inflict capital punishment under certain circumstances?"

Barani quoted in his reply a high Islamic authority who regarded capital punishment as permissible in seven circumstances. Otherwise it produced disturbances, trouble and insurrection, and inflicted injury on the country. These seven were:

Apostasy from the true religion; wilful murder; adultery of a married man with another man's wife; conspiracy against the king; heading a revolt; joining the enemies of the king and conveying information to them; and disobedience productive of injury to the state, but *no other disobedience*. The Prophet himself had condemned three of these offences, namely, apostasy, murder of a Musulman and adultery with a married woman. Punishment of the other four offences was more a matter of policy and good government. But the authorities, said Barani, had also stressed the fact that kings appoint wazirs, advance them to high dignity and place the management of their kingdoms in their hands in order that they may frame regulations and keep the country in such good order that the king is spared the necessity of staining his hands with human blood.

To this the Sultan replied "The punishments which were then prescribed were suited to the early ages of the world, but now there are more turbulent and wicked men. I visit them with chastisement on the suspicion or presumption of their rebellious or treacherous designs and I punish the most trifling act of contumacy with death. This I will do until I die, or until the people act honestly and give up rebellion and contumacy. I have no such wazir as will make rules to obviate the shedding of blood. I punish the people because they have all at once become my enemies and opponents. I have dispensed great wealth among them, but they have not become friendly and loyal. Their temper is well known to me and I see that they are disaffected and inimical to me."

In a later conversation he regretted that he had not had killed in time all those who later created so much trouble for him by their rebellions. On another occasion when he had just lost one of his most important cities—the one to which all the inhabitants of Delhi had been forced to move—he sent for Barani and asked him what remedies former kings had resorted to in such cases: his kingdom was diseased and no treatment cured it. Barani replied "Some kings, when they perceived that they did not retain the confidence of their people and had become the objects of general dislike, have abdicated and handed over the government to the most worthy of their sons. Others have taken to hunting, pleasure and wine, leaving all the business of the state to their wazirs and officers. If the people were satisfied with this and the king was not given to revenge, the disorders of the state could be cured. Of all political ills the greatest and the most dire is a general feeling of aversion and a want of confidence among all ranks of the people." But even this courageous and scarcely veiled advice of Barani had no effect on the Sultan. He said, if he could only settle the affairs of his kingdom as he wished, he would consign the government to three men and himself go on pilgrimage to Mecca. "But at present I am angry with my subjects and they are aggrieved with me. The people are acquainted with my feelings and I am aware of their misery and wretchedness, but no treatment I employ is of any use. My remedy for rebels, insurgents, opponents and disaffected people is the sword. I employ punishment and use the sword, so that a cure may be effected by suffering. The more people resist, the more I inflict chastisement."

But the number of rebellions and the general disaffection throughout his empire did have *one* effect on the Sultan's mind. He began to feel scruples, not about the mounds of corpses before his palace and in all the provinces and cities he visited, but about the legitimacy of his rule. He was, as will be sufficiently clear by now, a pious and moral man and he wanted his position as king sanctioned by the highest spiritual authority of Islam. In former centuries the Abbasid Khalifs, whose headquarters were in Bagdad, were regarded as such. But their empire no longer existed: in 1258 Bagdad had been conquered by the Mongols and the last Khalif killed. For Muhammad Tughlak, who ascended the throne in 1325 and whose scruples awoke about 1340 as province after province of his empire began to fall away from him, it was not at all easy to find out where the right of investiture lay. He had careful enquiries made; all travellers from the western countries of Islam who arrived at his court were diligently interrogated until, finally, he came to the conclusion that the Khalif in Egypt was his "Pope". He entered into negotiations with him, emissaries went to and fro and his letters to the Khalif contained flatteries so gross that even Barani, who must have been used to a good deal in this way, could not bring himself to repeat them. When the ambassador of the Khalif arrived, Muhammad, with all his nobles and scholars, went to meet him and walked barefoot before him for a considerable distance. He had his own name removed from the coinage and replaced by that of the Khalif, whom he regarded as the supreme ruler of Islam. The Khalif was named in the Friday prayer, but this was not enough to satisfy Muhammad: the names of all his predecessors who had not received the sanction of the Khalif were removed from the prayer and their authority retrospectively declared invalid. The name of the Khalif was inscribed on lofty buildings and no other name was permitted to stand beside it. After a correspondence lasting for several years a solemn document arrived from Egypt in which Muhammad was formally named the Khalif's Vicegerent for India. This document gave Muhammad so much pleasure that he had it skilfully put into verse by his court poets.

In every other respect he remained the same till the end, his severity increasing with his failures. He did not die by the hand of a murderer. After ruling for twenty-six years he died of a fever caught on a punitive expedition.

He is the purest case of a paranoiac ruler. The way he lived is strange and unfamiliar to a European; everything about him is striking and thus it is easier to see him as a whole; the extraordinary consistency of his nature is patent.

His mind was dominated by four kinds of crowds: his army, his treasure, his corpses and his court (and, with it, his capital). He juggled with them ceaselessly, but only succeeded in increasing one at the expense of another. He raises enormous armies, but in so doing exhausts his treasury. He banishes the entire population of his capital, and suddenly finds himself alone in the vast city, his anger appeased as he surveys the empty metropolis from the roof of his palace. He savoured to the full the exultation of the survivor.

Whatever he did there was always *one* crowd which he managed to preserve. In no circumstances did he ever cease to kill. All his prisoners were brought before him daily: as candidates for execution they were his most precious possessions. During the twenty-six years of his reign, famine and plague helping him, the heaps of corpses piled up in every province of his empire. The consequent loss of revenue certainly vexed him, but, so long as the numbers of his victims increased, nothing could seriously shake his self-confidence.

In order to maintain the force of his commands—which were nothing but death sentences—at its highest pitch, he sought to have his position confirmed by a higher authority. God, in whom as a pious Mohamedan he believed, was not sufficient for him. He also wanted confirmation from God's legal representative.

Muhammad Tughlak has been defended by modern Indian historians. Power has never lacked eulogists, and historians, who are professionally obsessed with it, can explain anything, either by the *times* (disguising their adulation as scholarship), or by *necessity*, which, in their hands, can assume any and every shape.

We must expect the same thing to happen in the case of rulers who are nearer to us than Muhammad Tughlak. It may be useful, therefore, as a preventive measure, to lay bare the inner processes of power, though in a man who, fortunately for the world, only possessed it in his delusions.

The Case of Schreber: I

THERE IS NO richer or more instructive document than the *Memoirs* of Daniel Paul Schreber, sometime *Senatspräsident* at the Court of Appeal in Dresden. He was an educated and intelligent man trained by his profession in the precise use of words. He had spent seven years in mental asylums as a paranoiac when he decided to write down in full detail what the world must call his delusional system. His *Memoirs of a Nervous Illness* became a whole book. He was so firmly convinced of the truth and importance of his self-created religion that, after he had been released from the asylum, he had the book published. The language at his command might have been made for the description of this singular intellectual structure, enabling him to grasp just enough of his experience for nothing essential to remain obscure. He pleads for his case, but is fortunately no poet, so that one can follow his thoughts without being seduced by them.

I want to consider some of the most striking characteristics of his system, so far as it is possible to do so in a limited space. I believe that this will enable us to come very close to an understanding of paranoia. If others who study the *Memoirs* should arrive at different conclusions this may simply be a proof of the richness of the material.

The magnitude of the claim Schreber puts forward is most obvious when he appears to limit it. "After all," he says, almost at the beginning. "I too am only a human being and therefore bound by the limits of human understanding. But on one point he has no doubts at all, namely that he has come infinitely closer to the truth than any other human beings. Thence he immediately passes on to *eternity*. The thought of it permeates his whole book; it means far more to him than to ordinary men. He feels at home in eternity and regards it not only as something which belongs to him by right, but as something which is part of him. He reckons in enormous spaces of time; his experiences stretch over centuries. It seemed to him "as though single nights had the duration of centuries, so that within that time there could very well have come about the most fundamental changes in the whole of mankind, in the earth itself and in the entire solar system." He is as much at home in universal space as he is in eternity. Certain constellations and individual stars, such as Cassiopeia, Vega, Capella and the Pleiades, are especially close to him; he speaks of them as though they were bus-stops just round the corner. But he is well aware of their real distance from the earth; he has some knowledge of astronomy and does not reduce the size of the universe. On the contrary, it is because they are so distant that the celestial bodies attract him. The immensity of space draws him; he wants himself to be as wide as space, so that he can extend all over it.

One feels that it is not the process of *growth* which matters to him so much as the actual *extension*. He needs space in order to establish and maintain his position in it. *Position* in itself is the important thing, and for him it can never be eternal and lofty enough. To him the supreme principle is "the Order of the Universe". This he ranks above God and, if God tries to act contrary to it, he runs into diffi-culties. Of his own human body Schreber often speaks as though it were a celestial body and, as other people are engrossed with the man-agement of their family, so he with the management of the planetary system. He wants to be part of it and anchored there. The change-lessness of the constellations over thousands of years may have been what particularly attracted him to them: a place among them was a place for eternity.

This sense of personal place, or position, is of cardinal importance for the paranoiac: there is always an exalted position to defend and make secure. By the very nature of power, the same must be true of the ruler. His sense of his own position is in no way different from that of the paranoiac; he, if he can, surrounds himself with soldiers and shuts himself in fortresses; Schreber, who also feels threatened in many ways, holds fast to the stars. As we shall see, his world is in a state of turmoil. In order to explain the dangers which threaten him it is necessary to say something about the inhabitants of his world.

According to Schreber the human soul is contained in the *nerves* of the body. While man is alive he is both body and soul, but when he dies the nerves remain as the soul. God is never body, but only nerve, and kin therefore to the human soul, but immensely superior to it, for the number of God's nerves is infinite and they are eternal. They have the faculty of transforming themselves into rays, the rays of the sun and of the stars for example. God has pleasure in the world which he created, but as a rule does not interfere directly in its destiny. After the creation he withdrew from it and now abides mostly at a distance. God *must* not come too near men, for the nerves of living human beings have such a power of attraction for him that he would not be able to free himself from them again and so would endanger his own existence. He is thus always on his guard against the living and if it should happen that a particularly fervent prayer or an inspired poet tempts him to approach too close he rapidly with-draws again before it is too late.

"Regular contact between God and human souls took place only after death. There was no danger for God in approaching *corpses* to draw their nerves out of their bodies and up to himself and so awaken them to new heavenly life." But before human nerves could be raised to a state of blessedness they had to be "sifted and purified". Only pure human nerves were of use to God, because it was their destiny to be attached to him and ultimately to become part of him as "forecourts of heaven". A complicated process of purification was necessary, which even Schreber could not describe exactly. Souls completely cleansed by this process ascended to heaven and there gradually forgot who they had been on earth, though not all equally quickly. The souls of great men such as Goethe or Bismarck retained the knowledge of their identity for centuries perhaps, but none, not even the greatest, for ever. Rather, it was the ultimate destiny of all souls *to merge with other souls and become integrated into higher unities,* conscious of nothing except that they were parts of God ("forecourts of heaven").

The merging of all souls into a single crowd is ordained as the highest form of blessedness, recalling the many Christian representations of angels and saints thronging together like a cloud, or sometimes actually *as* a cloud, only careful inspection enabling one to distinguish the separate heads. This image is so familiar that we never reflect on its meaning. It means that blessedness consists not only in closeness to God, but also in the close togetherness of equals. The expression "forecourts of heaven" is an attempt to attribute even greater density to this crowd of blessed souls: they are actually integrated into "higher unities".

God has very little knowledge of living human beings. In the later parts of the *Memoirs* Schreber repeatedly reproaches God with his inability to understand the living human being and, in particular, to judge his thinking correctly. He speaks of God's blindness and lack of knowledge of human nature; he is only used to corpses and takes great care not to come too near the living. God's eternal love is basically only for creation as a whole. He is not a being of such absolute perfection as most religions attribute to him, otherwise he would not have allowed himself to be enticed into the conspiracy against innocent human beings which was the real cause of Schreber's illness. For the "miraculous structure of the Universe", as Schreber described it, has suddenly been rent. The crisis which has broken over the "realms of God" is intimately connected with Schreber's personal fate.

What is at issue is nothing less than a case of soul murder. Schreber had been ill once before and had been treated by Professor Flechsig, the Leipzig psychiatrist. After a year he had been dis-

438 CROWDS AND POWER

charged as cured and had been able to resume his work. At the time he had been most grateful to the psychiatrist, and his wife even more so. "She worshipped Professor Flechsig as the man who had restored her husband to her; for this reason she kept his portrait on her writing table for many years." Schreber then spent eight healthy, happy and busy years with his wife. During the whole of this period he often had occasion to see the picture of Flechsig on his wife's desk and it must clearly have occupied his mind very much without his being aware of it. For when he fell ill a second time and, as was natural (since he had been successful before), Flechsig was again approached, it became apparent that, in Schreber's mind, he had become a really dangerous figure.

Perhaps Schreber who, as a judge, had himself possessed a certain authority, resented having been in the psychiatrist's power for a whole year. He certainly hated him now, for having him in his power again. He became convinced that Flechsig was practising "soul murder", or "soul theft" on him. He says that the idea that it is possible to take possession of another person's soul is widespread and very old. In this way one secures the intellectual powers of the victim or prolongs one's own life at another soul's expense. Inspired by ambition and the lust for power, Flechsig was plotting with God and was trying to convince him that the soul of one Schreber was of no importance. He adds that there may perhaps have already been rivalry between the two families: a Flechsig may suddenly have felt that some member of the Schreber family had outstripped his own. He therefore entered into "a conspiracy with the elements of the realms of God", working towards excluding the Schrebers from those professions which would lead to closer relations with God, for example, the profession of nerve specialist. Since nerves were the actual substance of which God and all other souls consisted it was obvious how much power a nerve specialist would possess. The result of this was that no Schreber had become a psychiatrist, whilst a Flechsig had. The way to soul theft was open to the conspirators; Schreber was in the power of the murderers of his soul.

At this point one should perhaps stress the importance which plots and conspiracies have for the paranoiac. They are continually with him and anything even remotely resembling one is immediately seized on. The paranoiac feels *surrounded*; his chief enemy is never content to attack him single-handed, but always tries to rouse a spiteful *pack* to set on him at the suitable moment. At first the members of this pack keep hidden and may be anywhere and everywhere; or else they pretend to be harmless and innocent, as if they were not lying in wait for anything. But the piercing intellect of the paranoiac always unmasks them. He has only to stretch out his hand to drag forth a conspirator. The pack is always there, even if not actually baying at the moment; and its hostility is unchangeable. Once won over to the enemy, they remain his faithful hounds, and he can do what he wants with them. Even at a distance he keeps them in leash to his wickedness and can direct them as it suits him. By preference he selects them so that they can attack the victim from all sides and in greatly superior numbers.

Once the conspiracy against Schreber had come into being, what form did the actual attack on him take? What were the conspirators' aims and what means did they use to attain them? Their real aim, the most important though not the only one, was the destruction of Schreber's reason, and this they persisted in for many years. They wanted to turn him into an imbecile, to push the illness of his nerves to the point where he would appear permanently incurable. Could there be any prospect more terrible for a human being as highly gifted as he thought himself?

His illness began with torturing sleeplessness, for which nothing could be done. Schreber held that, right from the beginning, there was a definite intention to prevent his sleeping and thus to bring about his mental collapse. For this purpose large numbers of *rays* were directed against him. At first these originated from Professor Flechsig, but later on departed souls who had not yet completed their purification ("tested souls" as Schreber calls them) began to take an increasing interest in him and penetrate him as rays. God himself took part in this operation. All these rays *spoke* to him, but so that they could not be heard by other people. It was like a prayer which one repeats silently, not speaking the words aloud. But the painful difference was that whereas in prayer what one says depends on one's own will, these rays which were forced on him from outside went on and on with what *they* wanted to say.

"I could cite here the names of hundreds if not thousands who, as souls, trafficked with my nerves . . . All these souls talked at me as 'voices', each unaware of the presence of the others. The ensuing tumult in my head can readily be imagined . . .

"My nervousness increased all the time, and with it my power of attraction, so that an ever growing number of departed souls felt

drawn to me, to evaporate on my head or in my body. In a great
number of cases the process ended with the souls concerned leading
a brief existence on my head as so-called 'little men'—tiny figures
in human form but perhaps only a few millimetres high—before
they vanished completely . . . I was very often told the names of the
stars or constellations from which they had set out, or 'under which
they hung' . . . There were nights in which the souls, as 'little men',
finished by dripping down onto my head in hundreds if not thousands. I always warned them against approaching me because previous occurrences had made me continually aware of my nerves'
immensely increased power of attraction, but at first they found it
quite impossible to believe in such a menacing power of attraction.

"In soul-language I was called 'the seer of spirits', that is a man
who sees and is in contact with spirits or departed souls . . . Since the
world began there can hardly have been a case like mine in which
a human being entered into continual contact, not only with single
departed souls, but with the totality of all souls and with the very
Omnipotence of God."

It is obvious that all these phenomena which Schreber describes
have something to do with crowds. As far as the distant stars, space
is populated with the souls of the departed. All have their place
assigned them, on this or that familiar star. Suddenly, through his illness, Schreber becomes their centre. In spite of his warnings they
throng close, irresistibly attracted to him. One could say that he
gathers them round him as a crowd and since, as he insists, they are
the totality of all souls, they represent the largest crowd that can be
imagined. But they do not simply continue to stand round him, like
an assembled crowd, a people round its leader; they immediately and
instantaneously experience what to a people only happens gradually
and over the course of years: by contact with him they grow smaller
and smaller. As soon as they reach him they shrink rapidly until they
are only a few millimetres high. The true relationship between them
comes out very clearly here: the one a giant and the others tiny
creatures fussing around him. But that is not the end. The great man
swallows the midgets; they literally go inside him and disappear completely. His effect on them is annihilating. He attracts them and
gathers them round him, reduces them in size and ends by consum-
ing them. Everything that they were now accrues to his own body.
Not that they came intending to benefit him. Their purpose had
actually been hostile; originally they were sent to confuse his reason

and thus destroy him. But it was precisely this threat which gave him the strength to grow; and once he knows how to master them, he feels proud of his power of attraction.

At a first glance, Schreber, in his delusion, could be taken for a man of some earlier period, when belief in spirits was universal and the souls of the dead flitted like bats past the ears of the living. It is as though he were a shaman, one who knows the worlds of the spirits inside out, can communicate directly with them and make use of them for all kinds of human purposes; and he likes to be called a "seer of spirits". But the power of a shaman is not nearly as great as that of Schreber. It is true that the shaman does sometimes detain spirits within him, but they never dissolve there; they never lose their separate identity and it is part of the bargain that he always lets them go again. With Schreber, on the other hand, they vanish, disappearing as completely as if they had never existed in their own right. Disguised as one of the old conceptions of the universe which presupposed the existence of spirits, his delusion is in fact a precise model of *political* power, power which feeds on the crowd and derives its substance from it. An attempt at a conceptual analysis of power can only blur the clarity of Schreber's vision. This contains all the real elements of the situation: the strong and lasting attraction exercised over the individuals who are to form a crowd; the ambiguous attitude of these individuals; their subjection through being reduced in size; the way they are taken into the man who in his own person, in his *body*, represents political power; the fact that his greatness must continually *renew* itself in this way; and finally, a very important point not so far mentioned, the sense of catastrophe which is linked with it, of danger to the world order arising from its sudden and rapid increase and unexpected magnetism.

There is in the *Memoirs* abundant evidence of this sense of catastrophe. There is always a certain magnificence in Schreber's visions of the end of the world, as in the passage I want to quote now, which deals directly with his power of attracting souls. They drip down on him in crowds and thereby endanger the celestial bodies from which they originate. It appears that the stars are actually composed of souls, so that when they leave in large numbers to get to Schreber the whole universe is in danger of dissolution.

"From all sides came tidings of disaster: now that this or that star, or this or that constellation, had had to be abandoned; now that Venus had been 'flooded'; now that soon the entire solar system

would have to be 'uncoupled'; now that soon Cassiopeia—the whole
constellation—would have to be pulled together into a single sun;
that soon only the Pleiades might perhaps still be saved."

Apprehension about the continued existence of the celestial
bodies was, however, only one aspect of Schreber's feelings of impending catastrophe. Much more important was the supposition with
which his illness began. This did not refer to the souls of the departed, with whom, as we know, he was in constant communication,
but to his fellow-men. These did not exist any more: *the whole of
mankind had perished.* The few human figures he still saw, such as
his doctor, the attendants at the asylum, or the other patients, he took
for appearances: they were "fleeting makeshift men", fabricated
solely in order to confuse him. They came and went like shadows, or
pictures, and he naturally did not take them seriously. All real people
had perished; *he was the only man left alive.* Not only did he have
special visions which revealed this fact, but he was at all times firmly
convinced of it; he believed it for years. All his visions of the end of
the world were coloured by it.

He thought it possible that the whole of Flechsig's asylum, and
perhaps the city of Leipzig with it, had been "scooped up" and removed to some other celestial body. The voices which talked to him
sometimes asked whether Leipzig were still standing. In one of his
visions he was taken in a lift into the depths of the earth, thus re-
living all prehistoric and geological periods. In the upper regions
there were still forests of leaf-bearing trees. Lower down everything
became progressively darker and blacker. When he left the "lift" for
a time, he seemed to be wandering through a cemetery. He came to
the part where the inhabitants of Leipzig lay buried, and passed the
grave of his own wife. His wife, one should add, was alive at this
time and frequently visited him in the asylum.

Schreber pictured various different ways in which the destruction
of mankind might have come about. He thought of a decrease in the
heat of the sun, due to its moving further away from the earth and a
consequent general glaciation. He thought of an earthquake: he
received news that the great earthquake of 1755 in Lisbon had
occurred in connection with a seer of spirits, similar to himself. "I
envisaged the further possibility of news having spread that something like a magician—namely Professor Flechsig—had appeared in
the modern world, and that I myself, a figure known after all in
wider circles, had disappeared. This had spread terror and dismay

amongst men, destroying the foundations of religion and giving rise to universal nervousness and immorality. Epidemics had followed, devastating mankind. There was talk of leprosy and plague, two diseases scarcely known in Europe any more." He noticed signs of the plague on his own body. There were different varieties of plague; there was the blue, the brown, the white and the black plague.

But while everyone else was perishing from these terrible maladies, Schreber himself was cured by beneficent rays. For there was a distinction to be made between two kinds of rays, the "searing" and the "blessing" ones. The former were laden with the poison of corpses or other putrid matter and therefore carried a germ of disease into the body or wrought some other damage in it. The "blessing", or pure rays, healed this damage.

We do not get the impression that these disasters came upon mankind against Schreber's will. On the contrary, he appears to feel a certain satisfaction in the fact that the persecution he was exposed to by Professor Flechsig should have had such appalling consequences. The whole of mankind suffers and is exterminated because Schreber thinks there is someone who is against him. He alone is protected in the epidemics by the agency of the "blessing" rays.

Schreber is left as the sole survivor because this is what he himself wants. He wants to be the only man left alive, standing in an immense field of corpses; and he wants this field of corpses to contain all men but himself. It is not only as a paranoiac that he reveals himself here. To be the last man to remain alive is the deepest urge of every real seeker after power. Such a man sends others to their death; he diverts death on to them in order to be spared it himself. Not only is he totally indifferent to their deaths, but everything within him urges him to bring them about. He is especially likely to resort to this radical expedient of mass death when his dominion over the living is challenged. Once he feels himself threatened his passionate desire to see *everyone* lying dead before him can scarcely be mastered by his reason.

It may be objected that this "political" interpretation of Schreber is implausible; that his apocalyptic visions are inherently religious and that he claims no dominion over the living; that the power of a "seer of spirits" is essentially different from political power; and that, since his delusion starts from the idea that all men are dead, there is no justification for attributing to him any interest in worldly power.

The fallaciousness of this objection will soon become clear. We shall find in Schreber a political system of a disturbingly familiar kind. But before discussing that we ought to know something about his conception of divine rule.

It must be God himself, he says, "who determined the whole direction of the policy pursued against me". . . . "God would at all times have been able to annihilate any human being who inconvenienced him by sending him a fatal illness or striking him with lightning". . . . "As soon as his interests collide with those individual men, or groups of men, or perhaps even with the entire population of a planet, the instinct of self-preservation will be aroused in God, as in any other living being. Think of Sodom and Gomorrah! . . . It is quite inconceivable that God would deny any single human being his due share of Blessedness, for every addition to the 'forecourts of heaven' serves only to heighten his own power and to strengthen the bulwarks against the dangers which arise from his approaching mankind. As long as men acted in accordance with the Order of the Universe, no collision could occur between their interests and those of God. That such a collision of interests did none the less occur in my case was due to a conjunction of circumstances so far unique in the history of the world and, I hope, never to be repeated." He speaks of the "restoration of God's absolute rule in Heaven" and of a "sort of confederacy between Flechsig's soul and parts of God" directed against himself and bringing about "a change in the relationship of the parties which has remained essentially the same to this day". He mentions the "colossal powers on the side of God's omnipotence" and his own "hopeless resistance". He conjectures that "Professor Flechsig's authority as administrator of one of God's provinces must have reached as far as America". Flechsig also appeared to govern England. He mentions a Viennese nerve specialist "who seemed to be a sort of administrator of God's interests in another of God's provinces, namely the Slavonic parts of Austria". Between him and Professor Flechsig a struggle for supremacy had arisen.

These extracts, taken from many different parts of the *Memoirs,* give us a very distinct picture of God: he is a despot and nothing else. His realm contains provinces and factions. "God's interests", as they are bluntly and summarily designated, demand the increase of his power. This, and this only, is why he would not deny any human being the share of blessedness due to him; human beings who hinder him are done away with. It cannot be denied that this is a God who sits in the web of his policy like a spider. From this it is only a step to Schreber's own policy.

It should perhaps be mentioned at this point that Schreber grew up in the old Protestant tradition of Saxony and was therefore highly suspicious of Catholics and their proselytizing zeal. His first reference to the Germans is in connection with the victorious war against France of 1870–71.

He claimed to have been given fairly definite hints that the bitter winter of 1870–71 was a deliberate move on the part of God to turn the war in the Germans' favour. God also had a weakness for the language of the Germans. "While undergoing purification souls learnt the so-called 'basic language' spoken by God himself, a somewhat archaic but powerful German . . . This should not be taken to mean that Blessedness was reserved only for Germans. Nevertheless, in more recent times, probably since the Reformation and perhaps even since the Migration of Peoples, the Germans had been *God's Chosen People,* whose language he used by preference. In the course of history God's chosen people in this sense (meaning the most moral at a given time), had been successively the old Jews, the old Persians, the 'Greco-Romans' and, finally, the Germans."

The chosen people of the Germans was naturally threatened with dangers, first among which were the machinations of the Catholics. The reader will remember those hundreds if not thousands of names Schreber could have mentioned, all of souls who were in contact with his nerves and were continually talking to him. "Many of the bearers of these names had special interests in religion; a great many were Catholics who were expecting [from me] the advancement of Catholicism, in particular the Catholicizing of Saxony and Leipzig. Among these were the Priest S. in Leipzig, '14 Leipzig Catholics' (presumably a Catholic club), the Jesuit Father S. in Dresden, the Cardinals Rampolla, Galimberti and Casati, the Pope himself and finally numerous monks and nuns. On one occasion 240 Benedictine monks led by a Father moved as souls into my head to perish there." But there were other souls too, among them a Viennese nerve specialist, a baptized Slavophile Jew who wanted to make Germany Slavonic through Schreber and "at the same time wanted to set up there the rule of Judaism."

Schreber cites a complete cross-section of Catholicism. Not only are there simple believers who join ominous sounding clubs in Leipzig, but the whole Catholic hierarchy is represented. There is a Jesuit Father (conjuring up visions of intrigue and conspiracy) and, for the high dignitaries of the church, three Italian cardinals with euphonious names, and finally the Pope in person. Monks and nuns appear in large numbers; even in the building in which Schreber is living they swarm like vermin. In a vision from which I have not quoted he sees how the women's department of the University Nerve Clinic is being fitted up as a nunnery and, on another occasion, as a Catholic chapel. In the rooms under the roof of the asylum he sees Sisters of Mercy. But most striking of all is the procession of 240 Benedictine monks under the leadership of a Father. No form of self-expression is better suited to Catholicism than a procession. Here the close group of the monks acts as a crowd crystal for the totality of Catholic believers. The sight of a procession re-activates in the spectators their own latent belief and they suddenly feel a desire to join on behind it. Thus the procession tends to be increased by all those who see it pass; ideally it should be endless. By swallowing the procession he sees, Schreber symbolically does away with the whole of Catholicism.

In the agitated early period of his illness, which he called his holy time, one particular fortnight stands out by reason of the intensity of what he experienced then. This was the time of "the first Divine Judgement". "The first Divine Judgement" was a series of visions, continuous by day and night and all based, as he himself says, on one general idea. The core of this idea is essentially political, even though its urgency is messianic.

"The conflict between Professor Flechsig and myself had led to a crisis which endangered the existence of God's realms. This meant that the German people, particularly Protestant Germany, could no longer be left with the leadership as God's chosen people. They might even have to be excluded from the occupation of other globes (inhabited planets?) unless a champion for the German people came forward to prove their continued worthiness. Sometimes I myself was to be this champion, sometimes another person designated by me. At the insistence of the voices which talked to me in nerve-contact I named a number of outstanding men whom I considered fit for such a contest. Linked with the basic idea of the first Divine Judgement was the advance of Catholicism, Judaism and Slavism which I have mentioned before." He was also considerably influenced at this time by intimations he received of what he would be in future reincarnations. "Several successive roles were allotted to me ... 'a Jesuit novice in Osseg', a 'Burgomaster of Klattau', an 'Alsatian girl who had to defend her honour against a victorious French officer', and finally a 'Mongol Prince'. In all these predictions I believed I recognized a connection with the general picture resulting from my other visions.

My designation as a Jesuit novice in Osseg, a Burgomaster of Klattau and an Alsatian girl in the position specified above I took as prophecies that Protestantism either already had been, or shortly would be, worsted in the struggle with Catholicism, and the German people in the struggle with their Latin and Slav neighbours. The final prospect before me, that of becoming a Mongol Prince, seemed to me an indication that all the Aryan peoples had shown themselves unfitted to be pillars of God's realms and that a last refuge must now be found with non-Aryan peoples."

Schreber's "holy time" falls in the year 1894; he had a passion for exactness about time and place and gives precise dates for the period of "the first Divine Judgement." In 1900, six years later, when his delusion had become clarified and established, he started composing the *Memoirs,* using the shorthand notes he had made before. In 1904 they were published. As no-one today is likely to deny, his political system had within a few decades been accorded high honour: though in a rather cruder and less literate form it became the creed of a great nation, leading, under "a Mongol Prince", to the conquest of Europe and coming within a hair's breadth of the conquest of the world. Thus Schreber's claims were posthumously vindicated by his unwitting disciples. We are not likely to accord him the same recognition, but the amazing and incontrovertible likeness between the two systems may serve to justify the time we have devoted to this single case of paranoia; nor have we finished with it yet.

On some points Schreber was even further in advance of his century. The occupation of other inhabited planets is still only a possibility and no chosen people has as yet been worsted in the venture. But we have already seen the "later champion", not named by him, who experienced Catholics, Jews and Slavs as hostile crowds in the same personal manner as he did, hating them for their very existence and ascribing to them the marked urge to increase inherent in all crowds. No-one has a sharper eye for the attributes of the crowd than the paranoiac or the despot who—as will perhaps be more readily admitted now—are one and the same. But the only crowds which he (to indicate both with the same pronoun) is concerned with are those he wants to attack or to rule; these all have the same features.

It is worth noticing the future existence Schreber chooses for himself. Of the five he mentions only the first (which I omitted) has a nonpolitical character. Each of the three following ones is a focus of violent conflict. He insinuates himself among the Jesuits as a novice;

he becomes the burgomaster of a town in Bohemia where there was fighting between the Germans and the Slavs; and as an Alsatian girl he defends his honour against an officer of a victorious French army: this "honour" sounds suspiciously like the "racial honour" of his successor. Most significant of all, however, is his re-incarnation as a "Mongol Prince". He is slightly apologetic about this, as though he were ashamed of this "non-Aryan" existence, and seeks to justify it by the alleged failure of the Aryan people. Actually the Mongol prince he has in mind is none other than Genghis Khan. He is fascinated by the Mongols' pyramids of skulls. (The reader will remember his preoccupation with accumulations of corpses.) He approves of their straightforward method of dealing with enemies wholesale. The man who exterminates his enemies has none to fear and can gloat over their defenceless corpses. Of all these four re-incarnations envisaged by Schreber it was as the Mongol Prince that he was most successful.

There is one immediate conclusion to be drawn from this close examination of a paranoiac delusion, namely that in it religion and politics are inextricably intermingled; the Saviour of the World and the Ruler of the World are one and the same person. At the core of it all is the lust for power. Paranoia is an *illness of power* in the most literal sense of the words and exploration of this illness uncovers clues to the nature of power clearer and more complete than those which can be obtained in any other way. One should not allow oneself to be confused by the fact that, in a case such as Schreber's, the paranoiac never actually attained the monstrous position he hungered for. Others *have* attained it. Some of them have succeeded in covering the traces of their rise and keeping their perfected system secret. Others have been less fortunate or had too little time. Here, as in other things, success depends entirely on accidents. The attempt to reconstruct these accidents under the illusion that they are governed by laws calls itself history. For every great name in history a hundred others might have been substituted. There is never any dearth of men who are both talented and wicked. Nor can we deny that we all eat and that each of us has grown strong on the bodies of innumerable animals. Here each of us is a king in a field of corpses. A conscientious investigation of power must ignore success. We must look for its attributes and their perversions wherever they appear, and then compare them. A madman, helpless, outcast and despised, who drags out a twilight existence in some asylum, may, through the insights he procures us, prove more important than Hitler or Napoleon, illuminating for mankind its curse and its masters.

The Case of Schreber: II

THE AIM OF the conspiracy against Schreber was not only soul murder and the destruction of his reason. His enemies also wanted to do something else to him, which would make him almost equally contemptible: they proposed to change his body into that of a woman. As a woman he was to be "sexually abused and then simply 'left lying there', in other words, left to rot". The idea of his transformation into a woman occupied him continually during the years of his illness. He felt female nerves being sent into his body as rays and gradually gaining the upper hand.

At the beginning of his illness he tried to take his own life in many different ways in order to escape so terrible a degradation. Every time he took a bath he thought of drowning and he several times demanded poison. But his despair about his proposed transformation into a woman did not last indefinitely. A conviction gradually grew up in him that this would be the best way of guaranteeing the continued existence of mankind. As we know, he thought all human beings had perished in some terrible catastrophe and he was the only one left alive. If he were a woman he would be able to bring forth a new generation. The only possible father for his children was God, so he must win his love. To be united with God was a high honour; to change more and more into a woman for his sake, to dress up so as to attract him and to lure him with feminine wiles no longer seemed a disgrace and degradation to this bearded man, once chief judge of a court of appeal. In addition he thought it would foil Flechsig's plot; God's favour would be won; more and more strongly attracted by the beautiful woman Schreber, the Almighty would come to depend on him. By such means, however obnoxious, as he admits, they may appear to others, Schreber succeeded in "attaching God to his person", though it was not without resistance that the latter surrendered to this somewhat ignominious fate. Time and again God withdrew from Schreber, and he doubtless wanted to free himself completely. But Schreber's attraction had grown too strong.

References to this theme are to be found in many parts of the *Memoirs* and at first the reader may feel tempted to regard the idea of his transformation into a woman as the myth at the core of his delusional system. It is certainly the point which has attracted most attention, including a well-known attempt to find the origin of his particular illness, and of paranoia in general, in repressed homosexuality. There could scarcely, however, be a greater mistake. Paranoia may be occasioned by anything; the essence of each case is the *structure* of the delusional world and the way it is *peopled*. Processes of power always play a crucial part in it. Even with Schreber, where certain elements might seem to point to the interpretation I have mentioned, closer examination would cast considerable doubt on it. Even, however, if we were to take Schreber's homosexual disposition as proved, the particular use he makes of it in his system would be much more important than the fact itself. For Schreber the central point of his system was the attack on his reason. Everything he thought and did was a defence against this attack. It was in order to disarm God that he wanted to transform himself into a woman; to become a woman for his sake was to flatter him and submit to him. Just as others kneel before him, Schreber offered himself for God's enjoyment. To win him over to his side and to make sure of him, he lured him to approach and then used every means to keep him there.

"The predicament in question is not only one which has no parallel in human experience, but also one which was never even anticipated in the Order of the Universe. Who in such a situation would want to hazard conjectures about the future? Of one thing only am I certain, namely that God will never succeed in his purpose of destroying my reason. I have been absolutely clear on this point for years, and it removes the chief danger which seemed to threaten me in the first year of my illness."

This statement appears in the last chapter of the *Memoirs*. In writing them Schreber seems largely to have regained his peace of mind. That he had managed to finish them and that those who read them in manuscript were impressed by them finally restored his faith in his reason. All that remained for him to do was to mount a counter-attack by having his book published. By doing so he would make it accessible to the general public and so be able, as he certainly wished, to convert it to his faith.

How was the attack on Schreber's reason actually prosecuted? We know that he was beset by innumerable rays, all talking at him. But which of his intellectual faculties and defences were they trying to destroy? What did they say when they spoke, what was the precise object of their attack? It is worth going into this more closely. Schreber defended himself against his enemies with the utmost tenacity. His description of them and of his defence is as exhaustive as one could wish. We must take it out of the context of his self-created world, his "delusion", as we habitually call such phenomena, and translate it into our own more ordinary language. Inevitably some of its unique quality will be lost in the process.

The first thing one should mention is his "compulsive thinking"— to use his own term. Only when he talked aloud was there "peace in his head". Then everything else became deathly quiet and he had the impression that he moved among walking corpses. All the people around him, attendants and fellow-patients, seemed to have lost the ability to speak even a single word. As soon as he himself became silent, the voices returned and forced him back to his endless thinking.

Their aim in this was to prevent him sleeping or resting. They talked to him incessantly and it was impossible not to hear them, or to ignore them. He was at their mercy and forced to pay close attention to everything they said. The voices had different methods, which they used in turn. A favourite one was to put a direct question to him: "What are you thinking of now?" He did not want to answer these questions, but, if he kept silent, they would tell him what he should reply, saying for instance, "You should be thinking about the Order of the Universe". This seemed to him to be a system of deliberate "thought-falsification". Not only did the voices question him in an inquisitorial manner, but they also wanted to dictate his thoughts. Even the questions with which they tried to penetrate his secret thoughts aroused his opposition, and still more the answers dictated to him. Both questions and commands were an infringement of his personal freedom. Both are familiar means to power and he, as a judge, had himself made frequent use of them.

The ways in which Schreber was tried were varied and inventive. First he was interrogated; then various thoughts were dictated to him; then, from his own words and sentences, a further catechism was constructed. His every thought was controlled; not one was allowed to pass unnoticed; every word he used was examined to determine exactly what it meant to him. His lack of privacy in relation to the voices was complete; everything was searched, everything brought into the light. He was the objective of a power which insisted on being omniscient. But though he had to submit to all this, he never really surrendered. One of his defences was to rehearse his own knowledge. He learned poems by heart to prove to himself how well his memory functioned, counted aloud in French and repeated the names of all the "Russian Governments" and "French Departments".

By the preservation of his reason Schreber chiefly meant the safe-guarding of everything he had stored up in his memory; the thing most important to him was the safety of *words*. To him all sounds were voices; the universe was full of words: railways, birds and paddle-steamers *spoke*. When he was not uttering words himself they immediately came from others. *Between* words there was nothing. The peace he spoke of and longed for would have been a *freedom from words*. But this was not to be found. Whatever happened to him was simultaneously communicated to him in words. The harmful as well as the beneficent rays were all endowed with speech, and were compelled to use it, as was he himself. "Do not forget that rays must speak!" It is impossible to overrate the importance of words for the paranoiac. They are everywhere, like vermin, always on the alert. They unite to form a world order which leaves nothing outside itself. Perhaps the most marked trend in paranoia is that towards a complete seizing of the world through words, as though language were a fist and the world lay in it.

It is a fist which never opens again. But how does it come to clench? Here one should point out that the paranoiac exhibits a mania for finding causal relations, which finally becomes an end in itself. Nothing that happens to him is chance or coincidence; there is always a reason, which can be found if searched for. Everything unknown can be traced back to something known. Every strange object which approaches can be unmasked and revealed as something one already possesses. Every fresh mask hides something familiar and all one needs is the courage to see through the mask and tear it off boldly. Finding "reasons" becomes a passion and is let loose on everything. Schreber is completely lucid about this aspect of his compulsive thinking. Whilst he complains bitterly about all the other operations he describes, he sees this mania as a kind of recompense for the wrong done him. Among the unfinished sentences "thrown into his nerves" conjunctions and adverbial phrases expressing causal relations figure prominently: "Why", "Why, since...", "Why, since I...". These, like everything else he hears, he has to complete and so they, too, act on him as compulsions. "But they forced me to ponder many things which most human beings carelessly pass over, and thus contributed to deepening my thought." Thus Schreber on the whole approves of this mania for causality. Indeed it gives him positive pleasure and he finds plausible arguments to justify it. He leaves the original act of creation to God, but everything else to do with the world is drawn into his private net of reasons and made his own.

But the mania is not always so reasonable. Schreber meets a man he has often seen and immediately recognizes him as a Mr. Schneider. Mr. Schneider is a man who does not dissemble, but innocently appears as the person he is generally supposed to be. But the simple process of recognition does not satisfy Schreber. He wants there to be something *behind* "Mr. Schneider" and cannot reconcile himself to the idea that there is nothing. Unmasking has become a habit with him and where there is no-one and nothing to practise it on he feels lost. The process of unmasking is of fundamental importance for the paranoiac, and not only for him, for from it derives the mania for identifying causes; and originally all causes were sought for in *persons*. The process of unmasking has already been mentioned several times in this book and this seems the best place to analyse it in more detail.

We have all on occasion, in a street perhaps, suddenly picked out from among the faces of strangers one face that seems familiar. Very often we turn out to have been wrong; the presumed acquaintance approaches, or we go up to him, and it is someone we have never seen before. No–one gives the mistake much thought. There will have been some incidental resemblance in his walk, his hair or the way he holds his head, which explains it. But there are times when such confusions multiply. We seem to see one particular person everywhere. He stands in front of the restaurant we are about to enter, or at a busy street corner; he will turn up several times in the course of a single day. It is, of course, someone who is on our mind, someone we love or, more often perhaps, hate. We may know that he has moved to another town, or gone abroad, but we think, none the less, that we see him; and we make the mistake repeatedly; we persist in it. It is clear that we *want* to find this one man behind all the faces we see. We think of the others as deceptions, hiding reality. There can be many faces which lend themselves to this process and behind them all we suspect the one that matters to us. There is an urgency in it; a hundred faces are stripped off like masks in order that the one face may appear behind them. If we were asked the main difference between this one and the hundred others we should have to say: the hundred are strange to us, the one is known. It looks as though we could only acknowledge the face which is familiar. But it has hidden itself and we have to search for it among strangers.

With the paranoiac this process is concentrated and heightened. He suffers from the atrophy of transformation; it begins in himself, in his own person, and is most marked there, but gradually it affects the whole world. Even things which are really different he tends to see as the same. In the most varied figures he finds the same enemy. Whenever he tears off a mask, there is that enemy, hiding behind it. For the sake of the unmasking itself, everything *becomes* a mask for him. But he is not deceived; he sees through everything; to him the many are one.

As the rigidity of his system increases the world grows poorer and poorer in real figures, until only those remain who have a part to play in his delusion. He can get to the bottom of everything and he ends by explaining everything away. Finally he is left only with himself and what he rules. What happens here is the exact opposite of the process of transformation. In unmasking, some creature is driven in on itself, limited to a single position and prescribed one particular attitude, which is then taken to be its only genuine one. One starts as a spectator, watching people transform themselves into different people. One may go on for some time like this, watching the masquerade though without approving of it or enjoying it, but then suddenly one shouts "stop" and the whole thing is brought to a halt. "Masks off" is the next command and there the players stand, each as his real self, never to change again. The play is over. The masks have been revealed for what they are. This process of *undoing* transformations is seldom found in a pure form. Generally it is coloured by the expectation of finding an enemy. The paranoiac assumes that the masks were intended to deceive; that the transformations had a purpose; that the most important thing to the actors was concealment and what they changed into or were meant to represent was of secondary importance to them, their main concern being to make themselves unrecognizable. They are felt as threatening and thus the response to them, the tearing down of the masks, is harsh and spiteful and, in the paranoiac, can be so impressive in its violence that one can easily overlook the transformations which aroused it.

On this point Schreber's *Memoirs* take us very close to the heart of the matter. He remembers the time at the beginning of his illness when everything within him was still in a state of flux. During the first year, in his "holy time", he spent a week or two in a small private asylum which his voices called "The Devil's Kitchen". This, he says, was the time of the "maddest miracle-mischief". His experience of transformation and unmasking during this period, long before his delusions grew clear and rigid, is a perfect illustration of my argument.

"I usually spent the day in the Common Room where there was a constant coming and going of other supposed patients. There seemed to be a special attendant appointed to supervise me, whom, because of a possibly accidental likeness, I thought I recognized as the officer of the High Court who used to bring official papers to my house during the six weeks of my professional activity in Dresden . . . This 'officer of the High Court' had a habit of wearing my clothes now and again. From time to time, generally in the evening, there appeared a gentleman who was supposed to be the Medical Director of the Institution. He, again because of a certain resemblance, reminded me of the Dr O. I had consulted in Dresden . . . I only once went for a walk in the garden of the Institution. On that occasion I saw several ladies, among them Mrs W., the wife of Pastor W. from Fr., and my own mother, as well as several gentlemen, including K., a High Court Judge from Dresden—though now he had a misshapen, enlarged head . . . I could understand such likenesses occurring in two or three cases, but not the fact that *almost all the patients in the Institution*, that is to say at least several dozen people, looked like persons who had been more or less close to me during my life."

As patients he saw "only outlandish figures, among them sooty ruffians in linen overalls . . . One after the other they came noiselessly into the Common Room and, equally noiselessly, went away again, apparently without taking any notice of each other. I repeatedly observed that, during their time in the Common Room, some of them *changed heads,* that is to say, without leaving the room and whilst I was watching them, they suddenly ran around with a different head."

"The number of patients I saw in the 'pen' "—Schreber's name for the courtyard where they went for air—"and in the Common Room, sometimes simultaneously, sometimes consecutively, was, as far as I could judge, out of all proportion to the size of the building. I was, and still am, convinced that it was impossible for all the forty to fifty people who were driven into the pen at the same time as myself, and who pressed back towards the door of the house on the signal for return, to have found sleeping accommodation there for the night . . . Most of the time the ground floor *swarmed* with human shapes."

Among the shapes he remembers as being in the pen, he mentions a cousin of his wife, "who had shot himself as early as 1887"; and "B., the senior Public Prosecutor, who always adopted a bowed, devout posture as though praying and remained motionless like that". Other people he recognized were a Privy Councillor, a Chief Judge of a Court of Appeal, another High Court Judge, a lawyer from Leipzig who had been a friend of his youth, his nephew Fritz and a casual summer acquaintance from Warnemünde." Once he noticed from the window his father-in-law in the drive leading to the Asylum.

"Another thing that happened repeatedly was that I saw a whole group of people(4-5), and once even some ladies, pass through the Common Room and go into the corner rooms, where they must have vanished. At these times I repeatedly heard the peculiar death-rattle connected with the dissolution of the 'fleeting makeshift men'."

"It was not only human forms which were bewitched, but also inanimate objects. However sceptical I try to be now when examining my recollections, I cannot expunge certain impressions from my memory: articles of clothing on the bodies of human beings were *transformed* under my eyes; similarly the food on my plate during meals (for instance pork into veal or vice versa)."

There are several striking things in this account. Schreber sees more people than there can possibly be room for, and they are all driven together into a pen. In common with them he feels (as the word "pen" shows) degraded into an animal. This is the nearest he ever comes to a crowd experience. But even in the "pen" he, of course, never becomes completely merged with the other patients. He watches the play of transformations closely, critically indeed, but without actual hostility. Even food and clothes undergo transformation. What occupies him most, however, are his acts of *recognition*. Everyone turns out to be someone he used to know well; he takes care that there shall be no real strangers there. But his unmaskings are as yet relatively good-tempered; the only person he speaks of with hatred (in a passage not quoted here) is the senior attendant. He recognizes a large number of very different people; his "system" has not yet become tight and exclusive. Instead of taking off their masks people simply change heads—the grandest and most amusing way of unmasking which can be imagined.

But only rarely were Schreber's experiences of this entertaining and liberating kind. During his "holy time" he repeatedly had an entirely different kind of vision and this, I think, leads us directly into the prototypal situation of paranoia.

The paranoiac feels surrounded by a pack of enemies who are all after him. This is his basic experience. It is most clearly expressed in visions of *eyes*; he sees eyes everywhere and all round him; they are interested only in him and their interest is menacing in the extreme. The creatures to whom the eyes belong intend to take their revenge on him. For a long time he has made them suffer and has gone un-punished; if they are animals they are relentlessly hunted and, threat-ened with extermination, have now suddenly risen against him. This, the prototypal situation of paranoia, is compellingly portrayed in many people's legends about their great hunters.

But the animals do not always keep the shape in which man knows them as prey. They change into more dangerous creatures which he has always feared, and when they press towards him, fill his room and occupy his bed, his terror becomes overwhelming. Schreber at night was beset by bears.

At this period he frequently got out of bed and sat on the floor of his room, clad only in a shirt. His hands, which he pressed firmly on the floor behind his back, were sometimes perceptibly lifted up by bear-like shapes—*black bears;* other "black bears", both greater and smaller, sat round him with glowing eyes; his bedclothes became "white bears". At times, whilst he was still awake, he saw cats with glowing eyes in the trees of the asylum garden.

But these *animal* packs were not the only ones. Schreber's arch-enemy, the psychiatrist Flechsig, had a particularly treacherous and dangerous habit of forming *celestial* packs to attack him. This was done by a process which Schreber called the *partition of souls.* He maintained that Flechsig's soul split, in order that the whole heav-enly vault might be occupied by "soul-parts" and the divine rays meet resistance on all sides; there were nerves strung out all over it, con-stituting a mechanical obstacle to the divine rays which it was impos-sible to surmount. They were like a besieged fortress protected by walls and moats against the assault of the enemy. This was why Flechsig's soul had split into a great number of "soul-parts". (For some time there were between forty and sixty, amongst them many tiny ones.)

It seems that other "tested souls", taking Flechsig as a model, then began to split too. The parts became more and more numerous and led, as is the nature of packs, a life of assaults and ambushes. A large proportion of them were occupied almost entirely with "circumven-tory movements", manoeuvres whose purpose was to attack the inno-cently approaching divine rays from behind and so force them to surrender. Most of these "tested soul-parts" eventually became a nuis-ance even to God's Omnipotence. One day, when Schreber had suc-ceeded in attracting a considerable number of them to himself, God's Omnipotence staged a raid on them and destroyed them all.

There may have been a connection in Schreber's mind between this "partition of souls" and the multiplication of cells through division, which, of course, he knew about. The employment as celestial packs of the large numbers originating in this way is one of the most characteristic conceptions of his delusion and it is impossible to find a clearer expression of the importance of *hostile packs* for the structure of paranoia.

The complicated and ambiguous nature of Schreber's relationship with God and with the "soul-policy" whose victim he felt himself to be did not prevent him from experiencing God's omnipotence as *splendour,* from outside, as it were, and as a whole. But in all the years of his illness he only had this experience once, during a few consecutive days and nights; and he was entirely aware of its preciousness and rarity.

Once only, in one single night, did God manifest himself. "As I lay wide awake in bed the shining image of his rays became visible to my spiritual eye. Simultaneously I heard his voice. It was not a soft whisper, but a mighty bass which resounded as though directly outside my bedroom windows."

On the following day he saw God with his "bodily eye". It was the sun, although not the sun in its usual appearance, but surrounded by a silver sea of rays which covered a sixth or eighth part of the sky. The sight was of such overwhelming splendour and magnificence that he did not dare look at it continuously, but tried to avert his gaze from the phenomenon. That radiant sun *spoke* to him.

He experienced this radiance not only as coming from God, but sometimes as coming also from himself—which was not surprising considering his importance and his close connection with God. "Owing to the massive confluence of rays my head was frequently encircled by a shimmer of light, similar to the halo of Christ in pictures, but incomparably richer and brighter: the so called 'crown of rays'."

But Schreber elsewhere describes the sacred aspect of power even more impressively. His experience of it reached its culmination in what he calls his period of *immobility*.

During this period his outward life was extremely monotonous. Apart from daily morning and afternoon walks in the garden, he sat motionless the whole day at his table, never even moving to look out of the window. Even in the garden he preferred to remain seated in one place the whole time. This absolute passivity he considered a kind of religious duty.

The idea was induced by the voices which spoke to him. Over and over again they repeated "Not the slightest movement!" Schreber explained this demand by the fact that God did not know how to treat a living man, being accustomed to dealing only with corpses—hence the monstrous demand that Schreber should behave continuously as though he himself were a corpse.

"I considered this immobility a duty incumbent on me both in the interests of self-preservation and towards God, to free him from the quandary he had got into owing to the 'tested souls'. I had reached the conclusion that the loss of rays would be greater if I moved about much. Being at that time still filled with holy awe towards the divine rays, and being also uncertain whether eternity really existed, or whether the rays might not suddenly come to an end, I considered it my duty to do whatever I could to prevent their being wasted in any way." He added that it was much easier to draw the "tested souls" down and force them to spend themselves in his body if he kept completely still. Only in this way could God's absolute rule in Heaven be restored. He had therefore made the incredible sacrifice of desisting from every movement for weeks and months. Since the arrival of "tested souls" was mostly to be expected during sleep, he did not even dare to change his position in bed at night.

This self-petrifaction lasting for months is among the most extraordinary things that Schreber recounts. His reason for it is twofold: it is both for God and for himself. That he, for the sake of God, should have kept still as a corpse sounds even odder to our modern European ears than it actually is. This is mainly because of our puritanical attitude to a corpse. Our customs require it to be removed quickly; we do not pay much attention to it in itself and, though we know how soon it will decay, we very seldom do anything to prevent this. We dress it up a little, and may put it on show for a short time, but make subsequent access to it impossible. Whatever the pomp of a funeral, the corpse itself does not appear at all; the funeral is the feast of its concealment and suppression. To understand Schreber we must think of the mummies of the Egyptians, in whom the personality of the corpse was conserved, cherished and admired. It was not really as a corpse that Schreber sought for months to behave for love of God, but as a mummy. In this case the word he uses is not really accurate.

His second motive for remaining motionless was dread of wasting the divine rays. This dread he shared with the many widely separate civilizations which have evolved a conception of power as something sacred. He experiences himself as a vessel in which the divine essence slowly collects. The smallest movement could lead to his spilling some of it and therefore he must not move at all. Here the man who holds power holds it in the most literal sense and also holds onto it, because he feels, either that it is an actual substance which can be exhausted by use, or because a higher authority expects this parsimony from him as an act of veneration. He slowly petrifies in the posture which seems to him most likely to conserve his precious substance; any change may be dangerous and fills him with anxiety. Only by conscientious avoidance of all movement can it be safeguarded. In some cases these postures of conservation, by virtue of their sameness throughout centuries, have come to determine the shape of society. The core of the political structure of many peoples is the rigid and meticulously ordered behaviour of one individual.

Schreber, also, makes provision for "a people", though he is not their king, but rather their "National Saint". He describes how an attempt was actually made on a distant star to create a new human world out of "the Schreber spirit". These new human beings were of much smaller stature than earthly men. He was told that they had achieved a fairly high level of culture and kept small cattle proportionate to their own size. He was also told that as their 'National Saint' he had become an object of veneration, as if his physical posture were of some significance for their faith.

Here we see very clearly how a particular posture can become significant. These human beings are not only created out of Schreber's substance, but their religion depends on his posture.

It was not only Schreber's reason which, during his illness, was exposed to every refinement of attack. His body was interfered with too, and in ways that beggar description. Scarcely any of it was spared. The rays overlooked nothing, but dealth with every part in turn. The effects of their interference were so sudden and unexpected that he could only regard them as "miracles".

First of all there were the manifestations of his coming transformation into a woman. This he had accepted and ceased to resist. But the other things which happened to him were almost unbelievable. A lung worm was sent into his lungs. His ribs were temporarily smashed. In place of his healthy natural stomach the Viennese nerve specialist mentioned above inserted a very inferior "Jew's stomach". Altogether the vicissitudes of his stomach were amazing. Frequently he had to exist without one and would tell the attendant that he could not eat because he had no stomach. If he ate in spite of this the food simply poured into the abdominal cavity and thence into the thighs. He became used to this state of affairs, however, and continued to eat unperturbed without a stomach. His gullet and intestines were often lacerated or made to vanish and more than once he swallowed part of his larynx.

"Little men" were planted in his feet to pump out his spinal cord; when he walked in the garden it issued from his mouth as little clouds. He frequently had the sensation that his whole skull had become thinner. When he played the piano or wrote, attempts were made to paralyze his fingers. Some souls took the form of tiny human figures, a few millimetres high, and played havoc with his body, both inside and outside. Some of these busied themselves with opening and shutting his eyes, taking up their positions in his eyebrows and from there pulling the eyelids up and down as they pleased with fine filaments like cobwebs. Almost always there were large numbers of little men assembled on his head. They literally walked about on it, nosing around to see if there was any fresh damage. They even shared his meals, helping themselves to a portion, though naturally only a tiny one, of whatever he ate.

He suffered considerable pain from caries in the region of the heel and the coccyx. This was intended to make walking, standing, sitting and lying equally impossible for him. He was not allowed to remain for long in any one position or at any one occupation. If he walked about attempts were made to force him to lie down and if he lay down to chase him from his bed again. "The rays did not seem to understand that an actual, existing human being *must be some-where*".

At this point one should notice one thing which all these phenomena have in common: they all have to do with the *penetration* of his body. The principle of the impenetrability of matter no longer applies. Just as he himself wants to extend and penetrate everywhere, even right through the earth, so, in the same way, everything penetrates through him and plays tricks *in* him as well as on him. He often speaks of himself as though he were a celestial body, but he is not even sure of his ordinary human body. The period of his extension, the very time in which he was asserting his claims, seems also to have been the period of his penetrability. For him *greatness* and *persecution* are intimately connected and both are expressed through his body.

Since, however, he went on living in spite of all the assaults on him, he came to the conclusion that these same rays also *healed* him. They soaked up all the impure matter in his body, which was why he could afford to eat, although he had no stomach. The rays planted the germs of diseases in him, but also removed them again.

Thus one cannot help suspecting that the real purpose of the attacks on Schreber's body was to prove his invulnerability; they were meant to show him how much he could overcome. The more he was injured and shaken, the more secure he ultimately became.

He began to doubt whether he was mortal at all. What were the strongest poisons compared with the injuries he had surmounted? If he were to fall into water and drown, his circulation and the action of his heart would be re-started and he would revive. If he put a bullet through his head, the inner organs and bones it destroyed would be restored. After all, had he not lived for a long time deprived of various vital organs which had then all grown again? Nor could any common disease endanger him. After much pain and suffering and many doubts the violence of his craving for invulnerability had resulted in his acquiring it.

I have already shown how the craving for invulnerability and the passion for survival merge into each other. In this, too, the paranoiac is the exact image of the ruler. The only difference between them lies in their position in the world. In their inner structure they are identical. One might even think the paranoiac the more impressive of the two because he is sufficient unto himself and cannot be shaken by failure. The opinion of the world is nothing to him. It is his delusion set against the whole of mankind.

"Everything that happens", says Schreber, "is in relation to me. I became for God *the* human being, or the one human being to whom everything that happens must be related and who therefore, from his own standpoint too, must relate all things to himself."

The idea that all other human beings had perished dominated him for years and this of course meant that he thought of himself as being the only one. Gradually, however, this idea was superseded by something less extreme: from being the only man alive he became the only one who mattered.

It is difficult to resist the suspicion that behind paranoia, as behind all power, lies the same profound urge: the desire to get other men out of the way so as to be the only one; or, in the milder, and indeed often admitted, form, to get others to help him *become* the only one.

EPILOGUE

The End of the Survivor

AFTER THIS DETAILED study of a paranoiac delusion which found only one adherent, namely its originator, it is time to consider what we have learnt about power in general. For every individual case, however valuable the clues it provides, arouses the same doubt in us. The more we learn about it the more conscious we become of its uniqueness, so that we suddenly catch ourselves hoping that it is only in *this* case that things are as they are and that in others, therefore, they may be different. This is particularly true in the case of the insane. Here our unshakeable arrogance clings to the inefficacy of their ideas. Even if it were possible to prove that every idea in the head of a Schreber were identical with those held by some dreaded ruler, we should still continue to hope that somehow, somewhere, there must be a fundamental difference between the two. Respect for the "great" of the world is not easily abandoned, and man's need to worship is limitless.

Fortunately, we have not had to confine ourselves to a single Schreber. Some, indeed, may think that too much ground has been covered in this enquiry, even though some points have only been touched on and others, which may very well be important, not mentioned at all. These omissions I hope to supply later, but none the less the reader cannot be blamed for wanting to know *now* what he can regard as established.

We can start by saying that it is clear which of the four different types of pack dominate our time. The power of the great religions of lament is declining. They have become overgrown and stifled by *increase*. In modern industrial production the ancient substance of the increase pack has undergone such a colossal expansion that, compared with it, all the other elements of life seem to be on the wane. Production happens here, in this life. It grows and proliferates all the time and with ever-increasing speed, so that we are left with no moment for reflection. Terrible wars have not halted it and, whatever the nature of the various opposing camps, it is rampant in all of them. If there is now one faith, it is faith in production, the modern frenzy of increase; and all the peoples of the world are succumbing to it one after the other.

One of the consequences of this increase in production is that more

and more people are wanted. The more goods we produce, the more
consumers we need. The point of business is the winning of as many
customers as possible; and ideally everyone. In this respect it resèmbles,
if only superficially, those universal religions which lay claim to every
single soul. It looks forward to an equality of willing and solvent
buyers. But even that would not really be enough, for all potential
customers might have been induced to buy and still production would
seek to increase. Thus what it really wants is more *men*. Through the
multiplication of goods it finds its way back to the original sense of
increase, the increase of man himself.

Production cannot but be peaceful. War and destruction mean
decrease and thus, by definition, harm it. Here capitalism and socialism
are at one, twin rivals in the same faith. For both of them production
is the apple of their eye and their main concern. Their very rivalry has
contributed to the ferocity of advance. They are becoming more and
more similar and in each there is a perceptible growth of respect for
the other, though confined almost exclusively to success in production.
It is no longer true that they want to destroy each other. What they
want is to *surpass* each other.

There exist today several very large centres of increase, which are
all both highly efficient and rapidly growing. They are distributed
between different languages and cultures; none of them is strong
enough to monopolize power and none of them dare stand alone
against a combination of any number of the others. There is a clear
trend towards the formation of enormous double crowds, named after
whole quarters of the globe—East and West. These contain so much
within themselves that there is less and less remaining outside them; and
what there is seems powerless. The rigidity of these opposed double
crowds, the fascination each has for the other, the fact that they are
both armed to the teeth and rivals for the moon, have awakened in
the world an apocalyptic fear: war between them could be the end of
mankind. But it is now apparent that the trend towards increase has
become so strong that it takes precedence over that towards war.
War is now nothing but a nuisance. As a means to rapid increase it
is played out. The Germany of National Socialism was the scene of its
final eruption in its primitive form. One can safely assume that never
again will war be waged for this purpose.

Today countries are more anxious to protect their productivity
than their people. Nothing appears more justified or more certain of
general approbation. Even in this century there are going to be more
goods produced than men can use. War can be replaced by other

systems of double crowds. We have learned in parliaments that it is possible to eliminate death from the activities of double crowds and a similar peaceful and regular rotation of power could be established between nations. In ancient Rome we already have an example of how, to a considerable extent, sport can replace war as a crowd phenomenon. It is on the point of regaining the same importance today, but this time on a worldwide scale. War is certainly dying and its end could be predicted as imminent, but for the fact that we still have to reckon with the *survivor*.

What, meanwhile, remains of the religions of lament? In the blind and contrary extremes of destruction and production which have so far characterized the century the religions of lament, in so far as they still exist in an organized form, present a picture of utter helplessness. Reluctantly or willingly, though with occasional dissentients, they give their blessing to whatever happens.

Their legacy is, nevertheless, greater than might be supposed. The image of him whose death Christians have lamented for nearly two thousand years has become part of the consciousness of mankind. He is the dying man and the man who ought not to die. With the increasing secularization of the world his divinity has become less important, but he remains as an individual, suffering and dying. The centuries of his divinity have endowed the *man* with a kind of earthly immortality. They have strengthened him and everyone who sees himself in him. There is no-one who suffers persecution, for whatever reason, who does not in part of his mind see himself as Christ. Mortal enemies, even when both are fighting for an evil and inhuman cause, experience the same feeling as soon as things go badly with them. The image of the sufferer at the point of death passes from one to the other according to who is winning or losing and the one who in the end proves weaker can see himself as the better. But even one too weak ever to have acquired a real enemy has a claim to the image. He may die for nothing at all, but the dying itself makes him significant. Christ lends him his lament. In the midst of all our frenzy of increase, which includes men too, the value of the individual has become not less, but more. The events of our times appear to have proved the opposite, but even they have not really altered man's image of himself. The value that has been put on his soul has helped man to the assurance of his earthly value. He finds his desire for indestructibility justified. Each feels himself a worthy object of lament; each is stubbornly convinced that he ought not to die. Here the legacy of Christianity, and, in a rather different way, of Buddhism, is inexhaustible.

What has radically changed in our time, however, is the situation of the survivor. Few readers can have finished the chapters on the survivor without some feeling of disgust. But it was my intention to hunt him out in all his hiding-places and show him for what he is and always has been. He has been glorified as a hero and obeyed as a ruler, but fundamentally he is always the same. His most fantastic triumphs have taken place in our own time, among people who set great store by the idea of humanity. He is not yet extinct, nor ever will be until we have the strength to see him clearly, whatever disguise he assumes and whatever his halo of glory. The survivor is mankind's worst evil, its curse and perhaps its doom. Is it possible for us to escape him, even now at this last moment?

In the world today his activities have become so terrifying that we scarcely dare look at them: a single individual can easily destroy a good part of mankind. To bring this about he can use technical means he does not understand; he can himself remain completely hidden; and he does not even have to run any personal risk in the process. The contrast between his singleness and the numbers of those he can destroy is so great that we can no longer find a meaningful image to express it. One man today has the possibility of surviving at a single stroke more human beings than could generations of his predecessors together. The precepts of earlier rulers are there to be studied and it is not difficult to learn from them. Rulers profit from all our discoveries, as though it were expressly for them that they had been made. Today the stakes are immensely higher: there are many more people and they are all much closer together. The means have increased a thousandfold, but the victims, if not as submissive, are fundamentally as defenceless as ever.

All the terror of a supernatural power which comes to punish and destroy mankind has now attached itself to the idea of the "bomb"; and this is something an individual can manipulate. It lies in his hands. An earthly ruler can now unleash destruction surpassing all the plagues with which God visited the Egyptians. Man has stolen his own God. He has seized him and taken for himself his armoury of doom and terror.

The most audacious dreams of those earlier rulers in whom the desire to survive had become a passion and a vice, seem meagre today. Seen in retrospect, history appears innocent and almost comfortable. Everything lasted for so long then and in an unexplored world there was so little to be destroyed. Today there is only a moment between decision and effect, and, measured by our potentialities, Genghis Khan, Tamerlane and Hitler seem pitiful amateurs.

Whether there is any way of dealing with the survivor, who has grown to such monstrous stature, is the most important question today; one is tempted to say that it is the only one. The fragmentation and fluidity of modern life blind us to the simplicity and urgency of this one fundamental issue. Hitherto the only answer to man's passionate desire for survival has been a creative solitude which earns immortality for itself; and this, by definition, can be the solution only for a few.

To set against this growing danger which we all feel in our bones, there is one other new fact which should be remembered. Today the survivor is himself afraid. He has always been afraid, but with his vast new potentialities his fear has grown too, until it is almost unendurable. His triumph, when it comes, may last only for hours or minutes. For nowhere in the world is safe, even for him. There is nowhere the new weapons cannot reach, including whatever refuge he may make himself. His greatness and his invulnerability have become incompatible. He has over-reached himself. Rulers tremble today, not, as formerly, because they are rulers, but as the equals of everybody else. The ancient mainspring of power, the safe-guarding of the ruler at the cost of all other lives, has been broken. Power is greater than it has ever been, but also more precarious. Today either everyone will survive or no-one.

What is really required, however, is to deal with the survivor himself; and for this we must learn to see him for what he is even when his activity appears most natural. The most unquestioned and therefore the most dangerous thing he does is to give commands. We have seen that the command, even in the domesticated form found in any community, is no less than a suspended death sentence; and we know that strict and effective systems of commands are in force everywhere. Anyone who works his way to the top too quickly, or, by any other means, suddenly seizes control of such a system, will acquire an abnormal measure of the anxiety of command and will inevitably try to get rid of it. The threat which he uses continually, and which constitutes the real essence of the system of commands, finally turns against himself. Whether or not he is actually in danger from enemies, he always feels himself menaced. The most dangerous threat comes from his own people, those to whom he habitually gives orders, who are close to him and know him well. The ultimate means of deliverance, which he never wholly renounces (though he may hesitate to use it), is the sudden command for mass death. He starts a war and sends his people where they are supposed to kill, but if large numbers of them die there he will not regret them. However much he may dissemble, he is never free of a deep and hidden need to see the ranks of his own people thinned. To free him from the anxiety of command what is really necessary is that not only his enemies should die, but also many of those who fight for him. The forest of his fears has grown so dense that he cannot breathe and he longs for it to be thinned. If he waits too long his vision becomes blurred and he may do something which will seriously weaken his position. The anxiety of command increases in him until it results in catastrophe. But before catastrophe overtakes *him* it will have engulfed innumerable others.

The system of commands is acknowledged everywhere. It is perhaps most articulate in armies, but there is scarcely any sphere of civilized life where commands do not reach and none of us they do not mark. Their threat of death is the coin of power, and here it is all too easy to add coin to coin and amass wealth. If we would master power we must face command openly and boldly, and search for means to deprive it of its sting.

Notes

NOTES

32f   The description of the Haka is taken from J. S. Polack, *New Zealand, A Narrative of Travels and Adventure*, London, 1838, Vol. I, pp. 81-4.

37f   There are many descriptions of the "Standing on Arafat"; the fullest is in M. Gaudefroy-Demombynes, *Le Pèlerinage à la Mekke*, Paris, 1923, pp. 241-55.

42   Bechuana. S. S. Dornan, *Pygmies and Bushmen of the Kalahari*, London, 1925, p. 291.

  Boloki. Weeks, *Among Congo Cannibals*, London, 1913, p. 261.

  Pygmies in Gaboon. The song about the cave of the dead is given in Trilles, *Les Pygmées de la Forêt Equatoriale*, Anthropos, Paris, 1931.

43   Auxiliary spirits of the Chukchee Shaman. A. Ohlmarks, *Studien zum Problem des Schamanismus*, Lund, 1939, p. 176.

  Vision of the Eskimo Shaman. Rasmussen, *Thulefahrt*, Frankfurt, 1926, pp. 448-9.

  The Aurora Borealis. O. Höfler, *Kultische Geheimbunde der Germanen*, Frankfurt, 1934, pp. 241-2.

44   "The space between heaven and earth is not empty." M. J. bin Gorion, *Die Sagen der Juden*, Frankfurt, 1919, Vol. I, p. 348.

  The ancient Persians' host of demons. J. Darmesteter, *The Zend-Avesta*, Oxford, 1883, Vol. II, p. 49.

  Caesarius of Heisterbach, *The Dialogue of Miracles*, trans. Scott and Bland, Routledge, London, 1929, Vol. I, pp. 322-3, p. 328, Vol. II, pp. 294-5.

45   God and his court. *Ibid*, Vol. II, p. 343.

46   Locusts. A. Waley, *The Book of Songs*, Allen and Unwin, London, 1937, p. 173.

58   Mme. Jullien to her son. Letter of 2nd August 1791. G. Landauer, *Briefe aus der Französischen Revolution*, Frankfurt, 1919, Vol. I, p. 339.

59   Camille Desmoulins to his father. *Ibid.*, Vol. I, p. 144.

60f   Revivals. F. N. Davenport, *Primitive Traits in Religious Revivals*, New York, 1905. One of the most famous of these preachers wrote his own life: *The Backwoods Preacher. An Autobiography*, by Peter Cartwright, London, 1858.

  Pains of Hell. F. N. Davenport, *op. cit.*, p. 67.

  Meeting at Cane Ridge. Jerks, barking, holy laugh. *Ibid.*, pp. 73-81.

62   The various stages of a Papuan feast are the subject of a lively book by André Dupeyrat, *Jours de Fête chez les Papous*, Paris, 1954.

64f   A feast among the Tupinambu. Jean de Léry, *Le Voyage au Brésil*, new edition, Payot, Paris, 1927, pp. 223-4.

65   War dance of the women among the Kafirs of the Hindu-kush.
      W. Crooke, *Things Indian*, London, 1906, p. 124.
      War dance of the Jivaro women. R. Karsten, *Blood Revenge, War and
      Victory Feasts among the Jibaro Indians of Eastern Ecuador*, Washington,
      1922, p. 24.

66   Mirary in Madagascar. R. Decary, *Moeurs et Coutumes des Malgaches*,
      Paris, 1951, pp. 178-9.

68   Jeremiah, Ch. 25, v. 33.
      Mohammed's sermon to his dead enemies. A. Guillaume, *The Life of
      Muhammad. A Translation of Ibn Ishaq's Sirat Rasul Allah*, Oxford,
      1955, pp. 305-6.

69   Une's report. A. Erman, *Ägypten und Ägyptisches Leben im Altertum*,
      Tübingen, 1885, p. 689.
      Hymn to Rameses II. A. Erman, *Die Literatur der Ägypter*, Leipzig, 1923.
      (Trans. Blackman, *The Literature of the Ancient Egyptians*, Methuen,
      London, 1927, p. 259.)
      Battle of Kadesh. *Ibid.*, p. 267.

70   Merenptah's victory over the Libyans. Erman, *Ägypten und Ägyptisches
      Leben im Altertum*, pp. 710-11.
      Rameses III and the Libyans. *Ibid.*, p. 711.
      The counting of heads among the Assyrians. The relief contemporary
      with King Assurbanipal is schematically reproduced in G. Maspéro,
      Au Temps de Ramsès et d'Assourbanipal, Paris, 1927, p. 370.

76   Fire in the Vedas. H. Oldenberg, *Die Religion des Veda*, Stuttgart, 1917,
      p. 43.

78   The Fire-dance of the Navajos. W. D. Hambly, *Tribal Dancing and
      Social Development*, London, 1926, pp. 338-9.

79f   Incendiarism. E. Kräpelin, *Einführung in die Psychiatrische Klinik*,
      Leipzig, 1921, Vol. II, Case 62, pp. 235-40.

86   Storm Gods in the Vedas. A. A. Macdònnell, *Hymns from the Rigveda*,
      Calcutta, pp. 56-7.

89   Plutarch. *The Parallel Lives*: Pompey. (Trans. Rex Warner in *Fall of the
      Roman Republic*, Penguin Classics, 1958, p. 148.)

98   Distribution. E. Lot-Falck, *Les Rites de Chasse chez les Peuples Sibériens*,
      Paris, 1953, pp. 179-83.

99ff Expedition of the Taulipang against the Pishauko. T. Koch-Grünberg,
      Vom Roroima zum Orinoco, Ethnographie, Vol. III, Stuttgart, 1922,
      pp. 102-5.

103ff Lament of the Warramunga. B. Spencer and F. J. Gillen, *Northern
      Tribes of Central Australia*, Macmillan, London, 1904, pp. 516-22.

109f Totems of the Australian aborigines. Apart from the older works of
      Spencer and Gillen and of C. Strehlow, the most important publica-
      tions are: A. P. Elkin, *The Australian Aborigines*, 1943, and *Studies in
      Australian Totemism*, Oceania Monographs, 1933.

111f Buffalo dance of the Mandan. George Catlin, *The North American Indians*, Edinburgh, 1926, Vol. I, pp. 143-4.

118f Ungutnika and the wild dogs. Spencer and Gillen, *The Arunta*, Macmillan, London, 1927, p. 169.

119f Hunting pack and kangaroo. *Ibid.*, pp. 170-1.

121ff Lying on top of the candidate. *Ibid.*, pp. 192-3; single file. *ibid.*, p. 160; running in a circle; *ibid.*, p. 273 and *passim*; lying in a row, p. 280, fig. 100; swaying cylinder, pp. 261-2; two opposing lines, p. 189; dense square, p. 278; heap on the ground, pp. 286, 290, 292; ordeals by fire, p. 294; throwing of burning boughs, pp. 279 and 289; circumcision, p. 210.

128ff Mary Douglas, *The Lele of Kasai*, in *African Worlds*, edited by C. Daryll Forde, Oxford University Press, 1954, pp. 1-26.

129 Prestige of the forest. *Ibid.*, p. 4.

130ff The communal hunt. *Ibid.*, pp. 15-16.

132ff R. Karsten, *op. cit.* The two conjurations quoted have been slightly abridged. See also the more recent study by M. W. Stirling, *Historical and Ethnographical Material on the Jivaro Indians*, Washington, 1938.

135ff Ruth Benedict, *Patterns of Culture*, Houghton Mifflin, Boston, 1934, pp. 57-130.

139f Dahomey. A. Dalzel, *The History of Dahomey*, London, 1793. This old but invaluable book also contains the first full description of the "Annual Custom", pp. xx f.

Other books on Dahomey are: R. Burton, *A Mission to Gelele, King of Dahomey*, London, 1864; A. B. Ellis, *The Ewe-speaking Peoples of the Slave Coast of West Africa*, London, 1890; A. Le Hérissé, *L'Ancien Royaume du Dahomey*, Paris, 1911; M. J. Herskovits, *Dahomey, an Ancient West African Kingdom*, New York, 1938.

142 *The Travels of Ibn Jubayr*. Trans. R. J. C. Broadhurst, Cape, London, 1952. Mecca's faculty of expansion, p. 174.

The prophet of fighting and of war. I. Goldziher, *Vorlesungen über den Islam*, Heidelberg, 1910, pp. 22, 25.

143 "Slay the Idolaters." *The Koran*, Surah 9, verse 5.

Cybele raving. Lucian, *Dialogues of the Gods*. VII.

Lament of Isis. Erman, *Religion der Ägypter*, Berlin, 1909, p. 39.

146ff In addition to Goldziher, I have used the following books for this chapter: Gobineau, *Religions et Philosophies dans l'Asie Centrale*, new edition, Paris, 1957; D. M. Donaldson, *The Shiite Religion*, Luzac, London, 1933; G. E. von Grunebaum, *Muhammadan Festivals*, Abelard-Schuman, London, 1958; C. Virolleaud, *Le Théâtre Persan*, Paris, 1950.

146f The Sufferings of Husain. Donaldson, *op. cit.*, pp. 79-87.

147f The Afflictions of the Family of the Prophet. Goldziher, *op. cit.*, pp. 212-13.

147f To weep for Husain. *Ibid.*, pp. 213-14.
148   Husain's grave in Kerbéla. Donaldson, *op. cit.*, pp. 88-100.
      The great festival of the Shiites. Von Grunebaum, *op. cit.*, pp. 85-94.
149f Two kinds of fraternities. Gobineau, *op. cit.*, pp. 334-8.
151f "The theatre is brim-full". Gobineau, *op. cit.*, pp. 353-6.
153   "Go thou and deliver from the flames". Grunebaum, *op. cit.*, p. 94.
      The Day of Blood. Titayna, *La Caravane des Morts*, Paris, 1930 (quoted in P. de Félice, *Foules en Délire*, Paris, 1947, pp. 170-1).
158ff A. P. Stanley, *Sinai and Palestine*, London, 1864, pp. 354-8.
160ff R. Curzon, *Visits to Monasteries in the Levant*, London, 1850, pp. 230-50.
167ff *The Crowd in History.* I did not want to discuss earlier crowd movements here, before the reader had become familiar with the conclusions on power reached in the later part of the book. Thus it may rightly be objected that the title, *The Crowd in History*, is too wide. There is, however, no doubt that my conclusions on the Crowd and the Pack can be applied to earlier movements. I am reserving this for another work, which is already nearing completion.
193ff The account of the self-destruction of the Xosas is from G. McCall Theal, *History of South Africa from 1795-1872*, Vol. III, Allen and Unwin, London, 1927. There is also a short and very graphic account in an article (now difficult to obtain) by the German missionary A. Kropf: *Die Lügenpropheten des Kaffernlandes* (*Neue Missionsschriften, 2. Auflage, Nr. 11*, Berlin, 1891). The relevant passages from this are given by Katesa Schlosser in her book, *Propheten in Afrika*, Braunschweig, 1949, pp. 35-41. The most detailed modern account, containing much new material, is to be found in the book of a South African writer, which has remained unknown in Europe: A. W. Burton, *Sparks from the Border Anvil*, King Williams Town, 1950, pp. 1-102.
214ff S. Zuckerman, *The Social Life of Monkeys and Apes*, Kegan Paul, London, 1932, pp. 57-58.
215f *Ibid.*, pp. 268-9 and 300-4.
229f Genghis Khan. B. Vladimirzov, *The Life of Chingis Khan*, Routledge, London, 1930, p. 168.
230f Caesar. Plutarch, *op. cit.*, p. 230.
233f The Funeral Banquet of Domitian. Dio Cassius, *Roman History*, VIII, trans. E. Cary, Loeb Classical Library, Epitome of Book LXVIII, ch. 9, pp. 334-9.
235ff Josephus, *The Jewish War*, III, 8.
238   "At last—let us say that it was either by chance or by divine providence —only Josephus was left with one other man." In the Slavonic version of *The Jewish War*, which, according to some scholars, is based on an earlier text, there is a strikingly different sentence instead: "After saying this, he counted the numbers cunningly and so deceived them all." On this point, see the appendix on the Slavonic additions to the

new English translation by G. A. Williamson (Penguin Classics), p. 403.

242 Muhammad Tughlak. See also the later chapter on this ruler.

243 The capture of Mudkal. Sewell, *A Forgotten Empire*, London, 1900, p. 34.

Hakim. P. Wolff, *Die Drusen und ihre Vorläufer*, Leipzig, 1845, p. 286.

244f For a concise account of the Mogul Emperors see V. A. Smith, *The Oxford History of India*, 1923, pp. 321-468.

The Jesuits on Prince Salim. Du Jarric, *Akbar and the Jesuits*, trans. C. H. Payne, Routledge, London, 1926, p. 182.

245f Shaka. The best contemporary account is contained in the *Diary of Henry Francis Fynn*, ed. J. Stuart and D. M. Malcolm, Shuter and Shooter, Pietermaritzburg, 1950. This was only published a hundred years after it was written and when it had already been frequently used. The only modern biography of any value is by E. A. Ritter, *Shaka Zulu*, Longmans Green, London, 1955. This makes use of oral traditions as well as of all the written sources.

249f The century of the Etruscans. A. Grenier, *Les Religions Etrusque et Romaine*, Paris, 1948, p. 26.

251f *Mana* in the Marquesas. E. S. C. Handy, *Polynesian Religion*, Honolulu, 1927, p. 31.

252f The killer among the Murngin. F. Lloyd Warner, *A Black Civilization*, Harper and Brothers, New York, 1958, pp. 163-5. This work, first published in 1937, is the most important account there is of an Australian tribe.

254 The hero in the Fiji Islands. Lorimer Fison, *Tales from Old Fiji*, London, 1904, pp. 51-53 and p. xx.

255ff The hero in the belly of the giant snake. K. T. Preuss, *Religion und Mythologie der Uitoto*, Göttingen, 1921, Vol. I, pp. 220-9.

257f A survivor among the Taulipang. T. Koch-Grünberg, *Indianermärchen aus Sudamerika*, Jena, 1921, pp. 109-10.

259f The origin of the Kutenai. F. Boas, *Kutenai Tales*, No. 74, Washington, 1918, *The Great Epidemic*, pp. 269-70.

260f Mass suicide among the Ba-ila. E. W. Smith and A. M. Dale, *The Ila-speaking Peoples of Northern Rhodesia*, Macmillan, London, 1920, Vol. I, p. 20.

261 Cabres and Caraibs. A. von Humboldt, *Reise in die Äquinoctial-Gegenden des neuen Continents*, Stuttgart, 1861, Vol. V, p. 63.

263f Death of an Indian child in Demerara. W. E. Roth, *An Enquiry into the Animism and Folklore of the Guiana Indians*, Washington, 1915, p. 155.

264ff The ancestor cult of the Zulus: the dead man and his brother. H. Callaway, *The Religious System of the Amazulu*, Natal, 1870, pp. 146-59.

269f The King's medium in Uganda. N. K. Chadwick, *Poetry and Prophecy*, Cambridge, 1942, pp. 36-8.

270f   The ancestor cult of the Chinese. M. Granet, *La Civilisation Chinoise*, Paris, 1929, pp. 300-2; Henri Maspéro, *La Chine Antique*, new edition, Paris, 1955, pp. 146-55; Jeanne Cuisinier, *Sumangat. L'âme et son culte en Indochine et en Indonésie*, Gallimard, Paris, 1951, pp. 74-85.

273   The plague in Athens. Thucydides, *The Peloponnesian War*, trans. Rex Warner, Penguin Classics, pp. 123-7.

283   Genghis Khan. His descent from a heavenly wolf is proclaimed at the beginning of *The Secret History of the Mongols* (A. Haenisch, *Die Geheime Geschichte der Mongolen*, Leipzig, 1948). The soul of the Roman Emperor as an eagle. There is a wonderful account of the apotheosis of Septimius Severus in Herodian, IV. 2.

        The Mongols' fear of lightning. The Journal of Rubruck in *Contemporaries of Marco Polo*, edited by M. Komroff, London, 1928, p. 91. Fulguratores. A. Grenier, *op. cit.*, pp. 18-19. Power and lightning. F. Kuhn, *Altchinesische Staatsweisheit*, Zürich, 1954, p. 105. Disappearance of Romulus in a thunder-storm, Livy, I. 16; Tullus Hostilius killed by lightning, *ibid.*, I. 31; Romulus Silvius, an earlier king of Alba Longa, killed by lightning, *ibid.*, I. 3.

287   Children's questions. O. Jespersen, *Language, its Nature, Development and Origin*, Allen and Unwin, London, 1949, p. 137.

289   The noon-woman. *Wendische Sagen*, edited by F. von Sieber, Jena, 1925, p. 17.

290f   The medicine-man among the Aranda. Spencer and Gillen, *The Arunta*, Vol. II, pp. 391-420.

292f   The last Visconti. Pier Candido Decembrio, German translation by P. Funk, *Leben des Filippo Maria Visconti*, Jena, 1913, pp. 29-30.

293f   Chosroes II tests the discretion of his courtiers. French translation by C. Pellat, *Le Livre de la Couronne, attribué à Ğahiz*, Paris, 1954, pp. 118-20.

313f   Wukuf and Ifadha. Gaudefroy-Demombynes, *op. cit.*, pp. 235-303.

319   Lucian, *On the Syrian Goddess*.

        The Skoptsy. K. Grass, *Die Russischen Sekten*, Vol. II, *Die Weissen Tauben oder Skopzen*, Leipzig, 1914. This is the most comprehensive book on the subject, though somewhat ponderous. Grass also edited a German translation of their short sacred scripture: *Die geheime heilige Schrift der Skopzen*, Leipzig, 1904. A more recent work containing useful material is J. Rapaport's *Introduction à la Psychopathologie Collective. La Secte mystique des Skoptzy*, Paris, 1948.

321   The Assassins. The older literature on the Assassins may now be said to have been superseded by M. G. S. Hodgson's definitive work, *The Order of Assassins*, The Hague, 1955.

322   "Suggestion-slavery." Kräpelin, *Psychiatrie*, III, p. 723.

323   "The mosquitoes talking", etc. *Ibid.*, pp. 673-4.

324ff   Hermann Lommel published his paper *Bhrigu im Jenseits* in *Paideuma*, Vol. IV (1950), adding a supplement in Vol. V (1952). I am greatly indebted to his translations of the wanderings of Bhrigu, from the *Shatapatha-Brahmana*, and of other relevant passages from ancient Indian literature.

326   *The Laws of Manu*, translated by G. Bühler, Oxford, 1886, V. 55, p. 177.

337ff   W. H. J. Bleek and L. C. Lloyd, *Specimens of Bushman Folklore*, Geo. Allen, London, 1911. Bushman Presentiments, pp. 330-9.

343   The *Loritja* Myth. C. Strehlow, *Die Aranda- und Loritja-Stämme in Zentral-Australien*, Frankfurt, 1910, II, pp. 2-3. See also L. Lévy-Bruhl, *La Mythologie Primitive*, Paris, 1955. This important book contains much suggestive material for the study of transformation. Being mainly confined to the mythical world of the Australians and Papuans, it has space for long quotations from the best books on its subject, so that the reader is allowed to think for himself. Of all the books of Lévy-Bruhl it is the one I have found most valuable.

The Master and his apprentice. A. Dirr, *Kaukasische Märchen*, Jena, 1922.

344   Proteus. *Odyssey*, IV, 440-60.

345f   Hysteria. Kräpelin, *Psychiatrie*, IV, pp. 1547-1606.

E. Bleuler, *Lehrbuch der Psychiatrie*, pp. 392-401.

(English translation by A. A. Brill, *Textbook of Psychiatry*, London, 1924.) Kretschmer, *Uber Hysterie*, Leipzig, 1927.

346   Shamans. Czaplicka, *Aboriginal Siberia*, Oxford, 1914; Ohlmarks, *op. cit.*; M. Eliade, *Le Chamanisme*, Paris, 1951; G. V. Ksenofontov, *Schamanengeschichten aus Sibirien*, Munich, 1955; H. Findeisen, *Schamanentum*, Stuttgart, 1957.

347f   Mania and melancholia. Kräpelin, *Psychiatrie*, III, Das manisch-depressive Irresein, pp. 1183-1395. See also Bleuler, *op. cit.*

348ff   T. G. H. Strehlow, *Aranda Traditions*, Melbourne University Press, 1947.

Bandicoot myth. *Ibid.*, pp. 7-10.

350f   Lukara myth. *Ibid.*, pp. 15-16.

353   "The ancestor represents the sum total. . . ." *Ibid.*, p. 17.

356   The ancestor from Mboringka. *Ibid.*, p. 12.

358ff   Delirium Tremens. Kräpelin, *Psychiatrie*, II, pp. 132ff.

Bleuler, *op. cit.*, pp. 227-8 and 233. (English edition, pp. 328-30.)

364f   The innkeeper. Kräpelin, *Einführung in die Psychiatrische Klinik*, II, Case 43, pp. 157-61.

366f   Schizophrenic patient suffering from an attack of Delirium Tremens. Bleuler, *op. cit.*, pp. 234-5 (English edition, pp. 337-8.)

371   The donkey in the lion's skin. J. Hertel, *Indische Märchen*, Jena, 1921, pp. 61-2.

401   Liudprand of Cremona. *The Works of Liudprand of Cremona*, trans. F. A. Wright, Routledge, London, 1930. The story of the Rising Throne is in *Antapodosis*, VI, 5, pp. 207-8.

402ff   General Paralysis. Kräpelin, *Einführung in die Psychiatrische Klinik*, II, Case 26, pp. 93-7.

404f   Second case of Paralysis. *Ibid.*, Case 28, pp. 101-2.

411ff   D. Westermann, *Geschichte Afrikas*, Cologne, 1952—a book which draws on a vast quantity of material—was consulted throughout this chapter.

Death of an old king in Gaboon and the election of his successor. P. Du Chaillu, *Explorations and Adventures in Equatorial Africa*, London, 1861, pp. 18-20.

413ff   The King of Jukun. C. K. Meek, *A Sudanese Kingdom*, Kegan Paul, London, 1931, pp. 120-77 and 332-53.

415f   Attributes of African kings. Westermann, *op. cit.*, pp. 34-43.

416f   The imitation of kings. Monomotapa: Westermann, *op. cit.*, pp. 413-14; Ethiopia: Diodorus Siculus, III. 7 and Strabo, XVII. 2 and 3; Darfur: *Travels of an Arab Merchant in Soudan*, London, 1854, p. 78; Uganda, Boni, China: J. G. Frazer, *The Dying God*, London, 1913, pp. 39-40.

418   The king himself determines the length of his reign. Monteil, *Les Bambara du Ségou*, Paris, 1924, p. 305.

Beating of the prospective king among the Yoruba. Westermann, *ibid.*, p. 40; in Sierra Leone: *ibid.*, p. 41.

419   Lawlessness after the death of a king. Among the Mosi of Wagadugu: Westermann, *op. cit.*, p. 185; in Ashanti: *ibid.*, p. 222; in Uganda: J. Roscoe, *The Baganda*, London, 1911, pp. 103-4.

The Hima states originated through the gradual conquest of what is now Uganda and the territory south of it. Warlike pastoralists of Hamitic origin, called Hima, migrated into the country from the north and made the native Bantu agriculturalists their serfs. These Hima kingdoms are among the most interesting in Africa. They are distinguished by a sharp caste-division between masters and serfs.

Succession in Ankole. K. Oberg, *The Kingdom of Ankole in Uganda*, in *African Political Systems*, edited by M. Fortes and E. E. Evans-Pritchard, Oxford University Press, 1954, pp. 121-62 and especially pp. 157-61. A much more diffuse work, but nevertheless worth reading, is Roscoe, *The Banyankole*, Cambridge, 1923. There is an excellent study of Ruanda, further to the south, by J. J. Maquet, *The Kingdom of Ruanda*, in *African Worlds*, pp. 1-26.

420f   Sacrifice of a young prince in Kitara. Roscoe, *The Bakitara*, Cambridge, 1923, pp. 129-30.

421   The royal bow of Kitara. *Ibid.*, pp. 133-4.

"I shoot the nations". *Ibid.*, p. 134.

Uganda: drums. Roscoe, *The Baganda*, London, 1911, p. 188.

422   "I am the king to live longer than my ancestors". *Ibid.*, p. 194.

Two passers-by seized. *Ibid.*, p. 197.

Scapegoat and overseer. *Ibid.*, p. 200.

422   Presentation of victims in pairs. *Ibid.*, p. 210.

423   "You are now Ata". Westermann, *op. cit.*, p. 39.

      "The Lion eats alone". Roscoe, *The Baganda*, p. 207.

      The king of Kitara fed by his cook. Roscoe, *The Bakitara*, p. 103.

      Summary justice. Roscoe, *ibid.*, pp. 61, 63.

424ff   Ibn Batuta. *Travels in Asia and Africa, 1325-1354*, translated and selected by H. A. R. Gibb, Routledge, London, 1929, ch. VI, pp. 183-213.

      The History of Ziau-d din Barani can be found in Vol. III of *The History of India as told by its own Historians*, H. M. Elliot and J. Dowson, 1867-1877. It has also been published separately as *Later Kings of Delhi*, by S. Gupta, Calcutta. The account of Muhammad Tughlak's reign is on pp. 159-192.

434   A modern defender of the Sultan is the Indian historian Ishwari Prasad (*L'Inde du VIIe au XVIe siècle*, in the series *Histoire du Monde*, Paris, 1930, pp. 270-300). He calls him an "unfortunate idealist", "without doubt the most able man of the Middle Ages".

434ff   *Denkwürdigkeiten eines Nervenkranken*, by Daniel Paul Schreber, Leipzig, 1903. [Additional note to the English translation.] I am of course aware of Freud's paper on the subject and of the conclusions he reached, but my close acquaintance with the *Denkwürdigkeiten* inclines me to believe that these conclusions were too narrow and, indeed, misleading. For this reason, I have made no use of his study. It should, however, be borne in mind that Freud wrote in 1911, before the great wars and revolutions of our century.

Bibliography

BIBLIOGRAPHY

It is impossible to give a full list here of all the books which, during the course of years, have had some influence on this work. The following selection has been made according to three principles. It contains, first, all the books from which I have quoted; second, all the books which have played a decisive part in shaping my thought: those without which I could not have arrived at certain conclusions. Most of these are, or contain, original documents of a widely diverse nature, relating to myth, religion, history, anthropology, biography and psychiatry. Among them there are, of course, various books belonging to the first group. Finally I have listed a few recent works which contain reliable surveys of unfamiliar civilizations, which may prove as useful to my readers as they were to me.

Albert von Aachen. *Geschichte des ersten Kreuzzugs.* Übersetzt von H. Hefele. Jena, 1923.

Ammianus Marcellinus. 3 vols. Loeb Classical Library. London, 1950.

Appian. *Roman History.* 4 vols. Loeb Classical Library. London, 1933.

Arabshah, Ahmed Ibn. *Tamerlane,* translated by Sanders. London, 1936.

Baumann, H., Thurnwald, R., and Westermann, D. *Völkerkunde von Afrika.* Essen, 1940.

Benedict, Ruth. *Patterns of Culture.* Boston, 1934.

Bernier, F. *Travels in the Moghul Empire 1656-1668.* London, 1914.

Bezold, F. v. *Zur Geschichte des Hussitentums.* Munich, 1874.

Bland, J. O. P., and Backhouse, E. *China under the Empress Dowager.* Boston, 1914.

Bleek, W. H. J., and Lloyd, L. C. *Bushman Folklore.* London, 1911.

Bleuler, E. *Lehrbuch der Psychiatrie.* Reprint, Berlin, 1930. (*Textbook of Psychiatry.* Translated by A. A. Brill. London, 1924.)

Boas, F. *Kutenai Tales.* Washington, 1918.

Bouvat, L. *L'Empire Mongol (2ème phase).* Paris, 1927.

Brandt, O. H. *Die Limburger Chronik.* Jena, 1922.

—— *Der grosse Bauernkrieg.* Jena, 1925.

Browne, E. G. *A Literary History of Persia.* Vols. I-IV. Cambridge, 1951.

Brunel, R. *Essai sur la Confrérie Religieuse des Aissoua au Maroc.* Paris, 1926.

Bryant, A. *Olden Times in Zululand and Natal.* London, 1929.

Bücher, K. *Arbeit und Rhythmus.* Leipzig, 1909.

Bühler, G. *The Laws of Manu.* Oxford, 1886.

Burckhardt, Jacob. *Griechische Kulturgeschichte*, Vols. I-IV.
—— *The Civilization of the Renaissance in Italy*.
—— *The Age of Constantine the Great*.
—— *Reflections on History*.
Burton, A. W. *Sparks from the Border Anvil*. King William's Town, 1950.
Burton, Richard. *A Mission to Gelele, King of Dahomey*. London, 1864.
Bury, J. B. *History of the Later Roman Empire*. 2 vols. New edition. New York, 1958.
Cabeza de Vaca. *Naufragios Y Comentarios*. Buenos Aires, 1945.
Caesarius of Heisterbach. *The Dialogue on Miracles*. 2 vols. London, 1929.
Callaway, H. *The Religious System of the Amazulu*. Natal, 1870.
Calmeil, L. F. *De la Folie*. 2 vols. Paris, 1845.
Carcopino, J. *Daily Life in Ancient Rome*. London, 1941.
Cartwright, Peter. *The Backwoods Preacher. An Autobiography*. London, 1858.
Casalis, E. *Les Bassoutos*. Paris, 1860.
Catlin, George. *The North American Indians*. London, 1841; reprint, Edinburgh, 1926.
Chadwick, N. K. *Poetry and Prophecy*. Cambridge, 1942.
Chantepie de la Saussaye. *Lehrbuch der Religionsgeschichte*. 4th ed. Tübingen, 1925.
Chamberlain, B. H. *Things Japanese*. London, 1902.
Cieza de Leon, Pedro de. *The Incas*. Translated by Harriet de Onis. Oklahoma, 1959.
Codrington, R. H. *The Melanesians*. Oxford, 1891.
Cohn, Norman. *The Pursuit of the Millennium*. London, 1957.
Commynes, P. de. *Mémoires*. Vols. I-III. Paris, 1925.
Contenau, G. *La Divination chez les Assyriens et les Babyloniens*. Paris, 1940.
Gonstantin VII. Porphyrogénète, *Le Livre des Cérémonies*. Traduit par A. Vogt. Vols. I et II. Paris, 1935-9.
Cortes, Hernando. *Five Letters 1519 to 1526*. Translated by Morris. London, 1928.
Coxwell, C. F. *Siberian and Other Folk-Tales*. London, 1925.
Crooke, W. *Things Indian*. London, 1906.
Cuisinier, Jeanne. *Sumangat. L'Âme et son Culte en Indochine et Indonésie*. Paris, 1951.
Cunha, Euclides da. *Rebellion in the Backlands*. Translated by Putnam. Chicago, 1944.
Cumont, Franz. *The Mysteries of Mithra*. Reprinted, New York, 1956.
—— *Oriental Religions in Roman Paganism*. Reprinted, New York, 1956.
Curzon, Robert. *Visits to Monasteries in the Levant*. London, 1850.
Czaplicka, M. A. *Aboriginal Siberia*. Oxford, 1914.
Dalzel, A. *The History of Dahomey*. London, 1793.
Darmesteter, J. *The Zend-Avesta*. Part II. Oxford, 1883.
Davenport, F. N. *Primitive Traits in Religious Revivals*. New York, 1905.

Decary, R. *Moeurs et Coutumes des Malgaches.* Paris, 1951.

Decembrio, Pier Candido. *Leben des Filippo Maria Visconti.* Übersetzt von Funk. Jena, 1913.

Depont, O., et Coppolani, X. *Les Confréries Religieuses Musulmanes.* Alger, 1897.

Dhorme, E. *Les Religions de Babylonie et d'Assyrie.* Paris, 1945.

Diaz del Castillo, Bernal. *The Discovery and Conquest of Mexico.* Translated by A. P. Maudsley. Reprinted, New York, 1956.

Dio Cassius. *Roman History.* Loeb Classical Library. 9 vols. London, 1955.

Dirr, A. *Kaukasische Märchen.* Jena, 1922.

Donaldson, D. M. *The Shiite Religion.* London, 1933.

Dornan, S. S. *Pygmies and Bushmen of the Kalahari.* London, 1925.

Douglas, Mary. *The Lele of Kasai,* in *African Worlds.* Edited by C. Daryll Forde. Oxford, 1954.

Dubois, Abbé. *Hindu Manners, Customs and Ceremonies.* Oxford, 1906.

Du Chaillu, P. B. *Explorations and Adventures in Equatorial Africa.* London, 1861.

Du Jarric. *Akbar and the Jesuits.* Translated by Payne. London, 1926.

Dumézil, Georges. *Mitra-Varuna.* Paris, 1948.

—— *Mythes et Dieux des Germains.* Paris, 1939.

Dupeyrat, André. *Jours de Fête chez les Papous.* Paris, 1954.

Eisler, R. *Man into Wolf.* London, 1951.

Eliade, M. *Le Chamanisme.* Paris, 1951.

—— *Traité d'Histoire des Religions.* Paris, 1953.

Elkin, A. P. *Studies in Australian Totemism.* Oceania Monographs No. 2. Sydney, 1933.

—— *The Australian Aborigines.* Sydney, 1943.

Elliot H. M., and Dowson, J. *The History of India as told by its own Historians.* 8 vols. London, 1867-77.

Ellis, A. B. *The Ewe-speaking Peoples of the Slave Coast of West Africa.* London, 1890.

Erman, A. *Ägypten und ägyptisches Leben im Altertum.* Tübingen, 1885.

—— *Die ägyptische Religion.* Berlin, 1909.

—— *Die Literatur der Ägypter.* Leipzig, 1923. Translated into English by A. M. Blackman, *The Literature of the Ancient Egyptians.* London, 1927.

Evans-Pritchard, E. E. *Witchcraft, Oracles and Magic among the Azande.* Oxford, 1937.

Félice, Philippe de. *Foules en Délire. Extases Collectives.* Paris, 1947.

Findeisen, H. *Schamanentum.* Stuttgart, 1957.

Fison, Lorimer. *Tales from Old Fiji.* London, 1904.

Florenz, Karl. *Geschichte der japanischen Literatur.* Leipzig, 1909.

Forde, C. Daryll. *Habitat, Economy and Society.* London, 1950.

—— Editor: *African Worlds.* London, 1954.

Fortes, M., and Evans-Pritchard, E. E. *African Political Systems.* Oxford, 1940.

Fortune, R. G. *Sorcerers of Dobu.* London, 1932.

Fox, George. *The Journal.* Cambridge, 1952.

Franke, O. *Studien zur Geschichte der konfuzianischen Dogmas und der chinesischen Staatsreligion*. Hamburg, 1920.

—— *Geschichte des chinesischen Reiches*. 5 vols. Berlin, 1930–52.

Frankfort, Henri. *Kingship and the Gods*. Chicago, 1948.

Frazer, J. G. *The Golden Bough*. Vols. I–XI. London, 1913 ff.

—— *The Fear of the Dead in Primitive Religion*. Vols. I–III. London, 1933–6.

—— *The Belief in Immortality and the Worship of the Dead*. Vols. I–III. London, 1913–24.

Friedländer, L. *Darstellungen aus der Sittengeschichte Roms*. Vols. I–IV. Leipzig, 1922.

Frobenius, Leo. *Atlantis, Volksmärchen und Volksdichtungen Afrikas*. Vols. I–XII. Jena, 1921–8.

—— *Kulturgeschichte Afrikas*. Vienna, 1933.

Fung Yu-Lan. *A History of Chinese Philosophy*. Vols. I–II. Princeton, 1952–3.

Fynn. *The Diary of Henry Francis Fynn*. Pietermaritzburg, 1950.

Garcilasso de la Vega, *Comentarios Reales*. Buenos Aires, 1942.

Gaudefroy-Demombynes, M. *Le Pèlerinage à la Mekke*. Paris, 1923.

—— *Les Institutions Musulmanes*. Paris, 1921.

Gesell, A. *Wolf Child and Human Child*. London, 1941.

Gobineau, *Religions et Philosophies dans l'Asie Centrale*. 1865. New edition. Paris, 1957.

Goeje, M. J. de. *Mémoire sur les Carmathes du Bahrein*. Leiden, 1886.

Goldenweiser, A. *Anthropology*. New York, 1946.

Goldziher, J. *Vorlesungen über den Islam*. Heidelberg, 1910.

Gorion, M. J. bin. *Die Sagen der Juden: I Von der Urzeit*. Frankfurt, 1919.

Granet, M. *La Civilisation Chinoise*. Paris, 1929.

—— *La Pensée Chinoise*. Paris, 1934.

Grass, K. *Die russischen Sekten*. 2 vols. Leipzig, 1907 and 1914.

—— *Die geheime heilige Schrift der Skopzen*. Leipzig, 1904.

Gregory of Tours. *History of the Franks*. Translated by O. M. Dalton, 2 vols. Oxford, 1927.

Grenier, A. *Les Religions Etrusque et Romaine*. Paris, 1948.

Grey, G. *Polynesian Mythology*. London, 1855.

Grousset, R. *L'Empire des Steppes*. Paris, 1939.

—— *L'Empire Mongol. Ière phase*. Paris, 1941.

Grube, W. *Religion und Kultus der Chinesen*. Leipzig, 1910.

Grunebaum, G. E. von. *Muhammadan Festivals*. London, 1958.

Guillaume, A. *The Life of Muhammad. A translation of Ibn Ishaq's Sirat Rasul Allah*. Oxford, 1955.

Guyard, S. *Un Grand Maître des Assassins au temps de Saladin*. Paris, 1877.

Haenisch, Erich. *Die Geheime Geschichte der Mongolen*. Leipzig, 1948.

Hambly, W. D. *Tribal Dancing and Social Development*. London, 1946.

Handy, E. S. C. *Polynesian Religion*. Honolulu, 1927.

Harris, Sarah. *The Incredible Father Divine*. London, 1954.

Hecker, J. C. F. *The Epidemics of the Middle Ages*. London, 1859.

Hepding, Hugo. *Attis, seine Mythen und sein Kult*. Giefsen, 1903.

Herodian. *History of the Roman Empire*. Translated by E. C. Echols. Cambridge, 1961.

Herodotus. *The Histories*. Translated by Aubrey de Selincourt. Penguin Classics, 1954.

Herskovits, M. J. *Dahomey, an Ancient West African Kingdom*. 2 vols. New York, 1938.

Hertel, J. *Indische Märchen*. Jena, 1921.

Histoire Anonyme de la Première Croisade. Traduite par L. Bréhier. Paris, 1924.

Historiae Augustae Scriptores. 3 vols. Loeb Classical Library. London, 1930.

Hitti, P. K. *History of the Arabs*. London, 1951.

Hodgson, M. G. S. *The Order of Assassins*. The Hague, 1955.

Höfler, O. *Kultische Geheimbünde der Germanen*. Frankfurt, 1939.

Hofmayr, W. *Die Schilluk*. Mödling, 1925.

Huizinga, J. *The Waning of the Middle Ages*. Penguin, 1955.

—— *Homo Ludens*. London, 1949.

Humboldt, A von. *Reise in die Äquinoctial-Gegenden des neuen Continents*. Stuttgart, 1861.

Hutton, J. H. *Caste in India*. Cambridge, 1946.

Ibn Batuta. *Travels in Asia and Africa, 1325-1354*. Translated and selected by Gibb. London, 1939.

Ibn Ishaq. *The Life of Muhammad*. Translated by G. Guillaume. Oxford, 1955.

Ibn Jubayr. *The Travels*. Translated by Broadhurst. London, 1952.

Ideler, K. W. *Versuch einer Theorie des religiosen Wahnsinns*. Halle, 1848.

James, William. *The Varieties of Religious Experience*. London, 1911.

Jeanmaire, H. *Dionysos. Histoire du Culte de Bacchus*. Paris, 1951.

Jeanne des Anges, Soeur. *Autobiographie d'une Hystérique Possédée*. Paris, 1886.

Jensen, A. E. *Hainuwele. Volkserzählungen von der Molukken-Insel Ceram*. Frankfurt, 1939.

—— *Mythus und Kult bei Naturvölkern*. Wiesbaden, 1951.

Jespersen, O. *Language, its Nature, Development and Origin*. London, 1949.

Jezower, J. *Das Buch der Träume*. Berlin, 1928.

Josephus. *The Jewish War*. Translated by G. A. Williamson. Penguin Classics. London, 1959.

Joset, P. E. *Les Sociétés Secrètes des Hommes Léopards en Afrique Noire*. Paris, 1955.

Junod, H. A. *The Life of a South African Tribe*. 2 vols. London, 1927.

Juvaini. *The History of the World Conqueror*. Translated from the Persian by J. A. Boyle. 2 vols. Manchester, 1958.

Kalevala. *The Land of the Heroes*. Translated by W. F. Kirby. 2 vols. Everyman. 1956.

Karsten, R. *Blood Revenge, War, and Victory Feasts among the Jibaro Indians of Eastern Ecuador*. Washington, 1922.

Kautilya. *Arthashastra*. Translated by R. Shamasastry. Mysore, 1929.

Koch-Grünberg, T. *Vom Roroima zum Orinoco*. Vols. I-V. Stuttgart, 1917-28.

—— *Zwei Jahre unter den Indianern Nordwest-Brasiliens*. Stuttgart, 1923.

—— *Indianermärchen aus Südamerika*. Jena, 1921.

Komroff, M. *Contemporaries of Marco Polo*. London, 1928.

Kräpelin, E. *Psychiatrie*. 8th ed. Vols. I-IV. Leipzig, 1910-15.

—— *Einführung in die psychiatrische Klinik*. Vols. II-III. Leipzig, 1921.

Kremer, A. V. *Culturgeschichte des Orients unter den Chalifen*. 2 vols. Vienna, 1875.

Kretschmer, E. *Über Hysterie*. Leipzig, 1927.

—— *Der sensitive Beziehungswahn*. Berlin, 1918.

Krickeberg, W. *Indianermärchen aus Nordamerika*. Jena, 1924.

—— *Märchen der Azteken und Inkaperuaner, Maya und Muisca*. Jena, 1928.

Kropf, A. *Das Volk der Xosa-Kaffern*. Berlin, 1889.

—— *Die Lügenpropheten des Kaffernlandes*. Neue Missionsschriften. 2nd ed. No. 11. Berlin, 1891.

Kuhn, F. *Altchinesische Staatsweisheit*. Zürich, 1954.

Landa, Fr. D. de. *Relacion de las cosas de Yucatan*. Paris, 1864.

Landauer, Gustav. *Briefe aus der Französischen Revolution*. 2 vols. Frankfurt, 1919.

Landtman, G. *The Origins of the Inequality of the Social Classes*. London, 1938.

Lane, E. W. *Manners and Customs of the Modern Egyptians*. London, 1895.

Lane-Poole, S. *A History of Egypt in the Middle Ages*. London, 1901.

O'Leary, De Lacy. *A Short History of the Fatimid Khalifate*. London, 1923.

Leenhardt, M. *Gens de la Grande Terre.—Nouvelle Calédonie*, Paris, 1937.

Lefebvre, G. *La Grande Peur de 1789*. Paris, 1932.

—— *La Révolution Française*. Paris, 1957.

—— *Etudes sur la Révolution Française*. Paris, 1954.

Legge, J. *The Sacred Books of China*. Part I: *The Shu-King*. Oxford, 1899.

Le Hérissé, A. *L'Ancien Royaume du Dahomey*. Paris, 1911.

Leiris, Michel. *La Possession et ses Aspects Théâtraux chez les Éthiopiens de Gondar*. Paris, 1958.

Léry, Jean de. *Le voyage au Brésil 1556-1558*. Paris, 1927.

Lévy-Bruhl, I. *L'Âme Primitive*. Paris, 1927.

—— *La Mythologie Primitive*. Paris, 1935.

Lewis, B. *The Origins of Ismailism*. Cambridge, 1940.

Lindner, K. *Die Jagd der Vorzeit*. Berlin, 1937.

Liudprand of Cremona. *The Works of*. Translated by F. A. Wright. London, 1930.

Livy. *The Early History of Rome*. Translated by A. de Selincourt. Penguin Classics. 1960.

Löffler, K. *Die Wiedertäufer in Münster*. Jena, 1923.

Lommel, H. *Bhrigu im Jenseits*. Paideuma 4. Bamberg, 1950. Paideuma 5. Bamberg, 1952.

Lot-Falck, E. *Les Rites de Chasse chez les Peuples Sibériens*. Paris, 1953.

Lowie, R. H. *Primitive Society*. London, 1920.

—— *Primitive Religion*. London, 1924.

Lucian. *Works.* 8 vols. Loeb Classical Library.

Ludwig II. von Bayern. *Tagebuch-Aufzeichnungen.* Liechtenstein, 1925.

Macdonnell, A. A. *Hymns from the Rigveda.* The Heritage of India Series. Calcutta.

Machiavelli, Niccolo. *The Discourses of.* Translated by L. J. Walker. 2 vols. London.

Malinowski, B. *Magic, Science and Religion.* New York, 1955.

Maquet, J. J. *The Kingdom of Ruanda,* in *African Worlds.* Edited by Daryll Forde. London, 1954.

Marco Polo. *The Travels of.* London, 1939.

Mason, J. A. *The Ancient Civilisations of Peru.* London, 1957.

Maspéro, Georges. *Au Temps de Ramsès et d'Assourbanipal.* Paris, 1927.

Maspéro, Henri. *La Chine Antique.* Paris, 1955.

—— *Les Religions Chinoises.* Paris, 1950.

Mas'udi. *Les Prairies d'Or.* Texte et traduction par Barbier de Meynard et Pavet de Courteille. 9 vols. Paris, 1861-77.

Mathieu, P. F. *Histoire des Miraculés et Convulsionnaires de Saint-Médard.* Paris, 1864.

Mathiez, A. *La Révolution Française.* Vols. I-III. Paris, 1922-7.

Meek, C. K. *A Sudanese Kingdom.* London, 1931.

Misson, Maximilien. *Le Théâtre Sacré des Cévennes.* London, 1707.

Mooney, J. *The Ghost-Dance Religion.* Washington, 1896.

Morley, S. G. *The Ancient Maya.* Stanford, 1946.

Nadel, S. F. *A Black Byzantium. The Kingdom of Nupe in Nigeria.* London, 1946.

Nihongi, Chronicles of Japan. Translated by W. G. Aston. London, 1956.

Nizam Al-Mulk. *The Book of Government, or Rules for Kings.* Translated from the Persian by H. Drake. London, 1960.

Oberg, K. *The Kingdom of Ankole in Uganda,* in *African Political Systems,* edited by Fortes and Evans-Pritchard. Oxford, 1940.

Ohlmarks, A. *Studien zum Problem des Schamanismus.* Lund, 1939.

D'Ohsson, C. *Histoire des Mongols.* 4 vols. The Hague, 1834-5.

Oldenberg, H. *Die Religion des Veda.* Stuttgart, 1917.

Olmstead, A. T. *History of the Persian Empire.* Chicago, 1948.

Pallottino, M. *The Etruscans.* London, 1955.

Pan-Ku. *The History of the Former Han Dynasty.* Translated by Homer H. Dubs. Vols. I-III. 1938-55.

Paris, Matthew. *Chronicles.* 5 vols. London, 1851.

Pellat, C. *Le Livre de la Couronne, attribué a Ğahiz.* Paris, 1954.

Pelliot, P. *Histoire Secrète des Mongols.* Paris, 1949.

Plutarch. *The Parallel Lives.* 11 vols. Loeb Classical Library.

—— *Fall of the Roman Republic. Six Lives.* Translated by Rex Warner. Penguin Classics, 1958.

Polack, J. S. *New Zealand, A Narrative of Travels and Adventure.* 2 vols. London, 1838.

Polybius. *The Histories.* 6 vols. Loeb Classical Library. London, 1954.

Prasad, Ishwari. *L'Inde du VIIe au XVIe Siècle.* Paris, 1930.

Preuss, K. T. *Religion und Mythologie der Uitoto.* 2 vols. Göttingen, 1921.

Pritchard, J. B. *The Ancient Near East.* An Anthology of Text and Pictures. Princeton, 1958.

Procopius. *History of the Wars.* 5 vols. *The Anecdota or Secret History,* 1 vol. Loeb Classical Library. London, 1954.

Psellus, Michael. *The Chronographia.* Translated from the Greek by E. K. A. Sewter. London, 1953.

Puech, H. *Le Manichéisme.* Paris, 1949.

Radin, P. *Primitive Man as a Philosopher.* New York, 1927.

—— *Primitive Religion.* New York, 1937.

—— *The Trickster.* London, 1956.

Radloff, W. *Aus Sibirien.* 2 vols. Leipzig, 1884.

Rambaud, A. *Le Sport et L'Hippodrome à Constantinople.* 1871, in *Études sur l'Histoire Byzantine.* Paris, 1912.

Rapaport, J. *Introduction à la Psychopathologie Collective. La Secte mystique des Skoptzy.* Paris, 1948.

Rasmussen, Knud. *Rasmussens Thulefahrt.* Frankfurt, 1926.

Rattray, R. S. *Ashanti.* Oxford, 1923.

—— *Religion and Art in Ashanti.* Oxford, 1927.

Recinos, A., Goetz D., and Morley, S. G. *Popol Vuh. The Sacred Book of the ancient Quiché Maya.* London, 1951.

Ritter, E. A. *Shaka Zulu.* London, 1955.

Roscoe, J. *The Baganda.* London, 1911.

—— *The Bakitara.* Cambridge, 1923.

—— *The Banyankole.* Cambridge, 1923.

Roth, W. E. *An Inquiry into the Animism and Folk-Lore of the Guiana Indians.* Washington, 1915.

Runciman, S. *The Medieval Manichee.* Cambridge, 1947.

Sacy, S. de. *Exposé de la Religion des Druses.* 2 vols. Paris, 1836.

Sahagun, Bernardino de. *Historia General de las Cosas de Nueva Espana.* 5 vols. Mexico, 1938.

—— *Einige Kapitel aus dem Geschichtswerk des Fray Bernardino de Sahagun.* Übersetzt von Eduard Seler. Stuttgart, 1927.

Salimbene von Parma. *Die Chronik des S. v. P.,* bearbeitet v. A. Doren. 2 vols. Leipzig, 1914.

Sansom, G. *Japan. A Short Cultural History.* London, 1936.

Schlosser, Katesa. *Propheten in Afrika.* Braunschweig, 1949.

Schmidt, K. *Histoire et doctrine de la secte des Cathares ou Albigeois.* 2 vols. Paris, 1848-9.

Schnitzer, J. *Hieronymus Savonarola. Auswahl aus seinen Predigten und Schriften.* Jena, 1928.

Schreber, Daniel Paul. *Denkwürdigkeiten eines Nervenkranken.* Leipzig, 1903.

—— *Memoirs of My Nervous Illness.* Translated and edited, with Introduction, Notes and Discussion, by Ida Macalpine and Richard A. Hunter. London, 1955.

Seligman, C. G., and B. C. *The Veddas.* Cambridge, 1911.

Sénart, E. *Caste in India.* Translated by E. Denison Ross. London, 1930.

Sewell. *A Forgotten Empire (Vijayanagar).* London, 1900.

Shapera, J. *The Khoisan Peoples of South Africa.* London, 1930.

—— Editor: *The Bantu-Speaking Tribes of South Africa.* London, 1937.

Sighele, S. *La Foule Criminelle.* Paris, 1901.

Singh, T. A. L., and Zingg, R. M. *Wolf Children and Feral Man.* Denver, 1943.

Sjoestedt, M. L. *Gods and Heroes of the Celts.* Translated by Myles Dillon. London, 1949.

Smith, V. A. *The Oxford History of India.* Oxford, 1923.

Smith, E. W., and Dale, A. M. *The Ila-Speaking Peoples of Northern Rhodesia.* 2 vols. London, 1920.

Spencer, B., and Gillen, F. J. *The Arunta.* London, 1927.

—— *The Northern Tribes of Central Australia.* London, 1904.

Sprenger, Jacob. *Malleus Maleficarum.* English Translation by Montague Summers. London, 1928.

Stählin, K. *Der Briefwechsel Iwans des Schrecklichen mit dem Fürsten Kurbsky (1564-1579).* Leipzig, 1921.

Stanley, A. P. *Sinai and Palestine.* London, 1864.

Steinen, K. von den. *Unter den Naturvölkern Zentral-Brasiliens.* Berlin, 1894.

Stirling, M. W. *Historical and Ethnographical Material on the Jivaro Indians.* Washington, 1938.

Stoll, O. *Suggestion and Hypnotismus in der Völkerpsychologie.* Leipzig, 1904.

Strehlow, C. *Die Aranda- und Loritja-Stamme in Zentral-Australien.* Vols. I-III. Frankfurt, 1908-10.

Strehlow, T. G. H. *Aranda Traditions.* Melbourne, 1947.

Suetonius. *The Twelve Caesars.* Translated by Robert Graves. Penguin Classics. 1957.

Tabari. *Chronique de Tabari,* traduit par H. Zotenberg. 4 vols. Paris, 1867-79.

Tacitus. *The Annals of Imperial Rome.* Translated by Michael Grant. Penguin Classics. 1956.

Talbot, P. A. *In the Shadow of the Bush.* London, 1912.

Tavernier, J. B. *Travels in India.* 2 vols. London, 1925.

Te Rangi Hiroa (Peter H. Buck). *The Coming of the Maori.* Wellington, 1952.

Tertullian. *De Spectaculis.* Loeb Classical Library. London, 1931.

Titayna. *La Caravane des Morts.* Paris, 1930.

Theal, G. McCall. *History of South Africa from 1795-1872.* Vol. III. London, 1927.

Thucydides. *History ·of the Peloponnesian War*. Translated by Rex Warner. Penguin Classics. 1954.

Thurnwald, R. *Repräsentative Lebensbilder von Naturvölkern*. Berlin, 1931.

Tremearne, A. J. N. *The Ban of the Bori*. London, 1914.

Trilles, R. P. *Les Pygmées de la Forêt Equatoriale*. Paris, 1931.

Trotter, W. *The Instincts of the Herd in Peace and War*. London, 1919.

Turi, Johan. *The Book of the Lapp*. London, 1931.

Turner, G. *Samoa*. London, 1884.

Tylor, E. B. *Primitive Culture*. London, 1924.

Ungnad, A. *Die Religionen der Babylonier und Assyrer*. Jena, 1921.

Vaillant, G. C. *The Aztecs of Mexico*. London, 1950.

Vedder, H. *Die Bergdama*. 2 vols. Hamburg, 1923.

Vendryès, J., Tonnelat, E., and Unbegaun, B. O. *Les Religions des Celtes, des Germains et des Anciens Slaves*. Paris, 1948.

Virolleaud, C. *Le Théâtre Persan ou le Drame de Kerbéla*. Paris, 1950.

Volhardt, E. *Kannibalismus*. Stuttgart, 1939.

Waley, Arthur. *The Travels of an Alchemist*. London, 1931.

—— *The Book of Songs*. London, 1937.

—— *The Analects of Confucius*. London, 1938.

—— *Three Ways of Thought in Ancient China*. London, 1939.

—— *The Real Tripitaka*. London, 1952.

Waliszewski, K. *Ivan le Terrible*. Paris, 1904.

—— *Peter the Great*. London, 1898.

Warneck, J. *Die Religion der Batak*. Göttingen, 1909.

Warner, F. Ll. *A Black Civilisation*. New York, 1958.

Weeks, J. H. *Among Congo Cannibals*. London, 1913.

Weil, Gustav. *Geschichte der Chalifen*. Vols. I-III. Mannheim, 1846-51.

Wendische Sagen, herausgegeben von F. Sieber. Jena, 1925.

Wesley, John. *The Journal*. London, 1836.

Westermann, D. *The Shilluk People*. Berlin, 1912.

—— *Geschichte Afrikas*. Cologne, 1952.

Westermarck, E. *Ritual and Belief in Morocco*. 2 vols. London, 1926.

Wilhelm, Richard. *Li Gi. Das Buch der Sitte*. 1958.

—— *Mong Dsi*. Jena, 1921.

—— *Frühling und Herbst des LüBu We*. Jena, 1928.

Williams, F. E. *Orokaiva Magic*. London, 1928.

—— *The Vailala Madness and the Destruction of Ceremonies*. Port Moresby, 1923.

—— *The Vailala Madness in Retrospect*, in: *Essays Presented to C. G. Seligman*. London, 1934.

Winternitz, M. *Geschichte der Indischen Literatur*. 3 vols. Leipzig, 1909-22.

Wirz, Paul. *Die Marind-anim von Holländisch-Süd-Neu-Guinea*. Vols. I and II. Hamburg, 1922 and 1925.

Wladimirzov, B. *The Life of Chingis-Khan*. London, 1930.

Wolff, O. *Geschichte der Mongolen oder Tataren, besonders ihres Vordringens nach Europa.* Breslau, 1872.

Wolff, P. *Die Drusen und ihre Vorläufer.* Leipzig, 1845.

Worsley, P. *The Trumpet Shall Sound: A Study of "Cargo" Cults in Melanesia.* London, 1957.

Zuckerman, S. *The Social Life of Monkeys and Apes.* London, 1932.